上海市浦东新区统计局
SHANGHAI PUDONG NEW AREA STATISTICAL BUREAU
国家统计局浦东调查队
PUDONG SURVEY TEAM OF NATIONAL STAT ISTICS BUREAU

上海浦东新区统计年鉴 2013

SHANGHAI PUDONG NEW AREA STATISTICAL YEARBOOK

（总第20期 No.20）

中国统计出版社
China Statistics Press

新区生产总值(亿元)
Gross Output Value of Pudong New Area (100 million yuan)

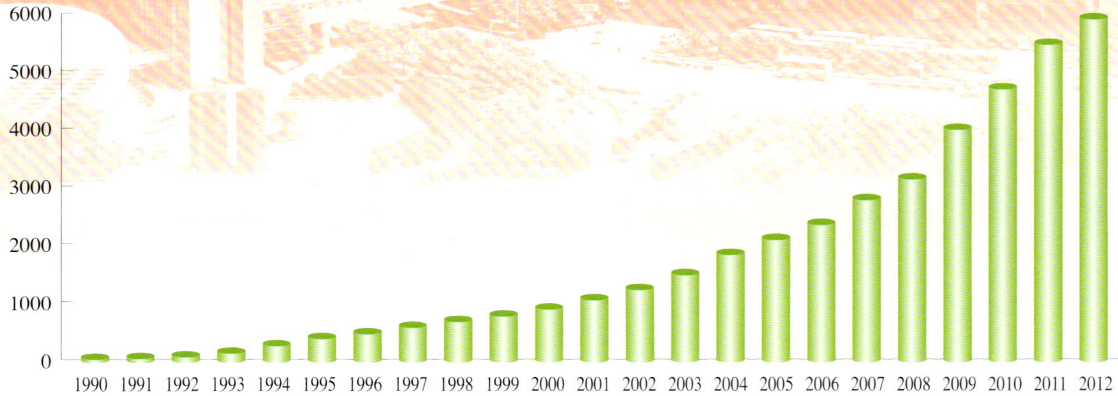

新区生产总值构成(%)
Composition of GDP of PNA (%)

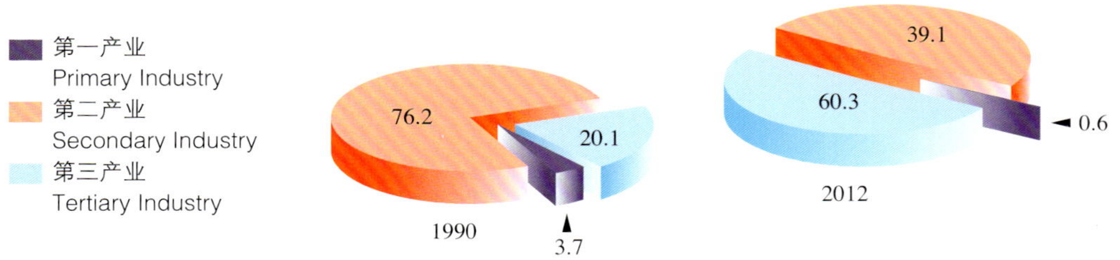

第三产业增加值构成(%)
Composition of Value Added of Tertiary Industry (%)

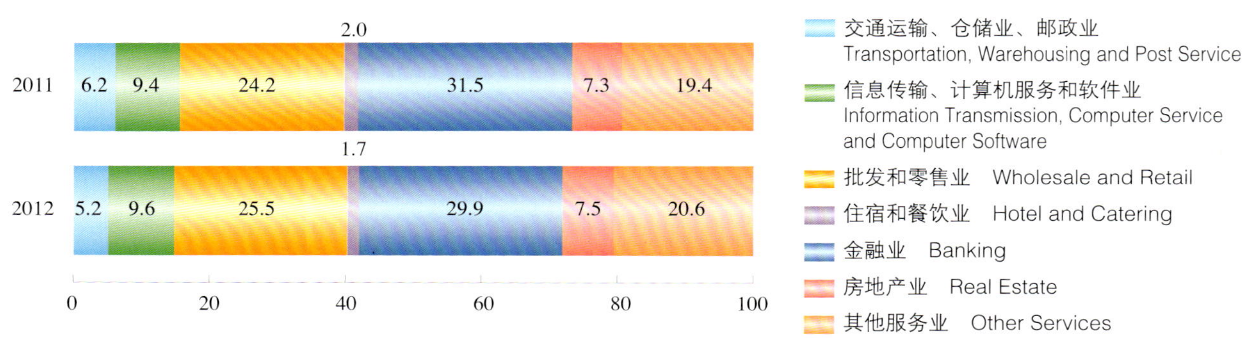

财政收入(亿元)
Financial Revenue (100 million yuan)

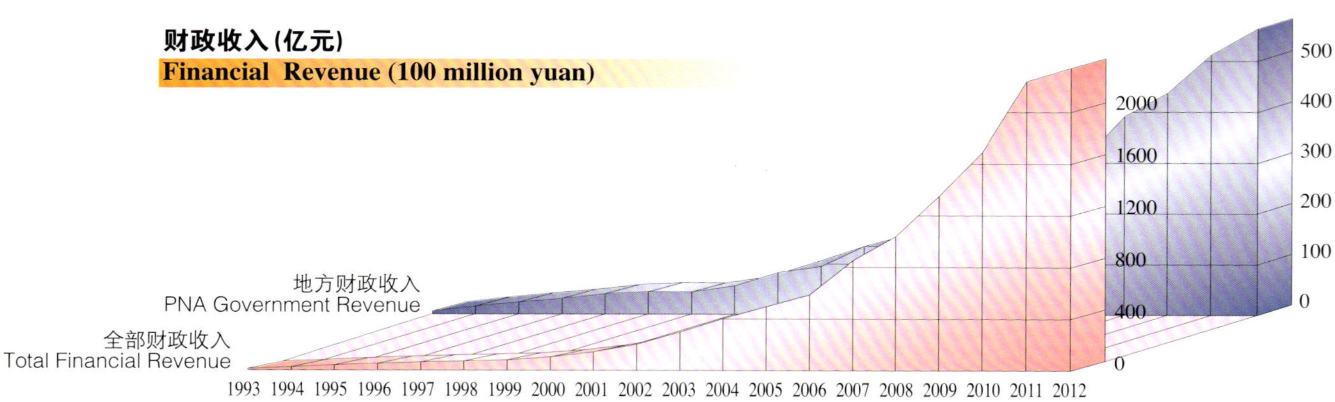

农业总产值(亿元)

Gross Output Value of Agriculture (100 million yuan)

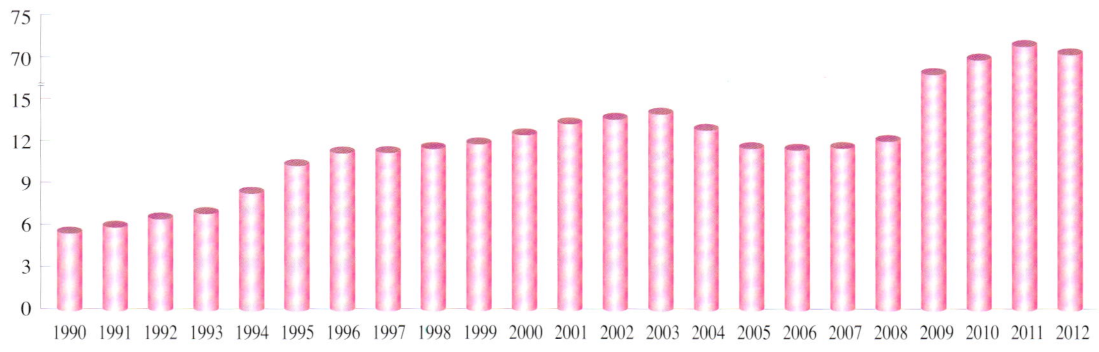

进出口货物总值(亿美元)

Total Value of Imports and Exports (USD 100 million)

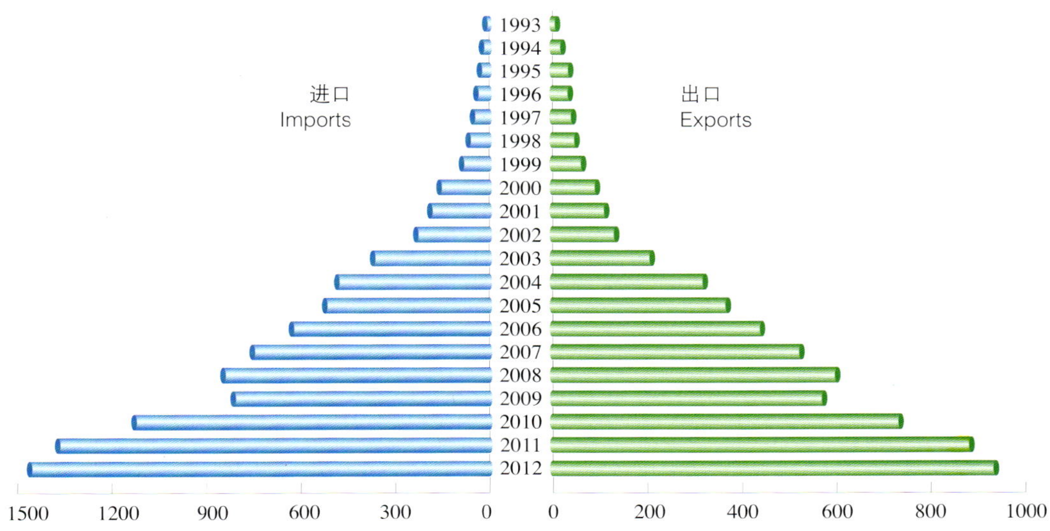

2012年六个工业重点发展行业产值构成(%)

Composition of Gross Output Value of Six Key Industries in 2012 (%)

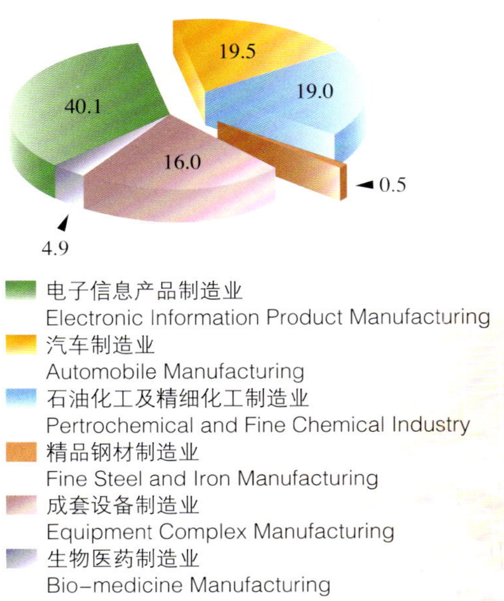

城市基础设施投资额构成(%)

Composition of Urban Infrastructure Investment (%)

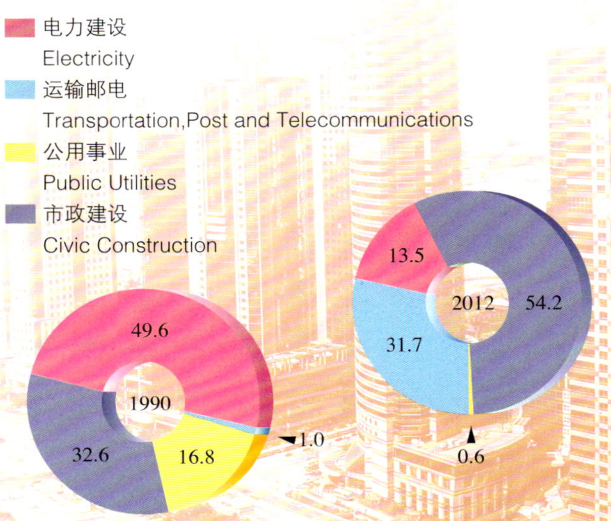

固定资产投资和城市基础设施投资(亿元)
Total Investment in Fixed Assets and Urban Infrastructure (100 million yuan)

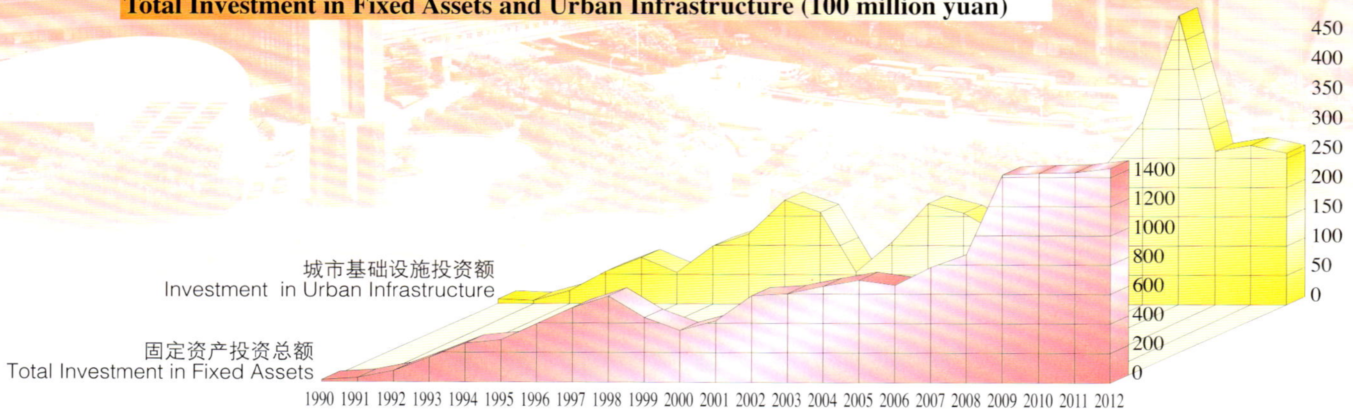

中外资银行本外币存贷款年末余额(亿元)
Balance of RMB and Foreign Currencies Deposits and Loans in Chinese and Foreign Banks (100 million yuan)

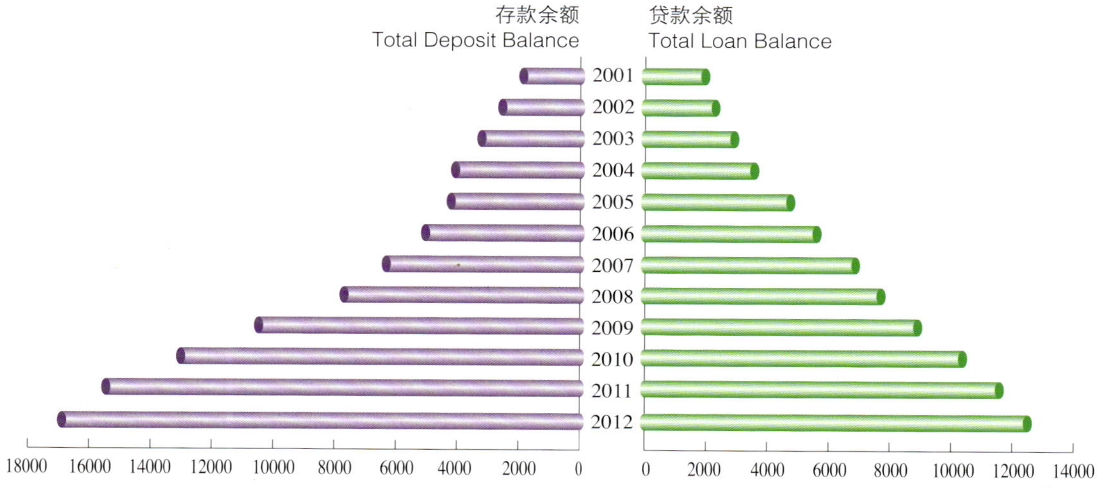

上海证券交易所市价总值(亿元)
Market Value of Shanghai Stock Exchange (100 million yuan)

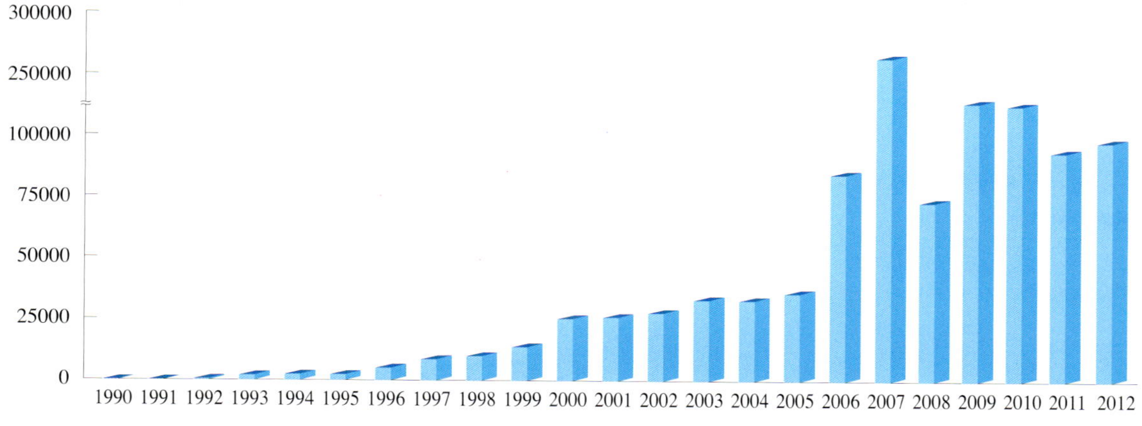

社会消费品零售总额(亿元)
Total Retail Sales of Consumer Goods (100 million yuan)

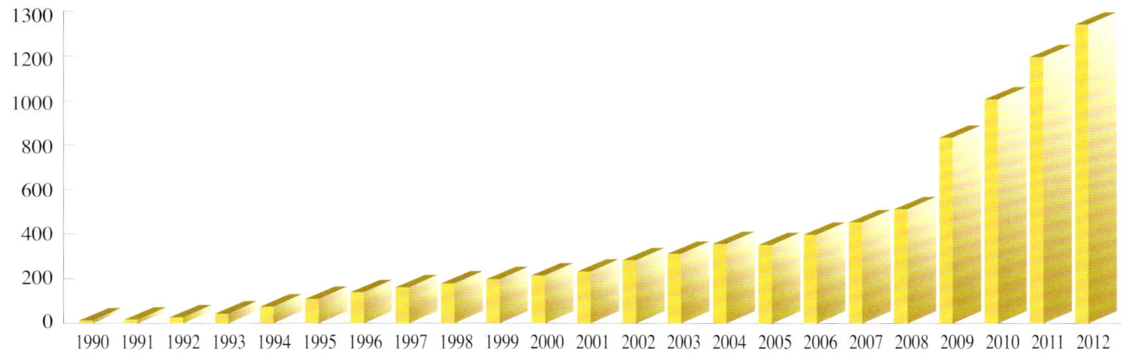

外商合同投资额的投资方式构成(%)
Composition of Contract Value of Foreign Investment by Ways of Investment (%)

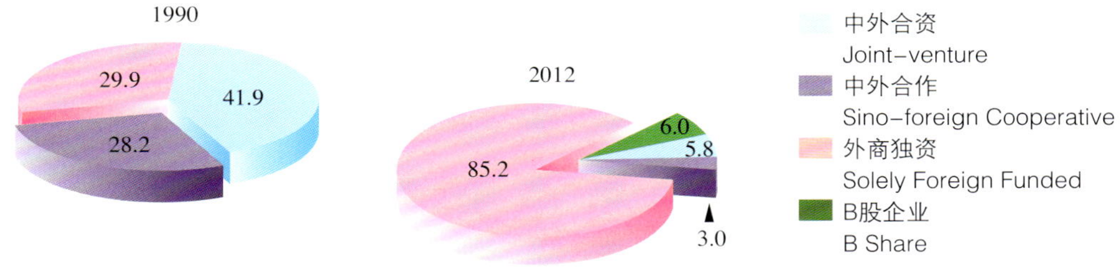

居民储蓄存款年末余额(亿元)
Resident Savings Deposit (100 million yuan)

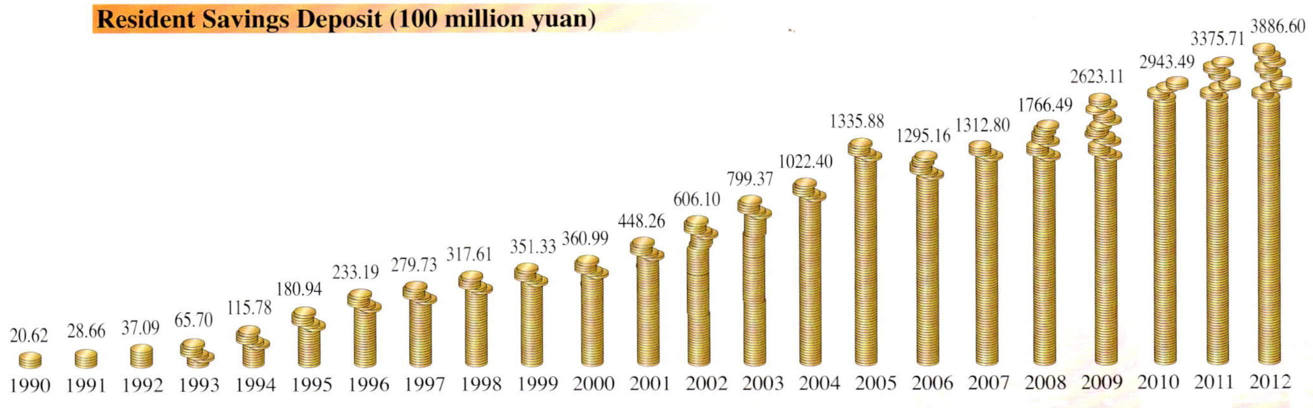

2012年城镇居民家庭消费支出构成(%)
Composition of Consumption Expenditure of Urban Families in 2012 (%)

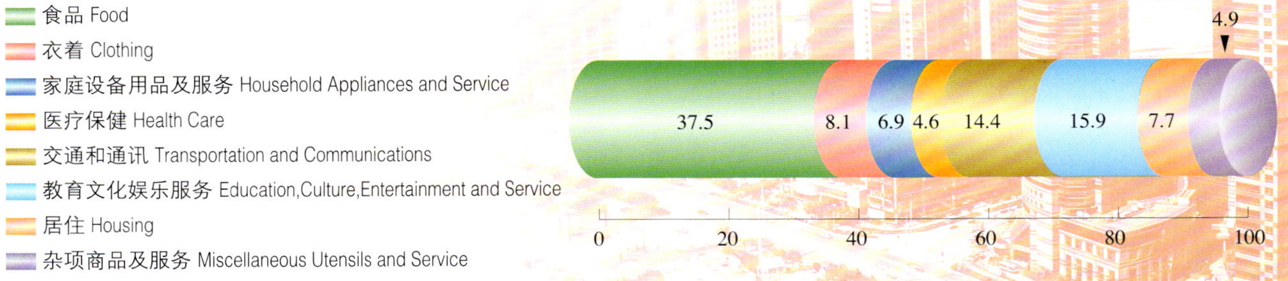

浦东功能 Functions In Pudong

2012年郊区居民家庭收入构成(%)
Income Composition of Suburban Residents in 2012(%)

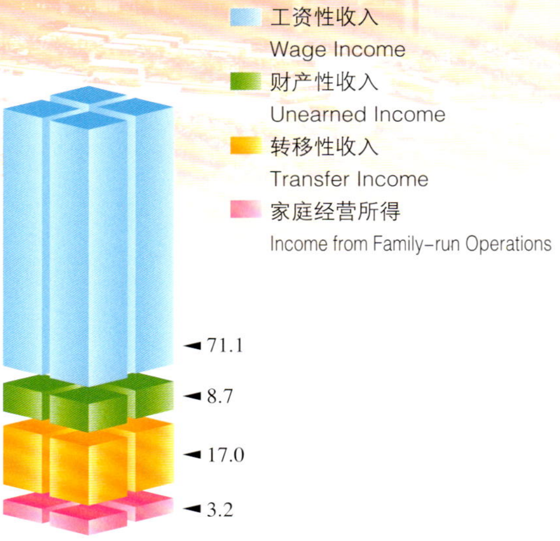

从业人员三次产业构成(%)
Employed Persons by Industry (%)

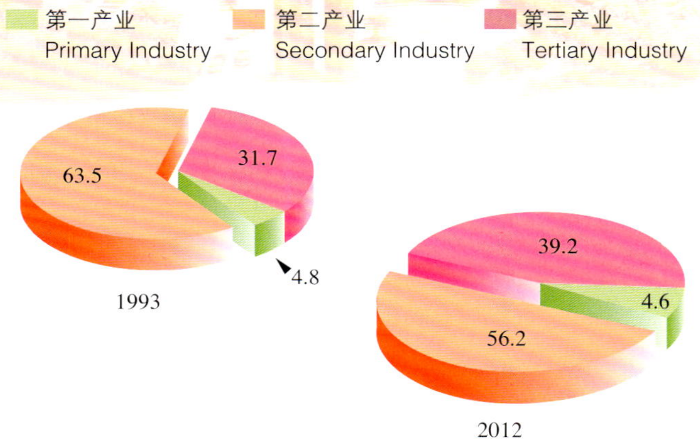

人口自然增长率和净迁移率(‰)
Natural Growth Rate and Net Migration Rate of Population (‰)

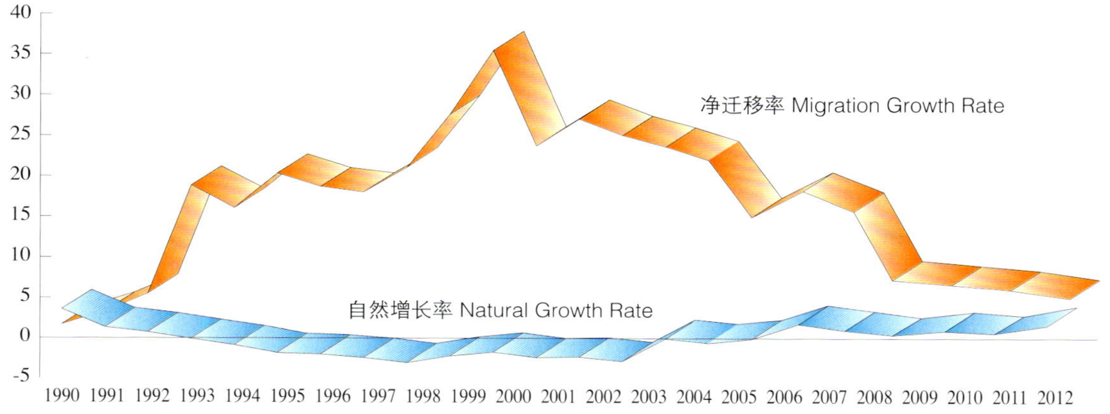

集装箱吞吐量(万标箱)
Container Handling Capacity (10000TEU)

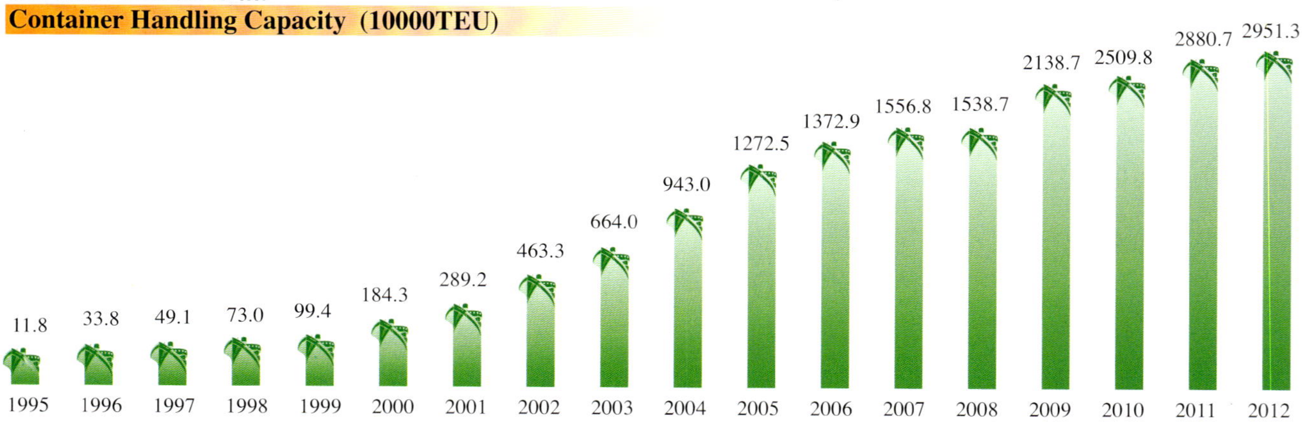

人均公共绿地面积(平方米)
Public Green Space Per Capita (sq.m)

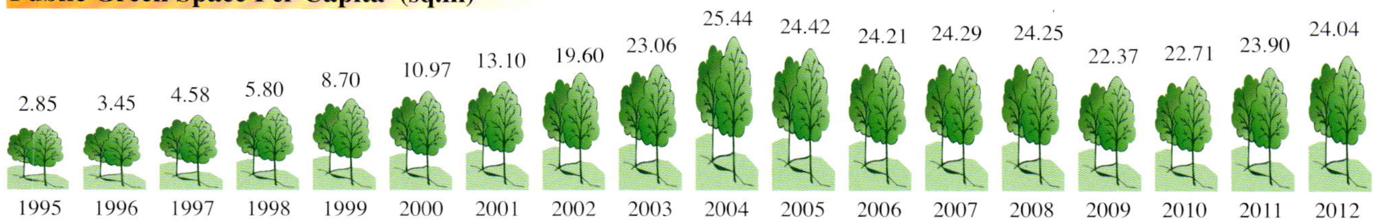

水电消耗情况
Consumption of Tap Water and Electricity

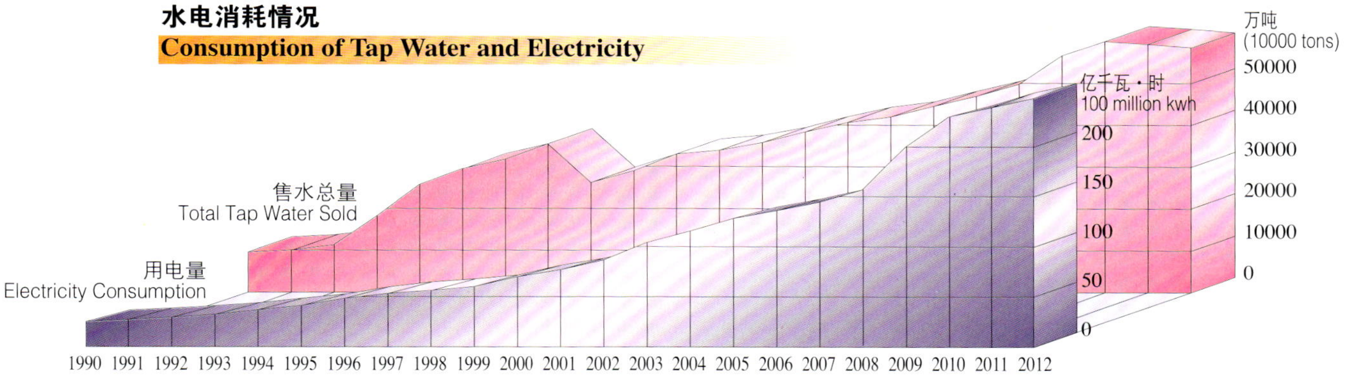

2012年前十位疾病死亡原因构成(%)
Composition of Top 10 Death-Causing Diseases in 2012 (%)

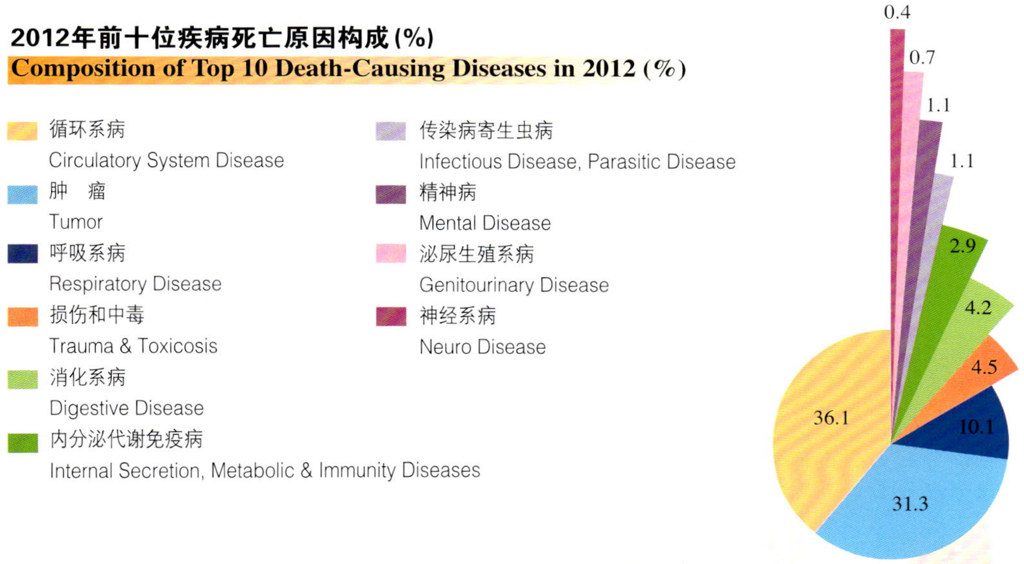

各级学校在校学生数构成(%)
Composition of Students Enrollment by Various Schools (%)

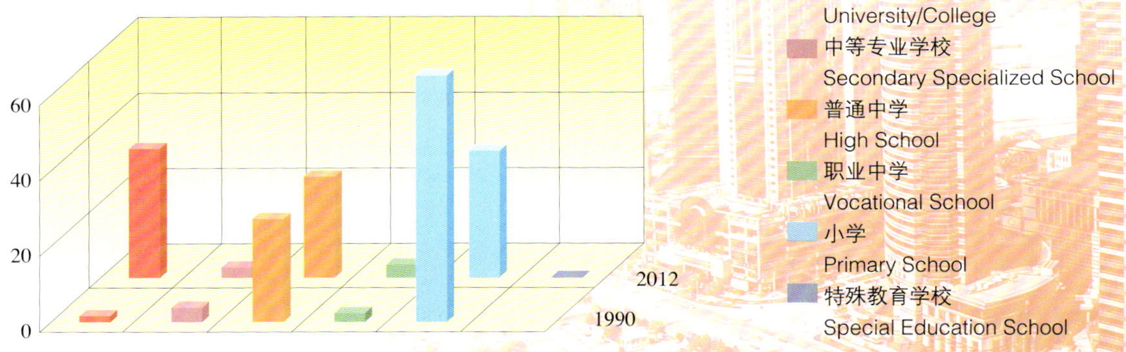

《上海浦东新区统计年鉴——2013》编辑委员会

《上海浦东新区统计年鉴——2013》编辑部

Editorial Board

Editorial Department

编者说明

一、《上海浦东新区统计年鉴－2013》是一部集浦东新区资料于一体的大型工具书。全书通过大量的统计数据，以中英文对照的形式记录了浦东新区开发开放以来社会经济发展的历程，全面展示了2012年浦东新区在二次创业的新阶段中，经济、社会、科技和重点开发区等各方面的发展变化。年鉴为各级领导、理论研究和实际工作者，以及国内外各界关心浦东开发开放的人士了解浦东、研究浦东、参与浦东开发建设提供了案头工具。

二、2009年，浦东新区行政体制发生重大变化。4月24日，国务院批准南汇区行政区域划入浦东新区。5月6日，上海市人民政府正式宣布两区合并。由于两区以前年度很多数据在统计方法、统计口径、统计范围等方面的不一致，数据无法简单相加，追溯存在一定难度。因此除特别注明外，本年鉴自2009年起，统计数据均为新浦东数据（即含原南汇地区），以前年度仍为原浦东数据。

三、2011年和2012年，浦东新区进行部分镇行政区划调整。2011年10月28日，上海市人民政府批准撤销川沙新镇、六灶镇建制，设立新的川沙新镇；撤销祝桥镇建制，设立新的祝桥镇，其行政区域范围作相应调整。2012年8月30日，经批准撤销申港街道、芦潮港镇建制，设立南汇新城镇，同时行政区域范围也作相应调整。

四、本年鉴中平均增长速度根据每年的环比增长速度相乘再开方得到。

五、全书内容分为十九个篇目。内含：1. 综合；2. 人口；3. 固定资产投资；4. 招商引资；5. 农业；6. 工业；7. 建筑业；8. 金融业及要素市场；9. 房地产；10. 国内外贸易；11. 服务、旅游和住宿业；12. 科学技术；13. 人民生活；14. 就业与社会保障；15. 教育、文化、体育和卫生；16. 法律、社会治安及其他；17. 城市建设和环境保护；18. 重点开发区和街镇；19. 上海市统计资料。

六、资料中使用的度量衡单位均采用国际统一标准计量单位。

七、本年鉴部分数据总计数或相对数由于单位取舍不同，产生的计算误差均未作机械调整。

八、浦东新区在行政管理体制上于1995年11月撤乡建镇，实行镇管村体制。因此，本年鉴中有关“镇”和“镇及镇以上工业”等指标含义与全国的“乡”和“乡及乡以上工业”等指标的含义相同。

九、本年鉴中的符号使用说明：“#”表示某一指标的其中主要项；“…”表示数据不足本表最小计量单位数；“空格”表示该项统计指标数据不详或无该项数据或数据为零。

十、根据国务院和国家统计局有关我国GDP核算和数据发布制度的规定，浦东新区国内生产总值自2004年起更名为“浦东新区生产总值”，简称“新区生产总值”。

十一、本年鉴中各项增加值和总产值绝对数均按当年价格计算，增长速度按可比价格计算。

十二、在使用统计资料时，凡与本年鉴有出入的，均以本年鉴为准。

十三、《上海浦东新区统计年鉴》公开出版以来，受到国内外广大读者的爱护和支持，对此我们深表谢意，并竭诚欢迎读者继续对本年鉴的不足之处给予批评和指正。

本年鉴的编制得到了上海市统计局、浦东新区各委、办、局及各开发区管委会等有关单位的大力支持，在此一并表示谢意。

EDITO ' S NOTE

Ⅰ. Statistical Yearbook of Shanghai Pudong New Area (PNA) – 2013 is a large, comprehensive reference book. With great amount of data and in both Chinese and English versions, it records recent years' social and economic development in PNA. It describes the changes in economy, society, science and technology, and key development zones in PNA's new stage of "Second Startup for Business" in 2012. It is a desktop tool – book meant for leaders at all levels, theorists, practitioners, and people at home and abroad who are interested in PNA, want to do research work on Pudong and intend to participate in its development and its construction.

Ⅱ. Great changes happened to the administrative system of Pudong New Area in 2009. On April 24, the State Council approved to add the administrative area of Nanhui District into Pudong New Area. On May 6, the Shanghai Municipal government formally announced the combination of these two districts. Because of data of previous years in these two districts can not be added simply while they had been produced with different statistical methods, approached and areas and it is hard to trace them. Unless specified, the statistical data in this Yearbook are those of new PNA (including former Nanhui District) since 2009, and the data of previous years are those of former PNA.

Ⅲ. In 2011 and 2012, administrative divisions of some towns in PNA were readjusted. On October 28, 2011, Shanghai People's Government approved the establishment of the new Chuansha New Town after rescinding the former Chuansha New Town and Liuzao Town, approved the establishment of the new Zhuqiao Town after rescinding the former Zhuqiao Town, and readjusted the administrative divisions of these two new towns. On August 30, 2012, the municipal government approved the establishment of the new Nanhui New Town after rescinding Shengang Sub – district and Luchaogang Town, and readjusted the administrative division of its administrative division.

Ⅳ. The annual average growth rate in this Yearbook is extracted from the multiplication of the annual chain growth rates.

Ⅴ. This book falls into nineteen chapters: 1. General Survey; 2. Population; 3. Investment in Fixed Assets; 4. Business Promotion and Foreign-fund Attraction; 5. Agriculture; 6. Industry; 7. Construction; 8. Finance and Banking, and Factor Markets; 9. Real Estate; 10. Domestic and Foreign Trades; 11. Services, Tourism and Hotels; 12. Science and Technology; 13. People's Livelihood; 14. Employment and Social Security; 15. Education, Culture, Sports and Public Health; 16. Laws, Public Order and Others; 17. Urban Construction and Environmental Protection; 18. Key Development Zones and Sub-districts and Towns; 19. Statistics of Shanghai Municipality.

Ⅵ. The units of measurement in this book are consistent with international standards.

Ⅶ. No adjustment has been made to correct the deviations of some of the figures in the Yearbook caused by different methods used in rounding.

Ⅷ. In November 1995, PNA rescinded village system and adopted town system. Villages are supervised by towns in the town system. Therefore, in this book, the meanings of "town" and "town and town-above industry" are the same as "township" and "township and township-above industry" in other Chinese statistical books.

Ⅸ. Notations used in this Yearbook:

"#" indicates the major item of a certain indicator,

"…" indicates the figure which is too small to be measured by the smallest unit in the table,

"blank" indicates the data unavailable or none in certain statistical indicator.

Ⅹ. According to relevant stipulations by the State Council and National Bureau of Statistics, GDP of Pudong New Area is to be renamed as Gross Output Value of Pudong New Area, shortened as PNA Gross Output Value starting from 2004.

Ⅺ. All added values and gross output vales in the Yearbook are listed in terms of current prices while growth rates listed in terms of comparable prices.

Ⅻ. If any statistical data from other sources conflict with the data in the present Yearbook, data in the present Yearbook shall apply.

XⅢ. The publication of Pudong New Area Statistical Yearbook has received great attention. Our gratitude and appreciation go to all the readers who have offered their comments. We welcome and are open to more comments and suggestions from our readers when presenting this new edition.

We appreciate the great support and efforts of Shanghai Statistics Bureau, all the commissions, offices and bureaus, and administrations of all the development zones in PNA during compilation of the present Yearbook.

目　　录
CONTENTS

综　述
ABSTRACT

第一篇　综　合
CHAPTER 1 GENERAL SURVEY

第二篇　人　口

CHAPTER 2 POPULATION

第三篇　固定资产投资

CHAPTER 3 INVESTMENT IN FIXED ASSETS

第四篇　招商引资
CHAPTER 4　BUSINESS PROMOTION AND FOREIGN-FUND ATTRACTION

第五篇　农　业
CHAPTER 5　AGRICULTURE

第六篇 工 业
CHAPTER 6 INDUSTRY

第七篇　建筑业
CHAPTER 7 CONSTRUCTION

第八篇　金融业及要素市场
CHAPTER 8 FINANCE AND BANKING, AND FACTOR MARKETS

第九篇　房地产

CHAPTER 9 REAL ESTATE

第十篇　国内外贸易

CHAPTER 10 DOMESTIC AND FOREIGN TRADES

第十一篇　服务、旅游和住宿业
CHAPTER 11 SERVICES, TOURISM AND HOTELS

第十二篇　科学技术
CHAPTER 12 SCIENCE AND TECHNOLOGY

第十三篇　人民生活
CHAPTER 13　PEOPLE'S LIVELIHOOD

第十四篇　就业与社会保障

CHAPTER　14　EMPLOYMENT AND SOCIAL SECURITY

第十五篇　教育、文化、体育、卫生

CHAPTER　15　EDUCATION, CULTURE, SPORTS AND PUBLIC HEALTH

第十六篇　法律、社会治安及其他
CHAPTER 16 LAWS, PUBLIC ORDER AND OTHERS

第十七篇　城市建设和环境保护
CHAPTER 17 URBAN CONSTRUCTIONS AND ENVIRONMENTAL PROTECTION

第十八篇　重点开发区和街镇

CHAPTER　18　KEY DEVELOPMENT ZONES AND SUB – DISTRICTS AND TOWNS

第十九篇　上海市统计资料

CHAPTER　19　STATISTICS OF SHANGHAI MUNICIPALITY

2012年浦东新区经济和社会发展情况

2012年是深入推进"十二五"规划实施的关键一年，在区委、区政府的领导下，浦东新区积极应对复杂严峻的国内外形势，深入贯彻落实科学发展观和国家宏观调控政策，牢牢把握"稳中求进"的总基调，坚持"创新驱动、转型发展"，积极推进区委、区政府年初确定的各项目标任务，经济社会发展平稳有序，较好地完成了年初预期目标。

一、经济保持平稳增长，转型效益进一步显现

1. 经济质量与效益不断提升。全年实现生产总值5929.91亿元，增长10.1%，高于全市2.6个百分点，其中第三产业增长14.9%；地方财政收入550.30亿元，增长10.0%；全社会固定资产投资1454.98亿元。区属单位增加值能耗下降6.6%。

2. 产业结构继续优化。三产比重进一步提高，占地区生产总值比重达60.3%。金融业和批发零售业保持两位数增长，信息服务业、商务服务业、旅游会展业等新兴服务业平稳发展。受国内外宏观经济形势影响，工业增速趋缓，全年完成工业总产值9424.67亿元，增长1.1%，三大新兴产业产值增长7.3%，其中，生物医药和航空航天制造业分别增长9.9%和25.5%；高技术产业产值增长8.9%，高技术产业产值率31.5%。

3. 创新能力不断增强。以创建张江国家自主创新示范区为契机，不断提升区域自主创新能力。每百万人发明专利授权数达510件。经认定的高新技术企业和研发机构分别新增207家和85家，累计总数突破1100家和500家；新认定技术先进性服务企业14家，总数达到170家。

4. 招商引资稳步推进。全年引进合同外资和实到外资分别为72.9亿美元和48.3亿美元，引进内资注册资本超过1000亿元。新推出14条支持总部经济发展的举措，引进跨国公司地区总部22家，占全市44%，累计已达193家，占全市47.9%；新增内资大企业总部和区域性总部13家。巴斯夫总部和研发大楼、迪卡侬总部和旗舰店、黑石股权投资、华人文化等内外资大项目落地。

二、"四个中心"核心功能区建设加快推进，功能开发进一步深化拓展

1. 金融功能加速集聚。全年实现金融业增加值1069.11亿元，增长11.9%。金融市场成交额增长明显，上海证券交易所成交额增长20.4%，上海期货交易所成交额增长2.6%，中国金融期货交易所股指期货成交额增长73.3%。引进监管类金融机构45家（累计737家）、非监管类金融机构404家（累计1247家）、金融专业服务机构48家（累计578家）。中国银行上海人民币交易业务总部等一批重大功能性机构落户，上海股权托管交易中心正式开业，"金才优教"、"金才优护"及"金才安居"项目加快推进，成功举办第六届陆家嘴金融文化节。

2. 航运功能不断拓展。全年累计完成港口货物吞吐量超过2.72亿吨，增长3.4%；集装箱吞吐量2951.3万标箱，增长2.5%，其中国际中转箱量增长29.3%。启运港退税、保税船舶登记等政策试点正式实施，融资租赁规模进一步扩大，新引进8家融资租赁母公司和50家SPV（单船单机）项目公司。2012中国国际航运文化节、第三届国际航运战略发展研讨会等成功举办。

3. 贸易功能继续增强。全年实现进出口总额2398.93亿美元，增长6.1%；社会消费品零售总额增长12.1%，商品销售总额增长23.8%。电子商务发展迅猛，全年电子商务商品交易额3511亿元，增长13%。服务外包、服务贸易稳步发展，全年服务贸易进出口总额416亿美元，增长18.5%，占全市41.7%。贸易功能创新不断强化，新推出5项贸易便利化试点措施，新型国际贸易结算中心试点拓展至50家，国家进口贸易创新示范区、国家对外文化贸易基地、国家服务外包交易促进中心等加快建设。

三、重点区域加快建设，区域发展格局继续优化

1. 陆家嘴、张江、金桥、上海综合保税区等先发区域加快功能提升。陆家嘴金融城建设有力推进，浦东金融广场等9个项目开工，上海中心、塘东总部基地等项目加快推进，东方金融广场等7个工程顺利竣工；核心区内短驳公交和无线WIFI均实现全覆盖；金融城青年人才公寓建成启用，并推出“梯度补贴”政策。张江园区加快优化创新环境，“张江创新十条”深化落实，代持股试点通道形成，华虹设计等9家企业准备试点；推出人才公寓4万平方米、创业工坊100套；“张江金融街”加快建设；盛大、惠普、蒂森克虏伯等79个重大产业项目集中开工。金桥出口加工区加快推进“优二进三”（优化第二产业，加快发展第三产业），服务业综合配套改革试点、国家新型工业化产业示范基地创建等工作取得初步成效；金桥备用地Ⅳ地块项目完成前期手续，加紧启动征收工作。上海综合保税区发展空间进一步拓展，洋山保税港区6.02平方公里扩区建设有序推进，岛域部分实现开工；森兰商务商业区建设进一步加快，森兰外高桥一期项目约11万平方米开工建设，二期项目完成规划设计。

2. 临港、国际旅游度假区、世博等新兴区域开发提速。市委、市政府出台并发布《关于在临港地区建立特别机制和实行特殊政策的意见》，临港地区管理体制调整到位，中航商发等一批龙头项目开工建设，综合区开发规划编制与项目落地同步推进，南汇新城镇地铁16号线交通枢纽配套工程加快推进，100万平方米限价房全部实现开工。世博地区13家央企顺利落户；前滩控制性详细规划获得批复，市政道路、河道、学校等一批项目开工。国际旅游度假区项目建设进展顺利，迪士尼乐园及配套设施场地形成项目竣工并向业主公司移交，乐园及配套设施主体工程启动建设，《上海国际旅游度假区发展规划（2011－2030）》获市政府批准，度假区结构规划、综合交通等相关专项规划编制完成。

3. “强镇优街”工作取得重要进展。镇域经济发展平稳有序，街镇社会管理水平进一步增强。制定实施了《浦东新区“强镇优街”工作若干措施（暂行）》、《浦东新区关于推进“镇管社区”工作的指导意见（试行）》，着力完善区域管理体制机制，增强镇域发展活力，提高街镇社会管理能力。

四、重点领域和关键环节改革逐步深化，体制机制更加优化

根据“三个着力”要求，按照“三个导向”原则，综合配套改革试点工作围绕全年工作安排，聚焦重点、有序推进，重点领域、重点事项改革取得较大突破。推动“四个中心”核心功能提升的制度环境不断完善；科技创新环境继续优化，张江代持股计划有序推进，“两个1000”工程全面实施；推动临港、陆家嘴、世博、外高桥等重点区域管理体制创新，大型居住区社会管理体制进一步优化；“局镇合作”、“办学联合体”、全科医师家庭责任制、新型农村合作医疗（以下简称“新农合”）支付方式改革等公共服务领域改革试点工作加快推进，进一步推动城乡公共资源均衡化布局。

五、社会建设全面加强，民生福祉不断提升

1. 就业与民生保障等工作不断加强。居民收入稳步增长，全年城乡居民收入约为40901元和17641元，分别增长11.1%和11.2%，均快于经济增长。积极促进就业，推进青年启航计划、高技能人才培养计划、万千百人计划和创建创业型城区三年行动计划，全年新增就业岗位15.05万个，城镇登记失业人数45331人，控制在市下达指标内。深入推进“1116引才计划”，人才工作继续加强，浦东国际人才城9月开城。社会保障进一步增强，新农保月平均养老金水平提高至601.5元，共落实征地安置人数7272人，救助各类帮困对象159.14万人次。养老事业加快发展，新增养老床位801张，享受居家养老服务老人数达5.2万人，“全国老年友好城区”创建工作有序推进。全年新开工各类保障性住房463万平方米，竣工318万平方米。廉租住房新增受益家庭782户（累计受益7929户）。

2. 社会管理水平继续提高。社区治理机制不断完善，居（村）委会换届选举、“全国和谐社区建设示范街道”、“农村社区建设实验全覆盖区”创评工作有序推进。继续强化专业社会服务，市民中心政社合作平台、社工机构孵化、农村社工服务等项目顺利启动。社会组织健康发展，截至目前已有社会组织1550家。浦东新区社会团体和民办非企业单位规范化建设相关指导意见制定出台，浦东公益服务园项目获第六届“中国地方政府创新奖”，浦东公益一条街实现试运营。

3. 社会事业加快发展。全年社会民生方面财政投入249亿元，增长18.8%。教育方面，加快推进上师大附中、上南中学、曹路大居配套完中（复旦附中）等项目建设，完成校安工程97个。上海纽约大学10月正式成立并全面开工建设。继续扩展优质高中资源，新增三所市实验性示范性高中。努力缓解来沪从业人员同住子女入学难、入园难。卫生方面，东方医院南院、第六人民医院东院建成开业，公利医院门急诊新大楼、孙桥社区卫生服务中心交付使用，国际医学中心(一期)项目加快建设。全科医师家庭责任制在45家社区卫生服务中心推开，新农合参合农民住院报销比例超过70%，最高报销限额达20.5万元，新农合“按人头支付”实施方案制定并启动。获评“国家慢性病综合防控示范区”。文化方面，加快推进新区广播电视中心、吴昌硕纪念馆、临港艺术中心(谢陈艺术馆)等项目；成功举办第二届浦东文化艺术节、首届上海民俗文化节等大型文化活动，启动第二批文保修缮(养护)项目。文化创意产业加快发展，全年实现增加值609亿元，增长11.2%，张江国家文化产业园成为首批“国家级文化与科技融合示范基地”。体育方面，三林体育中心等项目加快建设，短道速滑世锦赛等一批大型赛事成功举办，国际体育仲裁院上海听证中心落户浦东。

4.“三农”工作稳步推进。农业经济运行总体平稳，农村居民可支配收入保持稳步增长。全年农业总产值71亿元。5个国家现代农业示范基地加快建设，5个镇级为农综合服务中心基本建成，成功举办浦东新区第四届农博会。全年投入村庄改造资金约15亿元，共惠及14个镇57个行政村约4万农户。

5. 实事项目全面完成。围绕增强为老服务、推进新农村建设、加快旧住房改造、促进就业、方便市民出行、提升公共服务水平等与群众生活密切相关的重点领域，积极推进市、区两级实事项目建设，13项由新区实施的市政府实事项目和34项新区实事项目圆满完成。

六、城区建设管理水平不断提高，生态环境持续改善

1. 城区建设加快推进。积极推进规划编制，集中建设区(扣除机场、外高桥港区、临港产业区后)控制性详细规划覆盖率达到92%。市、区两级共68个重大工程项目建设顺利推进，全年完成投资约126亿元。加快旧区改造，高桥镇北新村五队(厂中村)等3个地块完成清盘，11个地块启动改造，全年共完成居民签约2020户。

2. 生态环境质量继续优化。顺利完成“国家环保模范城区”复核检查。启动第五轮三年环保行动计划项目103个，推进生态镇、生态村以及绿色学校、企业、宾馆等绿色细胞创建。开展各类环保专项执法行动，共出动1.6万人次，检查重点监控企业6000多户次。加快推进黎明资源再利用中心、滨江森林公园二期等重大环卫设施和绿化林业项目建设。继续推进生活垃圾分类减量和废旧衣物、电子垃圾、建筑装潢垃圾等专项回收，推进污水管网建设与河道整治等工作。环境质量进一步改善，全年空气质量优良率达96.2%，创历史最佳水平。

3. 城市管理水平不断提高。城管执法进一步加强，共出动38万人次开展11次“春风”系列专项执法行动。努力做好防汛防台工作，成功抵御“苏拉”等台风暴雨灾害侵袭。积极推进水利改革发展，推进临港地区供水集约化建设，完成全区青草沙水源地切换，成功创建上海市首个国家节水型示范城区。继续增强公共安全管理，安全生产有序可控，全年生产安全事故数和死亡人数分别同比下降8.7%和12.5%；社会治安状况良好，“110”报警类警情同比下降21.1%，十八大安保、钓鱼岛事件应急工作等均较好完成；加强食品药品安全管理，全区未发生集体性食物中毒和责任性药害事件。

4. 智慧浦东建设加快推进。智慧浦东发展研究院组建成立。基础网络能级快速提升，城市光网、无线城市、三网融合等主要信息基础设施指标均高于全市平均水平，“陆家嘴无线金融城应用平台”正式上线运行。潍坊街道、金桥镇等10家单位开展浦东新区智慧社区试点。智慧化应用深入推广，人口库、法人库等基础信息资源库基本建成，自助式医疗服务终端大大降低患者就医时间，“智慧公交”试点共启动建设60多个公交电子站牌。

ECONOMIC AND SOCIAL DEVELOPMENT OF SHANGHAI PUDONG NEW AREA IN 2012

The year of 2012 is one of the important years when we have deeply promoted the implementation of the "Twelfth Five-year Planning". Under the leadership of Pudong New Area (PNA) Communist Party Committee and PNA Government, we have actively dealt with the complicated and severe situation at home and abroad, deeply adopted a scientific outlook on development and the national macro-control policies, closely held the general tone of "steady progress", upheld the theory of "driving by innovations, developing by changes", and actively promoted all the targeted tasks determined by the PNA Communist Party Committee and PNA Government at the beginning of this year. As a result, we have well developed our national economy and society and successfully completed the expected targets set at the beginning of the year.

Ⅰ. Economy kept smooth growth, benefits after changes gradually appeared

Ⅰ. Economic quality and benefits increasingly promoted. The total output value reached 592. 991 billion yuan, an increase of 10. 1% over the previous year, 2. 6% higher than that of the municipality, in which the growth rate in the tertiary industry was 14. 9%. The local fiscal revenue reached 55. 030 billion yuan, an increase of 10. 0%, and the total social investment on fixed assets amounted to 145. 498 billion yuan. The power consumption of added value in PNA organizations decreased by 6. 6%.

Ⅱ. Industrial structure continuously optimized. With the ratio of the output value of the tertiary industry in the total further increased, it occupied 60. 3% of the local output value. The output value of the financial industry and that of the wholesale and retail kept a two-digit growth, and newly-emerging services, such as information, commerce, tourism, convention and exhibition, steadily developed. Affected by the macro-economic situations both home and abroad, the industry increased slowly. The total output value of industry achieved 942. 467 billion yuan last year, an increase of 1. 1%, the output value of three large new industries achieved an increase of 7. 3%, in which the manufacturing of bio-medicine and that of aviation and aerospace achieved an increase of 9. 9% and 25. 5%, respectively, and the output value of high-tech industry achieved a rise of 8. 9%, with an output rate of 31. 5%.

Ⅲ. Capability for innovations continuously enhanced. We have increasingly promoted our capability of self-independent innovations during the moment when we created Zhangjiang as one of national self-independent demonstration areas. The number of authorized patents for inventions per one million persons reached 510. The number of approved high-tech enterprises and that of R&D institutions increased by 207 and 85, respectively, which made a breakthrough of the accumulated number of 1100 and 500. The number of newly acknowledged technically-advanced service enterprises was 14, with the total number amounting to 170.

Ⅳ. Investment attraction steadily proceeded. The number of introduced foreign investment contracts and that of paid foreign investment reached USD 7. 29 billion and USD 4. 83 billion in the whole year, respectively, and the number of domestically-introduced registered capital assets exceeded 100 billion yuan. We have carried out 14 measures to support the development of the headquarters economy, and introduced 22 regional headquarters of transnational corporations, which occupied 44% of that in the municipality. The total number of headquarters in PNA reached 193, which was 47. 9% of that in the municipality. The number of newly-introduced headquarters of large domestic enterprises and regional headquarters reached 13. Large projects with domestic and foreign investment, such as the headquarters and R&D building of BASF, the headquarters and flagship store of Decathlon, Blackstone investment and Chinese Culture, have made process in PNA.

Ⅱ. Construction of "Four Centers" nuclear functional areas quickened to promote, functional development further exploited

Ⅰ. Financial function quickened to combine. The added value of the financial industry reached 106.911 billion yuan in the whole year, an increase of 11.9%. As the business volume in the financial market increased obviously, the turnover of business in Shanghai Stock Exchange increased by 20.4%, that in Shanghai Futures Exchange, 2.6%, and that of stock index futures in China Financial Futures Exchange, 73.3%. We have introduced 45 regulatory financial institutions (accumulated to the number of 737), 404 non-regulatory financial institutions (accumulated to the number of 1247), and 48 professional financial service institutions (accumulated to the number of 578). Some important functional institutions such as Shanghai RMB Business Headquarters of Bank of China were settled in PNA, Shanghai Equity Exchange formally operated. We quickened to promote the projects of Excellent Teaching, Excellent Nursing and Comfortable Living for Gold Talents, and successfully held the sixth Lujiazui Financial Culture Festival.

Ⅱ. Shipping function continuously exploited. The Volume of cargo handling at ports achieved 272 million tons in the whole year, an increase of 3.4%. The container handling capacity achieved 29.513 million TEUs, an increase of 2.5%, in which the number of international transit containers increased by 29.3%. Trial policies such as tax refund at departure ports and registration of bonded ships formally implemented. With the financial and leasing scale further enlarged, we have introduced 8 mother companies with financial and leasing business and 50 SPV (single ship single machinery) companies. We also successfully held the 2012 China International Shipping Culture Festival and the third International Shipping Strategic Development Forum.

Ⅲ. Trade function continuously enhanced. The total import and export volume achieved USD 239.893 billion in the whole year, an increase of 6.1%, the total retail volume of social consuming goods increased by 12.1%, and the total sales of commodities increased by 23.8%. With the steady development on E-business, the trading amount of E-business goods reached 351.1 billion yuan in the whole year, increased by 13%. As the services outsourcing and services trade steadily proceeded, the total import and export value of the services trade achieved USD 41.6 billion in the whole year, an increase of 18.5%, which was 41.7% of that of the municipality. As innovations of the trade function continuously strengthened, we have carried out 5 new measures for the trial of trade facilitation, expanded the trial of new international trade settlement centers which added up to 50, and quickened the construction of the national import trade innovation demonstration area, the national base of foreign culture trade, and the national promotion center for services outsourcing trade.

Ⅲ. Important zones quickened to construct, regional structure of development continuously optimized

Ⅰ. First-moving zones such as Lujiazui, Zhangjiang, Jinqiao and Shanghai Free Trade Zones quickened to improve their functions. With the powerful pushing for the construction of Lujiazui Financial City, we have started the construction of nine projects such as Pudong Financial Plaza, quickened to carry forward the projects such as Shanghai Center and the base of Tangdong headquarters, and successfully completed seven projects such as the Oriental Financial Plaza. We have also covered the nuclear zones with short-distance shuttle buses and WIFI network. We have completed the construction of the Youth Talent Apartment in the Financial City, started its operation, and come out the policy of gradient subsidies to its lodgers. With the innovative environment optimized in Zhangjiang Park, we have deeply implemented Ten Innovations in Zhangjiang, formed the route to share-holding agents, prepared the trial of nine enterprises such as Huahong Design, and put 40,000 sq. m talent apartment and 100 start-up workshops into operation. Zhangjiang Finance Street was quickened to construct. 79 important industrial projects have been constructed together, such as Shanda, HP and Thyssen Krupp. In Jinqiao Export Processing Zone, we have advanced the policy of "Optimizing the Secondary Industry, Quickly Developing the Tertiary Industry", made preliminary progress on the trial of comprehensive supporting reforms to the services and the construction of the national new industry demonstration base, completed the preliminary procedures for the project of Plot IV of Jinqiao standby land, and quickened the step of commencing the land requisition. As the development space for Shanghai Free Trade Zones further exploited, we have in an orderly manner proceeded the expansion construction of Yangshan Bonded Port with an area of 6.02 sq. km, started some projects on part of the island. With the construction of Senlan business and commercial district further quickened, we have started the construction of Phase I Project of Senlan Waigaoqiao with a floor space of about 110,000 sq. m, and completed the planning and design for Phase II project.

Ⅱ. Newly-emerging zones such as Lingang, International Tourism Resort and World Exposition fastened their development. After Shanghai Communist Party Committee and Shanghai Municipality Government published and released the Opinion on Establishing Special Mechanism and Implementing Special Policies in Lingang Region, the administrative system in Lingang region has been adjusted in place, some leading projects, such as AVIC ACAE, have started the construction, the compilation of development and planning and the implementation of projects in the bonded zone have simultaneously been promoted, supporting projects to the traffic hub for Metro Line 16 in Nanhui New Town have quickened to proceed, and the construction of price-limited buildings of one million sq. m has been started. In World Exposition zone, we have smoothly settled down 13 central enterprises, approved the regulatory detailed planning of Qiantan, and started the construction of some projects such as municipal roads, river courses and schools. On the other hand, we have smoothly promoted the construction of the international tourism resort project, finished the forming project of Disneyland Park and its supporting facilities and grounds and turned them over to the proprietary company, and started the construction of main work of the park and its supporting facilities. The Development Planning of Shanghai International Tourism Resort (2011 – 2030) was approved by the Municipality Government, and some relevant special plans, such as planning on the structure of resorts and integrated transportation, have been worked out.

Ⅲ. Work of "strong towns and optimal sub-districts" made progress. Town economy developed in an orderly way, and the administrative level of the sub-district and town societies further enhanced. We have formulated and carried out Some Measures on Work of "Strong Towns and Optimal Sub-districts" (Temporary) in PNA, the Guiding Opinion on Advancing Work of "Towns Supervising Communities" (Trial Implementation) in PNA, put more efforts on the system and mechanism of regional management, enhanced the development vitality of towns, and improved the social management ability of sub-districts and towns.

Ⅳ. Reforms on important fields and key links gradually deepened, system and mechanism more optimized.

According to the requirements of "Three Focus on" and in accordance with the principle of "Three Guides", the trial work of comprehensive supporting reforms has been focusing on the important work and made an orderly pushing forward, and some reforms on key fields and important items have made great breakthroughs around the annual work arrangement. We have continuously made perfect of the systematic environment that can promote the nuclear function of "Four Centers". The environment for technology innovations continued to be optimized, the program of share-holding agents in Zhangjiang was advanced in an orderly way, and "Two One-thousand" projects have been fully implemented. We have promoted administrative system innovations in key zones such as Lingang, Lujiazui, World Exposition and Waigaoqiao, and further optimized the social management system of large-scaled residential communities. We have quickened the pace to promote the trial work on fields of public services such as the Cooperation between Bureau and Town, the Educational Combine, family-oriented general practitioners, and the payment reform of new rural cooperative medical system (hereinafter referred to as the "New Rural Cooperation"), and further promoted the balanced layout of public resources in urban and suburban areas.

Ⅴ. Social construction completely strengthened, people's livelihood and welfare continuously improved.

Ⅰ. Employment and welfare guarantee continuously strengthened. With the steady increase of the earning of the residents, the income of urban and suburban residents reached about 40,901 yuan and 17,641 yuan, respectively in the whole year, an increase of 11. 1% and 11. 2% , both of which were faster than that of the economic growth. We have actively promoted the employment, and advanced the Youth Sailing Program, High-skill Talents Training Plan, Ten-thousand-Thousand-Hundred Persons Program, and the Three-year Action Program for Creating Innovative City. We created 150,500 new posts for the jobless in the whole year, and had 45,331 persons registered as unemployment living in urban and suburban areas, which was lower than that of the limit determined by the municipality. We have deeply promoted the 1116 Talents-introduction Program and continued to strengthen the work on talents. Pudong International Talents City operated last September. With further enhancement of the social guarantee, we have increased the average monthly pension for persons with the new rural insurance to RMB 601. 5 yuan, compensated 7272 persons who have been expropriated from their land, and salvaged 1. 5914 million person-times for all kinds of poor people. With the rapid development of the old-age care work, we have newly increased 801 beds for the old people, the number of the old who have enjoyed the service of living in their own houses with certain care reached 52,000, and we have in an orderly way promoted the creation of the National Old Friendly City. We started the construction of all kinds buildings for indemnificatory housing with a floor space of 4. 63 million sq. m, finished the construction with a floor space of 3. 18 million sq. m in the whole year. Another 782 households were benefited from the low-rent housing policy. (The number of accumulated households was 7929.)

Ⅱ. Social administrative level continuously enhanced. With the increasing improvement of management mechanism in communities, we have in an orderly way promoted the new election of residents (villagers) committees and the creation and evaluation work of National Demonstration Sub-district for Harmonious Communities and that of Construction and Experiment of Whole-coverage for Village Communities. We have continued to strengthen the professional social services, and smoothly started the projects such as the cooperative platform between the government and the communities in citizens' center, the incubation of social workers' institutions, and social workers' services in rural areas. Social organizations well developed. There have been 1550 social organizations by far. We have formulated relevant guiding opinions on the standard construction of social organizations and private non-enterprise entities in PNA. The project of Pudong Public Services Park was rewarded the sixth award of China Local Government Innovations, and Pudong Public Interests on One Street has started its trial operation.

Ⅲ. Social undertakings quickly developed. The financial investment on social livelihood aspects was 24. 9 billion yuan in the whole year, an increase of 18. 8%. As for education, we have quickly promoted the construction of projects such as the school affiliated to Shanghai Normal University, Shangnan Middle School, the complete high school (the high school affiliated to Fudan University) of supporting facilities to the Caolu large-scaled residents' area, and finished 97 projects for the campus security. New York University Shanghai was formally established last October and started its construction. High quality resources for high schools continued to exploit. We have added three municipal experimental demonstration high schools to relieve the difficulties that children of migrant workers who live together are facing with when they want to go to kindergartens and schools. As for healthcare, we have started the operation of South Branch of Oriental Hospital and East Branch of Shanghai No. 6 People's Hospital, and put into use the new emergency building of Gongli Hospital and Healthcare Service Center of Sunqiao Community, and quickened the construction of Project of International Medical Center (Phase I). We have fully practiced the system of family-oriented general practitioners in 45 community healthcare service centers. Farmers who have participated the new rural cooperation can have more than 70% of the refund during their hospitalization, with the maximum reimbursement limit worthy of 205,000 yuan. We have formulated and started the scenario of Pay to Individual according to the new rural cooperation and been rewarded National Chronic Disease Comprehensive Prevention and Control Demonstration District. As for culture, we have promoted the projects such as PNA Broadcasting and TV Center, Wu Changshuo Memorial Hall, Lingang Arts Center (Xie and Chen Museum). We have successfully held large cultural activities such as the second Pudong Culture and Arts Festival and the first Shanghai Folk Culture Festival, and started the second batch of cultural relics repair (protection) projects. The culture and creative industry quickly developed. The added value of this industry realized 60. 9 billion yuan in the whole year, an increase of 11. 2% , and

Zhangjiang National Culture Industrial Park became the first of National Combination of Culture and Technology Demonstration Bases. As for sports, we have quickened the construction of projects such as Sanlin Sports Center, and successfully held some large sports events such as Short Track Speed Skating World Championships. Shanghai Hearing Center of International Sports Arbitration Court was settled in PNA.

Ⅳ. "Three Agriculturals" work steadily promoted. As the agricultural economy operated steadily, the disposal income of the rural residents kept a steady growth. The total agricultural output value achieved 7. 1 billion yuan in the whole year. We have quickened the construction of five national modern agricultural demonstration bases, almost finished the construction of five town-level comprehensive service centers for agriculture, and successfully held the fourth Pudong Agriculture Fair. We have transformed the villages with an investment of about 1. 5 billion yuan in the whole year, from which 57 administrative villages and about 40,000 rural households from 14 towns have been benefited.

Ⅴ. Practical projects fully completed. Around the key fields that are closely related to the lives of the people, such as increasing the services for the old, promoting the construction of new villages, quickening the reformation of old buildings, promoting the employment, facilitating the public traffic, and enhancing the service level to the public, we have actively advanced the construction of practical projects both in PNA and the municipality, and fully completed 13 municipal practical projects and 34 practical projects conducted by PNA government.

Ⅵ. Urban construction and management level continuously advanced, ecological environment improved

Ⅰ. Construction of urban area quickened to proceed. We have actively promoted the compilation of the planning with the coverage of regulatory detailed planning reaching 92% for concentrated areas (excluding Pudong International Airport, Waigaoqiao Port Area and Lingang Industrial Park). We smoothly promoted the construction of 68 key projects of municipal and PNA level, and completed an investment of about 12. 6 billion yuan in the whole year. Old quarters were quickened to transform. We have cleared three plots of land such as Team No. 5 (village within factories) of Beixin Village in Gaoqiao Town, started reforming 11 plots of land, and signed contracts with about 2020 households in the whole year.

Ⅱ. Quality of ecological environment continuously optimized. We have smoothly finished the review for the title of National Model City for Environment Protection. We have also started 103 projects of the fifth round of Three-year Environment Protection Action Plan, and promoted the creation of ecological towns and villages and Green Cells such as green schools, enterprises and hotels. We have carried out all kinds of law enforcement activities for special purposes with 16,000 person-times, and inspected key-monitored enterprises for more than 6,000 unit-times. We have quickened to promote the construction of large sanitation facilities and green forest projects such as Liming Recycling of Resources Center and Phase II of Binjiang Forest Park. We have continued to promote the special-purposed recycling activities such as classification and decrease of domestic garbage, used and old clothes, electronic waste, building and decoration garbage, and promoted the work of construction of the sewage pipe network and river course regulation. With the further improvement of air quality, the excellent rate of air quality reached 96. 2% in the whole year, which set the best record in the history.

Ⅲ. Level of urban management continuously increased. Law enforcement by Chengguan further strengthened. We have altogether sent out 380,000 person-times to conduct 11 specific enforcement activities named the series of "Spring Breeze". Managing hard to do the work of preventing from flood and typhoons, we have successfully defended the invasion of natural disasters such as Typhoon Saola. Actively promoting the development of reforms on water conservancy, we have promoted the construction of concentrated water supply in Lingang area, finished switching to Qingcaosha water source for the whole PNA, and successfully created the first national water-saving demonstration area in Shanghai. We continued to strengthen the management on public security, made the safe production in an orderly way and under control. The number of accidents related to safety and that of death toll during the production decreased by 8. 7% and 12. 5% over the same period in the previous year, respectively. As the social order was in good condition, we have decreased 21. 1% of the alarms called to the emergency number of 110 that need the police over the previous year, and favorably completed the emergency operations such as the security work during the conferences of the 18th National Congress of the Communist Party of China and Fishing Island incident. We have strengthened the management of the security on food and drugs, and we have not had any incidents of collective food poisoning or any responsible drug injuries in PNA.

Ⅳ. Construction of a wise Pudong quickened to promote. Wise Pudong Development and Research Institute was established. With the fundamental network level rapidly improved, all of the indicators of main information infrastructure, such as MONET, Wireless City, Tri-networks Integration, have been higher than those of the municipality, and the Platform of Lujiazui Wireless Financial City Applications have formally put into online operation. We have conducted the trial of wise communities in ten units such as Weifang Sub-district and Jinqiao Town. With the intelligent applications deeply promoted, we have almost completed some basic information resources databases such as the population and legal person databases. Self medical service terminals have greatly decreased the time that patients consult the doctor, and the trial of Intelligent Public Transportation have started the construction of more than 60 electronic bus-stop boards.

第一篇

CHAPTER 1

综合

GENERAL SURVEY

表 1-1 气象概况
Climate
(2012)

月 份 Month		气 温(℃) Temperature(℃)			35℃以上高温日数(天) >35℃(day)	0℃以下低温日数(天) <0℃(day)
		平均气温 Average Temperature	平均最高气温 Average Highest Temperature	平均最低气温 Average Lowest Temperature		
年平均	**Annual Average**	**16.7**	**20.5**	**13.5**	**14**	**27**
1 月	January	4.7	7.6	2.0		8
2 月	February	4.5	7.3	2.1		10
3 月	March	9.5	13.5	6.1		1
4 月	April	17.1	21.8	13.1		
5 月	May	20.8	25.4	16.8		
6 月	June	24.1	27.6	21.8		
7 月	July	29.4	33.5	26.2	11	
8 月	August	28.7	32.3	26.3	3	
9 月	September	23.6	27.6	20.6		
10 月	October	19.3	23.8	15.3		
11 月	November	12.1	16.2	8.3		
12 月	December	6.4	9.7	3.2		8

表 1-1 续表 Continued

月 份 Month		日 照(小时) Sunshine (hour)	降 水 Rainfall		蒸发量(毫米) Evaporation (mm)	平均相对湿度(%) Relative Humidity(%)
			雨 量(毫米) Rainfall(mm)	雨 日(天) Rainy Day(day)		
全年总计	**Annual Total**	**1 798.4**	**1 343.9**	**176.0**	**1 175.5**	**73**
1 月	January	92.4	62.8	14	41.8	66
2 月	February	68.9	81.2	18	37.7	70
3 月	March	145.7	119.4	18	70.6	70
4 月	April	176.4	92.5	17	112.3	69
5 月	May	166.9	107.1	13	129.2	74
6 月	June	104.2	214.0	20	96.5	84
7 月	July	219.7	132.9	14	174.3	76
8 月	August	203.8	218.8	12	156.7	78
9 月	September	166.1	74.7	11	126.1	73
10 月	October	193.4	20.9	12	116.0	71
11 月	November	147.7	130.4	13	70.0	72
12 月	December	113.2	89.2	14	44.3	70

注：2012 年极端最高气温 37.7℃，出现在 7 月 6 日；极端最低气温 -5℃，出现在 1 月 26 日；初霜日 11 月 24 日，终霜日 3 月 21 日，无霜期 241 天。

Note: In 2012, the utmost highest temperature amounted to 37.7℃ on July 6 and the utmost lowest temperature came to -5℃ on January 26. The frost season started on November 24 and ended on March 21. There were 241 frost-free days in 2012

表 1-2 行政区划
Administrative Regions
(2012)

单位:个 (unit)

地 区 Subdistrict/Town		居民委员会 Neighborhood Committee	村民委员会 Village Committee	地 区 Subdistrict/Town		居民委员会 Neighborhood Committee	村民委员会 Village Committee
街镇总计(36 个)	**Total (36)**	**799**	**372**				
街 道(12 个)	**Subdistricts (12)**						
潍坊新村街道	Weifangxincun Subdistrict	27		沪东新村街道	Hudongxincun Subdistrict	33	
陆家嘴街道	Lujiazui Subdistrict	30		金杨新村街道	Jinyangxincun Subdistrict	48	
周家渡街道	Zhoujiadu Subdistrict	32		洋泾街道	Yangjing Subdistrict	38	
塘桥街道	Tangqiao Subdistrict	23		浦兴路街道	Puxinglu Subdistrict	40	
上钢新村街道	Shanggang xincun Subdistrict	23		东明路街道	Dongminglu Subdistrict	37	
南码头路街道	Nanmatoulu Subdistrict	27		花木街道	Huamu Subdistrict	41	
镇(24 个)	**Towns(24)**						
川沙新镇	Chuansha New Town	39	43	周浦镇	Zhoupu Town	15	10
高桥镇	Gaoqiao Town	28	14	新场镇	Xinchang Town	6	13
北蔡镇	Beicai Town	46	9	大团镇	Datuan Town	4	16
合庆镇	Heqing Town	6	29	康桥镇	Kangqiao Town	28	12
唐 镇	Tangzhen Town	10	17	航头镇	Hangtou Town	9	13
曹路镇	Caolu Town	15	32	祝桥镇	Zhuqiao Town	22	40
金桥镇	Jinqiao Town	9	3	泥城镇	Nicheng Town	9	11
高行镇	Gaohang Town	28	4	宣桥镇	Xuanqiao Town	5	12
高东镇	Gaodong Town	13	12	书院镇	Shuyuan Town	5	13
张江镇	Zhangjiang Town	21	9	万祥镇	Wanxiang Town	3	7
三林镇	Sanlin Town	43	16	老港镇	Laogang Town	2	7
惠南镇	Huinan Town	23	29	南汇新城镇	Nanhui New Town	11	1

注:2012 年,撤销芦潮港镇、申港街道,建南汇新城镇,辖原芦潮港镇、申港街道以及老港镇大治河以南、两港大道以东区域。
Note: In 2012, after Luchaogang Town and Shengang Subdistrict werecancelled, we established Nanhui New Town, which governed the former Luchaogang Town and Shengang Town, Shengang Subdistrict, the southern part of Dazhi River in Laogang Town and the eastern part of Lianggang Avenue.

表 1-3 主要年份经济发展主要指标
Major Indicators of Economic Development in Main Years

指 标	Indicators	1993	2005	2010	2011	2012
新区生产总值(亿元)	**Gross Domestic Product of PNA (100 million yuan)**	**164.00**	**2 108.79**	**4 707.52**	**5 484.35**	**5 929.91**
第一产业	Primary Industry	2.12	6.09	31.47	34.46	32.89
第二产业	Secondary Industry	114.45	1 070.96	2 036.58	2 306.32	2 320.75
第三产业	Tertiary Industry	47.43	1 031.74	2 639.47	3 143.57	3 576.27
财 政	**Finance**					
财政收入(亿元)	Financial Revenue (100 million yuan)	11.15	494.94	2 046.17	2 256.13	2 360.81
#地方财政收入	Local Financial Revenue	5.53	155.31	428.82	500.26	550.30
地方财政支出(亿元)	Local Financial Expenditure (100 million yuan)	9.53	198.79	524.06	615.24	666.63
固定资产投资总额(亿元)	**Total Investment in Fixed Assets (100 million yuan)**	**164.56**	**693.61**	**1 432.30**	**1 435.39**	**1 454.98**
#房地产开发投资	Investment in Real Estate Development		287.92	555.74	589.45	600.30
#城市基础设施投资额	Investment in Urban Infrastructure	54.73	125.95	261.92	272.02	261.86
招商引资	**Business Promotion and Foreign-Fund Attraction**					
外商直接投资合同项目(项)	Projects of Foreigin Direct Investment(unit)	924	1 734	906	995	976
外商直接投资合同金额(亿美元)	Project Amount of Foreign Direct Investment (USD 100 million)	17.57	56.54	56.25	65.97	72.86
期末内资企业注册数(个)	Number of Registered Domestically-Funced Enterprises at End of Term (unit)			10 961	10 636	10 633
科技创新	**Technological Innovations**					
研发机构数(个)	Number of R&D Institutions (unit)		161	393	393	440
申请专利数(项)	Patent Claiming(item)		3 141	17 587	18 819	21 972
授权专利数(项)	Number of Authorized Patents (Piece)		1 204	12 764	12 685	11 226

注:1. 2005 年至 2008 年,"港口货物吞吐量"和"集装箱吞吐量"为外高桥港区数据;2009 年起"港口货物吞吐量"和"集装箱吞吐量"为外高桥港区和洋山深水港区数据。
2. "中外资保险机构原保费收入"与历年年鉴中的"保费收入"统计口径相同,下同。

Note: 1. The items of "Volume of Cargo Handled at Port" and "Container Handling Capacity" are the data at Waigaoqiao Port from 2005 to 2008. These two items are the data at Waigaoqiao Port and Yangshan Deepwater Port since 2009.
2. The item of "Former premium income of insurances by Chinese and foreign insurance institutions" has the same statistical approach with that of "Premium income" of previous years. The below are the same.

表 1-3 续表 Continued

指 标	Indicators	1993	2005	2010	2011	2012
工业总产值(亿元)	**Gross Output Value of Industry (100 million yuan)**	**604.40**	**4 242.47**	**8 591.50**	**9 553.79**	**9 424.67**
#高技术工业	Industrial Output of High Technologies		1 190.72	2 259.08	2 704.33	2 913.52
国内外贸易	**Domestic and Foreign Trades**					
商品销售总额(亿元)	Aggregate Sales of Commodities (100 million yuan)		2 807.47	8 263.56	10 502.98	14 546.69
社会消费品零售总额(亿元)	Total Retail Sales of Consumer Goods (100 million yuan)	41.92	353.69	1 036.88	1 204.04	1 349.73
外贸进出口总额(亿美元)	Total Imports and Exports (USD 100 million)	25.92	894.75	1 865.62	2 260.00	2 398.93
出口总额	Total Exports	12.02	372.12	738.79	888.98	939.83
进口总额	Total Imports	13.90	522.63	1 126.83	1 371.02	1 459.10
功能开发	**Functional Development**					
中外资金融机构数(个)	Number of Chinese and Foreign Financial Institutions (unit)		369	649	692	737
中外资银行本外币存款余额(亿元)	Balance of RMB and Foreign Currencies Deposits in Chinese and Foreign Banks (100 million yuan)		4 244	13 079	15 553	17 045
中外资银行本外币贷款余额(亿元)	Balance of RMB and Foreign Currencies Loans in Chinese and Foreign Banks (100 million yuan)		4 668	10 436	11 672	12 621
期末认定跨国公司地区总部入驻数(户)	Settled Headquarters of Transnational Companies at End of Term (in number)		64	150	171	193
举办展览(博览)(次)	Number of Exhibitions Hosted (time)		114	120	156	184
举办国际性会议(次)	Number of International Conferences Hosted (time)		199	26	1 949	2 930
接待国内外游客总数(万人次)	Foreign and Domestic Tourists Received (10 000 person-times)		1 660	3 215	3 133	2 780
浦东国际机场旅客吞吐量(万人次)	Passenger Capacity at Pudong International Airport (10 000 person-times)		2 358	4 041	4 144	4 486
浦东国际机场货邮吞吐量(万吨)	Volume of Cargo Handled at Pudong International Airport (10 000 tons)		185	322	311	295
港口货物吞吐量(万吨)	Volume of Cargo Handled at Ports (10 000 tons)	9 017	10 646	22 470	26 332	27 232
集装箱吞吐量(万标箱)	Container Handling Capacity (10 000 TEUs)		1 272.5	2 509.8	2 880.7	2 951.3

表 1-4 主要年份社会发展主要指标
Major Indicators of Social Development in Main Years

指 标	Indicators	1993	2005	2010	2011	2012
人 口	**Population**					
年末常住人口(万人)	Permanent Population at Year end (10 000 persons)		279.19	504.44	517.50	526.39
年末户籍总人口(万人)	Registered Population at Year end (10 000 persons)	143.73	184.81	275.80	278.53	281.12
年末总户数(万户)	Total Households at Year end(10 000 households)	48.63	68.95	106.08	107.32	108.43
自然增长率(‰)	Natural Growth Rate(‰)	-0.08	-0.58	1.06	0.77	1.85
劳动就业	**Labor and New Jobs**					
从业人员(万人)	Employed Persons (10 000 persons)	104.40	144.08	235.11	280.68	297.01
第一产业	Primary Industry	4.98	1.99	14.78	14.37	13.71
第二产业	Secondary Industry	66.37	57.07	123.90	147.36	166.99
第三产业	Tertiary Industry	33.05	85.02	96.43	118.95	116.31
职工人数(万人)	Staff and Workers (10 000 persons)	78.88	70.16	85.02	138.53	145.14
新增就业岗位(万人)	Number of New Jobs (10 000 persons)		11.50	14.04	15.40	15.05
期末城镇登记失业人数(万人)	Number of Registered Unemployed Persons in Towns at End of Term (10 000 persons)		4.29	4.35	4.48	4.53
人民生活	**People's Livelihood**					
城镇居民人均年可支配收入(元)	Annual Disposable Income Per Capita of Urban Residents (yuan)		19 089	32 330	36 815	40 901
农村居民人均年可支配收入(元)	Annual Disposable Income Per Capita of Rural Residents (yuan)		9 779	13 898	15 861	17 641
职工工资总额(亿元)	Total Wages of Staff and Workers (100 million yuan)	47.26	235.03	765.95	1 243.20	1 331.81
职工年平均工资(元)	Average Annual Wages of Staff and Workers (yuan)	5 999	33 186	89 424	90 721	92 040
城镇居民人均住宅建筑面积(平方米)	Floor Space of Urban Residents Per Capita (sq·m)		32.73	39.26	36.30	36.50
平均期望寿命(岁)	Life Expectancy (year)	76.10	80.85	82.57	82.62	82.53

表 1-4 续表 Continued

指 标 Indicators		1993	2005	2010	2011	2012
教 育	**Education**					
高等学校在校学生数(人)	Student Enrollment of Higher Education (person)	3 776	41 034	167 746	184 831	177 954
中等学校在校学生数(人)	Student Enrollment at High Schools(person)	79 751	149 407	171 968	172 446	170 431
小学在校学生数(人)	Student Enrollment at Primary Schools (person)	131 204	92 062	165 009	176 328	183 060
市实验性、示范性高中和区重点高中就读学生比例(%)	Rate of Students Enrolled in Municipal Experimental and Demonstration High Schools and District-Key High Schools(%)			73.2	74.3	77.6
学龄儿童入学率(%)	Rate of School-age Child Enrollment (%)	99.2	100.0	100.0	100.0	100.0
幼儿园幼儿数(人)	Young Child Enrollment at Kindergartens (person)	42 378	44 554	83 313	94 727	103 321
卫 生	**Health**					
医疗机构数(个)	Healthcare Institutions (unit)	378	630	1 057	1 074	1 091
#医 院	Hospitals	47	57	56	59	60
医院病床(张)	Hospital Bed (bed)	4 840	6 520	15 164	17 731	18 151
卫生技术人员(人)	Healthcare Professionals (person)	7 717	9 794	18 925	23 099	24 466
#执业医生	Medical Practitioners	4 102	4 726	7 644	8 864	9 230
注册护士	Registered Nurses	2 179	3 390	7 448	9 631	10 391
城市建设、环境保护	**Urban Construction and Environmental Protection**					
建成区绿化覆盖率(%)	Coverage of Urban Green Areas in PNA (%)		37.8	36.1	36.1	36.1
城镇污水纳管率(%)	Rate of Sewage Pipe in Towns(%)		70.4	81.9	82.5	83.9
空气质量优良率(%)	Rate of Fine Air Quality (%)		89.3	92.6	94.2	96.2
人均公共绿地(平方米)	Public Green Space Per Capita (sq·m)	3.40	24.42	22.71	23.94	24.04

表1-5　历年社会经济主要指标增长率(以上年为基期)
(1993～2012)

单位:%

指　标	Indicators	1993	1994	1995	1996	1997	1998	1999
年末总户数	Total Households at Year-end		2.6	3.1	3.1	2.8	3.4	3.1
年末户籍总人口	Registered Population at Year-end	2.2	1.7	1.7	1.7	1.5	1.8	2.5
男	Male	2.3	1.9	1.8	1.8	1.5	2.0	2.6
女	Female	2.0	1.6	1.5	1.6	1.5	1.7	2.4
年末常住人口	Permanent Population at Year-end							
新区生产总值	Gross Output Value of PNA	30.2	28.6	22.0	20.2	18.3	16.8	16.1
第一产业	Primary Industry	-8.5	5.1	14.2	1.9	5.3	5.9	3.8
第二产业	Secondary Industry	22.0	21.6	21.9	17.4	16.3	14.0	13.5
第三产业	Tertiary Industry	46.6	42.8	22.6	30.0	24.3	24.2	22.5
工业总产值	Gross Domestic Product of Industry	28.7	20.1	19.3	18.2	18.4	15.1	17.3
财政收入	Financial Revenue		1.2倍(times)	62.9	30.5	21.4	13.0	13.2
#地方财政收入	Local Financial Revenue		1.8倍(times)	51.6	32.1	30.0	10.2	-0.5
地方财政支出	Local Financial Expenditure		1.1倍(times)	93.9	10.1	18.2	10.8	4.8
固定资产投资总额	Total Investment in Fixed Assets	1.2倍(times)	58.7	9.2	38.6	27.7	15.6	-24.9
#房地产开发投资	Investment in Real Estate Development							
城市基础设施投资额	Investment in Urban Infrastructure	1.5倍(times)	43.9	-32.2	84.7	20.9	48.5	-11.7
商品销售总额	Aggregate Sales of Commodities			16.7	21.2	28.3	-1.6	93.8
社会消费品零售总额	Total Retail Sales of Consumer Goods	48.5	97.4	32.9	27.5	15.7	10.3	10.8
外贸进出口总额	Total Imporst and Exports		82.7	52.0	12.2	22.6	21.0	28.2
出口总额	Total Exports		93.1	70.8	-2.2	18.3	15.1	26.3
进口总额	Total Imports		73.7	33.9	30.0	26.5	26.1	29.8

注：凡财政指标均为2004年财税体制改革后的同口径对比数,后续相关指标口径相同。
Note: Every financial indicator is the comparative number with the same approach after reforms of finance and taxation system in 2004. Hereinafter are the same.

Growth Rate of Major Indicators of Social Economy in Main Years (the Previous Year as Base)

(%)

2000	2001	2002	2003	2004	2005	2006	2007	2008	2009	2010	2011	2012
4.1	2.3	2.4	2.6	2.3	3.3	1.7	1.8	1.3	1.3	2.6	1.2	1.0
3.0	2.2	2.6	2.2	2.4	2.2	1.5	1.9	1.6	1.4	1.3	1.0	0.9
3.2	2.3	2.7	2.4	2.4	2.1	1.4	1.8	1.4	1.3	1.2	0.9	0.9
2.8	2.0	2.5	2.1	2.3	2.2	1.5	2.1	1.9	1.4	1.4	1.0	0.9
	3.1	3.0	3.0	3.1	3.1	2.2	7.0	0.1	1.7	20.4	2.6	1.7
16.5	16.1	16.7	17.5	16.4	12.1	13.4	15.2	11.6	10.5	12.4	11.1	8.1
4.9	6.1	4.9	1.6	-7.3	-4.0	-5.1	-5.4	-5.8	-2.7	-2.7	-0.9	-4.6
15.2	16.3	16.4	19.3	17.2	10.5	12.1	10.1	9.1	6.3	15.3	9.5	0.6
19.6	16.1	17.1	15.8	15.7	14.0	15.0	20.4	14.0	14.5	10.3	12.4	13.8
18.9	20.1	21.0	26.4	22.4	11.8	13.3	14.3	9.4	6.7	21.1	11.2	-1.4
30.1	39.1	41.2	46.1	25.7	10.5	18.7	45.4	22.0	5.8	25.4	10.3	4.6
27.6	47.2	14.6	41.6	20.9	13.0	14.8	46.3	16.0	9.1	12.0	16.7	10.0
19.1	26.9	36.9	32.6	20.7	2.7	12.0	29.1	28.9	7.1	10.2	17.4	8.4
-19.9	18.5	41.1	2.5	8.3	6.4	-4.8	18.8	11.3	16.2	0.8	0.2	1.4
6.6	6.5	93.6	13.9	13.7	3.0	-10.5	-4.0	13.1	6.2	28.8	6.1	1.8
-65.2	93.3	62.6	-9.2	-22.1	3.9	23.9	50.3	32.7	33.3	-46.6	3.9	-3.7
26.9	33.5	77.9	35.5	21.0	-4.3	4.9	22.7	28.6	13.7	39.9	27.1	38.5
8.5	8.3	22.0	10.2	14.4	13.2	13.1	14.0	15.5	14.4	20.6	16.1	12.1
65.9	16.9	21.9	57.5	39.0	10.7	19.9	19.3	13.2	-12.9	34.2	21.1	6.1
43.7	15.0	18.2	55.8	52.8	14.9	19.5	18.8	14.4	-16.9	28.2	20.3	5.7
82.9	17.9	24.2	58.6	31.1	7.9	20.2	19.7	12.4	-9.8	38.5	21.7	6.4

单位:%　　　　表1－5 续表 Continued

指 标	Indicators	1993	1994	1995	1996	1997	1998	1999
浦东国际机场旅客吞吐量	Passenger Capacity at Pudong International Airport							
浦东国际机场货邮吞吐量	Volume of Cargo Handled at Pudong International Airport							
港口货物吞吐量	Volume of Cargo Handled at Port	21.8	-7.8	-27.6	19.7	2.9	-5.8	-1.3
集装箱吞吐量	Container Handling Capacity				1.9倍 (times)	45.3	48.7	36.2
外商直接投资合同项目	Projects of Foreigin Direct Investment	63.0	12.0	-19.0	-4.3	-23.2	-9.9	-15.2
外商直接投资合同金额	Actual Paid Amount of Foreign Direct Investment	29.9	47.6	25.6	-44.4	-0.5	55.0	-61.5
中外资银行本外币存款余额	Balance of RMB and Foreign Currencies Deposits in Chinese and Foreign Banks							
中外资银行本外币贷款余额	Balance of RMB and Foreign Currencies Loans in Chinese and Foreign Banks							
城镇居民人均年可支配收入	Annual Disposable Income Per Capita of Urban Residents							
农村居民人均年可支配收入	Annual Disposable Income Per Capita of Rural Residents							
居民储蓄存款年末余额	Residents' Savings Deposit Balance (Year End)	77.1	76.2	56.3	28.9	20.0	13.5	10.6
高等学校在校学生数	Student Enrollment of Higher Education	26.4	11.3	13.0	6.6	11.9	29.0	21.7
中等学校在校学生数	Student Enrollment at High Schools	9.6	17.1	15.6	8.2	5.0	5.9	6.2
小学在校学生数	Student Enrollment at Primary Schools	7.7	0.2	-1.8	-0.1	1.3	-2.7	-6.7
幼儿园幼儿数	Young Child Enrollment at Kindergartens		-12.0	-3.5	-9.0	0.5	-0.5	1.0
医院病床	Hospital Beds	3.1	3.7	4.8	2.8	-1.2	3.4	9.8
卫生技术人员	Healthcare Professionals	3.4	4.0	2.3	4.4	5.2	3.1	1.2
#执业医生	Medical Practitioners	6.6	5.1	3.0	6.4	4.5	2.6	1.6
注册护士	Registered Nurses	3.7	4.9	2.6	3.7	7.6	5.1	2.7
期末认定跨国公司地区总部入驻数	Settled Headquarters of Transnational Companies at End of Term							

(%)

2000	2001	2002	2003	2004	2005	2006	2007	2008	2009	2010	2011	2012
		64.9	36.3	39.7	12.1	13.1	8.6	-2.8	13.4	26.2	2.5	8.3
		79.5	81.8	38.5	-1.1	16.8	16.2	4.8	-2.4	26.8	-3.4	-5.1
10.1	20.9	36.9	16.5	36.0	33.2	6.6	15.3	0.4	-4.9	14.3	17.2	3.4
85.4	56.9	60.2	43.3	42.0	34.9	7.9	13.4	-1.2	-9.7	17.4	14.8	2.5
47.4	27.0	9.5	73.4	1.0	2.7	-16.6	-13.3	-36.0	-12.1	16.2	9.8	-1.9
1.7倍 (times)	-30.6	33.3	7.8	12.1	75.4	-14.4	2.2	0.9	0.3	1.7	17.3	10.4
					25.3	18.8	25.0	22.2	22.9	24.2	18.9	9.6
					21.4	20.2	23.8	12.0	7.6	16.9	11.8	8.1
					12.4	12.4	13.2	14.5	9.3	11.0	13.9	11.1
					11.4	11.6	12.2	12.5	9.2	12.1	14.1	11.2
2.7	24.2	35.2	31.9	27.9	30.7	17.1	1.4	34.6	18.2	12.2	14.7	15.1
34.4	28.0	86.2	21.3	9.6	8.5	5.9	8.2	19.0	4.7	29.5	10.2	-3.7
0.8	-1.0	0.2	-1.5	12.3	-2.0	-4.1	-3.8	-3.0	-0.5	-0.7	0.3	-1.2
-6.7	-6.3	-2.3	-0.6	-11.4	3.3	3.5	3.3	3.1	17.3	3.2	6.9	3.8
3.0	-1.9	11.0	6.4	7.3	5.4	4.2	9.9	5.5	9.1	10.6	13.7	9.1
2.2	5.3	6.0	4.6	-0.6	-5.4	17.4	5.6	2.7	2.5	7.8	16.9	2.4
1.4	0.9	-1.3	-0.1	12.3	0.1	6.5	19.6	10.5	3.2	-1.8	22.1	5.9
1.5	0.5	-8.4	-0.2	3.7	-0.1	1.4	9.9	9.6	1.8	2.8	16.0	4.1
2.6	3.9	9.9	0.6	7.4	1.6	18.0	18.2	8.4	8.9	4.4	29.3	7.9
						29.7	15.7	19.8	17.4	11.1	14.0	12.9

表1-6 社会经济主要指标年均增长速度
Average Annual Growth Rate of Main Social Economic Indicators

单位:% (%)

指 标	Indicators	平均每年增长 Annual Growth Rate 1993~2012	1991~1995	1996~2000	2001~2005	2006~2010
年末户籍总人口	Registered Population at Year-end	1.9	2.1	2.1	2.3	1.5
新区生产总值	Gross Domestic Product in PNA	16.4	23.0	17.6	15.7	13.1
第一产业	Primary Industry	0.2	2.4	4.4	0.1	0.5
第二产业	Secondary Industry	14.1	20.0	15.3	15.9	11.6
第三产业	Tertiary Industry	20.2	29.8	24.1	15.7	14.9
工业总产值	Gross Output Value of Industry	16.4	20.3	17.6	20.3	14.9
*财政收入	Financial Revenue	28.7		21.4	36.8	22.8
* #地方财政收入	Local Financial Revenue	27.5		19.2	22.5	18.9
*地方财政支出	Local Financial Expenditure	23.9		12.5	23.4	17.1
社会消费品零售总额	Total Retail Sales of Consumer Goods	20.0	50.4	14.4	14.0	16.7
*外贸进出口总额	Total Imports and Exports	26.2		28.8	28.6	15.8
* #出口总额	Total Exports	24.6		19.3	31.2	14.7
* #进口总额	Total Imports	27.3		37.5	26.9	16.6
中外资银行本外币存款余额	Balance of RMB and Foreign Currencies Deposits in Chinese and Foreign Banks					20.8
中外资银行本外币贷款余额	Balance of RMB and Foreign Currencies Loans in Chinese and Foreign Banks					19.2
居民储蓄存款年末余额	Balance of Residents' Savings Deposits at Year-end	25.9	54.4	14.8	29.9	21.6

注:1. 带"*"指标宾栏第一栏年均增长速度的年份为"1994~2012"。
2. 带"*"指标宾栏第二栏因仅有二年增长速度,故不再计算该指标的年均增长速度。

Note: 1. The year with the annual growth rate in the first horizontal column that is indicated with the symbol of "*" is from 1994 to 2012.
2. Because the second column in the field of indicators with the sign of "*" only have the growth rate of the recent two years, we will not calculate the annual growth rate of this indicator.

表 1-7 社会经济结构主要指标
Main Indicators of Economic and Social Structures

单位:% (%)

指 标	Indicators	2005	2010	2011	2012
第三产业增加值占 GDP 比重	Ratio of Added Value of the Tertiary Industry in GDP	48.9	56.1	57.3	60.3
新区财政收入相当于 GDP 比例	Ratio of PNA Financial Revenue in GDP	23.5	36.1	41.1	39.8
地方财政收入相当于 GDP 比例	Ratio of Local Financial Revenue in GDP	7.4	9.0	9.1	9.3
固定资产投资相当于 GDP 比例	Ratio of Fixed Capital Investment in GDP	32.9	30.4	26.2	24.5
外贸进出口总额相当于 GDP 比例	Ratio of Total Volume of Foreign Trade in GDP	342.4	262.5	259.6	254.3
外贸出口总额相当于 GDP 比例	Ratio of Total Exports of Foreign Trade in GDP	142.4	103.9	102.1	99.6
社会消费品零售总额相当于 GDP 比例	Ratio of Total Volume of Retail Sales for Social Consumer Goods in GDP	16.8	22.0	22.0	22.8
六个重点发展行业总产值占工业总产值比重	Ratio of Total Output Value of Six Key Industries in Total Value of Industrial Output	68.1	70.0	70.6	71.3
高技术产业工业总产值占工业总产值比重	Ratio of Total Output Value of Hi-tech Industries in Total Value of Industrial Output		26.3	28.3	30.9
城市基础设施投资占固定资产投资总额比重	Ratio of Investment for Urban Infrastructure in Gross Investment in Fixed Assets	18.2	18.3	19.0	18.0
房地产开发投资占固定资产投资总额比重	Ratio of Investment for Real Estate Development in Gross Investment in Fixed Assets	41.5	38.8	41.1	41.3
机电产品出口占外贸出口商品总额比重	Ratio of Exports of Machinery and Electrical Equipment in Total Exports of Foreign Trade	61.0	66.4	65.5	66.9
高新技术产品出口占外贸出口商品总额比重	Ratio of Export of High and New Technological Products in Total Export of Foreign Trade	33.4	36.6	38.4	41.0
第三产业实到外资占新区实到外资金额比重	Ratio of Foreign Investment in Place for the Tertiary Industry in Total of Foreign Investment in Place in PNA	71.8	86.8	90.6	88.3
发明专利申请量占专利申请量比重	Ratio of the Number of Applications for Invention Patents in the Volume of Patent Applications	57.1	37.4	49.0	58.7
城镇居民家庭人均食品支出占人均消费支出比重	Ratio of Expenses for Food per Capita of Urban Families in Consumption Expenditure Per Capita	36.2	34.9	34.5	37.5
城镇居民家庭人均服务性消费支出占人均消费支出比重	Ratio of Expenses for Service Consumptions Per Capita of Urban Families in Consumption Expenditure Per Capita	32.7	31.0	30.1	31.8

表1-8 主要年份社会经济部分指标平均每天水平
Daily Average Level of Major Economic and Social Indicators in Main Years

指 标	Indicators	单 位 Unit	2005	2010	2011	2012
新区生产总值	Gross Output Value in PNA	万元 10 000 yuan	57 775	128 973	150 256	162 463
工业总产值	Gross Output Value of Industry	万元 10 000 yuan	116 232	235 384	261 748	258 210
财政收入	Financial Revenue	万元 10 000 yuan	13 560	56 059	61 812	64 680
#地方财政收入	Local Financial Revenue	万元 10 000 yuan	4 255	11 748	13 706	15 077
固定资产投资额	Total Investment in Fixed Assets	万元 10 000 yuan	19 003	39 241	39 326	39 862
新增固定资产	Newly Acquired Fixed Assets	万元 10 000 yuan	10 409	17 066	21 637	18 185
商品销售总额	Total Sales of Commodities	万元 10 000 yuan	76 917	226 399	287 753	398 539
社会消费品零售额	Retail Sales of Consumer Goods	万元 10 000 yuan	11 370	28 408	32 987	36 979
外贸出口货物总额	Total Exports Value of Commodities in Foreign Trade	万美元 USD 10 000	10 195	20 241	24 356	25 749
外商直接投资合同项目	Projects of Foreigin Direct Investment	个 unit	4.75	2.48	2.73	2.67
外商直接投资合同金额	Contracted Amount of Foreign Direct Investment	万美元 USD 10 000	1 549	1 541	1 807	1 996
港口货物吞吐量	Volume of Cargo Handled at Port	万吨 10 000 tons	29.17	61.56	72.14	74.61
函 件	Mails	万份 10 000 pieces	14.82	41.40	55.35	57.73
自来水售水量	Sales of Tap Water	万立方米 10 000 cu·m	114.87	164.62	162.79	160.81
售电量	Electricity Sales	万千瓦·时 10 000 kwh	3 512	6 293	6 548	6 788
管道燃气售气量	Sales of Pipelined Gas	万立方米 10 000 cu·m	121.37	175.89	183.01	190.41
公交车辆乘客人数	Passengers Carried by Public Vehicles	万人次 10 000 person-times	173.12	206.02	218.75	171.55
医院诊疗人数	Outpatients Treated	万人次 10 000 person-times	3.49	8.12	9.56	10.44
出生人数	Birth	人 person	34	61	61	73
死亡人数	Death	人 person	37	53	55	59

表1-9 主要年份社会经济人均指标
Annual Average Level of Major Social and Economical Indicators Per Capita in Main Years

指标	Indicators	单位 Unit	2005	2010	2011	2012
工业总产值	Gross Output Value of Industry	元 yuan	154 244	186 066	186 974	180 568
财政收入	Financial Revenue	元 yuan	17 995	44 314	44 154	45 231
#地方财政收入	Local Financial Revence	元 yuan	5 647	9 287	9 790	10 543
固定资产投资额	Total Investment in Fixed Assets	元 yuan	25 218	31 019	28 091	27 876
新增固定资产	Newly Acquired Fixed Assets	元 yuan	13 813	13 490	15 456	12 717
社会消费品零售额	Total Retail Sales of Consumer Goods	元 yuan	12 859	22 456	23 564	25 860
外贸出口总额	Total Exports Value of Foreign Trade	美元 USD	13 529	16 000	17 398	18 006
外贸进口总额	Total Imports Value of Foreign Trade	美元 USD	19 001	24 404	26 832	27 955
居民年末储蓄存款余额	Balance of Savings Deposits at Year-end	元 yuan	40 209	63 747	66 065	74 464
职工年平均工资	Annual Average Wage of Staff and Workers	元 yuan	33 186	89 424	90 721	92 040
城镇居民年人均可支配收入	Annual Disposable Income Per Capita of Urban Residents	元 yuan	19 089	32 330	36 815	40 901
农村居民年人均可支配收入	Annual Disposable Income Per Capita of Suburban Residents	元 yuan	9 779	13 898	15 861	17 641
公共绿地占有面积	Public Green Area	平方米 sq·m	24.42	22.71	23.94	24.04
邮政订销报刊数	Total Circulation of Newspapers and Magazines	份 in number	43	16	35	35
城镇居民人均住房建筑面积	Building Area of Housing Per Capita	平方米 sq·m	32.73	39.26	36.30	36.50
每万人拥有病床数	Number of Sick-beds per 10 000 Persons	张 bed	23.35	32.84	34.70	34.80
每万名中小学生拥有教职员工数	Number of Teaching Staff per 10 000 Primary and Middle School Students	人 person	882	821	796	795
实有人口万人发案率	Ratio of Criminal Cases per 10 000 Persons	起/万人 in number /10 000 persons	61.76	50.93	51.02	52.79
每万人拥有律师数	Number of Lawyers per 10 000 Persons	人 person	5.4	6.4	6.4	6.8

注：1. 上述指标除特别注明外，人均水平均采用常住人口计算。
2. 居民年人均可支配收入为住户调查资料。

Note：1. The average level per capita has been calculated in the permanent population except the above-mentioned indicators are otherwise specified.
2. The data of annual disposable income per capita are surveyed from household residents.

表 1-10 历年新区生产总值
Gross Domestic Product in PNA in Main Years
(1990 ~2012)

单位:亿元 (100 million yuan)

年 份 Year	新区生产总值 Gross Domestic Product of PNA	第一产业 Primary Industry	第二产业 Secondary Industry	#工 业 Industry	第三产业 Tertiary Industry	#金 融 Banking	房地产 Real Estate
1990	60.24	2.22	45.89	43.13	12.13	3.07	
1991	71.54	2.41	53.45	50.46	15.68	4.46	
1992	101.49	1.89	73.72	70.25	25.88	6.96	
1993	164.00	2.12	114.45	108.16	47.43	16.40	
1994	291.20	3.19	197.13	177.45	90.88	23.73	
1995	414.65	4.22	283.92	260.07	126.51	28.59	36.52
1996	496.47	4.57	320.31	286.32	171.59	39.08	40.61
1997	608.22	4.95	376.87	325.38	226.40	69.10	46.20
1998	704.27	5.30	412.82	349.97	286.15	101.31	52.68
1999	801.36	5.47	435.66	388.88	360.23	138.35	47.26
2000	923.51	5.72	488.60	445.43	429.19	159.88	55.36
2001	1 087.53	6.06	560.29	508.62	521.18	170.12	70.39
2002	1 244.00	6.38	635.54	579.86	602.08	166.04	100.51
2003	1 510.32	6.67	767.53	708.98	736.12	183.48	129.12
2004	1 850.13	6.00	952.25	894.13	891.88	218.13	168.25
2005	2 108.79	6.09	1 070.96	1 009.47	1 031.74	249.69	174.48
2006	2 365.33	5.88	1 194.47	1 133.76	1 164.98	313.98	169.24
2007	2 793.39	6.06	1 306.49	1 237.36	1 480.84	474.83	185.38
2008	3 150.99	5.88	1 430.25	1 351.44	1 714.86	553.46	181.49
2009	4 001.39	30.61	1 706.29	1 581.82	2 264.49	708.28	258.94
2010	4 707.52	31.47	2 036.58	1 899.04	2 639.47	825.78	250.08
2011	5 484.35	34.46	2 306.32	2 154.27	3 143.57	991.61	229.71
2012	5 929.91	32.89	2 320.75	2 171.00	3 576.27	1 069.11	269.46

表1-11 历年新区生产总值结构
Structure of Total Gross Domestic Product in PNA in Main Years (1990～2012)

单位:% (%)

年 份 Year	新区生产总 值 Gross Domestic Product of PNA	第一产业 Primary Industry	第二产业 Secondary Industry	#工 业 Industry	第三产业 Tertiary Industry	#金 融 Banking	房地产 Real Estate
1990	100.0	3.7	76.2	71.6	20.1	5.1	
1991	100.0	3.4	74.7	70.5	21.9	6.2	
1992	100.0	1.9	72.6	69.2	25.5	6.9	
1993	100.0	1.3	69.8	66.0	28.9	10.0	
1994	100.0	1.1	67.7	60.9	31.2	8.1	
1995	100.0	1.0	68.5	62.7	30.5	6.9	8.8
1996	100.0	0.9	64.5	57.7	34.6	7.9	8.2
1997	100.0	0.8	62.0	53.5	37.2	11.4	7.6
1998	100.0	0.7	58.6	49.7	40.7	14.4	7.5
1999	100.0	0.7	54.4	48.6	44.9	17.3	5.9
2000	100.0	0.6	52.9	48.2	46.5	17.3	6.0
2001	100.0	0.6	51.5	46.8	47.9	15.6	6.5
2002	100.0	0.5	51.1	46.6	48.4	13.4	8.1
2003	100.0	0.5	50.8	46.9	48.7	12.1	8.6
2004	100.0	0.3	51.5	48.3	48.2	11.8	9.1
2005	100.0	0.3	50.8	47.9	48.9	11.8	8.3
2006	100.0	0.2	50.5	47.9	49.3	13.3	7.2
2007	100.0	0.2	46.8	44.3	53.0	17.0	6.6
2008	100.0	0.2	45.4	42.9	54.4	17.6	5.7
2009	100.0	0.8	42.6	39.5	56.6	17.7	6.5
2010	100.0	0.7	43.2	40.3	56.1	17.5	5.3
2011	100.0	0.6	42.1	39.3	57.3	18.1	4.2
2012	100.0	0.6	39.1	36.6	60.3	18.0	4.5

表1-12 主要年份新区生产总值(新行业分类)
Gross Domestic Product in Main Years(Grouped by New Sectors)

单位:亿元 (100 million yuan)

指 标	Indicators	2005	2010	2011	2012
新区生产总值	**Gross Gross Domestic Production of PNA**	**2 108.79**	**4 707.52**	**5 484.35**	**5 929.91**
第一产业	Primary Industry	6.09	31.47	34.46	32.89
第二产业	Secondary Industry	1 070.96	2 036.58	2 306.32	2 320.75
工 业	Industry	1 009.47	1 899.04	2 154.27	2 171.00
建筑业	Construction	61.49	137.54	152.05	149.75
第三产业	Tertiary Industry	1 031.74	2 639.47	3 143.57	3 576.27
交通运输、仓储业、邮政业	Transportation, Warehousing and Post Service	88.88	170.97	196.27	187.10
信息传输、计算机服务和软件业	Information Transmission, Computer Service and Computer Software	73.34	233.07	294.47	343.06
批发和零售业	Wholesale and Retail	212.05	608.27	762.72	910.69
住宿和餐饮业	Hotel and Catering	28.13	53.03	58.33	60.78
金融业	Banking	249.69	825.78	991.61	1 069.11
房地产业	Real Estate	174.48	250.08	229.71	269.46
其他服务业	Other Services	205.17	498.27	610.46	736.07
构 成(%)	**Composition (%)**	**100.0**	**100.0**	**100.0**	**100.0**
第一产业	Primary Industry	0.3	0.7	0.6	0.6
第二产业	Secondary Industry	50.8	43.2	42.1	39.1
工 业	Industry	47.9	40.3	39.3	36.6
建筑业	Construction	2.9	2.9	2.8	2.5
第三产业	Tertiary Industry	48.9	56.1	57.3	60.3
交通运输、仓储业、邮政业	Transportation, Warehousing and Post Service	4.2	3.6	3.6	3.2
信息传输、计算机服务和软件业	Information Transmission, Computer Service and Computer Software	3.5	5.0	5.4	5.8
批发和零售业	Wholesale and Retail	10.1	12.9	13.9	15.4
住宿和餐饮业	Hotel and Catering	1.3	1.2	1.0	1.0
金融业	Banking	11.8	17.5	18.1	18.0
房地产业	Real Estate	8.3	5.3	4.2	4.5
其他服务业	Other Services	9.7	10.6	11.1	12.4

表 1-13 历年新区生产总值指数

Gross Domestic Product Indexes of PNA in Main Years (1991 ~2012)

（以 1990 年为 100） (Taking1990 as 100)

年 份 Year	新区生产总值 Gross Domestic Product of PNA	第一产业 Primary Industry	第二产业 Secondary Industry	#工 业 Industry	第三产业 Tertiary Industry	#金 融 Banking	房地产 Real Estate
1991	113.9	101.2	113.1		119.5	141.0	
1992	138.0	102.3	137.6		143.8	179.1	
1993	179.7	93.6	167.9	121.9	210.7	332.7	
1994	231.1	98.4	204.2	148.0	301.0	408.5	
1995	282.0	112.4	248.9	172.1	369.0	440.0	105.2
1996	339.0	114.5	292.2	199.8	479.7	576.9	111.6
1997	401.0	120.6	339.9	227.4	596.2	856.7	120.8
1998	468.3	127.7	387.4	256.7	740.5	1 210.5	132.1
1999	543.8	132.6	439.7	301.4	907.1	1 571.2	105.4
2000	633.5	139.1	506.5	352.9	1 084.9	1 850.9	127.7
2001	735.5	147.6	589.1	406.2	1 259.6	1 937.9	157.4
2002	858.3	154.8	685.7	473.3	1 475.0	1 941.7	214.3
2003	1 008.5	157.3	818.0	570.3	1 708.1	2 145.6	250.3
2004	1 173.9	145.8	958.7	678.1	1 976.3	2 488.9	276.5
2005	1 315.9	140.0	1 059.4	752.0	2 253.0	2 854.8	273.5
2006	1 492.2	132.9	1 187.6	849.0	2 591.0	3 565.6	261.7
2007	1 719.0	125.7	1 307.5	935.6	3 119.5	4 963.3	267.7
2008	1 918.5	118.3	1 426.7	1 019.8	3 555.9	5 712.8	257.0
2009	2 119.9	115.1	1 516.6	1 080.9	4 071.6	7 369.5	314.1
2010	2 382.8	112.0	1 748.6	1 253.8	4 491.0	7 819.0	282.7
2011	2 647.3	111.0	1 914.7	1 381.8	5 047.8	8 663.5	257.5
2012	2 914.7	103.5	1 985.6	1 435.7	5 799.9	9 694.5	299.3

注：工业增加值以 1992 年为 100，房地产增加值以 1994 年为 100。
Note: The added industrial value takes the data of 1992 as 100, and the added real estate value takes the data of 1994 as 100.

表1-14　历年新区生产总值指数
Gross Domestic Product Indexes of PNA in Main Years
(1991～2012)

(以上年为环比基期)　　　(Previous Year as Chain Base)

年　份 Year	新区生产总值 Gross Domestic Product of PNA	第一产业 Primary Industry	第二产业 Secondary Industry	#工　业 Industry	第三产业 Tertiary Industry	#金　融 Banking	房地产 Real Estate
1991	113.9	101.2	113.1	113.8	119.5	141.0	
1992	121.2	101.1	121.7	120.1	120.3	127.0	
1993	130.2	91.5	122.0	121.9	146.6	185.8	
1994	128.6	105.1	121.6	121.4	142.8	122.8	
1995	122.0	114.2	121.9	116.3	122.6	107.7	105.2
1996	120.2	101.9	117.4	116.1	130.0	131.1	106.1
1997	118.3	105.3	116.3	113.8	124.3	148.5	108.2
1998	116.8	105.9	114.0	112.9	124.2	141.3	109.4
1999	116.1	103.8	113.5	117.4	122.5	129.8	79.8
2000	116.5	104.9	115.2	117.1	119.6	117.8	121.1
2001	116.1	106.1	116.3	115.1	116.1	104.7	123.3
2002	116.7	104.9	116.4	116.5	117.1	100.2	136.1
2003	117.5	101.6	119.3	120.5	115.8	110.5	116.8
2004	116.4	92.7	117.2	118.9	115.7	116.0	110.5
2005	112.1	96.0	110.5	110.9	114.0	114.7	98.9
2006	113.4	94.9	112.1	112.9	115.0	124.9	95.7
2007	115.2	94.6	110.1	110.2	120.4	139.2	102.3
2008	111.6	94.2	109.1	109.0	114.0	115.1	96.0
2009	110.5	97.3	106.3	106.0	114.5	129.0	122.2
2010	112.4	97.3	115.3	116.0	110.3	106.1	90.0
2011	111.1	99.1	109.5	110.2	112.4	110.8	91.1
2012	110.1	93.2	103.7	103.9	114.9	111.9	116.2

表1-15 历年第三产业增加值指数(旧行业分类)

Indexes of Value Added in Tertiary Industry in Main Years (Grouped By Old Sectors) (1991 ~2000)

(以上年为环比基期) (Previous Year as Chain Base)

年 份 Year	第三产业增加值 Value Added in Tertiary Industry	#交通、运输、仓储、邮电通讯业 Transportation, Warehousing, Post and Telecommunications	批发和零售贸易、餐饮业 Wholesale, Retail and Catering	金融保险 Banking and Insurance	房地产 Real Estate
1991	119.5	108.8	108.1	141.0	
1992	120.3			127.0	
1993	146.6	137.3	124.8	185.8	
1994	142.8	105.4	154.1	122.8	
1995	122.6	115.2	172.8	107.7	105.2
1996	130.0	128.4	158.9	131.1	106.1
1997	124.3	112.2	118.5	148.5	108.2
1998	124.2	117.0	118.3	141.3	109.4
1999	122.5	122.1	129.1	129.8	79.8
2000	119.6	117.9	119.1	117.8	121.1

表1-16 历年第三产业增加值指数(新行业分类)

Index of Value Added in Tertiary Industry in Main Years(Grouped by New Sectors) (2001 ~2012)

(以上年为环比基期) (Previous Year as Chain Base)

年 份 Year	第三产业增加值 Value Added in Tertiary Industry	#交通运输、仓储业、邮政业 Transportation, Warehousing and Post Service	信息传输、计算机服务和软件业 Information Transmission, Computer Service and Computer Software	批发和零售业 Wholesale and Retail	金融业 Banking	房地产业 Real Estate
2001	116.1	127.5	109.4	121.6	104.7	123.3
2002	117.1	127.1	109.7	116.9	100.2	136.1
2003	115.8	115.8	164.3	113.6	110.5	116.8
2004	115.7	122.2	121.4	112.6	116.0	110.5
2005	114.0	118.6	118.3	114.8	114.7	98.9
2006	115.0	115.2	119.1	112.9	124.9	95.7
2007	120.4	115.7	116.4	114.7	139.2	102.3
2008	114.0	110.9	120.3	115.4	115.1	96.0
2009	114.5	94.7	105.4	114.3	129.0	122.2
2010	110.3	116.5	110.9	120.1	106.1	90.0
2011	112.4	112.3	118.4	116.6	110.8	91.1
2012	114.9	103.4	116.3	118.2	111.9	116.2

表1-17 社会经济主要指标占全市比重

The Proportion of Major Economic and Social Indicators in Shanghai

指 标	Indicators	2011 浦东新区 PNA	2011 全市 Shanghai	2011 浦东新区占全市比重(%) Proportion of PNA in Shanghai(%)	2012 浦东新区 PNA	2012 全市 Shanghai	2012 浦东新区占全市比重(%) Proportion of PNA in Shanghai(%)
土地面积(平方公里)	Land Area (sq·km)	1 291.64	6 340.50	20.4	1 373.82	6 340.50	21.7
年末常住人口(万人)	Permanent Population at Year-end (10 000 persons)	517.50	2 347.46	22.0	526.39	2 380.43	22.1
年末户籍总人口(万人)	Registered Population at Year-end (10 000 persons)	278.53	1 419.36	19.6	281.12	1 426.93	19.7
从业人员(万人)	Employment (10 000 persons)	280.68	1 104.33	25.4	297.01	1 115.50	26.6
职工人数(万人)	Staff and Workers(10 000 persons)	138.53	868.42	16.0	145.14	944.47	15.4
生产总值(亿元)	Gross Domestic Product (100 million yuan)	5 484.35	19 195.69	28.6	5 929.91	20 181.72	29.4
第一产业	Primary Industry	34.46	124.94	27.6	32.89	127.80	25.7
第二产业	Secondary Industry	2 306.32	7 927.89	29.1	2 320.75	7 854.77	29.5
#工 业	Industry	2 154.27	7 208.59	29.9	2 171.00	7 097.76	30.6
第三产业	Tertiary Industry	3 143.57	11 142.86	28.2	3 576.27	12 199.15	29.3
#金 融	Banking	991.61	2 277.40	43.5	1 069.11	2 450.36	43.6
房地产	Real Estate	229.71	1 019.68	22.5	269.46	1 147.04	23.5
工业总产值(亿元)	Gross Output Value of Industry (100 million yuan)	9 553.79	33 834.44	28.2	9 424.67	33 186.41	28.4
固定资产投资总额(亿元)	Total Investment in Fixed Assets (100 million yuan)	1 435.39	5 067.09	28.3	1 454.98	5 254.38	27.7
城市基础设施投资额(亿元)	Investment in Urban Infrastructure (100 million yuan)	272.02	1 157.34	23.5	261.86	1 038.61	25.2
地方财政收入(亿元)	Local Government Revenue (100 million yuan)	500.26	3 429.83	14.6	550.30	3 743.71	14.7
地方财政支出(亿元)	Local Government Expenditure (100 million yuan)	615.24	3 914.88	15.7	666.63	4 184.02	15.9

表 1-17 续表 Continued

指 标 Indicators		2011			2012		
		浦东新区 PNA	全市 Shanghai	浦东新区占全市比重(%) Proportion of PNA in Shanghai(%)	浦东新区 PNA	全市 Shanghai	浦东新区占全市比重(%) Proportion of PNA in Shanghai(%)
商品销售总额(亿元)	Aggregate Sales of Commodities (100 million yuan)	10 502.98	46 075.87	22.8	14 546.69	53 795.10	27.0
社会消费品零售总额(亿元)	Retail Sales of Consumer Goods (100 million yuan)	1 204.04	6 814.80	17.7	1 349.73	7 412.30	18.2
年末居民储蓄存款余额(亿元)	Savings Deposit Balance of Rural and Urban Residents (100 million yuan)	3 375.71	17 958.22	18.8	3 886.60	20 247.24	19.2
外贸进出口商品总额(亿美元)	Total Value of Imports and Exports (USD 100 million)	2 260.00	4 374.36	51.7	2 398.93	4 367.58	54.9
#出口总额	Value of Exports	888.98	2 097.89	42.4	939.83	2 068.07	45.4
外商直接投资合同项目(个)	Projects of Foreigin Direct Investment (unit)	995	4 329	23.0	976	4 043	24.1
外商直接投资合同金额(亿美元)	Project Amount of Foreign Direct Investment (USD 100 million)	65.97	201.03	32.8	72.86	223.38	32.6
外商直接投资实际到位金额(亿美元)	Foreign Direct Investment Actually Absorbed (USD 100 million)	52.97	126.01	42.0	48.30	151.85	31.8
港口货物吞吐量(万吨)	Volume of Cargo Handled at Port (10 000 tons)	26 332	72 758	36.2	27 232	73 559	37.0
集装箱吞吐量(万标箱)	Container Handling Capacity (10 000 TEUs)	2 880.7	3 173.9	90.8	2 9513	3 252.9	90.7
各级各类学校在校学生数(万人)	Student Enrollment by Level and Type of Schools (10 000 persons)	53.44	197.64	27.0	53.26	185.74	28.7
医院病床(张)	Number of Hospital Beds (bed)	17 731	87 548	20.3	18 151	89 971	20.2
专业卫生技术人员(万人)	Medical Technical Personnel (10 000 persons)	2.31	13.91	16.6	2.45	14.61	16.8
#执业医生	Medical Practitioners	0.89	5.21	17.1	0.92	5.42	17.0
申请专利(项)	Patent Claiming (item)	18 819	80 215	23.5	21 972	82 682	26.6

表1-18 财政收支
Financial Revenue and Expenditure

单位:万元 (10 000 yuan)

指 标	Indicators	2000	2010	2011	2012
全部财政收入	**Total Financial Revenue**	**1 032 077**	**20 461 744**	**22 561 309**	**23 608 119**
地方财政收入	**PNA Government Revenue**	**564 020**	**4 288 216**	**5 002 592**	**5 503 035**
区级财政收入	**PNA Financial Revenue**	**355 863**	**6 866 283**	**6 933 355**	**6 645 262**
#增值税	Value Added Tax	44 293	695 060	695 307	1 197 899
营业税	Business Income Tax	122 200	1 478 656	1 512 511	1 231 271
企业所得税	Enterprise Tax	72 712	911 281	1 119 566	1 191 426
个人所得税	Individual Income Tax	77 662	447 612	541 489	573 089
城市维护建设税	Tax on Urban Construction and Maintenance	11 603	64 066	98 026	127 214
房产税	Tax on Real Estate	13 418	78 264	99 360	122 284
印花税	Stamp Tax	3 588	124 409	150 480	181 974
契 税	Contract Tax	7 107	315 205	323 867	251 281
地方财政支出	**PNA Government Expenditure**	**695 999**	**5 240 626**	**6 152 362**	**6 666 275**
#一般公共服务	Ordinary Community Services		337 484	372 136	368 144
公共安全	Public Security		217 982	231 784	242 954
教 育	Education		493 988	692 047	917 618
科学技术	Technology		239 029	326 331	394 437
文化体育与传媒	Culture, Sports and Media		55 135	91 315	76 838
社会保障和就业	Social Security and Employment		456 319	510 653	538 441
医疗卫生	Healthcare		260 061	286 751	267 673
节能环保	Lower Power Consumption and Environment Protection		61 191	33 877	30 110
城乡社区事务	Urban and Suburban Community Affairs		1 475 828	1 802 289	1 713 512
农林水事务	Agricultural, Forest and Water Affairs		285 049	294 139	402 787
交通运输	Traffic and Transportation		153 107	133 429	237 326
资源勘探电力信息等事物	Resource Exploration and Electric Power Information, etc		879 267	1 099 532	1 186 349
商业服务业等事物	Business Services, etc		63 436	39 206	37 261
金融监管等事物支出	Expenditure such as Supervision on Financial Affaires		88 000	58 400	64 000

注：1. 2007 年财政部进行财税体制改革,起用新科目,2000 及 2005 年口径数据无法提供。
2. 2010 年起财政收入数按“十二五”市财税体制改革确定的新体制口径填列。

Note: 1. This table is provided by PNA Financial Bureau. The Financial Department has started the reform of the finance and taxation system since 2007, which began to use the new subject. Data approached in 2000 and those in 2005 are not available.
2. The number of financial revenue are filled in according to the new system approach determined by the municipal financeand system reforms during the “Twelfth – Five – Year Planning” since the year of 2010.

主要统计指标解释

气　温

气温是指空气的温度，一般以摄氏度(℃)为单位表示。气象观测的温度表是放在离地面约1.5米处通风良好的百叶箱里测量的，因此，通常说的气温指的是离地面1.5米处百叶箱中的温度。其统计计算方法为：

月平均气温是将全月各日的平均气温相加，除以该月的天数而得。

年平均气温是将12个月的月平均气温累加后除以12而得。

降水量

降水量是指从天空降落到地面的液态或固态(经融化后)水，未经蒸发、渗透、流失而在地面上积聚的深度。其统计计算方法为：

月降水量是将全月各日的降水量累加而得。

年降水量是将12个月的月降水量累加而得。

日照时数

日照时数是指太阳实际照射地面的时间。其统计方法与降水量相同。

生产总值(原国内生产总值)

国内生产总值是指按市场价格计算的一个地区所有常住(驻)单位在一定时期内生产活动的最终成果。生产总值有三种表现形态，即价值形态、收入形态和产品形态。从价值形态看，它是所有常驻单位在一定时期内所生产的全部货物和服务价值超过同期投入的全部非固定资产货物和服务价值的差额，即所有常住(驻)单位的增加值之和；从收入形态看，它是所有常住(驻)单位在一定时期内所创造并分配给常住(驻)单位和非常住(驻)单位的初次(分配)收入之和；从产品形态看，它是所有常住单位在一定时期内最终使用的货物和服务减去进口货物和服务。在实际核算中，生产总值有三种计算方法(其三种表现形态体现为三种计算方法)，即生产法、收入法和支出法。三种方法分别从不同的方面反映生产总值及其构成。根据国务院和国家统计局有关我国GDP核算和数据发布制度的规定，浦东新区国内生产总值自2004年起更名为“浦东新区生产总值”，简称“浦东新区GDP”。

三次产业

根据社会生产活动历史发展的顺序对产业结构的划分，产品直接取自自然界的部门称为第一产业，对初级产品进行再加工的部门称为第二产业，为生产和消费提供各种服务的部门称为第三产业。

第一产业：农林牧渔业(包括农业、林业、畜牧业、渔业和农林牧渔服务业)。

第二产业：包括采矿业、制造业、电力、燃气及水的生产和供应业与建筑业。

第三产业：除第一、第二产业以外的其他各业。

指　数

指数是一种表明社会经济现象动态的相对数。运用指数可以测定不能直接相加和直接对比的社会经济现象的总动态；可以分析社会经济现象总变动中各因素变动的影响程度；可以研究总平均指标变动中各组标志水平和总体结构变动的作用。它是在把各个年份的产值换算成可比价格的基础上，根据定基数等于相应各个环比指数的连乘积这个换算关系计算出来的。

平均每年增长速度

在我国计算平均增长速度有两种方法，一种是习惯上经常使用的“水平法”，又称几何平均法，是各以间隔期最后一年的水平同基期水平对比来计算平均每年增长(或下降)速度。另一种是"累计法"，又称代数平均法或方程法，是以间隔期内各年水平的总和同基期水平对比来计算平均每年增长(或下降)速度。

在一般正常情况下，两种方法计算的平均每年增长速度比较接近，但在经济发展不平衡，出现大起大落时，两种方法计算的结果差别较大。

本年鉴内所列的平均每年增长速度，除固定资产投资、直接吸收外资是用“累计法”计算以外，其余均用“水平法”计算。

财政收入

指国家财政参与社会产品分配所取得的收入，是实现国家职能的财力保证。财政收入所包括的内容几经变化，目前主要包括：

(1)各项税收：包括增值税、营业税、消费税、土地增值税、城市维护建设税、资源税、城市土地使用税、企业所得税、个人所得税、关税、证券交易印花税、车辆购置税、农牧业税和耕地占用税等。

(2)专项收入：包括排污费收入、城市水资源费收入、矿产资源补偿费收入、教育费附加收入等。

(3)其他收入：包括利息收入、基本建设贷款归还收入、基本建设收入、捐赠收入等。

(4)国有企业亏损补贴：此项为负收入，冲减财政收入。主要包括对工业企业、商业企业、粮食企业的补贴。

中央财政收入和地方财政收入

指按现行分税制财政体制划分的中央本级收入和地方本级收入。1994 年实行分税制财政体制以后，属于中央财政的收入包括关税、海关代征消费税和增值税，消费税，中央企业所得税，地方银行和外资银行及非银行金融企业所得税，铁道部门、各银行总行、各保险总公司等集中缴纳的营业税、利润和城市维护建设税，车辆购置税，船舶吨税，增值税的 75% 部分，证券交易税（印花税）94% 部分，个人所得税中的利息所得税，利息所得税之外的个人所得税中央分享的部分，海洋石油资源税。属于地方财政的收入包括营业税，地方企业所得税，利息所得税之外的个人所得税地方分享的部分，城镇土地使用税，固定资产投资方向调节税，城镇维护建设税，房产税，车船使用税，印花税，屠宰税，农牧业税，农业特产税，耕地占用税，契税，土地增值税、国有土地有偿使用收入，增值税 25% 部分，证券交易税（印花税）6% 部分和除海洋石油资源税以外的其他资源税。

地方财政支出

地方财政支出指根据政府在经济和社会活动中，按照政府的责权划分确定的支出。地方财政支出主要包括地方行政管理和各项事业费，地方统筹的基本建设、技术改造支出，支援农村生产支出，城市维护和建设经费，价格补贴支出等。

港口货物吞吐量

指经水运进出港区范围，并经过装卸的货物数量，包括邮件及办理托运手续的行李、包裹以及补给运输船舶的燃、物料和淡水。货物吞吐量按货物流向分为进口、出口吞吐量，按货物交流性质分为外贸货物吞吐量和国内贸易货物吞吐量。货物吞吐量的货类构成及其流向，是衡量港口生产能力大小的重要指标。

国际标准集装箱吞吐量

凡经过水运进、出港区范围，并经过装卸的集装箱箱数和重量（含集装箱自重），通常是按进港和出港分别统计。

TEU 是“折合 20 英尺标准箱”的英文缩写。它是指各种尺寸的国际标准集装箱的自然箱数，按各自的换算比例，折算为 20 英尺标准箱的换算箱数。其换算比例为：40 英尺箱 1 : 2；35 英尺箱 1 : 1.75；20 英尺箱 1 : 1；10 英尺箱 1 : 0.5。

EXPLANATORY NOTES TO MAJOR STATISTICAL INDICATORS

Temperature

Temperature refers to the air temperature. It often uses centigrade as the unit. The thermometry used for weather observation is put in a breezy shutter, which is 1.5 meters high from the ground. Therefore, the commonly used temperature refers to the temperature in the breezy shutter 1.5 meters away from the ground. The calculation method is as follows:

Monthly average temperature is the summation of average daily temperature of one month divided by the actual days of that particular month.

Annual average temperature is the summation of monthly average of a year divided by 12 months.

Volume of Precipitation

Volume of Precipitation refers to the deepness of liquid state or solid state (thawed) water falling from the sky to the ground that has not been evaporated, infiltrated or run off. The calculation method is as follows:

Monthly precipitation is the summation of daily precipitation of a month.

Annual precipitation is the summation of 12 months precipitation of a year.

Sunshine Hours

Sunshine Hours refer to the actual hours of sun irradiating the earth. The calculation method is the same as that of the precipitation.

Gross Domespic Product

Gross Domespic Product refers to the final products at market prices by (of) all resident units of a region during a certain period of time. Gross product is expressed in three different forms, i. e value, income, and products respectively. The form of value added refers to the total value of all products and services produced by all resident units during a certain period of time minus the total value of inputs of non fixed-assets products and services or the summation of the value added of all resident units; the form of income includes all the income items produced by all resident units and distributed primarily to all resident and non-resident units; the form of product refers to all final goods and services minus imports of goods and services. In the practice of national accounting, it is calculated by three approaches, i. e. product approach, income approach, and expenditure approach, respectively, to reflect Gross Product and its composition of different aspects. According to the regulations of GDP national accounting and data release issued by the State Council and National Bureau of Statistics, since 2004 Pudong New Area Gross Domestic Product has been renamed as Pudong New Area Gross Product Value, for short PNA GDP.

Three Industries

Three Industries have been classified according to the historical sequence of development. Primary industry refers to extraction of natural resources; secondary industry involves processing of primary products; and tertiary industry provides services of various kinds for production and consumption.

Primary industry: Agriculture, forestry, animal husbandry and fishery. (including farming, forestry, animal husbandry, fishery industry and service industry for farming, forestry, animal husbandry and fishery).

Secondary industry: Mining, manufacturing, power, steam and water production and supply and construction.

Tertiary industry: All other industries not included in primary or secondary industries.

Index

Index refers to the relative figures indicating social and economic phenomena and developments. Index is used to evaluate the overall development of social and economic phenomena which can not be determined by simple addition or direct comparison. It is also used to analyze the outcome of various changes in the general phenomenon movement of social and economic development, and to study the level of each sub-index in the changes of general average index and the role of the changes of the overall structure. It is calculated at the comparable prices conversed from the output value of each year, using the formula of index number with fixed base period equal to the continuous product of its relative chain index.

Average Annual Growth Rate

Two methods for calculating Average Annual Growth Rate are applied in China, one is often called "level approach" or geometry average, which is derived by comparing the growth rate for the last year of the interval with that of the beginning year; the other is called "accumulating approach" or algebraic average or equation method, which is calculated by comparing the total growth rate of each year for the interval with that of base year.

Usually the results calculated by the two methods are fairly close, but they differ sharply when imbalance occurred in economic development with striking fluctuations in growth.

The Average Annual Growth Rates listed in this statistical yearbook are calculated by "level approach" except for the growth rate of investment in fixed assets and foreign capital absorbed.

Government Revenue

Government Revenue refers to the revenue of the government finance by means of participating in the distribution of the social products, which is the financial resources for ensuring the government to function. The contents of government revenue have been changed several times. Now it includes the following main items:

(1) Various tax revenues, including value added tax, business tax, consumption tax, land value added tax, tax on city maintenance and construction, resources tax, tax on use of urban land, enterprise income tax, personal income tax, tariff, stamp tax on security transactions, tax on purchase of motor vehicles, tax on agriculture and animal husbandry and tax on occupancy of cultivated land, etc.

(2) Special revenues, including revenues from the fee on sewage treatment, fee on urban water resources, fee for the compensation of mineral resources and extra-charges for education, etc.

(3) Other revenues, including revenue from interest, revenue from the repayment of capital construction loan, revenue from capital construction projects, and donations and grants.

(4) Subsidies for the losses of the state-owned enterprises. This is an item of negative revenue, consisting of subsidies to industrial, commercial and grain purchasing and supply enterprises.

Revenue of the Central Government and Revenue of the Local Government

Revenue of the central government and revenue of the local governments: refers to the revenue of the central government and that of the local governments as defined by the decentralized taxation system starting from 1994. In accordance with this system, the revenue of the central government includes tariff, consumption tax and value added tax levied by the customs, consumption tax, income tax of the enterprises subordinate to the central government, income taxes of the local banks, foreign-funded banks and non-bank financial institutions, business tax and profits of railways, head offices of banks, head office of insurance company , which are handed over to the government in a centralized way, tax on city maintenance and construction, tax on purchasing motor vehicles, tonnage tax of ships, 75% of the value added tax, 94% of the tax on stock dealing (stamp tax), interest income tax in the personal income tax, proportion of the personal income tax (other that interest income tax) to be shared by the central government, and tax on ocean petroleum resources. The revenue of the local governments includes business tax, income tax of the enterprises subordinate to the local government, proportion of the personal income tax (other that interest income tax) to be shared by the central government, tax on the use of urban land, tax on the adjustment of the investment in fixed assets, tax on town maintenance and construction, tax on real estates, tax on the use of vehicles and ships, stamp tax, slaughter tax, tax on agriculture and animal husbandry, tax on special agricultural products, tax on the occupancy of cultivated land, contract tax, value-added tax on land, income from charges on use of state-owned land, 25% of the value added tax, 6% of the tax on stock dealing (stamp tax) and tax on resources other than the ocean petroleum resources.

Expenditure of the Local Government

Expenditure of the local government includes mainly the administrative expenses and various operating expenses at the level of local governments, the expenditure for capital construction and technological innovation with the funds raised by the local government, expenditure for supporting rural production, expenditure for city maintenance and construction and expenditure for price subsidies, etc.

Volume of Freight Handled in Ports

Volume of Freight Handled in Ports refers to the volume of cargo passing in and out the harbor area of the ports and having been loaded and unloaded. The volume includes that of the postal matters, registered luggage and fuels, materials and fresh water as supplies of the ships. The volume of freight handled may be classified by direction of flow as freight for import and freight for export, or by nature of cargo as freight for domestic trade and freight for foreign trade. As an important indicator, the volume of freight handled by type of cargo and by main flow direction reflects the production capacity of ports.

International Container Throughput Capacity

International Container Throughput Capacity refers to number and weight of containers which are loaded or unloaded within port area via water carriage. It is often calculated by entering and leaving port, respectively. TEU was the abbreviation of twenty foot equivalent unit, which refers to converted number of all kinds of containers. The conversion method is based on respective conversion ratio and the number of all kinds of container is converted to the standard number of twenty foot equivalent unit. The conversion ratio is: 40 feet container 1 : 2, 35 feet container 1 : 1.75, 20 feet container 1 : 1, 10 feet container 1 : 0.5.

第二篇

CHAPTER 2

人口

POPULATION

表2-1　历年常住人口、户籍人口、流动人口情况
(1990～2012)

单位:万人

年　份 Year	年末常住人口 Permanent Population at year-end	常住人口密度 (人/平方公里) Density of Permanent Population (Persons/sq·km)	年末户籍人口 Registered Population at Year-end	按户籍 Grouped by Types of
				非农业 Non-agriculture
1990			133.94	81.67
1991			137.34	85.45
1992			140.67	89.65
1993			143.73	97.78
1994			146.20	104.63
1995			148.63	109.73
1996			151.11	113.84
1997			153.40	119.20
1998			156.18	123.70
1999			160.08	128.51
2000	240.23	4 503	164.87	134.57
2001	247.56	4 641	168.45	139.85
2002	255.11	4 782	172.82	146.25
2003	262.89	4 616	176.69	153.46
2004	270.91	4 756	180.90	160.13
2005	279.19	4 902	184.81	170.17
2006	285.30	5 009	187.56	175.24
2007	305.35	5 361	191.16	179.90
2008	305.70	5 367	194.29	183.62
2009	419.05	3 462	272.28	240.32
2010	504.44	3 908	275.80	245.06
2011	517.50	4 007	278.53	248.63
2012	526.39	3 832	281.12	252.24

Permanent Population, Household Registered Population and Migrating Population in Main Years

(10 000 Persons)

性质分 Residence Registration	按性别分 Grouped by Sex		户籍人口密度 (人/平方公里) Population Density (persons/sq · km)	期末登记流动人口数 Number of Registered Migrating Population
农 业 Agriculture	男 Male	女 Female		
52.27	66.41	67.53	2 584	
51.89	68.22	69.12	2 650	
51.02	69.96	70.71	2 714	
45.95	71.59	72.14	2 749	
41.57	72.92	73.28	2 797	
38.90	74.23	74.40	2 843	
37.27	75.53	75.58	2 891	
34.20	76.70	76.70	2 934	
32.48	78.21	77.97	2 988	
31.57	80.22	79.86	3 001	
30.30	82.75	82.12	3 091	
28.60	84.66	83.79	3 158	
26.57	86.97	85.85	3 240	67.94
23.23	89.03	87.66	3 102	80.16
20.77	91.20	89.70	3 176	82.58
14.64	93.12	91.69	3 245	93.73
12.32	94.45	93.11	3 293	119.75
11.26	96.13	95.03	3 356	130.97
10.67	97.48	96.81	3 411	127.30
31.96	136.00	136.28	2 249	169.53
30.74	137.60	138.20	2 137	218.33
29.90	138.87	139.65	2 156	206.50
28.88	140.18	140.94	2 046	238.32

表2-2　土地面积、户数、人口、人口密度及人口迁移情况
(2012年底)

单位:人

地　区	Subdistrict/Town	土地面积(平方公里) Land Area (sq. km)	户　数(户) Household (household)	年末人口 Year-end Population	按户籍性质分 Grouped by Types of Residence Registration 非农业 Non-agriculture	农　业 Agriculture
总　计	**Total**	**1 373.82**	**1 084 266**	**2 811 167**	**2 522 395**	**288 772**
街道小计	**Subdistrict Tot**	**84.64**	**436 920**	**1 153 581**	**1 153 529**	**52**
潍坊新村街道	Weifangxincun Subdistrict	3.74	31 739	91 050	91 050	
陆家嘴街道	Lujiazui Subdistrict	6.89	38 110	118 965	118 965	
周家渡街道	Zhoujiadu Subdistrict	5.52	43 603	115 815	115 815	
塘桥街道	Tangqiao Subdistrict	3.86	21 808	57 588	57 585	3
上钢新村街道	Shanggangxincun Subdistrict	7.54	37 347	103 944	103 944	
南码头路街道	Nanmatoulu Subdistrict	4.25	30 119	81 133	81 132	1
沪东新村街道	Hudongxincun Subdistrict	5.39	28 655	72 313	72 313	
金杨新村街道	Jinyangxincun Subdistrict	8.02	52 725	130 762	130 762	
洋泾街道	Yangjing Subdistrict	7.38	39 246	107 330	107 330	
浦兴路街道	Puxinglu Subdistrict	6.25	41 388	99 873	99 873	
东明路街道	Dongminglu Subdistrict	4.90	27 048	64 511	64 471	40
花木街道	Huamu Subdistrict	20.90	45 132	110 297	110 289	8
镇小计	**Town Tot**	**1 289.18**	**647 346**	**1 657 586**	**1 368 866**	**288 720**
川沙新镇	Chuansha New Town	96.70	55 151	149 799	111 812	37 987
高 桥 镇	Gaoqiao Town	39.02	34 309	88 166	82 487	5 679
北 蔡 镇	Beicai Town	23.71	49 298	125 910	122 282	3 628
合 庆 镇	Heqing Town	41.86	22 229	56 243	36 070	20 173
唐　　镇	Tangzhen Town	32.32	15 920	40 853	38 052	2 801
曹 路 镇	Caolu Town	45.48	24 504	73 113	61 668	11 445
金 桥 镇	Jinqiao Town	25.28	10 689	29 358	28 845	513
高 行 镇	Gaohang Town	22.85	20 009	51 090	51 040	50
高 东 镇	Gaodong Town	35.16	13 854	36 363	32 209	4 154
张 江 镇	Zhangjiang Town	45.02	25 665	74 016	74 001	15
三 林 镇	Sanlin Town	34.19	48 310	120 427	113 457	6 970
惠 南 镇	Huinan Town	59.08	46 067	114 886	100 274	14 612
周 浦 镇	Zhoupu Town	43.23	30 614	75 023	68 584	6 439
新 场 镇	Xinchang Town	53.45	21 261	51 619	32 888	18 731
大 团 镇	Datuan Town	50.58	28 900	66 941	34 723	32 218
康 桥 镇	Kangqiao Town	41.04	24 886	64 355	63 111	1 244
航 头 镇	Hangtou Town	59.96	24 585	59 537	43 612	15 925
祝 桥 镇	Zhuqiao Town	154.00	53 991	137 558	103 069	34 489
泥 城 镇	Nicheng Town	59.49	24 667	57 634	42 746	14 888
宣 桥 镇	Xuanqiao Town	45.73	18 542	42 584	34 135	8 449
书 院 镇	Shuyuan Town	66.91	22 283	51 959	27 267	24 692
万 祥 镇	Wanxiang Town	23.07	9 958	24 893	16 512	8 381
老 港 镇	Laogang Town	38.90	13 339	33 767	18 535	15 232
南汇新城镇	Nanhui New Town	152.15	8 315	31 492	31 487	5

注：南汇新城镇集体户口居多,因此不计算他的户规模。

Note: As the nubmer of collective households in Nanhui New Town is much more than that of urban households, we do not calculate its scale of households.

Land Area, Households, Population, Density of Population and Migration of Population (End of 2012)

(person)

按性别分 Grouped by Sex		平均每户人口 Average Persons Per Household	人口密度（人/平方公里） Population Density (persons/sq · km)	人口迁移情况 Population Mobility		
男 Male	女 Female			迁入 Population Moved-in	迁出 Population Moved-out	净迁入 Net Mobility
1 401 761	**1 409 406**	**2.59**	**2 046**	**25 253**	**11 238**	**14 015**
577 514	**576 067**	**2.65**	**13 629**	**10 283**	**2 344**	**7 939**
44 906	46 144	2.87	24 345	323	52	271
58 716	60 249	3.12	17 266	1 101	394	707
57 418	58 397	2.66	20 981	1 827	63	1 764
28 530	29 058	2.64	14 919	273	55	218
51 761	52 183	2.78	13 786	349	47	302
40 055	41 078	2.69	19 090	351	40	311
37 066	35 247	2.52	13 416	544	72	472
65 557	65 205	2.48	16 304	878	118	760
54 469	52 861	2.73	14 543	2 180	1 231	949
51 142	48 731	2.41	15 980	1 024	117	907
32 903	31 608	2.39	13 166	524	44	480
54 991	55 306	2.44	5 277	909	111	798
824 247	**833 339**	**2.54**	**1 286**	**14 970**	**8 894**	**6 076**
74 219	75 580	2.72	1 549	735	85	650
43 982	44 184	2.57	2 260	462	60	402
63 433	62 477	2.55	5 310	1 053	260	793
27 663	28 580	2.53	1 344	152	24	128
20 188	20 665	2.57	1 264	260	117	143
36 285	36 828	2.98	1 608	2 183	1 599	584
15 034	14 324	2.75	1 161	335	39	296
25 809	25 281	2.55	2 236	582	52	530
18 093	18 270	2.62	1 034	230	30	200
37 370	36 646	2.88	1 644	1 604	978	626
59 801	60 626	2.49	3 522	742	77	665
56 516	58 370	2.49	1 945	579	918	-339
37 039	37 984	2.45	1 735	429	403	26
25 401	26 218	2.43	966	96	19	77
33 325	33 616	2.32	1 323	131	32	99
32 189	32 166	2.59	1 568	1 173	834	339
29 371	30 166	2.42	993	197	31	166
67 959	69 599	2.55	893	249	48	201
28 421	29 213	2.34	969	64	24	40
21 043	21 541	2.30	931	95	23	72
25 710	26 249	2.33	777	94	32	62
12 354	12 539	2.50	1 079	36	10	26
16 756	17 011	2.53	868	42	27	15
16 286	15 206		207	3 447	3 172	275

表2-3 各街镇户籍人口自然变动
Natural Change of Registered Population in Subdistricts and Towns
(2012)

单位:人 (person)

指 标	Indication	出生人口 Birth Population 合 计 Total	男 Man	女 Female	死亡人口 Death Population 合 计 Total	男 Man	女 Female	自然增加人口 Natural Growth 合 计 Total	男 Man	女 Female
总 计	**Total**	**26 610**	**13 776**	**12 834**	**21 400**	**11 375**	**10 025**	**5 210**	**2 401**	**2 809**
街道小计	**Subdistrict Tot**	**11 260**	**5 876**	**5 384**	**9 551**	**5 139**	**4 412**	**1 709**	**737**	**972**
潍坊新村街道	Weifangxincun Subdistrict	785	393	392	771	407	364	14	-14	28
陆家嘴街道	Lujiazui Subdistrict	1 101	574	527	983	525	458	118	49	69
周家渡街道	Zhoujiadu Subdistrict	931	475	456	1 216	675	541	-285	-200	-85
塘桥街道	Tangqiao Subdistrict	554	263	291	395	203	192	159	60	99
上钢新村街道	Shanggangxincun Subdistrict	743	396	347	1 121	613	508	-378	-217	-161
南码头路街道	Nanmatoulu Subdistrict	660	329	331	727	388	339	-67	-59	-8
沪东新村街道	Hudongxincun Subdistrict	683	353	330	694	389	305	-11	-36	25
金杨新村街道	Jinyangxincun Subdistrict	1 186	633	553	998	531	467	188	102	86
洋泾街道	Yangjing Subdistrict	1 235	651	584	666	391	275	569	260	309
浦兴路街道	Puxinglu Subdistrict	1 109	584	525	731	377	354	378	207	171
东明路街道	Dongminglu Subdistrict	732	393	339	638	333	305	94	60	34
花木街道	Huamu Subdistrict	1 541	832	709	611	307	304	930	525	405
镇小计	**Town Tot**	**15 350**	**7 900**	**7 450**	**11 849**	**6 236**	**5 613**	**3 501**	**1 664**	**1 837**
川沙新镇	Chuansha New Town	1 426	743	683	1 005	535	470	421	208	213
高 桥 镇	Gaoqiao Town	764	396	368	660	357	303	104	39	65
北 蔡 镇	Beicai Town	1 298	673	625	1 116	587	529	182	86	96
合 庆 镇	Heqing Town	453	205	248	423	220	203	30	-15	45
唐 镇	Tangzhen Town	439	220	219	293	160	133	146	60	86
曹 路 镇	Caolu Town	604	305	299	484	246	238	120	59	61
金 桥 镇	Jinqiao Town	314	171	143	189	99	90	125	72	53
高 行 镇	Gaohang Town	689	370	319	345	196	149	344	174	170
高 东 镇	Gaodong Town	258	131	127	302	155	147	-44	-24	-20
张 江 镇	Zhangjiang Town	1 043	534	509	423	223	200	620	311	309
三 林 镇	Sanlin Town	1 314	695	619	963	514	449	351	181	170
惠 南 镇	Huinan Town	982	501	481	735	416	319	247	85	162
周 浦 镇	Zhoupu Town	763	388	375	582	319	263	181	69	112
新 场 镇	Xinchang Town	368	192	176	417	225	192	-49	-33	-16
大 团 镇	Datuan Town	416	207	209	482	233	249	-66	-26	-40
康 桥 镇	Kangqiao Town	872	448	424	469	246	223	403	202	201
航 头 镇	Hangtou Town	535	262	273	432	210	222	103	52	51
祝 桥 镇	Zhuqiao Town	1 019	526	493	1 026	534	492	-7	-8	1
泥 城 镇	Nicheng Town	440	227	213	397	211	186	43	16	27
宣 桥 镇	Xuanqiao Town	347	179	168	298	139	159	49	40	9
书 院 镇	Shuyuan Town	398	206	192	351	178	173	47	28	19
万 祥 镇	Wanxiang Town	175	88	87	142	72	70	33	16	17
老 港 镇	Laogang Town	249	131	118	211	102	109	38	29	9
南汇新城镇	Nanhui New Town	184	102	82	104	59	45	80	43	37

表2-4 主要年份户籍人口变动
Change of Registered Population in Main Years

单位:人 (person)

指 标	Indicators	1990	1993	2000	2005	2010	2011	2012
人口自然变动	**Natural Changes in Population**							
出生人口	Birth	13 459	9 785	8 229	12 363	22 337	22 336	26 610
出生率(‰)	Birth Rate (‰)	10.20	6.88	5.07	6.76	8.10	8.02	9.47
死亡人口	Death	8 711	9 899	11 007	13 423	19 415	20 202	21 400
死亡率(‰)	Death Rate (‰)	6.60	6.96	6.78	7.34	7.04	7.25	7.61
自然增长人口	Natural Growth	4 748	-114	-2 778	-1 060	2 922	2 134	5 210
自然增长率(‰)	Natural Growth Rate (‰)	3.60	-0.08	-1.71	-0.58	1.06	0.77	1.85
人口迁移变动	**Population Mobility**							
迁入人口	Population Moved-in	18 079	59 214	160 975	128 476	27 440	26 596	25 253
# 市外迁入	Non-Shanghai Population Moved-in	8 102	10 469	18 522	18 346	26 845	25 907	24 666
迁入率(‰)	Rate of Population Moved-in (‰)	13.50	41.20	99.10	70.26	9.95	9.54	8.98
迁出人口	Population Moved-out	15 820	32 457	103 486	88 315	9 119	9 816	11 238
# 迁出市外	Population Moved Out of Shanghai	5 843	3 356	5 734	2 612	8 434	9 239	10 646
迁出率(‰)	Rate of Population Moved-out (‰)	11.81	22.58	63.70	48.30	3.31	3.52	4.00
迁移增长人口	Growth of Population Mobility	2 259	26 757	57 489	40 161	18 321	16 780	14 015
# 市外迁移增长	Growth of Outward Mobility	2 259	7 113	12 788	15 734	18 411	16 668	14 020
净迁移率(‰)	Rate of Net Mobility (‰)	1.69	18.62	35.40	21.96	6.64	6.02	4.99

表2-5　年末流动人口登记情况

Registered Migrating Population at Year End

单位：人　　　　(person)

指　标	Indicators	2005	2009	2010	2011	2012
总　计	**Total**	**937 331**	**1 695 349**	**2 183 277**	**2 064 975**	**2 383 169**
潍坊新村街道	Weifangxincun Subdistrict	10 975	21 608	30 057	30 314	32 156
陆家嘴街道	Lujiazui Subdistrict	17 538	29 680	53 091	45 802	59 514
周家渡街道	Zhoujiadu Subdistrict	13 614	21 291	28 984	22 985	24 605
塘桥街道	Tangqiao Subdistrict	7 319	13 763	19 797	20 280	22 575
上钢新村街道	Shanggangxincun Subdistrict	9 998	14 886	17 907	15 551	16 855
南码头路街道	Nanmantoulu Subdistrict	9 295	18 356	19 957	24 170	27 492
沪东新村街道	Hudongxincun Subdistrict	11 559	21 045	23 289	23 218	24 995
金杨新村街道	Jinyangxincun Subdistrict	27 016	39 864	42 152	46 409	52 679
洋泾街道	Yangjing Subdistrict	19 041	40 767	50 032	38 520	44 428
浦兴路街道	Puxinglu Subdistrict	15 898	33 187	38 169	41 471	49 674
东明路街道	Dongminglu Subdistrict	14 981	23 812	26 787	25 946	28 008
花木街道	Huamu Subdistrict	36 626	50 779	60 266	56 620	64 506
申港街道	Shengang Subdistrict		5 937	11 759	5 975	
水上派出所	Boat Police Station	333				
世博园区	Shibo Park		16 811	14	4	1 379
外高桥保税区	Waigaoqiao Free Trade Zone	3 036	872	3 443	3 476	3 060
川沙新镇	Chuansha New Town	123 566	140 691	173 882	122 999	155 028
高 桥 镇	Gaoqiao Town	51 477	66 805	84 918	83 285	89 433
北 蔡 镇	Beicai Town	75 586	123 182	140 747	127 392	141 604
合 庆 镇	Heqing Town	40 144	60 093	72 050	76 309	78 948
唐　　镇	Tangzhen Town	49 296	66 496	79 778	84 491	93 221
曹 路 镇	Caolu Town	55 245	66 823	96 229	103 834	111 928
金 桥 镇	Jinqiao Town	69 312	57 515	65 756	41 661	49 398
高 行 镇	Gaohang Town	45 035	57 153	63 057	61 755	73 135
高 东 镇	Gaodong Town	59 380	60 210	71 851	68 811	76 862
张 江 镇	Zhangjiang Town	51 157	66 465	124 278	106 880	117 271
三 林 镇	Sanlin Town	119 904	167 460	196 584	165 690	194 911
惠 南 镇	Huinan Town		44 213	92 325	89 293	105 461
周 浦 镇	Zhoupu Town		45 682	67 239	73 402	86 931
新 场 镇	Xinchang Town		32 488	42 297	36 330	53 174
大 团 镇	Datuan Town		11 403	13 800	12 340	14 734
芦潮港镇	Luchaogang Town		7 194	12 406	13 026	
康 桥 镇	Kangqiao Town		122 636	152 304	159 611	191 631
航 头 镇	Hangtou Town		45 655	59 749	56 417	67 951
六 灶 镇	Liuzao Town		15 901	18 292		
祝 桥 镇	Zhuqiao Town		31 839	46 462	105 148	113 491
泥 城 镇	Nicheng Town		11 793	21 397	19 137	27 598
宣 桥 镇	Xuanqiao Town		15 846	26 775	23 983	28 854
书 院 镇	Shuyuan Town		14 322	19 569	17 410	19 188
万 祥 镇	Wanxiang Town		2 520	3 440	4 456	5 484
老 港 镇	Laogang Town		8 306	12 388	10 574	12 018
南汇新城镇	Nanhui New Town					22 989

表2-6 主要年份婚姻登记和计划生育情况
Marriage Registration and Family Planning in Main Years

单位:人 (person)

指 标	Indicators	1993	2000	2005	2009	2010	2011	2012
婚姻登记	**Marriage Registration**							
准予登记结婚(对)	Registered Marriage (couple)	7 362	11 083	14 602	28 515	23 831	28 976	28 102
离婚登记(对)	Registered Divorce (couple)	489	2 102	4 402	7 398	7 511	8 146	9 733
计划生育	**Planned Birth**							
出 生	**Birth**							
出生人数	Number of Births	9 785	9 958	12 363	20 379	22 337	22 336	26 610
第一孩	First Child	9 309	9 669	11 928	19 359	20 893	20 674	24 380
第二孩	Second Child	471	285	424	1 013	1 423	1 635	2 195
多 孩	≥ Third Child	5	4	11	7	21	27	35
符合计划生育人数	Planned Parenthood	9 760	9 903	12 323	20 281	22 273	22 284	26 565
计划生育率(%)	Rate of Planned Birth (%)	99.74	99.45	99.68	99.52	99.71	99.80	99.80
节 育	**Birth Control**							
已婚育龄妇女人数(万人)	Married Women at Child-bearing Age (10 000 persons)	31.69	32.34	29.33	44.88	45.08	45.51	45.79
已领独生子女证人数(万人)	Persons Who Have Applied for One-child Certificate (10 000 persons)	22.66	15.48	10.84	14.90	13.80	15.10	15.03
独生子女领证率(%)	Rate of One-child Certificate (%)	71.50	47.86	36.98	33.21	30.60	33.20	32.83
晚 婚	**Late Marriage**							
女性初婚人数	Number of First Marriage of Female	5 712	7 564	11 594	14 291	12 054	15 101	14 320
#23 岁以上	≥ 23 Years Old	2 115	4 217	8 941	12 029	10 289	13 467	12 998
晚婚率(%)	Rate of Belated Marriage (%)	37.03	55.75	77.12	84.17	85.36	89.18	90.77

主要统计指标解释

人口数

为每年 12 月 31 日的年末总人口。根据统计口径的不同,分为户籍人口和常住人口。户籍人口是指在公安部门办理了户籍登记的人口。常住人口是指实际上经常居住在一个地方(住所)的人口,一般都以在其住所居住半年以上者为常住人口。年鉴中除特别注明是常住人口、实有人口等统计口径外,其他均为户籍人口数。

农业人口、非农业人口

是人口按经济特征分组的主要指标。农业人口指依靠从事农业(包括种植业、林业、牧业、渔业)维持生活的全部人口,即包括从事农、林、牧、渔业生产的人口以及由他们抚养的人口。非农业人口指依靠从事农业以外职业的人口以及由他们抚养的人口。但长期来在户籍管理上,往往把在农村中就业并按工资形式获得劳动报酬及由其抚养的人口统计为非农业人口;在农村劳动并参加农村合作经济收益分配的人,及由其抚养的人口作为农业人口统计。

出生率(又称粗出生率)

指在一定时期内(通常为一年)一定地区的出生人数与同期平均人数(或期中人数)之比,一般用千分率表示。计算公式:

$$出生率 = \frac{年出生人数}{年平均人数} \times 1000‰$$

出生人数是指活产婴儿,即胎儿脱离母体时(不管怀孕月数),有过呼吸或其他生命现象。年平均人数是年初、年底人口数的平均数,也可用年中人口数代替。

死亡率(又称粗死亡率)

指在一定时期内(通常为一年)一定地区的死亡人数与同期平均人数(或期中人数)之比,一般用千分率表示。计算公式:

$$死亡率 = \frac{年死亡人数}{年平均人数} \times 1000‰$$

人口自然增长率

指在一定时期内(通常为一年)人口自然增加数(出生人数减死亡人数)与该时期内平均人数(或期中人数)之比,一般用千分率表示。计算公式:

$$人口自然增长率 = \frac{本年出生人数 - 本年死亡人数}{年平均人数} \times 1000‰$$

人口自然增长率 = 人口出生率 - 人口死亡率

EXPLANATORY NOTES TO MAJOR STATISTICAL INDICATORS

Population

Population refers to the total population by December 31 every year. According to different statistical approaches, there are two definitions of population named as population with registered residence and population with permanent residence. The former refers to the population with registration in the police while the latter refers to the population that actually reside in a place (residence) permanently ,usually longer than half a year. Unless the statistical approaches are specified as permanent population and present population, the others are the number of registered population in this Yearbook.

Agricultural Population, Non-agricultural Population

Agricultural Population, Non-agricultural Population are main indicators of population grouped by economic features. Agricultural Population refers to the total number of people who live on agriculture, including farming, forestry, husbandry and fishery, and their dependents. Non-agricultural Population refers to the number of people who live on non-agricultural jobs and their dependents. According to the resident registering control system, however, the people who are employed in rural area, receive income, and their dependents are actually registered as non-agricultural population. The people who work in rural area and receive their income from agricultural collective units and their dependents are statistically defined as agricultural population.

Birth Rate

Birth Rate (or gross birth rate) means the ratio of the number of births in a certain period (usually a year) to the average population in the same period (or mid-year figure). It is usually calculated in terms of permillage and its calculating formula is:

$$\text{Birth Rate} = \frac{\text{Number of Births}}{\text{Average Number of Popualtion}} \times 1000‰$$

Number of Births refers to live births, when babies have showed any vital phenomena regardless of the length of pregnancy.

Average Number of Population is the average of the number of population at the beginning of the year and, at the end of the year and sometimes is substituted for with mid-year population.

Death Rate

Death Rate (or Gross Death Rate) refers to the ratio of number of deaths to the average population (or mid-year population) during a certain period of time (usually a year), which is often presented as permillage. Its calculating formula is :

$$\text{Death Rate} = \frac{\text{Number of Deaths}}{\text{Average Number of Population}} \times 1000‰$$

Natural Growth Rate of Population

Natural Growth Rate of Population refers to the ratio of natural increase in population (number of births minus number of deaths) in a certain period of time (usually a year) to the average population (or mid-year population) of the same period, which is often presented as permillage. The following formula are applied:

$$\text{Natural Growth Rate of Population} = \frac{\text{Number of Births-Number of Deaths}}{\text{Average Number of Population}} \times 1000‰$$

Natural Growth Rate of Population = Birth Rate-Death Rate

第三篇

CHAPTER 3

固定资产投资

INVESTMENT IN FIXED ASSETS

表3-1　固定资产投资主要指标
(2012)

指标	Indicators	合计 Total	内资 Domestic Investment	国有 State-owned	集体 Collective-owned	股份合作 Share Holding
本年完成投资额(亿元)	**Completed Investment in This Year (100 million yuan)**	**1 454.98**	**1 175.34**	**416.23**	**17.09**	**0.20**
按构成分	**By Composition**					
建筑安装工程	Construction and Installation	758.86	638.44	201.31	13.18	
设备工具器具购置	Purchase of Equipment and Instrument	265.85	151.88	59.55	0.04	0.20
其他费用	Others	430.27	385.02	155.37	3.87	
按建设性质分	**By Type of Construction**					
#新　建	New Construction	532.55	448.44	281.67	7.08	
改　建	Reconstruction	171.83	113.75	59.21	0.11	0.20
扩　建	Expansion	41.21	24.14	8.84	1.48	
按三次产业分	**By Industry**					
第一产业	Primary Industry	5.80	5.70	0.30	0.62	
第二产业	Secondary Industry	356.68	198.30	66.51		0.20
第三产业	Tertiary Industry	1 092.50	971.34	349.42	16.47	
按主要行业分	**By Main Sector**					
#工　业	Industry	356.55	198.30	66.67		0.20
交通运输、仓储和邮政业	Transportation, Warehousing and Post Service	88.98	82.39	40.42		
信息传输、计算机服务和软件业	Information Transmission, Computer Service and Computer Software	11.48	8.02	1.85		
批发和零售业	Wholesale and Retail	27.18	27.04	4.29	1.68	
住宿和餐饮业	Hotel and Catering	12.82	12.42	1.27	3.53	
金融业	Banking	49.15	49.15	32.79		
新增固定资产	**Newly-increased Fixed Assets**	**663.74**	**463.65**	**155.92**	**7.77**	
固定资产交付使用率(%)	Rate of Fixed Assets Put into Use (%)	45.6	39.4	37.5	45.5	
房屋建筑面积(万平方米)	**Floor Area of Buildings (10 000 sq·m)**					
施工面积	Floor Area Under Construction	4 473.62	3 935.42	742.17	77.63	
#住　宅	Residential Housing	2 280.68	2 143.72	309.04	58.13	
竣工面积	Floor Area Completed	751.42	658.52	230.73	13.34	
#住　宅	Residential Housing	433.38	414.09	136.29	7.50	

Major Indicators of Investment in Fixed Assets

联 营 Jointly Operated	有限责任公司 Companies with Limited Liability	股份有限公司 Companies Limited by Shares	私营及个体 Private/Individual	其他 Others	港澳台商投资 Hong Kong/Macao/Taiwan Funded		外商投资 FIE	
						#独资企业 Solely Foreigner Funded Enterprises		#独资企业 Solely Foreigner Funded Enterprises
11.86	**431.41**	**74.79**	**223.06**	**0.70**	**56.82**	**26.69**	**222.82**	**99.76**
5.97	258.2	31.45	127.89	0.44	32.74	13.48	87.68	51.67
0.14	35.12	34.29	22.53	0.01	14.84	8.59	99.13	39.48
5.75	138.09	9.05	72.64	0.25	9.24	4.62	36.01	8.61
	86.12	26.1	47.13	0.34	5.18	3.37	78.93	29.92
0.60	42.22	1.47	9.94		12.06	4.32	46.02	7.66
0.62	1.53	2.88	8.79		1.07	1.07	16.00	12.12
0.10	1.77		2.85	0.06			0.10	0.10
0.50	74.98	17.67	38.24	0.20	19.41	11.53	138.97	70.34
11.26	354.66	57.12	181.97	0.44	37.41	15.16	83.75	29.32
0.50	74.98	17.66	38.09	0.20	19.41	11.53	138.97	70.34
0.62	4.96	26.11	10.28		2.17	1.23	4.42	0.86
	2.50	3.13	0.54		0.39	0.39	3.07	2.83
	8.47	0.12	12.48		0.14	0.14		
	6.98		0.64				0.40	0.30
	6.52	9.84						
44.52	**104.05**	**26.63**	**124.76**		**99.64**	**9.91**	**100.45**	**51.88**
375.4	24.1	35.6	55.9		175.4	37.1	45.1	52.0
87.63	1 699.63	297.13	1 022.71	8.52	221.49	56.14	316.71	220.95
74.51	1 139.16	78.54	484.34		69.58	23.85	67.38	34.31
68.27	146.68	32.13	167.37		75.43	0.05	17.47	8.14
56.37	107.03	21.60	85.30		19.29			

表3-2　历年固定资产投资总额

Total Investment in Fixed Assets in Main Years

(1990 ~2012)

单位:亿元　　(100 million yuan)

年　份 Year	投资总额 Total Investment	#城市基础设施 Investment in Urban Infrastructure	#房地产开发 Real Estate Development	#工　业 Industry
1990	14.15	7.50		
1991	28.95	5.42		
1992	75.00	21.84		
1993	164.56	54.73		
1994	261.13	78.76		
1995	285.07	53.42	18.26	
1996	395.04	98.68	95.45	112.55
1997	504.36	119.32	125.00	140.95
1998	583.22	177.24	134.87	209.11
1999	438.20	156.54	103.88	135.50
2000	351.06	54.51	110.74	140.65
2001	416.18	105.36	111.66	161.48
2002	587.20	147.00	215.80	192.87
2003	602.16	155.63	245.81	191.00
2004	651.94	121.21	279.49	200.29
2005	693.61	125.95	287.92	144.61
2006	659.97	156.04	257.81	139.56
2007	784.10	234.54	247.46	224.59
2008	872.68	311.30	279.97	158.59
2009	1 420.77	490.77	431.36	298.71
2010	1 432.30	261.92	555.74	336.72
2011	1 435.39	272.02	589.45	361.03
2012	1 454.98	261.86	600.30	356.55
1990 ~2012 年累计 Accumulated from 1990 to 2012	14 112.02	3 471.56	4 690.97	3 504.76

表3-3 各行业固定资产投资情况
Investment in Fixed Assets by Sector
(2012)

指 标	Indicators	施工项目(个) Projects Under Construction (unit)	竣工项目(个) Projects Completed (unit)	本年完成投资额(亿元) Investment (100 million yuan)	新增固定资产(亿元) Newly Increased Fixed Assets (100 million yuan)
总 计	**Total**	**1 458**	**269**	**1 454.98**	**663.74**
农、林、牧、渔业	Agriculture, Forest, Animal Husbandry and Fishery	34	14	5.80	3.40
工 业	Industry	559	117	356.55	145.02
#制造业	Manufacturing	523	96	325.70	133.12
电力、热力、燃气及水生产和供应业	Production and Supply of Electricity, Thermal Power, Gas and Water	36	21	30.85	11.90
建筑业	Construction	1	1	0.15	0.15
批发和零售业	Wholesale and Retail	28	7	27.18	5.55
交通运输、仓储和邮政业	Transportation, Warehousing and Postal Service	64	11	88.98	37.72
住宿和餐饮业	Hotel and Catering	16	5	12.82	6.55
信息传输、软件和信息技术服务业	Information Transmission, Computer Services and Software	24	1	11.48	1.10
金融业	Banking	20	2	49.15	0.15
房地产业	Real Estate	347	60	601.63	412.32
租赁和商务服务业	Leasing and Commercial Services	28	6	73.29	16.82
科学研究和技术服务业	Scientific Research and Technology Services	47	2	11.97	2.36
水利、环境和公共设施管理业	Water Conservancy, Environment and Public Facilities Management	177	25	142.39	19.09
居民服务、修理和其他服务业	Residents' Services, Repair and Other Services	5	3	5.79	5.38
教 育	Education	53	8	13.33	5.34
卫生和社会工作	Healthcare and Social Work	30	4	14.23	1.98
文化、体育和娱乐业	Culture, Sports and Entertainment	12	1	37.14	0.63
公共管理、社会保障和社会组织	Public Management, Social Guarantee and Social Organizations	13	2	3.11	0.20

表3-4　固定资产投资房屋建筑面积
Floor Space of Housing and Buildings in Fixed Assets Investment

单位:万平方米　　(10 000 sq·m)

指　标	Indicators	2005	2010	2011	2012	1990～2012年累计 Accumulated Investment (1990～2012)
房屋施工面积	**Floor Area Under Construction**					
合　计	**Total**	**2 483.56**	**4 322.59**	**4 558.16**	**4 473.62**	
住　宅	Residential Housing	1 510.04	2 086.26	2 296.52	2 280.68	
厂房仓库	Factory Building and Warehouse	120.52	308.28	312.56	397.97	
商业营业用房	Commerce	276.76	491.29	518.07	387.60	
办公楼	Offices	196.68	601.15	621.46	585.78	
教育用房	Education	20.35	48.36	49.82	55.09	
医疗用房	Healthcare	7.39	9.20	11.82	13.53	
其　他	Others	351.82	778.05	747.91	752.97	
房屋竣工面积	**Floor Area Completed**					
合　计	**Total**	**615.37**	**646.98**	**692.94**	**751.42**	**12 721.80**
住　宅	Residential Housing	408.44	297.89	286.14	433.38	7 664.09
厂房仓库	Factory Building and Warehouse	43.89	55.50	59.44	61.86	1 395.06
商业营业用房	Commerce	85.64	61.83	72.35	36.17	832.38
办公楼	Office	54.08	93.82	130.48	80.95	1 155.33
教育用房	Education	8.37	10.06	12.77	18.26	245.64
医疗用房	Healthcare		4.56	4.89	6.89	78.18
其　他	Others	14.95	123.32	126.87	113.91	1 351.12

表3-5 历年新增固定资产
Newly Increased Fixed Assets In Main Years (1994~2012)

指 标 Indicators		1994	1995	1996	1997	1998	1999
新增固定资产（亿元）	Newly Increased Fixed Assets(100 million yuan)	141.03	150.76	260.75	329.84	331.79	396.22
固定资产交付使用率(%)	Rate of Fixed Assets Transferred in Use (%)	54.0	52.9	66.8	65.4	56.9	90.4

表3-5 续表1 Continued

指 标 Indicators		2000	2001	2002	2003	2004	2005
新增固定资产（亿元）	Newly Increased Fixed Assets (100 million yuan)	379.60	261.82	279.79	407.66	633.37	379.92
固定资产交付使用率(%)	Rate of Fixed Assets Transferred in Use (%)	108.1	62.9	47.6	67.7	97.2	54.8

表3-5 续表2 Continued

指 标 Indicators		2006	2007	2008	2009	2010	2011	2012
新增固定资产（亿元）	Newly Increased Fixed Assets (100 million yuan)	522.56	380.96	638.70	656.15	622.81	789.74	663.74
固定资产交付使用率(%)	Rate of Fixed Assets Transferred in Use (%)	79.2	48.6	73.2	46.2	43.5	55.0	45.6

表3-6 主要年份固定资产投资资金来源
Capital Resources of Investment in Fixed Assets in Main Years

单位:亿元 (100 million yuan)

指 标 Indicators		2010	2011	2012
资金来源合计	**Total Capital Resources**	**2 045.60**	**2 050.04**	**2 254.92**
上年末结余资金	Balance at End of Previous Year	363.69	428.89	399.19
本年资金来源小计	Sub-total of Capital Resources in this Year	1 681.91	1 621.15	1 855.73
国家预算内资金	State Budgetary Funds	23.97	22.10	92.48
国内贷款	Domestic Loans	381.47	342.15	378.67
债 券	Bonds	8.00	3.47	
利用外资	Foreign Investment	79.00	54.70	43.42
#外商直接投资	Foreign Direct Investment	42.14	47.60	30.91
自筹资金	Self-Financed Capital	872.50	859.18	946.40
#企事业自有资金	Self-Financed by Enterprises and Institutions	515.87	552.39	477.04
其他资金	Other Capitals	316.97	339.55	394.76
#集 资	Raised Funds	2.86	0.50	
本年各项应付投资款	Investment Due to Pay in this Year	196.79	218.89	122.35
#工程款	Project Funds	85.70	82.05	34.77

表3-7　城市基础设施投资额
Investment in Urban Infrastructure

指　标	Indicators	2010	2011	2012	1990~2012年累计 Accumulated Investment (1990~2012)
投资额总计(亿元)	**Total Investment (100 million yuan)**	**261.92**	**272.02**	**261.86**	**3 495.93**
电力建设	Electricity	24.38	37.83	35.20	405.73
运输邮电	Transportation, Post and Telecommunications	116.85	154.52	83.07	1 572.81
#市内公共交通	Urban Public Transportation	31.48	57.88	10.62	474.96
公用设施	Public Facilities	120.69	79.67	143.59	1 517.38
公用事业	Public Utilities	3.85	3.62	1.61	145.10
自来水	Tap Water	2.56	2.08	1.16	72.66
燃　气	Gas	1.29	1.55	0.45	72.44
市政建设	Civic Construction	116.85	76.04	141.98	1 372.28
市政工程	Civic Projects	100.51	66.84	105.22	1 244.59
园林绿化	Garden/Park	14.08	8.28	31.18	94.01
环境卫生	Environmental Sanitation	2.10	0.89	0.11	27.32
其　他	Others	0.17	0.03	5.47	6.36
构　成(%)	**Composition(%)**				
投资额总计	**Total Investment**	**100.0**	**100.0**	**100.0**	**100.0**
电力建设	Electricity	9.3	13.9	13.5	11.6
运输邮电	Transportation, Post and Telecommunications	44.6	56.8	31.7	45.0
#市内公共交通	Urban Public Transportation	12.0	21.3	4.1	13.6
公用设施	Public Facilities	46.1	29.3	54.8	43.4
公用事业	Public Utilities	1.5	1.3	0.6	4.2
自来水	Tap Water	1.0	0.7	0.4	2.1
燃　气	Gas	0.5	0.6	0.2	2.1
市政建设	Civic Construction	44.6	28.0	54.2	39.3
市政工程	Civic Projects	38.3	24.6	40.2	35.6
园林绿化	Garden/Park	5.4	3.0	11.9	2.7
环境卫生	Environmental Sanitation	0.8	0.3	0.0	0.8
其　他	Others	0.1	0.1	2.1	0.2

表3-8 工业各行业投资主要指标
Main Indicators of Investment By Industrial Sectors (2012)

指标	Indicators	施工项目（个） Projects Under Construction (unit)	全部建成投产项目（个） Projects Completed and Put into Production (unit)	建成投产率（%） Rate of Projects Completed and Put into Use(%)	工业本年完成投资额(亿元) Completed Investment in Industry in This Year (100 million yuan)
总计	**Total**	**433**	**116**	**26.8**	**356.55**
#制造业	**Manufacturing**	**397**	**95**	**23.9**	**325.70**
农副食品加工业	Processing of Agricultural Side-line Food	4			1.05
食品制造业	Food Manufacturing	5			1.16
烟草制品业	Tobacco Manufacturing	1			7.54
纺织业	Textile Industry	1	1	100.0	0.29
纺织服装、服饰业	Textile Clothes and Accessories	2	1	50.0	0.35
皮革、毛皮、羽毛及其制品和制鞋业	Manufacturing of Leather, Furs, Down, Related Products and Shoes	1	1	100.0	0.25
家具制造业	Furniture Manufacturing	1	1	100.0	0.06
造纸和纸制品业	Paper-making and Paper Products	3	2	66.7	1.22
印刷业和记录媒介复制业	Manufacturing of Printing and Record Medium Reproduction	7	2	28.6	2.72
文教、工美、体育和娱乐用品制造业	Manufacturing of Stationery, Educational, Sports and Entertainment	3			3.12
石油加工、炼焦和核燃料加工业	Petroleum Processing, Coking and Processing of Nuclear Fuels	10	3	30.0	5.02
化学原料和化学制品制造业	Chemical Materials and Chemical Products	22	10	45.5	8.80
医药制造业	Medicine Manufacturing	34	4	11.8	25.80
化学纤维制造业	Chemical Fiber Manufacturing	1			0.17
橡胶和塑料制品业	Manufacturing of Rubber and Plastic Products	8	4	50.0	5.51
非金属矿物制品业	Manufacturing of Non-metal Mineral Products	7	4	57.1	6.42
黑色金属冶炼和压延加工业	Manufacturing of Smelting and Processing of Ferrous Metals	3	1	33.3	1.14
有色金属冶炼和压延加工业	Manufacturing of Smelting and Processing of Non-ferrous Metals	2			1.22
金属制品业	Manufacturing of Metal Products	11	4	36.4	6.05
通用设备制造业	Manufacturing of General-use Equipment	33	5	15.2	15.86
专用设备制造业	Manufacturing of Special Equipment	32	5	15.6	8.94
汽车制造业	Manufacturing of Automobiles	47	10	21.3	31.91
铁路、船舶、航空航天和其他运输设备制造业	Manufacturing of Railway, Ship, Aviation and Aerospace, and Other Transportation Equipment	12	6	50.0	13.66
电气机械和器材制造业	Manufacturing of Electric Machinery and Apparatus	23	6	26.1	12.76
计算机、通信和其他电子设备制造业	Manufacturing of Computer, Telecommunications and Other Electronic Equipment	74	13	17.6	117.39
仪器仪表制造业	Manufacturing of Instrument and Meter	3	1	33.3	0.54
其他制造业	Other Manufacturings	46	11	23.9	46.42
废弃资源综合利用业	Comprehensive Recycling of Discarded Resources	1			0.33
电力、热力、燃气及水生产和供应业	**Production and Supply of Electricity, Thermal Power, Gas and Water**	**36**	**21**	**58.3**	**30.85**
电力、热力生产和供应业	Production and Supply of Electricity and Thermal Power	30	19	63.3	29.23
燃气生产和供应业	Production and Supply of Gas	2	2	100.0	0.45
水的生产和供应业	Production and Supply of Tap Water	4			1.16

表3-9 主要年份建设改造投资主要指标
Major Indicators of Investment on Constructions and Transformations

指标	Indicators	2011	2012
投资总额(亿元)	**Total Investment (100 million yuan)**	**845.94**	**854.68**
按建设性质分	**Grouped by Type of Construction**		
#新建	New Construction	516.94	532.55
改建和技改	Reconstruction and Technologic Reforms	154.73	171.83
扩建	Expansion	58.08	41.21
按产业分	**Grouped by Type of Industry**		
第一产业	Primary Industry	9.21	5.80
第二产业	Secondary Industry	361.08	356.68
第三产业	Tertiary Industry	475.65	492.20
按行业分	**Grouped by Sectors**		
农、林、牧、渔业	Farming, Forestry, Animal Husbandry and Fishery	9.21	5.80
工业	Industry	361.03	356.55
建筑业	Construction	0.05	0.15
批发和零售业	Wholesale and Retail	21.00	27.18
交通运输、仓储和邮政业	Transportation, Storage and Post Service	158.68	88.98
住宿和餐饮业	Hotel and Catering	22.21	12.82
信息传输、软件和信息技术服务业	Information Transmission, Software and Information Technology Services	11.30	11.48
金融业	Financial Industry	21.55	49.15
房地产业	Real Estate Industry	32.98	1.33
租赁和商务服务业	Leasing and Business Service	19.48	73.29
科学研究和技术服务业	Scientific Research andTechnology Service	28.26	11.97
水利、环境和公共设施管理业	Water Conservancy, Environment and Public Facilities Management	88.00	142.38
居民服务、修理和其他服务业	Residents'Services, Repair and Other Services	1.99	5.79
教育	Education	16.96	13.33
卫生和社会工作	Healthcare and Social Work	28.55	14.23
文化、体育和娱乐业	Culture, Sports and Entertainment	13.70	37.14
公共管理、社会保障和社会组织	Public Management, Social Guarantee and Social Organizations	10.99	3.11
新增固定资产	**Newly Increased Fixed Assets**		
固定资产交付使用率(%)	Rate of Fixed Assets Transfered in Use(%)	56.2	29.5
房屋建筑面积(万平方米)	**Floor Space of Buildings(10 000 sq·m)**		
施工面积	Floor Space Under Construction	1 046.01	946.36
#住宅	Residential Housing	…	…
竣工面积	Floor Space Completed	204.79	124.46
#住宅	Residential Housing	…	…

表3-10 主要年份住宅投资(按经济类型分)
Investment in Residential Housing by Ownership in Main Years

单位:亿元 (100 million yuan)

指 标	Indicators	2010	2011	2012
住宅投资额总计	**Total Investment in Residential Housing**	**343.57**	**404.60**	**370.85**
占固定资产投资额比重(%)	Percentage of Investment in Fixed Assets (%)	23.8	28.2	25.5
内 资	Domestic Investment	309.32	341.98	339.50
国 有	State-owned	48.69	79.69	36.18
集 体	Collective-owned	30.06	4.50	7.58
股份合作	Share-holding			
联 营	Jointly-operated	26.31	0.60	9.08
有限责任公司	Companies with Limited Liability	115.45	165.83	211.62
股份有限公司	Companies Limited by Shares	0.92		2.59
私 营	Private	87.88	86.11	72.44
其 他	Others		5.25	
港澳台商投资	Hong Kong/Macao/Taiwan Invested	12.16	30.85	13.62
#港澳台商独资	Solely Hong Kong/Macao/Taiwan Funded	6.18		8.96
外商投资	FIE	22.09	31.76	17.73
#外商独资	Solely Foreigner Funded	21.37		7.81

表3-11 主要重大项目(浦东部分)投资完成额
Amount of Completed Investment in Key Civic Projects in PNA (2012)

单位:亿元 (100 million yuan)

序号 No.	指 标	Indication	计划总投资 Total Planned Investment	累计完成投资 Accumulated Investment	#2012 年完成投资 Investment Completed in 2012
	合 计	**Total**	**1 467.55**	**878.41**	**181.20**
1	轨道交通十一号线南段工程	Project of Southern Part in Line 11	160.84	142.64	10.00
2	上海通用汽车浦东轿车项目	Pudong Car Project of Shanghai GM	125.94	125.10	0.47
3	上海华力微电子有限公司“909”工程升级改造12英寸集成电路芯片项目	Reformation of 909 Project of Shanghai Huali Microelectronics Corporation	145.00	114.74	20.11
4	东西通道	Project of East-west Thoroughfare	71.95	50.52	1.94
5	申能临港电厂一期工程建设项目	Project of Phase I Construction of Shenneng Lingang Power Plant	46.67	44.43	5.22
6	上海通用汽车增资生产新一代中级、中高级轿车项目	New-generation Middle and High Grade Car Project with Newly-increased Investment of Sahnghai GM	52.00	36.36	3.50
7	浦东新区环城绿带开天窗补绿工程	Patch Green Project of PNA Green Belt	64.50	36.25	0.22
8	上海飞机制造有限公司C919大型客机研制保障条件能力建设项目	Research and Maintenance Capability Project for C919 Large Airplane of Shanghai Airplane Manufacturing Co., Ltd.	69.85	34.99	8.16
9	上海汽车临港基地自主品牌新产品技术改造项目	Technology Transformation of Self-branded Products Project of SAIC Lingang Base	36.72	28.87	2.67
10	上海迪斯尼乐园A-1、F-1地块开发项目	Land Plot A-1 and F-1 Development Projects of Shanghai Disneyland Park	26.43	26.43	26.43
11	上海迪士尼乐园前期配套项目	Pre-term Supporting Project of Shanghai Disneyland Park	244.80	25.74	25.74
12	南汇生态专项	Special Project of Hanhui Biology	30.09	22.80	2.80
13	申江南路(沪南公路-浦东区界)	Project of Shenjiangnan Road (Hunan Highway - Pudong Boundary)	22.44	22.11	0.30
14	中环线浦东段(军工路隧道-高科中路)	Pudong Section Project of Mid-ring Route (Jungong Road Tunnel - Gaokezhong Road)	122.55	20.42	9.66
15	上海通用汽车新一代大型直立四缸发动机项目	New Generation Large Vertical Four-Cylinger Engine Project of Shanghai GM	26.93	17.97	2.97
16	中国商用飞机有限责任公司中国商飞总部基地	Headquarters Base Project of Shanghai Commercial Plane Co., Ltd.	34.49	16.86	16.86
17	中国商用飞机有限责任公司大型客机研保条件建设项目	Large Airplane Research and Maintenance Projection of Shanghai Commerical Plane Co., Ltd.	23.85	15.55	2.99
18	招商银行信用卡中心	Credit Card Center of China Merchants Bank	18.90	14.38	1.19
19	中国人寿数据中心	Data Center Project of PLICC	15.75	13.86	3.25
20	上海国际金融中心上交所项目	SSE Project of Shanghai International Financial Center	35.00	12.98	12.98
21	轨道交通七号线浦江耀华站综合开发项目-环通商业广场	Huantong Commercial Plaza- Comprehensive Development Project at Yaohua Station of Pujiang Town for Line 7	16.35	12.37	1.72
22	上海通用汽车增资扩能生产高档轿车项目	High Grade Car Project with Newly-increased Investment of Shanghai GM	22.36	12.14	0.09
23	高南河水系建设工程	Water System Construction Projec of Gannan River	15.50	10.99	2.02
24	上海国际金融中心中金所项目	China Financial Futures Exchange Project of Shanghai Intenational Financial Center	20.00	10.35	10.35
25	罗山路(龙东大道-S20)	Luoshan Road Project (Longdong Avenue - S20)	18.64	9.56	9.56

表3-12 当年建成部分大项目一览表
Major Projects Completed in Current Year (2012)

单位:亿元 (100 million yuan)

序号 No.	指标 Indication		计划总投资 Total Planned Investment	累计完成投资 Accumulated Investment	#2012年完成投资 Investment Completed in 2012
1	浦江双辉大厦	Pujiang Shuanghui Building	50.43	50.43	1.21
2	上海通用汽车增资扩能生产高档轿车项目	High Grade Car Project with Increased Investment of Shanghai GM	22.36	12.14	0.09
3	东方金融广场	Oriental Financial Plaza	21.87	19.51	2.73
4	上海市保障性住房三林基地3号地块	Land Plot 3 Project of Sanlin Base for Shanghai Indemnificatory Housing	16.40	12.28	0.54
5	浦东新区川沙新镇C02-08、C02-15地块商品房	Land Plot C02-08 and C02-15 for Commercial Building Project in Chuansha New Town, PNA	10.09	10.09	4.20
6	川沙新镇杜坊C02-10配套商品房	Supporting Commerical Building of Dufang C02-10 Project in Chuanshan New Town	9.92	9.92	1.52
7	浦东现代产业园空港物流仓储作业区	Airport Logistics Warehouse Operation Area Project in Pudong Modern Industrial Park	9.32	9.32	1.79
8	嘉瑞国际广场	Jiarui International Plaza	9.30	9.20	1.29
9	张家浜楔形绿地商品住宅一期	Phase I Project of Green Wedge Commercial Building in Zhangjiabang	8.77	8.77	0.40
10	川沙新镇杜坊C02-21配套商品房	Supporting Commerical Building of Dufang C02-21 Project in Chuanshan New Town	8.74	8.74	1.22
11	配套商品房航头镇基地7号地块	Land Plot 7 Project of Supporing Commercial Building in Hangtou Town	7.79	7.79	2.27
12	万向大厦	Wanxiang Building	6.11	5.96	0.56
13	上海展讯中心二期工程	Phase II Project of Shanghai Spreadtrum Center	5.00	5.00	2.75
14	中芯国际12英寸相关设备购置及技改项目	Purchasing and Tehnology Reforms of 12-inch Related Equipment Project of SMIC	5.00	5.00	5.00
15	康梧路(周邓公路-原浦东区界)	Kangwu Road Project (Zhoudeng Highway - Former Pudong Boundary)	4.77	4.77	4.77
16	军民村D3-1-3地块配套商品房项目	Land Plot D3-1-3 Supporting Commercial Building Project in Junmin Village	4.50	4.08	1.69
17	逸亭佳苑	Yiting Garden	4.10	3.83	0.24
18	五隆·高东铭府配套商品房	Supporting Commercial Building Project of Wulong - Gaodong Mingfu Garden	3.84	3.84	0.31
19	竹园2-9地块办公楼	Land Plot 2-9 Office Building Project in Zhuyuan	3.68	2.68	0.16
20	名扬佳园	Mingyang Garden	3.65	3.65	0.85
21	竹园2-11地块办公楼	Land Plot 2-11 Office Building Project in Zhuyuan	3.54	3.25	0.20
22	江镇新都汇	Xindouhui Project in Jiangzhen Town	3.50	3.01	1.64
23	上海交运股份奥克斯科技园生产研发中心二期	Phase II Project of Production R&D Center of Aux Technology Park, Shanghai Jiaoyun Co., Ltd.	3.32	3.32	0.74
24	GF-6自动变速器换挡机构技术改造项目	Project of Technology Transformation of Gearshift in GF-6 Automatic Gearbox	3.06	2.69	0.09
25	云舒苑	Yunshu Garden	2.80	2.60	0.90

主要统计指标解释

全社会固定资产投资

固定资产投资是国民经济再生产活动的一个重要部分。固定资产投资额是以货币形式表现的在一定时期内建造和购置固定资产的工作量以及与此有关的费用总称。它是反映固定资产投资规模、结构和发展速度的综合性指标。按照现行国家统计制度，全社会固定资产投资包括建设改造、房地产开发、城乡集体经济单位、城乡私人建房和其他经济单位投资。

从2011年起，固定资产投资统计起点为500万元（含500万元）以上项目。

房地产开发投资

指各种登记注册类型的房地产开发公司、商品房建设公司及其他房地产开发法人单位和附属于其他法人单位实际从事房地产开发或经营活动的单位统一开发的包括统代建、拆迁还建的住宅、厂房、仓库、饭店、宾馆、度假村、写字楼、办公楼等房屋建筑物和配套的服务设施，土地开发工程（如道路、给水、排水、供电、供热、通讯、平整场地等基础设施工程）的投资；不包括单纯的土地交易活动。

固定资产投资按国民经济行业分

固定资产投资按国民经济行业分是根据建设项目建成投产后的主要产品或主要用途及社会经济活动性质来确定国民经济行业。一般情况下，一个建设项目或一个企业、事业单位只能属于一种国民经济行业。

固定资产投资按构成分

（1）建筑工程（建筑工作量）包括：

①各种房屋如厂房、仓库、办公室、住宅、商店、学校、医院、俱乐部、食堂、招待所等工程，包括列入房屋工程预算内的暖气、卫生、通风、照明、煤气等设备的价值及装饰油饰工程，列入建筑工程预算内的各种管道（如蒸汽、压缩空气、石油、给排水等管道）、电力、电讯电缆导线的敷设工程。

②设备基础、支柱、操作平台、梯子、烟囱、凉水塔、水池、灰塔等建筑工程；炼焦炉、蒸汽炉等各种窑炉的砌筑工程及金属结构工程。

③为施工而进行的建筑场地的布置、工程地质勘探，原有建筑物和障碍物的拆除，平整土地、施工临时用水、电、气、道路工程，以及完工后建筑场地的清理、环境绿化美化工作等。

④矿井的开凿，井巷掘进延伸，露天矿的剥离，石油、天然气钻井工程和铁路、公路、港口、桥梁等工程。

⑤水利工程，如水库、堤坝、灌溉以及河道整治等工程。

⑥防空、地下建筑等特殊工程。

（2）安装工程（安装工作量）包括：

①生产、动力、起重、运输、传动和医疗、实验等各种需要安装设备的装配和安装，与设备相连的工作台、梯子、栏杆等装设工程，附属于被安装设备的管线敷设工程，被安装设备的绝缘、防腐、保温、油漆等工作。

②为测定安装工程质量，对单个设备、系统设备进行单机试运，系统联动无负荷试运工作（投料试运工作不包括在内）。在安装工程中，不得包括被安装设备本身价值。

（3）设备、工具、器具购置：是指把工业生产的产品转为固定资产的购置活动，包括建设单位或在企、事业单位购置或自制达到固定资产标准的设备、工具、器具的价值。固定资产的标准按财务部门规定。新建单位及扩建单位的新建车间，按照设计和计划要求购置或自制的全部设备、工具、器具，不论是否达到固定资产标准均计入“设备、工具、器具购置”中。

①设备：指各种生产设备、传导设备、动力设备、运输设备等。分为需要安装的设备和不需要安装的设备两种。

需要安装的设备（简称“需安设备”）：是指必须将其整体或几个部位装配起来，安装在基础上或建筑物支架上才能使用的设备。如轧钢机、发电机、蒸汽锅炉、变压器、塔、换热器、各种泵、机床等。有的设备虽不要基础，但必须进行组装工作，并在一定范围内使用，如生产用电铲、塔吊、门吊、皮带运输机等也作为需要安装的设备统计。

不需要安装的设备（简称“不需安设备”）：指不必固定在一定位置或支架上就可以使用的各种设备，如电焊机、叉车、汽车、机车、飞机、船舶以及生产上流动使用的空压机、泵等。

②工具、器具：是指具有独立用途的各种生产用具、工作工具和仪器。如生产和维修用的切削工具、压延工具、铆焊工具、模压器、铸型、风镐等，检验、实验测量用的各种计量、分析、化验仪器，以及达到固定资产标准的包装容器等。

购置旧设备：是指从外单位购入的，已经使用过的各种设备。不包括从国外购进的旧设备。旧设备一般是指在国内其他单位作为固定资产使用过的设备（单纯购置旧设备不纳入固定资产投资统计）。

用于更新的设备：是指为更换陈旧设备而购置的投资。用于更新的设备与原有设备在台数和价值上不一定相等。购置的设备如不是用于更换原有设备，而是用于新增或扩大生产能力的，不能作为用于“更新的设备”统计。

（4）其他费用：指不属于上述几项的投资完成额。包括计入固定资产的费用（如农林建设单位牲畜购置费、各种经济林木营造费、办公和生活用家具、器具购置费、建设单位管理费、土地、青苗补偿和安置补偿费、勘察设计费、研究试验费、负荷联合试运费、引进技术和进口设备项目的其他费用）。

固定资产投资按建设性质分

按建设项目情况填写。

（1）新建：指从无到有"平地起家"开始建设的项目。现有企业、事业、行政单位投资的项目一般不属于新建。但如有的单位原有基础很小，经过建设后新增的固定资产价值超过该企业、事业、行政单位原有固定资产价值（原值）三倍以上的，也应作为新建。

（2）扩建：是指企（事）业单位在厂内或其他地点，为扩大原有产品的生产能力（或效益）或增加新的产品生产能力，而增建主要生产车间（或主要工程）独立的生产线、分厂等。行政、事业单位在原单位增建业务用房（如学校增建的教学用房、医院增建门诊部、病房）也作为扩建。

现有企、事业单位为扩大原有主要产品生产能力或增加新的产品生产能力，增建一个或几个主要生产车间（或主要工程）、总厂之下的分厂，如同时进行一些更新改造工程的建设，则也应作为扩建。

（3）改建和技术改造：是指现有企业、事业单位对原有设施进行技术改造或更新（包括相应配套的辅助性生产、生活福利设施）的建设项目。改建项目包括现有企业、事业单位为适应市场变化的需要，而改变企业的主要产品种类（如军工企业转民产品等）的建设项目，原有产品生产作业线由于各工序（车间）之间能力不平衡，为填平补齐充分发挥原有生产能力而增建不增加本企业主要产品设计能力的车间的建设项目。技术改造是指企业、事业单位在现有基础上，用先进的技术代替落后的技术，用先进的工艺和装备代替落后的工艺和装备，以改变企业落后的技术经济面貌，实现以内涵为主的扩大再生产，达到提高产品质量、促进产品更新换代、节约能源、降低消耗、扩大生产规模、全面提高社会经效益的目的。技术改造具体包括以下内容：机器设备和工具的更新改造；生产工艺改革、节约能源和原材料的改造；厂房建筑和公共设施的改造；保护环境进行的"三废"治理改造；劳动条件和生产环境的改造等。

（4）单纯建造生活设施：是指企（事）业及行政单位在不扩建、改建生产性工程和业务用房的情况下，单纯建造职工住宅、托儿所、子弟学校、医务室、浴室、食堂等生活福利设施。

（5）迁建：指为改变生产能力布局或由于城市环境保护和安全生产的需要等原因搬迁到另地建设的企、事业单位。在搬迁另地建设过程中，不论是维持原来规模还是扩大规模都按迁建统计。

（6）恢复：是指因自然灾害、战争等原因，使原有固定资产全部或部分报废，以后又投资恢复建设的单位。不论是按原规模恢复还是在恢复的同时进行扩建的都按恢复项目统计。尚未建成投产的基本建设项目，因自然灾害而损坏重建的，仍按原有建设性质划分。

（7）单纯购置：是指现有企、事业、行政单位单纯购置不需要安装的设备、工具、器具而不进行工程建设的单位。有些单位当年虽然只从事一些购置活动，但其设计中规定有建筑安装活动，应根据设计文件的内容来确定建设性质，不得作为单纯购置统计。

新增固定资产

新增固定资产又称交付使用的固定资产，是指已经完成建造和购置过程，并已交付生产或使用单位的固定资产价值。新增固定资产是表示固定资产投资成果的价值量指标，也是反映建设进度、计算固定资产投资效果的必要数据。

固定资产交付使用率

固定资产交付使用率又称固定资产运用系数，是指一定时期新增固定资产与同期完成投资额的比率。它反映各个时期固定资产动用速度，衡量建设过程中宏观投资效果的综合性指标。

施工项目

施工项目指报告期内进行过建筑或安装施工活动的项目。凡是报告期内施过工的建设项目，不论施工时间长短，均作为施工项目统计。施工项目个数可以反映一定时期固定资产投资的实际规模，与同期建成投产的建设项目个数相比，可以从建设速度的角度反映固定资产投资的效果。根据建设项目施工活动的不同性质，施工项目又分为：本年正式施工项目、本年收尾项目和以前年度全部停缓建项目。

全部投产项目

工业项目指设计文件规定形成生产能力的主体工程及其相应配套的辅助设施全部建成，经负荷试运转，证明具备生产设计规定合格产品的条件，并经过验收鉴定合格或达到竣工验收标准，与生产性工程配套的生活福利设施可以满足近期正常生产的需要，正式移交生产的建设项目。非工业项目指设计文件规定的主体工程和相应的配套工程全部建成，能够发挥设计规定的全部效益，经验收鉴定合格或达到竣工验收标准，正式移交使用的建设项目。

EXPLANATORY NOTES TO MAJOR STATISTICAL INDICATORS

Total Investment in Fixed Assets

Investment in Fixed Assets constitutes an important portion of the national economic reproduction. Fixed assets investment is a general term for both the work volume of production and purchase of fixed assets and relevant expenditure, in the form of currency, during a certain period. It is a comprehensive indicator of scale, structure and development speed of fixed assets investment. As stipulated in the current national statistics regulations, the social fixed assets investment includes the investment into infrastructure and reformation, real estate development, urban and rural collective economic bodies, private house construction in urban and rural areas and other economic bodies.

Since the year of 2011, the fixed assets items have only include those with an investment of 5 million yuan and above.

Investment in Real Estate Development

Investment in Real Estate Development refers to the investment by the real estate development companies, commercial buildings construction companies and other real estate development units of various types of ownership in the construction of house buildings, such as residential buildings, factory buildings, warehouses, hotels, guesthouses, holiday villages, office buildings, and the complementary service facilities and land development projects, such as roads, water supply, water drainage, power supply, heating, telecommunications, land leveling and other projects of infrastructure. It excludes the activities in pure land transactions.

Investment in Fixed Assets by Sector

Investment in Fixed Assets by Sector refers to determining the classification of construction projects by the major products or the purpose of the projects when they are put into production or use, and by the nature of their social economic activities. In general, one project or one enterprise or institution can only be classified into one sector.

Investment in Fixed Assets by Composition

(1) Construction Projects (work volume of construction) include:

① Various kinds of houses and buildings such as workshops, warehouses, offices, residential buildings, shops, schools, hospitals, clubs, canteens and hostels, including the value of equipment such as heating, sanitation, lighting, and gas that are covered by the budget of housing projects and some decoration and polishing projects, various kinds of pipelines such as steam, compressed air, petroleum, tap water and sewage that are covered by the budget of construction projects and the pavement for cable conductors of electricity and telecommunications.

② Construction projects such as equipment foundations, pillars, operating platforms, ladders, chimneys, cooling towers, pools and gray towers, the masonry of various kinds of kilns and stoves for coke and stream ovens, and the metal structure work.

③ Site layout and geological explorations for the construction, demolition of the old buildings and barriers, site leveling, projects of temporary tap water, electricity , gas and road for the construction, and clearing up and green environment after the construction.

④ The mine excavation, the excavation and extension of roadway, the stripping of open pits, drilling engineering works for petroleum and natural gas, and the projects of railway, highway, ports and bridges.

⑤ Projects of water conservancy, such as reservoirs, dams, irrigation and river regulation.

⑥ Special projects such as air-raid shelters and underground constructions.

(2) Installation Projects (work volume of installation) include:

① Various assembly and installations that need equipment for installation, such as production, power, lifting, transportation, transmission and medical experiments, decoration projects that are connected with the equipment, such as tables, ladders and railings, pipeline laying works that are attached with the installed equipment, and works such as isolation, anti-corrosion and painting for the installed projects.

② In order to determine the quality of the installation project, the system equipment will be operated on trial separately and the system will be connected without any load (excluding the trial with feeding). The installation project will not include the value of the installed equipment itself.

(3) Purchase of equipment, tools and instruments refers to the total value of equipment, tools, and instruments purchased or self-produced which come up to standards for fixed assets by the construction units or the enterprises or institutions. The standards for fixed assets are specified by the financial departments. All of the equipment, tools and instruments purchased or self-produced for new workshops by newly established or expanded units are categorized as "purchase of equipment, tools and instruments" no matter whether they come up to the standards for fixed assets.

① Equipment refers to various kinds of equipment for production, transmission, power and transportation. It is divided into two categories: one that need installation and the other that need not be installed.

Equipment that need installation refers to the equipment that must be assembled in whole or in several parts, and mounted on the base or on the brackets of the building for normal operation, such as rolling machines, generators, steam boilers, transformers, towers, heat exchangers, pumps and machine tools. Although some equipment need not a base, they need the job for assembly and can only be used in a certain scope, such as shovels, cranes, gantry cranes and belt conveyors for production.

Equipment that need not be installed refers to various kinds of equipment that are not necessarily installed at a certain place or bracket and can be put into use, such as welding machines, forklifts, cars, motorcycles, planes, ships, and air compressors and pumps that are used in a non-fixed place during the production.

② Tools and instruments refer to various production supplies, working tools and instruments with their independent uses, such as cutting, rolling and riveting tools, molded devices and picks for production and repair, various measurement, analysis, laboratory equipment for inspection and experiment, and containers that can meet the standards of fixed assets.

Purchase of old equipment refers to various kinds of used equipment that have been bought from other units, which exclude used equipment purchased from foreign countries. Old equipment generally refers to the equipment that other domestic units have used as fixed assets (Simple purchasing of old equipment will not be covered in the statistical investment of fixed assets).

Equipment for updating refers to the investment that is purchased for updating the old equipment. Equipment for updating does not necessarily have the same number and value as those of the original equipment. If the purchased equipment is not used to replace the old equipment but to increase or enlarge its production capability, it can not be identified as "Equipment for updating".

(4) Other Expenses refer to the completed investment that are other than those mentioned above, which include expenses that are covered by fixed assets, such as purchasing livestock, planting economic trees, furniture and appliances for office and living, manage-

ment, land, compensation for young crops, resettlement compensation, survey and design, research and test, joint trial for load and combination, introduction of foreign technology and imported equipment by construction units of agriculture and forest.

Investment in Fixed Assets by Property of Construction

It is filled out according to the specific construction project.

(1) New construction refers to completely new construction from scratch. Projects of the existing enterprises, institutions or administrative units are not considered as new construction. In case the assets of the existing unit are quite small, and the value of newly added fixed assets exceeds the original value of assets by three times, the expansion will also be considered as new construction.

(2) Expansion refers to construction of new major production workshop, branch factory or independent production line within a factory or in other locations, for the purpose of increasing the production capacity (or improving efficiency) of the original products. Newly constructed houses for the operation of institutions and administrative organizations (such as the newly constructed buildings for teaching in schools, buildings for clinics or wards in hospitals, etc.) are also classified as expansion.

Also included in the expansion are investments by existing enterprises or institutions in building major production line(s) or branch factory(ies) along with some work on innovation, for the purpose of expending the production capacity of original products or producing new products.

(3) Reconstruction and technological reforms refers to construction projects by existing enterprises or institutions in innovation or technical transformation of the old facilities (including auxiliary production equipment and welfare facilities). Also considered as reconstruction is the construction of new workshops by the existing enterprises or institutions to change the variety of products to meet the market demand (such as the production of civil products by defense industries), or to bring the designed production capacity into full play through a more balanced production process on production lines. Technological reforms refer to the fact that enterprises and institutions, on an ongoing basis, replace outdated technology with advanced technology and replace backward process and equipment with advance ones, in order to change the outdated technology of the enterprises and improve the economic benefits while lowering the consumption of the energy. Technological reforms include the following contents: renovation of the machinery and tools, reform of production process, saving energy and raw materials, reform of plant buildings and public facilities, protection of the environment, and reform of the working conditions and environment.

(4) Simple construction of living facilities refers to facilities for living and welfare, such as residential buildings, nurseries, schools, medical rooms, bathrooms and canteens for the staff and workers, simply built by enterprises and institutions without expanding or reconstructing production projects or business buildings.

(5) Relocation: Enterprises and institutions relocate their plants to other places because of the change of production layout or for reasons of protecting the urban environment and safe production. During the construction of relocation to other places, the original or expanded scale of construction will be covered in the statistics.

(6) Restoration: Enterprises and institutions restore the construction with investment after all or part of their original fixed assets has been scrapped due to natural disasters and wars. Restoration to their original scale or any expansion will be covered as restored projects.

(7) Simple purchase: Existing enterprises, institutions and administrative units simply purchase equipment, tools and instruments that need not be installed or any construction. Although some units purchased some equipment in the previous year, there are some construction and installation in their design. These constructions should be determined to the contents of the design files, not being covered as simple purchase.

Newly Increased Fixed Assets

Newly Increased Fixed Assets, also called fixed assets put into operation, refers to the value of fixed assets that has been put into production or handed over to the production units after the completion of the process of construction and purchase. The newly increased fixed asset is a value indicator of the result of investment. It is also the necessary data for reflecting the construction process and the result of investment in fixed assets.

Rate of Fixed Assets Completed and Put into Operation

Rate of Fixed Assets Completed and Put into Operation, also called the fixed assets operation ratio, refers to ratio of newly increased fixed assets to total investment completed in the same period, which is a comprehensive indicator, reflecting the development of fixed assets investment and investment efficiency.

Projects under Construction

Projects under Construction refer to projects with construction and installation activities undertaken in the reference period. All projects that have construction activities undertaken during the reference period are reported as projects under construction irrespective of the length of construction work. The number of projects under construction can reflect the actual size of investment in fixed assets during a given period, and when compared with the number of projects completed and put into use during the same period, it demonstrates the results of investment in fixed assets. Depending on the nature of construction activities, projects under construction can also be classified into projects under construction in current year, winding-up projects in current year and stopped or suspended projects in previous years.

Projects Completely Put into Use

Industrial projects refer to the major projects and accessory facilities completed which result in forming production capacity and have been checked and accepted while the living and welfare facilities have been completed and can ensure normal production and formally put into production. Non-industrial projects refer to the major projects and accessory facilities completed which possess the designed capacity and have been checked, accepted and formally put into production.

第四篇

CHAPTER 4

招商引资

BUSINESS PROMOTION AND FOREIGN-FUND ATTRACTION

表4-1 历年外商直接投资情况
(1990~2012)

年 份 Year	外商直接投资合同项目(项) Contracted Projects of Foreign Direct Investment(unit)	#中外合资 Joint-venture	中外合作 Sino-foreign Cooperative	外商独资 Solely Foreigner Funded
1990	28	22	2	4
1991	92	79	4	9
1992	567	467	38	56
1993	924	610	38	275
1994	1 035	547	51	432
1995	838	340	41	455
1996	802	285	38	479
1997	615	132	36	447
1998	554	88	30	435
1999	470	71	18	380
2000	693	109	21	563
2001	880	110	10	758
2002	964	119	14	829
2003	1 563	175	15	1 370
2004	1 688	188	9	1 489
2005	1 734	149	8	1 574
2006	1 446	143	7	1 292
2007	1 254	112	3	1 138
2008	803	90	3	710
2009	780	100	4	676
2010	906	140	1	765
2011	995	181	2	809
2012	976	207	2	763

注：从2004年起，外商直接投资实际到位金额中不包含间接吸收外资。
Note: The actual paid amount of foreign direct investment will not include the indirectly-attracted foreign capital after the year of 2004.

Foreign Direct Investment in Main Years

外商直接投资合同金额(亿美元) Contracted Value of Foreign Direct Investment (USD 100 million)	# 中外合资 Joint-venture	中外合作 Sino-foreign Cooperative	外商独资 Solely Foreigner Funded	外商直接投资实际到位金额(亿美元) Capital in Place of Foreign Direct Investment (USD 100 million)
0.34	0.29	0.01	0.05	0.13
1.01	0.92	0.03	0.06	0.68
13.53	7.28	0.82	2.77	2.49
17.57	13.08	1.53	2.78	4.29
25.93	14.14	4.10	7.32	6.85
32.56	10.47	2.56	17.43	12.81
18.09	5.04	5.84	7.21	14.25
18.00	13.39	0.82	3.79	10.13
27.90	13.77	0.63	2.90	15.37
10.73	2.95	0.55	6.91	5.92
28.84	2.73	0.47	25.63	8.85
20.02	4.51	1.12	14.16	23.04
26.68	5.72	1.36	17.22	18.47
28.75	6.47	0.12	21.19	18.01
32.24	5.05	0.56	26.08	23.78
56.54	7.84	0.38	42.20	31.11
48.42	7.67	0.32	39.46	32.20
49.49	5.08	0.39	41.30	33.06
49.92	5.87	0.12	43.12	34.35
55.29	4.80	1.22	47.13	39.08
56.25	8.57	0.01	45.35	38.56
65.97	9.31	0.59	55.00	52.97
72.86	4.21	2.17	62.09	48.30

表 4-2 外商直接投资合同项目

Number of Contracted Projects of Foreign Direct Investment

单位:个 (unit)

指 标	Indicators	2005	2010	2011	2012	至 2012 年末累计 Accumulated by the End of 2012
总 计	**Total**	**1 734**	**906**	**995**	**976**	**20 624**
按投资方式分	**By Way of Investment**					
中外合资	Joint-venture	149	140	181	207	4 515
中外合作	Sino-foreign Cooperative	8	1	2	2	402
外商独资	Solely Foreigner Funded	1 574	765	809	763	15 667
B 股企业	B Share	3		3	4	40
按投资行业分	**By Sector**					
#第二产业	Secondary Industry	209	52	42	23	4 032
#工 业	Industry	188	46	38	20	3 419
第三产业	Tertiary Industry	1 524	854	953	953	16 567
#批发零售业	Wholesale and Retail	672	476	551	536	9 125
交通运输、仓储和邮政业	Transportation, Warehousing, Post and Telecommunications	18	20	33	26	771
房地产业	Real Estate	25	3	11	8	340
租赁和商务服务业	Leasing and Commercial Services	295	216	241	227	3 226
按总投资规模分	**By Investment Scale**					
1000 万美元以上	>USD 10 million	59	51	80	117	1 302
500~1000 万美元	USD 5 ~ 10 million	51	33	25	40	592
300~500 万美元	USD 3 ~ 5 million	29	19	22	23	477
100~300 万美元	USD 1 ~ 3 million	150	128	142	140	2 624
50~100 万美元	USD 0.5 ~1 million	153	70	100	96	2 817
30~50 万美元	USD 0.3 ~0.5 million	97	69	75	76	1 881
30 万美元以下	<USD 0.3 million	1 195	536	551	484	10 931
按投资国别、地区分	**By Country/Region**					
#中国香港	Hong Kong, China	307	301	275	336	5 893
中国澳门	Macao, China	2		1	5	65
中国台湾	Taiwan, China	82	62	39	48	1 254
日 本	Japan	270	101	91	88	2 727
新加坡	Singapore	107	52	58	67	1 223
韩 国	Republic of Korea	80	29	23	25	590
英 国	United Kingdom	35	15	14	17	374
德 国	Germany	52	27	36	54	578
法 国	France	26	10	12	11	193
荷 兰	the Netherlands	24	10	7	5	233
瑞 士	Switzerland	14	8	8	9	185
美 国	United States of America	146	87	79	80	2 336
加拿大	Canada	19	10	10	18	312
澳大利亚	Australia	22	8	14	14	299
海外中资集团	Overseas Chinese Group Companies					72

注：当年增资部分不计算项目个数。
Note: The increase of investment in the current year is not listed as new project.

表 4-3 外商直接投资合同金额
Contract Value Capital of Foreign Direct Investment

单位:万美元 (USD 10 000)

指 标	Indicators	2005	2010	2011	2012	至 2012 年末累计 Accumulated by the End of 2012
总 计	**Total**	**565 369**	**562 487**	**659 727**	**728 551**	**7 069 042**
按投资方式分	**By Way of Investment**					
中外合资	Joint-venture	78 437	85 679	93 081	42 065	1 372 341
中外合作	Sino-foreign Cooperative	3 771	122	5 920	21 705	175 355
外商独资	Solely Foreigner Funded	421 985	453 504	550 004	620 944	5 152 572
B 股企业	B Share	61 176	23 182	10 722	43 837	368 774
按投资行业分	**By Sector**					
#第二产业	Secondary Industry	172 056	98 697	43 322	73 452	2 051 388
#工 业	Industry	162 312	95 872	40 942	71 890	1 573 935
第三产业	Tertiary Industry	393 242	463 790	616 405	655 043	5 015 616
#批发零售业	Wholesale and Retail	61 919	90 922	151 336	177 122	177 122
交通运输、仓储和邮政业	Transportation, Warehousing, Post and Telecommunications	114 776	18 896	23 108	48 217	398 338
房地产业	Real Estate	49 390	100 310	135 341	49 396	49 396
租赁和商务服务业	Leasing and Business Service	114 149	163 058	103 392	254 712	254 712
按总投资规模分	**By Investment Scale**					
1000 万美元以上	>USD 10 million	162 738	142 532	265 512	246 117	3 115 144
500~1000 万美元	USD 5~10 million	16 141	11 390	25 130	19 040	166 401
300~500 万美元	USD 3~5 million	5 620	4 486	12 566	4 890	72 602
100~300 万美元	USD 1~3 million	16 233	14 820	33 659	15 162	241 663
50~100 万美元	USD 0.5~1 million	6 972	3 316	8 369	4 900	98 316
30~50 万美元	USD 0.3~0.5 million	2 464	1 873	3 597	2 090	43 346
30 万美元以下	<USD 0.3 million	15 817	6 885	22 892	6 024	172 771
当年增资	Capital Increase in Current Year	339 384	401 546	376 467	478 223	3 319 520
按投资国别、地区分	**By Country/Region**					
#中国香港	Hong Kong, China	68 253	200 809	242 094	288 635	1 830 509
中国澳门	Macao, China	68		155	1 750	8 502
中国台湾	Taiwan, China	2 795	2 936	2 105	16 729	77 249
日 本	Japan	69 789	49 831	41 930	79 118	787 008
新加坡	Singapore	18 363	30 632	70 775	56 705	441 564
韩 国	Republic of Korea	5 438	4 463	11 816	5 421	88 854
英 国	United Kingdom	6 245	10 809	4 023	2 901	113 378
德 国	Germany	54 020	9 016	10 089	10 637	209 035
法 国	France	2 531	21 750	7 407	14 747	128 011
荷 兰	the Netherlands	8 424	9 744	13 107	32 486	219 177
瑞 士	Switzerland	1 340	1 037	11 142	4 351	53 485
美 国	United States of America	41 169	21 172	20 955	70 680	684 801
加拿大	Canada	1 101	-92	791	835	24 736
澳大利亚	Australia	787	1 024	620	1 493	21 936
海外中资集团	Overseas Chinese Group Companies					20 657
当年增资	**Capital Increase in Current Year**	**339 384**	**401 546**	**376 467**	**478 223**	**3 319 520**

注:资金负数是当年项目的投资不抵当年增资(减资)的数值。
Note: The negative figures in the table are the values that the investment of projects in that particular year. is not worth of that of the increase or decrease of investment in that year.

表4-4　当年签约投资2000万美元以上的外商投资企业
FIEs with Current Year Contracted Investment Over USD 20 Million (2012)

单位:万美元　　(USD 10 000)

序号 No.	指标 Indicators		国别(地区) Country/Region	总投资 Total Investment	外商合同投资 Contracted Foreign Investment
1	中华开发股权投资管理有限公司	China Kaifa Equity Investment Management Co. ,Ltd.	香港 Hong Kong	2 000	1 000
2	上海曜中能源科技有限公司	Shanghai Yaozhong Energy Technology Co. , Ltd.	英属维尔京群岛 British Virgin Islands	4 101	2 366
3	吴羽(中国)投资有限公司	Wuyu (China) Investment Co. , Ltd.	日本 Japan	5 000	5 000
4	第一三共(中国)投资有限公司	Daiichisankyo (China) Investment Co. , Ltd.	日本 Japan	3 000	3 000
5	上海挚信融资租赁有限公司	Shanghai Zhixin Financing and Leasing Co. , Ltd.	香港 Hong Kong	3 000	3 000
6	上海海晟融资租赁有限公司	Shanghai Haisheng Financing and Leasing Co. , Ltd.	香港 Hong Kong	2 000	600
7	上海盛时商贸有限公司	Shanghai Shengshi Commerce and Trade Co. , Ltd.	投资性公司投资 Investment Companies	3 600	3 600
8	上海宏泰融资租赁有限公司	Shanghai Hongtai Financing and Leasing Co. , Ltd.	香港 Hong Kong	5 000	1 250
9	上海迪赛诺药业有限公司	Shanghai Desano Pharmacy Co. , Ltd.	毛里求斯 Mauritius	9 129	1 506
10	科聚亚(中国)投资有限公司	Chemtura (China) Investment Co. , Ltd.	美国 USA	3 000	3 000
11	上海实业发展股份有限公司	Shanghai Shiye Development Co. , Ltd.	香港 Hong Kong	13 087	8 330
12	江铜国际贸易有限公司	Jiangtong International Trade Co. , Ltd.	香港 Hong Kong	29 966	1 577
13	摩科瑞(中国)金属资源有限公司	Mercuria (China) Metal Resources Co. , Ltd.	新加坡 Singapore	9 000	3 000
14	三一重通机械有限公司	Sany Zhongtong Mechinery Co. , Ltd.	美国 USA	2 966	2 038
15	上海思凯房地产开发有限公司	Shanghai SK Real Estate Development Co. , Ltd.	香港 Hong Kong	66 493	34 020
16	上海洛浦外仓储有限公司	Shanghai Luopuwai Warehousing Co. , Ltd.	新加坡 Singapore	18 000	6 000
17	中皓融资租赁(上海)股份有限公司	Zhonghao Financing and Leasing (Shanghai) Co. , Ltd.	香港 Hong Kong	4 731	1 183
18	上海赛飞航空线缆制造有限公司	Shanghai Saifei Aviation Cables Manufacturing Co. , Ltd.	法国 France	4 000	686
19	上海昊信光电有限公司	Shanghai Haoxin Optoelectronics Co. , Ltd.	英属维尔京群岛 British Virgin Islands	6 309	3 219
20	上海和誉融资租赁有限公司	Shanghai Heyu Financing and Leasing Co. , Ltd.	香港 Hong Kong	2 000	500

单位:万美元　　表4-4　续表　Continued　　(USD 10 000)

序号 No.	指标	Indicators	国别(地区) Country/Region	总投资 Total Investment	外商合同投资 Contracted Foreign Investment
21	路易达孚(上海)商贸有限公司	Louis Dreyfus (Shanghai) Commerce and Trade Co., Ltd.	新加坡 Singapore	4 500	1 500
22	上银融资租赁(中国)有限责任公司	Shangyin Financing and Leasing (China) Co., Ltd.	台湾省 Taiwan	2 000	2 000
23	康慧母婴专护服务(上海)有限公司	Kanghui Mother-and-baby Care Services (Shanghai) Co., Ltd.	香港 Hong Kong	9 463	3 864
24	上海盛时商贸有限公司	Shanghai Shengshi Commerce and Trade Co., Ltd.	投资性公司投资 Investment Companies	3 600	3 600
25	上海国际主题乐园配套设施有限公司	Shanghai International Theme Parks Supporting Facilities Co., Ltd.	美国 USA	68 706	20 680
26	爱德万测试(中国)管理有限公司	Advantest (China) Management Co., Ltd.	新加坡 Singapore	2 000	800
27	久保田(中国)融资租赁有限公司	Kubota (China) Financing and Leasing Co., Ltd.	投资性公司投资 Investment Companies	3 500	3 500
28	美药典标准研发技术服务(上海)有限公司	USP Standards R&D Technical Services (Shanghai) Co., Ltd.	美国 USA	2 900	1 200
29	波科医疗器械(上海)有限公司	Boston Science Medical Devices (Shanghai) Co., Ltd.	爱尔兰 Ireland	9 000	3 000
30	爱定客(上海)网络科技有限公司	IDX (Shanghai) Network Technologies Co., Ltd.	香港 Hong Kong	3 500	1 500
31	上海翡翠滨江艺术发展有限公司	Shanghai Feicui Bingjiang Arts Development Co., Ltd.	香港 Hong Kong	4 800	1 600
32	三井仓库(中国)投资有限公司	Mitsui Warehouse (China) Investment Co., Ltd.	日本 Japan	4 000	4 000
33	昇瑞光电科技(上海)有限公司	ShineRayTek Opto - electronics Technologies (Shanghai) Co., Ltd.	香港 Hong Kong	2 600	1 050
34	坤谷国际融资租赁有限公司	Kungu International Financing and Leasing Co., Ltd.	香港 Hong Kong	3 154	789
35	易可邦材料科技(上海)有限公司	Yikebang Materials Technology (Shanghai) Co., Ltd.	香港 Hong Kong	2 000	1 000
36	莲特贸易(上海)有限公司	Lindt Trade (Shanghai) Co., Ltd.	香港 Hong Kong	3 857	1 286
37	上海凯惠置业有限公司	Shanghai Kaihui Property Co., Ltd.	新加坡 Singapore	9 499	4 512
38	上海爱定客信息科技有限公司	Shanghai IDX Information Technology Co., Ltd.	香港 Hong Kong	3 000	1 500
39	上海盟科药业有限公司	Shanghai Mengke Pharmacy Co., Ltd.	香港 Hong Kong	8 631	1 668
40	三菱仓库(中国)投资有限公司	Mitsubishi Warehouse (China) Investment Co., Ltd.	日本 Japan	3 956	3 956
41	上海诚达融资租赁有限责任公司	Shanghai Chengda Financing and Leasing Co., Ltd.	香港 Hong Kong	4 766	1 192
42	纵横国际融资租赁有限公司	Zongheng International Financing and Leasing Co., Ltd.	香港 Hong Kong	4 766	1 192

表4-5 外商直接投资实际到位金额
Capital in Place of Foreign Direct Investment

单位：万美元 (USD 10 000)

指 标	Indicators	2010	2011	2012
总 计	**Total**	**385 567**	**529 736**	**483 036**
按投资方式分	**By Way of Investment**			
# 中外合资	Joint-venture	59 492	78 376	47 546
中外合作	Sino-foreign Cooperative	836	8 577	18 638
外商独资	Solely Foreigner Funded	325 239	442 783	416 852
按投资行业分	**By Sector**			
# 第二产业	Secondary Industry	50 926	49 931	56 377
# 工 业	Industry	48 603	48 889	55 574
第三产业	Tertiary Industry	334 516	479 793	426 659
# 批发和零售业餐饮业	Wholesale and Retail Catering	64 727	88 847	109 069
房地产业	Real Estate	64 706	136 141	62 810
租赁和商务服务业	Leasing and Business Service	118 916	92 014	112 126
按投资国别、地区分	**By Country/Region**			
# 中国香港	Hong Kong, China	116 495	272 308	181 401
日 本	Japan	37 506	34 687	51 549
新加坡	Singapore	61 672	53 452	21 459
英 国	United Kingdom	4 632	8 784	2 516
德 国	Germany	8 738	10 833	13 293
法 国	France	14 871	16 239	31 339
荷 兰	the Netherlands	27 020	13 218	14 953
开曼群岛	Cayman Islands	12 702	29 552	22 329
英属维尔京群岛	British Virgin Islands	17 901	18 008	31 097
美 国	United States of America	21 956	19 582	48 247
萨摩亚	Samoa	1 358	1 328	1 222

表4-6 内资企业工商注册情况
Registered Domestic Enterprises

指 标	Indicators	单 位 Unit	2011	2012
期末实有注册企业	**Actual Registered Enterprises at End of Term**	**个 unit**	**10 636**	**10 633**
第一产业	Primary Industry	个 unit	155	150
第二产业	Secondary Industry	个 unit	2 811	2 595
#制造业	Manufacturing	个 unit	2 191	2 080
建筑业	Construction	个 unit	477	449
第三产业	Tertiary Industry	个 unit	7 670	7 888
#交通运输、仓储和邮政业	Transportation, Warehousing and Post Service	个 unit	463	464
批发和零售业	Wholesale and Retail	个 unit	2 860	2 847
金融业	Banking	个 unit	90	128
房地产业	Real Estate	个 unit	881	876
期末实际注册资金总额	**Total of Actual Registered Capital at End of Term**	**亿元（100 million yuan）**	**7 482.42**	**8 184.49**
第一产业	Primary Industry	亿元（100 million yuan）	19.90	18.48
第二产业	Secondary Industry	亿元（100 million yuan）	2 163.62	2 202.64
#制造业	Manufacturing	亿元（100 million yuan）	1 352.84	1 431.97
建筑业	Construction	亿元（100 million yuan）	548.76	515.32
第三产业	Tertiary Industry	亿元（100 million yuan）	5 298.90	5 963.38
#交通运输、仓储和邮政业	Transportation, Warehousing and Post Service	亿元（100 million yuan）	573.81	593.63
批发和零售业	Wholesale and Retail	亿元（100 million yuan）	634.44	691.02
金融业	Banking	亿元（100 million yuan）	377.81	508.37
房地产业	Real Estate	亿元（100 million yuan）	950.96	1 043.02

注：内资注册数和注册资本含市局登记、不含分支机构。

Note: The number of domestic registered enterprises and that of registered capital included those registered in Shanghai municipal bureaus and excluded those registered in branch bureaus.

表 4-7　私营企业基本情况
Statistics of Private Enterprises
(2012)

	指　标 Indicators	户　数 (户) Number of Enterprises (unit)	投资人数 (人) Number of Investors (person)	雇工人数 (人) Employed Persons (person)	注册资金 (亿元) Registered Capital (100 million yuan)
总　计	**Total**	**92 727**	**197 639**	**695 854**	**3 504.61**
农、林、牧、渔业	Farming, Forestry, Animal Husbandry and Fishery	732	1 232	4 236	7.78
采掘业	Mining and Quarrying	4	10	6	1.31
制造业	Manufacturing	16 674	32 882	238 810	308.55
建筑业	Construction	3 404	7 352	44 661	132.55
交通运输业、仓储和邮政业	Transportation, Warehousing and Post Service	3 545	7 535	28 081	129.20
信息传输、计算机服务	Information Transmission and Computer Service	2 581	6 561	19 113	78.47
批发零售贸易业	Wholesale and Retail	32 646	66 425	173 255	764.34
住宿和餐饮业	Accommodation and Catering	1 841	3 333	17 719	13.51
居民服务和其他服务业	Resident Service and Other Services	2 806	4 988	16 030	40.25
房地产	Real Estate	2 392	4 749	23 919	315.94
其　他	Others	26 102	62 572	130 024	1 712.71

表4-8 个体工商户基本情况
Self-Employment Business
(2012)

指 标	Indicators	户 数(户) Number of Enterprises (unit)	从业人数(人) Employed persons (person)	注册资金(万元) Registered Capital (10 000 yuan)
总 计	**Total**	**68 015**	**72 102**	**159 395**
农、林、牧、渔	Farming, Forestry, Animal Husbandry and Fishery	429	454	2 671
制造业	Manufacturing	1 732	2 023	4 741
建筑业	Construction	72	79	201
交通运输业、仓储业	Transportation and Warehousing	508	525	3 094
批发零售贸易业、住宿和餐饮业	Wholesale, Retail and Catering Businesses	57 132	59 793	127 993
批发零售贸易业	Wholesale and Retail	53 493	55 089	115 015
住宿和餐饮业	Accommodation and Catering	3 639	4 704	12 978
居民服务和其他服务业	Resident Service and Other Services	7 233	8 254	17 782
其 他	Others	909	974	2 913

主要统计指标解释

外商直接投资

外商直接投资是指外国企业和经济组织或个人(包括华侨、港澳台胞以及我国在境外注册的企业)按我国有关政策、法规,用现汇、实物、技术等在我国境内开办外商独资企业、与我国境内的企业或经济组织共同举办中外合资经营企业、合作经营企业或合作开发资源的投资(包括外商投资收益的再投资)以及企业投资总额内直接投资者对企业的贷款,即外方股东贷款(需在报告期内将相应合同及贷款协议报商务部备案核查)。

合同投资额

是指经有关部门批准的我方与外商正式签订的合同规定的可使用的贷款额、外商投资额和中方对外发行债券、股票总值,以及"补偿贸易"外商提供的设备价款,"国际租赁"境外出租人提供的设备等价款总值。

外商实际投资额

是指按合同(章程)规定,外商以现金、实物及专有技术等工业产权计价的全部实缴资本额,包括经有关部门批准,外商用于扩大再生产、发展企业规模或补充基本建设资金不足而投入的追加资金。外商的实缴资本额一律折成美元计算。

EXPLANATORY NOTES TO MAJOR STATISTICAL INDICATORS

Foreign Direct Investment

Foreign Direct Investment refers to the investments made inside China by foreign enterprises and economic organizations or individuals (including overseas Chinese, compatriots in Hong Kong, Macao and Chinese enterprises registered abroad), in line with the relevant policies and laws of China, for the establishment of wholly foreign-owned enterprises, and joint ventures or development projects launched in China (including re-investment of profits from foreign businesses), and the funds that enterprises borrow from abroad in the total investment of projects which are approved by the relevant departments of the governments and the loans from the direct investors within the total investment of the projects, i. e., foreign shareholders' loans. (The related contracts and loans agreements in the report period should be filed with the Ministry of Commerce)

Agreed (Contracted) Investment

Agreed (Contracted) Investment includes usable loans which are approved by government departments and with contracts signed formally by Chinese units and foreign investors, investment of foreigners, total value of bonds and stocks issued in international market by Chinese units, the value of equipment provided by foreign investors for compensation trade, the value of equipment which are leased from foreign firms, etc.

Actual Investment of Foreign Investors

refers to all foreign investors paid-in capital, in cash, in kind or in special technique, based on contracts, which includes the additional funds used for extensional reproduction, expanding enterprise scale or complements to capital construction. All the foreigners paid-in capital is measured by or converted to US dollars.

第五篇

CHAPTER 5

农 业

AGRICULTURE

表5-1 主要年份农村户数、人口和劳动力
Rural Households, Population and Workforce in Main Years

指 标	Indicators	单 位 Unit	1990	2000	2005	2010	2011	2012
户 数	Household	万户 10 000 households	15.74	13.67	12.67	32.90	32.57	31.68
人 口	Population	万人 10 000 persons	47.00	36.82	35.57	82.96	80.94	76.89
劳动力使用	Workforce	万人 10 000 persons	27.70	19.86	19.66	48.70	48.67	46.49
第一产业	Primary Industry	人 person	68 339	40 430	16 725	106 229	102 452	94 508
第二产业	Secondary Industry	人 person	149 075	89 835	115 266	259 458	260 061	272 323
第三产业	Tertiary Industry	人 person	59 586	68 335	64 609	121 290	124 187	98 076
外省市流入劳动力	Migrant Workforce from Other Provinces	人 person	15 262	91 268	265 223	653 226	663 762	671 513
第一产业	Primary Industry	人 person	2 828	14 743	16 453	40 821	38 868	40 412
第二产业	Secondary Industry	人 person	11 846	52 715	184 437	433 208	404 303	419 329
第三产业	Tertiary Industry	人 person	588	23 810	64 333	179 197	220 591	211 772

注：表中涉及的户数、人口和劳动力是指居住在农村地区的本市户籍人口。
Note: The numbers of households, population and labor force involved in this table are referred to those that live in the rural area and are registered in Shanghai.

表5-2 各镇耕地面积
Cultivated Area by Town

单位:公顷 (hectare)

镇 Town		2011年末耕地面积 Cultivated Area (End of 2011)	2012年净减少耕地面积 Net Decrease in Cultivated Area in 2012	2012年末耕地面积 Cultivated Area (End of 2012)	水田 Paddy Field	水浇地 Irrigated Land
川沙新镇	Chuansha New Town	2 216.3	246.3	1 970.0	1 876.1	93.9
高桥镇	Gaoqiao Town	430.4		430.4	16.6	413.8
北蔡镇	Beicai Town	146.0		146.0	146.0	
合庆镇	Heqing Town	837.2		837.2	762.6	74.6
唐镇	Tangzhen Town	208.6	2.3	206.3	51.4	154.9
曹路镇	Caolu Town	601.5	74.8	526.7	521.4	5.3
金桥镇	Jinqiao Town	24.8		24.8	24.8	
高行镇	Gaohang Town	21.6		21.6		21.6
高东镇	Gaodong Town	261.3		261.3	239.6	21.7
张江镇	Zhangjiang Town	288.3	28.3	260.0	260.0	
三林镇	Sanlin Town	258.0	7.0	251.0		251.0
惠南镇	Huinan Town	1 791.6	163.4	1 628.2	1 628.2	
周浦镇	Zhoupu Town	621.8	22.4	599.4	513.9	85.5
新场镇	Xinchang Town	2 189.8	-121.1	2 310.9	2 257.7	53.2
大团镇	Datuan Town	1 910.0		1 910.0	1 741.3	168.7
康桥镇	Kangqiao Town	842.9	21.7	821.2	188.5	632.7
航头镇	Hangtou Town	2 921.1		2 921.1	2 123.4	797.7
祝桥镇	Zhuqiao Town	4 352.7	32.9	4 319.8	2 255.7	2 064.1
泥城镇	Nicheng Town	3 169.9		3 169.6	2 899.3	270.6
宣桥镇	Xuanqiao Town	2 027.6	-5.0	2 032.6	1 225.4	807.2
书院镇	Shuyuan Town	3 565.9		3 565.9	3 360.8	205.1
万祥镇	Wanxiang Town	1 462.7		1 462.7	1 430.1	32.6
老港镇	Laogang Town	1 810.5		1 810.5	1 810.5	
南汇新城镇	Nanhui New Town	956.9		956.9	873.0	83.9
农场	Farm	26.1		26.1	26.1	
棉种场	Cotton Farm	23.5		23.5	23.5	

注：各镇耕地面积南片为批准数，北片为实际经营数，两者不能加总。

Note: The number in the southern part of cultivated area in each town is what has been authorized, and that in the northern part is what has been operated. These two numbers cannot be accumulated.

表5-3 主要年份耕地面积增减情况
Increase and Decrease of Cultivated Land in Main Years

单位:公顷 (hectare)

指 标	Indicators	2005	2010	2011	2012
年初耕地面积	Cultivated Area (Year Beginning)	9 483	44 001	43 551	43 319
当年减少	Decrease in Current Year	634	450	245	470
年末耕地面积	Cultivated Area (Year End)	8 849	43 551	43 319	42 849

注：2011 年耕地面积为批准数。
Note: The number of cultivated area in 2011 is what has been authorized.

表5-4 主要年份农业总产值
Gross Output Value of Agriculture in Main Years

单位:万元 (10 000 yuan)

指 标	Indicators	1990	2000	2005	2010	2011	2012
按当年价格计算	**Calculated in Current Year**						
总 计	**Total**	**55 318**	**125 732**	**116 248**	**698 552**	**735 789**	**713 461**
种植业	Planting	24 015	59 584	66 809	396 127	425 407	432 362
林 业	Forestry	234	1 279	25 424	10 420	17 324	18 463
牧 业	Animal Husbandry	29 528	60 837	19 488	183 084	186 993	150 970
渔 业	Fishery	1 541	4 032	4 527	70 921	67 565	74 766
农、林、牧、渔服务业	Agriculture, forestry, animal husbandry and fishery			38 000	38 500	38 500	36 900
构 成(%)	**Composition (%)**						
总 计	**Total**	**100.0**	**100.0**	**100.0**	**100.0**	**100.0**	**100.0**
种植业	Planting	43.4	47.4	57.5	56.7	57.8	60.6
林 业	Forestry	0.4	1.0	21.9	1.5	2.4	2.6
牧 业	Animal Husbandry	53.4	48.4	16.8	26.2	25.4	21.1
渔 业	Fishery	2.8	3.2	3.8	10.2	9.2	10.5
农、林、牧、淮服务业	Agriculture, forestry, animal husbandry and fishery				5.4	5.2	5.2

表5-5 各镇农业总产值
Gross Output Value of Agriculture by Town
(2012)

单位:万元 (10 000 yuan)

指标	Indicators	农业总产值(按现行价格计算) Gross Output Value of Agriculture (at Current Price)	#种植业 Planting	林业 Forestry	牧业 Animal Husbandry	渔业 Fishery
总计	**Total**	**713 461**	**432 362**	**18 463**	**150 970**	**74 766**
川沙新镇	Chuansha New Town	51 239	28 668	5 308	12 859	2 104
高桥镇	Gaoqiao Town	1 744	1 691			53
北蔡镇	Beicai Town	733	673			60
合庆镇	Heqing Town	9 261	5 918		2 823	520
唐镇	Tangzhen Town	3 180	2 912	228		40
曹路镇	Caolu Town	24 613	9 235	597	14 516	215
金桥镇	Jinqiao Town	162	101	45		16
高行镇	Gaohang Town	400	400			
高东镇	Gaodong Town	1 737	1 679			58
张江镇	Zhangjiang Town	6 336	5 995	112		229
三林镇	Sanlin Town	4 508	1 968	262		133
惠南镇	Huinan Town	32 978	19 238		11 659	2 081
周浦镇	Zhoupu Town	16 903	12 905		3 541	457
新场镇	Xinchang Town	55 932	45 861		8 834	1 237
大团镇	Datuan Town	43 527	25 197		17 053	1 277
康桥镇	Kangqiao Town	3 825	3 324		413	88
航头镇	Hangtou Town	38 826	13 478	2 163	21 731	1 454
祝桥镇	Zhuqiao Town	66 948	50 117	180	12 599	4 052
泥城镇	Nicheng Town	41 406	24 864		5 166	11 098
宣桥镇	Xuanqiao Town	31 186	20 480		9 795	383
书院镇	Shuyuan Town	49 867	36 585	317	6 461	6 504
万祥镇	Wanxiang Town	14 209	8 900		2 796	2 513
老港镇	Laogang Town	58 815	43 091		12 608	3 116
南汇新城镇	Nanhui New Town	18 523	11 350		1 014	6 159
其他	Others	136 603	57 732	9 251	7 102	30 919

表5-6 各镇粮食和蔬菜作物播种面积和产量
Sown Area and Output of Grain Crops and Vegetables by Town (2012)

指 标 Indicators		粮食播种面 积（公顷） Sown Area (hectare)	粮食总产量（吨） Total Output of Grain Crops (ton)	夏 粮 Summer Harvested	秋 粮 Autumn Harvested	粮食单位面积产量（千克/公顷） Yield Per Unit (kg/hectare)	蔬菜播种面 积（公顷） Sown Area of Vegetables (hectare)	蔬菜总产量（吨） Total Output of Vegetables (ton)
总 计	**Total**	**25 011.1**	**167 767**	**38 395**	**129 372**	**6 708**	**25 618.3**	**848 994**
川沙新镇	Chuansha New Town	818.6	5 546	1 300	4 246	6 775	3 066.5	101 989
高 桥 镇	Gaoqiao Town						231.7	6 249
北 蔡 镇	Beicai Town						162.8	3 268
合 庆 镇	Heqing Town	238.8	1 653	433	1 220	6 922	407.5	17 147
唐 镇	Tangzhen Town	91.4	602	150	452	6 586	318.4	4 331
曹 路 镇	Caolu Town	196.5	1 424	377	1 047	7 247	1 293.5	44 731
金 桥 镇	Jinqiao Town						42.5	379
高 行 镇	Gaohang Town						58.6	1 941
高 东 镇	Gaodong Town						244.6	4 207
张 江 镇	Zhangjiang Town	149.1	1 027	322	705	6 888	152.3	5 893
三 林 镇	Sanlin Town						209.4	8 087
惠 南 镇	Huinan Town	1 192.9	8 691	1 906	6 785	7 286	1 764.7	44 823
周 浦 镇	Zhoupu Town	425.8	2 845	747	2 098	6 682	1 181.3	34 724
新 场 镇	Xinchang Town	1 211.2	8 943	952	7 991	7 384	2 250.2	84 528
大 团 镇	Datuan Town	1 628.5	11 858	1 826	10 032	7 282	464.3	69 385
康 桥 镇	Kangqiao Town	295.7	1 943	607	1 336	6 571	377.3	8 050
航 头 镇	Hangtou Town	619.1	4 785	996	3 789	7 729	2 366.1	53 824
祝 桥 镇	Zhuqiao Town	3 044.2	18 340	5 589	12 751	6 025	3 221.2	113 427
泥 城 镇	Nicheng Town	1 440.6	10 892	2 292	8 600	7 561	1 667.2	54 173
宣 桥 镇	Xuanqiao Town	807.2	4 562	1 122	3 440	5 652	2 214.7	61 864
书 院 镇	Shuyuan Town	5 417.6	39 031	9 605	29 426	7 204	1 390.8	53 241
万 祥 镇	Wanxiang Town	1 199.7	8 450	1 987	6 463	7 043	591.0	14 452
老 港 镇	Laogang Town	4 593.5	27 941	4 962	22 979	6 083	1 520.6	48 207
南汇新城镇	Nanhui New Town	1 640.7	9 234	3 222	6 012	5 628	421.1	10 074

表5-7 主要农产品产量
Output of Main Farm Products

指 标	Indicators	单 位 Unit	2005	2010	2011	2012
粮食作物	Grain Crops	吨 ton	13 671	148 707	148 599	167 767
夏熟作物	Summer Harvested	吨 ton	1 303	27 147	29 867	38 395
#小 麦	Wheat	吨 ton	1 064	20 291	22 322	23 774
秋熟作物	Autumn Harvested	吨 ton	12 368	121 560	118 732	129 372
#单季晚稻	Single-season Late Harvested Rice	吨 ton	10 580	116 437	112 968	122 382
油菜籽	Rapeseed	吨 ton	89	2 315	2 351	2 405
蔬 菜	Vegetables	万吨 10 000 tons	30	81	83	84.90
西甜瓜	Watermelons	万吨 10 000 tons	2	23	22	15.79
水果产量	Output of Fruits	吨 ton	4 219	108 714	88 191	93 847
#柑 桔	Mandarin Oranges	吨 ton	607	56 543	23 741	24 256
生 梨	Pears	吨 ton	274	7 829	8 889	12 486
葡 萄	Grapes	吨 ton	727	4 304	7 025	7 949
桃 子	Peaches	吨 ton		39 153	47 813	48 430
生猪饲养数	Stock of Hogs	万头 10 000 in number	16.72	96.61	96.35	84.60
生猪出栏数	Hogs on Market	万头 10 000 in number	8.80	56.36	54.59	48.00
猪肉产量	Pork Output	万吨 10 000 tons	0.77	3.66	4.11	3.72
牛奶产量	Milk Output	万吨 10 000 tons	1.27	4.43	4.43	4.60
家禽出栏数	Poultry on Market	万羽 10 000 in number	24.28	1 913.32	1 730.18	1 059.66
鲜蛋产量	Output of Fresh Eggs	万吨 10 000 tons	0.17	2.26	2.06	1.95
水产品产量	Output of Aquatic Products	万吨 10 000 tons	0.23	2.16	1.98	2.37
海水产品	Sea Products	万吨 10 000 tons		0.32	0.33	0.31
淡水产品	Fresh Water Products	万吨 10 000 tons	0.23	1.84	1.65	2.06

表5-8　农业机械拥有量
Farm Machinery Holding

指　标	Indicators	单　位　Unit	2010	2011	2012
农业机械总动力	**Total Power of Farm Machinery**	**千瓦 kw**	**112 420**	**117 169**	**129 062**
每公顷耕地拥有动力	Power Per Hectare	千瓦 kw	5	5	6
每万公顷耕地拥有拖拉机	Tractors Per 10 000 Hectare	台 set	842	876	825
#耕作机械动力合计	Total Power of Farm Machinery	千瓦 kw	46 605	47 251	47 370
大、中型拖拉机	Large/Medium Tractors	台 set	925	965	971
小型拖拉机	Walking Tractors	台 set	938	935	782
排灌机械动力合计	Total Power of Drainage and Irrigation Machinery	千瓦 kw	15 603	15 444	32 919
种植机械动力合计	Total Power of Cultivation	千瓦 kw	2 897	3 274	3 589
植物保护机械动力合计	Total Power of Crop Protection Machinery	千瓦 kw	6 141	7 445	7 683
#机动喷雾器	Motorized Sprayers	台 set 千瓦 kw	2 043 6 052	2 238 7 313	2 459 7 683
收获机械动力合计	Total Power of Harvest Machinery	千瓦 kw	14 293	15 338	14 321
#联合收割机	Combines	台/千瓦 set/kw	383/10 176	408/11 662	296/11 312
农产品加工机械动力合计	Power of Farm Processing Machinery	千瓦 kw	6 468	5 523	4 110
积肥机械动力合计	Power of Manure-Collecting Machinery	千瓦 kw	1 629	1 875	1 604
畜牧机械动力合计	Power of Animal Husbandry Machinery	千瓦 kw	2 831	2 962	2 930
渔业机械动力合计	Total Power of Fishery Machinery	千瓦 kw	9 673	9 902	8 981
园艺机械动力合计	Total Power of Horticultural Machinery	千瓦 kw	492	748	1 087
其他农业机械动力合计	Total Power of Other Agricultural Machineries	千瓦 kw	5 788	7 407	4 468
#农用载重汽车	Trucks for Agricultural Use	辆 in number	75	75	45
机动运输船	Transport Ships with Mechanical Power	艘 in number	43	41	25

表5-9 农田水利建设情况
Construction of Farmland Water Conservancy

指 标 Indicators		单 位 Unit	2010	2011	2012
有效灌溉面积	Effectively Irrigated Area	公顷 hectare	18 510	16 168	16 334
本年实灌面积	Actually Irrigated Area (Current Year)	公顷 hectare	11 939	12 411	12 405
当年新增改善灌溉面积	Increased and Improved Irrigated Area (Current Year)	公顷 hectare	242	833	598
旱涝保收面积	Ensured Area from Drought and Flood	公顷 hectare	11 939	12 411	12 405
易涝面积	Area Subjected to Flood	公顷 hectare		282	
水 闸	Dams	座 unit	11	16	16
堤 防	Dikes	公里 km	180.59	180.59	183.12
#郊区海塘	Rural/Suburban Sea Wall	公里 km	115.28	115.28	117.81
江 堤	Embankment	公里 km	65.31	65.31	65.31
小机口新增	Newly Increased Small Machinery	座/台套/千瓦 unit /set /kw	29/29/316.5	27/37/532.5	26/32/4 345
新增排涝泵站	Newly Built Pump Houses for Draining Water-logging Fields	座/台套/千瓦 unit /set /kw	1/3/10	2/5/37.5	1/3/22.5
新建排涝涵洞	Newly Built Culvert for Draining Water-logging Fields	座/米 unit /meter	57/2 681	68/3 627	45/2 540
改造地下渠道	Underground lrrigation Ditch Reformed	公里 km	101.74	110.33	90.79
改造渡槽倒虹吸	Siphon Aqueduct Transformed	条/米 unit/meter	192/3 851	272/5 369	282/5 520

表5-10 历年农田水利工程投资
Investment in Farmland Water Conservancy Projects in Main Years (1990~2012)

单位:万元 (10 000 yuan)

年 份 Year	合 计 Total	国家投资 State-invested	乡村自筹 Funded by Villages	乡村自筹所占比重(%) Percentage of Investment Funded by Villages(%)
1990	1 363.74	668.75	694.99	51.0
1991	906.70	354.80	551.90	60.9
1992	826.30	311.90	514.40	62.3
1993	1 517.22	357.80	1159.42	76.4
1994	2 673.15	1 253.61	1 419.54	53.1
1995	2 426.99	1 262.82	1 164.17	48.0
1996	3 357.97	1 766.90	1 591.07	47.4
1997	4 203.64	2 154.13	2 049.51	48.8
1998	4 849.08	2 419.01	2 430.07	50.1
1999	4 907.60	2 152.70	2 754.90	56.1
2000	6 321.21	2 333.20	3 988.01	63.1
2001	5 627.80	2 787.75	2 840.05	50.5
2002	7 975.97	3 423.95	4 552.02	57.1
2003	7 259.27	3 281.75	3 977.52	54.8
2004	7 137.29	3 583.26	3 554.03	49.8
2005	10 131.48	4 403.23	5 728.25	56.5
2006	15 053.70	6 661.95	8 391.75	55.7
2007	14 859.89	7 510.40	7 349.49	49.5
2008	43 846.67	21 908.07	21 938.60	50.0
2009	37 513.48	15 601.77	21 911.71	58.4
2010	68 474.03	52 745.21	15 728.82	23.0
2011	59 262.87	41 412.45	17 850.42	30.1
2012	89 338.99	66 015.05	23 323.94	26.1

表5－11 孙桥现代农业园区主要经济指标
Major Economic Indicators of Sunqiao Modern Agricultural Park

指标	Indicators	单位 Unit	2010	2011	2012
园区面积	**Area of the Park**				
规划面积	Planned Area	公顷 hectare	932	932	932
已开发利用面积	Area Put to Use	公顷 hectare	346	346	346
引进项目情况	**Projects Introduced**				
引进投资项目数	Number of Investment Projects Introduced	项 item	76	80	88
#引进外资项目数	Number of Foreign Investment Projects Introduced	项 item	7	7	7
外省市项目数	Number of Investment Projects Introduced From Other Provinces and Municipalities	项 item	22	22	25
引进投资项目金额	Amount of Investment Projects Introduced	万元 10 000 yuan	67 936	68 599	70 377
#引进外资项目金额	Amount of Foreign Investment Projects Introduced	万美元 10 000 USD	2 714	2 714	2 714
开发总投资	**Total Investment for Development**	**万元 10 000 yuan**	**95 039**	**96 727**	**100 563**
招商引资	Business Promotion and Foreign Funds Attraction	万元 10 000 yuan	68 563	69 223	70 541
政府扶持资金	Government Grants	万元 10 000 yuan	10 438	11 057	12 607
其　它	Others	万元 10 000 yuan	16 038	16 447	17 415
企业和从业人员	**Enterprises and Employed Persons**				
年末实有企业数	Number of Enterprises at Year End	个 unit	64	55	61
#农产品生产企业	Enterprises Producing Farm Products	个 unit	26	21	22
农产品加工企业	Enterprises Processing Farm Products	个 unit	12	10	11
农产品贸易服务企业	Enterprises Engaged in Trading and Service for Farm Products	个 unit	5	6	8
年末从业人员数	Employed Persons at Year End	人 person	2 007	2 138	1 985
#各类专业技术人员	All Kinds of Technical Professionals	人 person	165	168	170

表5－11 续表 Continued

指 标 Indicators		单 位 Unit	2010	2011	2012
品牌生产及认证	**Production and Autthentication of Branded Farm Products**				
品牌农产品生产企业	Enterprises Producing Branded Farm Products	个 unit	4	4	4
品牌农产品产值	Output Value of Branded Farm Products	万元 10 000 yuan	17 151	18 338	28 961
认证品牌生产个数	Number of Authenticated Branded Products	个 in number	3	3	3
认证品牌生产面积	Production Area of Authenticated Brands	公顷 hectare	142	142	142
认证品牌生产产值	Output Value of Authenticated Brands	万元 10 000 yuan	12 793	16 006	16 360
生产经营情况	**Operation**				
农业总产值	Output Value of Agriculture	万元 10 000 yuan	88 543	99 211	121 417
农产品出口总额	Total Value of Exported Farm Products	万元 10 000 yuan	8 590	10 179	12 760
农产品加工产值	Output Value of Processed Farm Products	万元 10 000 yuan	24 778	25 682	28 668
农产品服务贸易销售收入	Sales Revenue from Service and Trading of Farm Products	万元 10 000 yuan	8 037	8 146	8 547
利税总额	Total of Profits and Taxes	万元 10 000 yuan	5 316	1 238	7 115
园区产业化生产经营（辐射）能力	**Operating (Influential) Capacity of Park Industrialization**				
带动本市园区外农户户数	Number of Rural Households Outside the Park from Which Have Benefited	户 household	61 092	66 286	5 642
带动外省市农户户数	Number of Rural Households in Other Provinces and Municipalities from Which Have Benefited	户 household	57 124	61 330	57 010
对外省市产品及技术服务输出总额	Total Value of Products and Service Transferred to Other Provinces	万元 10 000 yuan	11 170	17 540	17 940

表5-12 南汇现代农业园区主要经济指标
Major Economic Indicators of Nanhui Modern Agricultural Park

指 标	Indicators	单 位 Unit	2010	2011	2012
园区面积	**Area of the Park**				
规划面积	Planned Area	公顷 hectare	1 030	1 030	1 030
已开发利用面积	Area Put to Use	公顷 hectare	349	349	349
引进项目情况	**Projects Introduced**				
引进投资项目数	Number of Investment Projects Introduced	项 item	22	22	20
#引进外资项目数	Number of Foreign Investment Projects Introduced	项 item	5	5	2
外省市项目数	Number of Investment Projects Introduced From Other Provinces and Municipalities	项 item	8	8	9
引进投资项目金额	Amount of Investment Projects Introduced	万元 10 000 yuan	249 831	249 831	231 231
#引进外资项目金额	Amount of Foreign Investment Projects Introduced	万美元 10 000 USD	2 164	2 164	318
开发总投资	**Total Investment for Development**	**万元 10 000 yuan**	**42 742**	**43 617**	**43 617**
招商引资	Business Promotion and Foreign Funds Attraction	万元 10 000 yuan	42 742	43 617	43 617
政府扶持资金	Government Grants	万元 10 000 yuan			
其 它	Others	万元 10 000 yuan			
企业和从业人员	**Enterprises and Employed Persons**				
年末实有企业数	Number of Enterprises at Year End	个 unit	7	8	8
#农产品生产企业	Enterprises Producing Farm Products	个 unit	3	4	4
农产品加工企业	Enterprises Processing Farm Products	个 unit	2	2	2
农产品贸易服务企业	Enterprises Engaged in Trading and Service for Farm Products	个 unit	1	1	1
年末从业人员数	Employed Persons at Year End	人 person	594	565	663
#各类专业技术人员	All Kinds of Technical Professionals	人 person	41	41	62

表5－12　续表　Continued

指　标 Indicators		单　位 Unit	2010	2011	2012
品牌生产及认证	**Production and Autthentication of Branded Farm Products**				
品牌农产品生产企业	Enterprises Producing Branded Farm Products	个 unit	5	6	4
品牌农产品产值	Output Value of Branded Farm Products	万元 10 000 yuan	12 710	15 765	17 364
认证品牌生产个数	Number of Authenticated Branded Products	个 in number	9	3	4
认证品牌生产面积	Production Area of Authenticated Brands	公顷 hectare	362	30	19
认证品牌生产产值	Output Value of Authenticated Brands	万元 10 000 yuan	5 946	9 924	5 684
生产经营情况	**Operation**				
农业总产值	Output Value of Agriculture	万元 10 000 yuan	4 898	11 859	21 565
农产品出口总额	Total Value of Exported Farm Products	万元 10 000 yuan	8 112	8 567	14 953
农产品加工产值	Output Value of Processed Farm Products	万元 10 000 yuan	9 412	4 206	16 286
农产品服务贸易销售收入	Sales Revenue from Service and Trading of Farm Products	万元 10 000 yuan	450	450	955
利税总额	Total of Profits and Taxes	万元 10 000 yuan	4 857	4 126	3 290
园区产业化生产经营(辐射)能力	**Operating (Influential) Capacity of Park Industrialization**				
带动本市园区外农户户数	Number of Rural Households Outside the Park from Which Have Benefited	户 household	240	70	4 085
带动外省市农户户数	Number of Rural Households in Other Provinces and Municipalities from Which Have Benefited	户 household	12 700	160	8 165
对外省市产品及技术服务输出总额	Total Value of Products and Service Transferred to Other Provinces	万元 10 000 yuan	244	244	544

表5-13 浦东临空出口农业园区主要经济指标
Major Economic Indicators of Pudong Linkong Exports-Oriented Agricultural Park

指 标	Indicators	单 位 Unit	2010	2011	2012
园区面积	**Area of the Park**				
规划面积	Planned Area	公顷 hectare	1 038	1 038	1 038
已开发利用面积	Area Put to Use	公顷 hectare	222	222	222
引进项目情况	**Projects Introduced**				
引进投资项目数	Number of Investment Projects Introduced	项 item	33	31	31
#引进外资项目数	Number of Foreign Investment Projects Introduced	项 item	2	2	2
外省市项目数	Number of Investment Projects Introduced From Other Provinces and Municipalities	项 item	15	14	14
引进投资项目金额	Amount of Investment Projects Introduced	万元 10 000 yuan	46 184	46 682	47 311
#引进外资项目金额	Amount of Foreign Investment Projects Introduced	万美元 10 000 USD	121	121	121
开发总投资	**Total Investment for Development**	**万元 10 000 yuan**	**46 184**	**46 682**	**47 311**
招商引资	Business Promotion and Foreign Funds Attraction	万元 10 000 yuan	39 679	39 979	40 448
政府扶持资金	Government Grants	万元 10 000 yuan	6 505	6 703	6 863
其 它	Others	万元 10 000 yuan			
企业和从业人员	**Enterprises and Employed Persons**				
年末实有企业数	Number of Enterprises at Year End	个 unit	33	31	31
#农产品生产企业	Enterprises Producing Farm Products	个 unit	9	9	9
农产品加工企业	Enterprises Processing Farm Products	个 unit	9	8	8
农产品贸易服务企业	Enterprises Engaged in Trading and Service for Farm Products	个 unit	12	11	12
年末从业人员数	Employed Persons at Year End	人 person	851	831	840
#各类专业技术人员	All Kinds of Technical Professionals	人 person	151	149	152

表5-13 续表 Continued

指 标 Indicators		单 位 Unit	2010	2011	2012
品牌生产及认证	**Production and Autthentication of Branded Farm Products**				
品牌农产品生产企业	Enterprises Producing Branded Farm Products	个 unit	1	1	1
品牌农产品产值	Output Value of Branded Farm Products	万元 10 000 yuan	7 739	7 200	8 710
认证品牌生产个数	Number of Authenticated Branded Products	个 in number	3	3	3
认证品牌生产面积	Production Area of Authenticated Brands	公顷 hectare	549	549	549
认证品牌生产产值	Output Value of Authenticated Brands	万元 10 000 yuan	7 900	8 150	8 710
生产经营情况	**Operation**				
农业总产值	Output Value of Agriculture	万元 10 000 yuan	11 000	16 035	14 376
农产品出口总额	Total Value of Exported Farm Products	万元 10 000 yuan	34 780	32 380	29 880
农产品加工产值	Output Value of Processed Farm Products	万元 10 000 yuan	17 660	15 886	16 455
农产品服务贸易销售收入	Sales Revenue from Service and Trading of Farm Products	万元 10 000 yuan	29 745	36 015	30 454
利税总额	Total of Profits and Taxes	万元 10 000 yuan	1 264	2 864	2 284
园区产业化生产经营(辐射)能力	**Operating (Influential) Capacity of Park Industrialization**				
带动本市园区外农户户数	Number of Rural Households Outside the Park from Which Have Benefited	户 household	8 388	5 188	5 188
带动外省市农户户数	Number of Rural Households in Other Provinces and Municipalities from Which Have Benefited	户 household	32 500	26 500	26 500
对外省市产品及技术服务输出总额	Total Value of Products and Service Transferred to Other Provinces	万元 10 000 yuan			

主要统计指标解释

农村从业人员

指乡村人口中16岁以上实际参加生产经营活动并取得实物或货币收入的人员，既包括劳动年龄内实际参加劳动人员，也包括超过劳动年龄但实际参加劳动的人员，但不包括户口在家的在外学生、现役军人和丧失劳动能力的人，也不包括待业人员和家务劳动者。劳动者年龄为16岁以上。

农业总产值

农业总产值是以货币表现的农、林、牧、渔业全部产品的总量和对农林牧渔生产活动进行的各种支持性服务活动的价值。它反映一定时期内农业生产的总规模和总成果。

农、林、牧、渔业的统计范围是：

（1）农业　包括农作物种植业和其他农业。

农作物种植业包括谷物、豆类、薯类、棉、油料、糖料、麻类、烟叶、蔬菜、药材、瓜类和其他农作物的种植，以及茶园、桑园、果园的生产经营。

其他农业包括采集野生植物的果实、纤维、树胶、树脂、油料以及柴草、野生药材、菌类等及农民家庭兼营的商品性工业。

（2）林业　包括林木的栽培（不包括茶园、桑园和果园的栽培、管理和收获等活动）、林产品的采集和村及村以下合作经济组织和农户的竹木采伐。

（3）牧业　包括除渔业养殖以外的一切动物饲养和放牧，以及野生动物的捕猎和饲养。

（4）渔业　包括水生动物和海藻类植物的养殖和捕捞。

（5）农林牧渔服务业　包括农林牧渔业生产活动进行的各种支持性服务活动。但不包括各种科学技术和专业技术服务活动。

从所有制看，包括国有经济的各种专业农（农、林、牧、渔）场以及国家各级机关团体学校、科研机构、部队经营的农业；集体所有制的乡镇村各级办农场；农村各种经济组织经营的农、林、牧、渔业以及工矿企业家属集体经营的农业；农民家庭自营的农林牧渔业及兼营商品性工业等。

农业总产值的计算方法通常是按农林牧渔业产品及其副产品的产量分别乘以各自单位产品价格求得，少数生产周期较长、当年没有产品或产品产量不易统计的，则采用间接方法匡算其产值，然后将四业产品产值和服务业产值相加即为农业总产值。

1957年以前的农业总产值中包括了厩肥和农民自给性手工业（如农民自制衣服、鞋、袜，自己从事粮食初步加工等）。1958年及以后的农业总产值，林业中增加了村及村以下竹木采伐产值；牧业中取消了厩肥产值；副业中取消了农民自给性手工业产值，增加了村及村以下办的工业产值；渔业中增加了海洋捕捞水产品产值。1980年及以后的农业总产值，在副业中增加了农民家庭兼营工业商品部分的产值。从1984年起村及村以下办工业产值划归工业。从1993年起，取消副业。将野生动物的捕猎划入牧业，野生植物采集和农民家庭兼营商品性工业划归农业。从2003年起，农业总产值中包括了农林牧渔服务业产值。

当年价格

当年价格（或现行价格）是指报告期的实际价格，如工业品的出厂价格、农产品的收购价格、商品零售价格等。用当年价格计算的一些以货币表现的物量指标或劳务总量指标，如国内生产总值、工农业总产值、社会商品零售额等，反映当年的实际情况，使国民经济各项指标互相衔接，便于考察当年社会经济效益，便于对生产和流通、生产和分配、生产和消费之间进行经济核算和综合平衡。

按当年价格计算的以货币表现的指标，在不同年份之间进行对比时，因包含各年间价格变动的因素，不能确切地反映实物量的增减变动，必须消除价格变动的因素后，才能真实反映经济发展动态。因此，在计算增长速度时都使用按可比价格计算的数字。

可比价格

可比价格指在对不同时期的价值指标对比时，扣除了价格变动的因素，以确切反映物量的变化。按可比价格计算有两种方法，一种是直接按产品产量乘其某一年的不变价格计算；另一种是用价格指数换算。

不变价格

指以同类产品某年的平均价格作为固定价格，用于计算各年的产品价值。按不变价格计算的产品价值消除了价格变动因素，不同时期对比可以反映生产的发展速度。新中国成立后，随着工农业产品价格水平的变化，国家统计局先后五次制定了全国统一的工业产品不变价格和农业产品不变价格。从1952年到1957年使用1952年工（农）业产品不变价格，从1957年到1970年使用1957年不变价格，从1971年到1980年使用1970年不变价格，从1981年到1990年使用1980年不变价格，从1991年到2000年使用1990年不变价格，从2001年开始使用2000年不变价格。

年末耕地面积

年末耕地面积指能够种植农作物，经常进行耕锄的田地。包括熟地、当年新开荒地、新开垦围垦地、连续撂荒未满三年的耕地和当年休闲地（轮歇地）。以种植农作物为主并附带种植桑树、茶树、果树和其他林木的土地，以及沿海、沿湖地区已围垦利用的“海涂”、“湖田”等也应包括在内，但不包括专业性桑园、茶园、果园、果木苗圃、林地、芦苇地、天然草原等。小于一米宽的渠、路、田埂,包括在耕地中。

农作物播种面积

农作物播种面积指报告期内收获农产品的作物的实际播种或移植有农作物的面积。凡是实际种植农作物的面积,不论种植在耕地上还是种植在非耕地上,均包括在农作物播种面积中。在播种季节基本结束后,因遭灾而重新改种和补种的农作物面积,也包括在内。

粮食产量

指全社会的产量。包括国有经济经营的、集体统一经营的和农民家庭经营的粮食产量,还包括工矿企业办的农场和其他生产单位的产量。粮食除包括稻谷、小麦、玉米、高粱、谷子及其他杂粮外,还包括薯类和豆类。其产量计算方法,豆类按去豆荚后的干豆计算;薯类(包括甘薯和马铃薯,不包括芋头和木薯)1963 年以前按每 4 公斤鲜薯折 1 公斤粮食计算,从 1964 年开始改为按 5 公斤鲜薯折 1 公斤粮食计算。城市郊区作为蔬菜的薯类(如马铃薯等)按鲜品计算,并且不作粮食统计。其他粮食一律按脱粒后的原粮计算。1989 年以前全国粮食产量数据主要靠全面报表取得,1989 年开始使用抽样调查数据。

水产品产量

指人工养殖的水产品和天然生长的水产品的捕捞量。包括海水的鱼类、虾蟹类、贝类和藻类以及内陆水域的鱼类、虾蟹类和贝类,不包括淡水生植物。水产品产量是通过各级水产和统计部门逐级上报取得数据。1995 年及以前,贝类中牡蛎按鲜肉计算;蚶、蛤、蛙按 5 斤鲜品折 1 斤计算。1996 年以后则统一按鲜品计算。

猪、牛、羊肉产量

指当年出栏并已屠宰、除去头蹄下水后带骨肉(即胴体重)的重量。包括全社会范围内的产量。1996 年前为各级逐级上报数据。1996 年第一次农业普查以后,由于畜牧业产品年报数据与普查数据之间存在一定的差距,国家统计局农调总队对畜牧业年报数据与普查数据进行衔接。1999 年以后,国家统计局开展了猪、牛、羊、禽等主要畜禽品种的抽样调查,并用抽样数据作为国家定案数据使用。未开展抽样调查的品种,仍使用各级统计部门逐级上报数据。

农业机械总动力

农业机械总动力指用于农、林、牧、渔业生产的各种动力机械的动力总和。动力机械包括耕作、排灌、种植、植物保护、收获、农产品加工、运输、畜牧、渔业、农田水利等各种机械。不包括专门用于乡办工业、基本建设、非农业运输、科学试验和教学等非农业生产方面用的动力机械与作业机械的数量。

农村经济收益分配主要指标

农村经济收益分配和效益指标,是为了全面观察农村经济收入分配情况,研究农村经济的规模、发展速度、多种经营、商品化程度,国家、集体和个人的分配关系及经济效益。其计算范围包括乡村企业、集体统一经营(含家庭承包)新经济联合体以及农民家庭经营(含家庭承包)四个部分。

(1)总收入:指本单位当年经营的收入中可用以抵偿本年开支并在国家、集体、农民之间进行分配的农、林、牧、渔业、工业、交通运输业、建筑业、商业、饮食业、服务业等各项经营收入和利息、租金等非生产收入,但不包括那些不能用来分配,属于借贷性质或暂收性质的收入,如贷款收入、预购定金、国家投资、农民投资等。

(2)总费用:是指为实现当年各项生产经营收入应由当年负担的各项费用开支,包括生产费用、管理费用和其他费用三项。

(3)净收入总额:是指当年"总收入"减去"总费用"后,当年所得的净收入部分。

(4)农村居民净收入:是指农村居民从当年的净收入中减去国家税金和集体提留以后,归个人支配的部分,包括现金和实物折款。

EXPLANATORY NOTES TO MAJOR STATISTICAL INDICATORS

Personnel Employed in Rural Areas

Personnel Employed in Rural Areas refers to people in rural areas who are older than 16 years and engaged in production and business activities that generate incomes in cash or in practicality. It includes all working laborers, no matter whether they are within the working age or not, whereas students studying outside but with their registered residence at home, active serviceman, people who lost their ability to work, unemployed people, and those engaged in housework are not included. The working age is defined as older than 16 years.

Gross Output Value of Agriculture

Gross Output Value of Agriculture refers to the total volume of products of farming, forestry, animal husbandry and fishery expressed in the monetary terms and output value of all kinds of service activities that support farming, forestry, animal husbandry and fishery production. It reflects the overall scale and achievements of agricultural production during a given period of time.

The scope of statistics on farming, forestry, animal husbandry, and fishery are as follows:

(1) Farming includes cultivation of farm crops and other agri-

cultural activities.

Cultivation of farm crops include cultivation of grain crops, legume crops, tuber-crops, cotton, oil-bearing crops, sugar crops, bastfiber plants, tobacco, vegetables, medicinal herbs, melon crops, and cultivation and management of tea plantations, mulberry fields and orchards.

Other agricultural activities include harvesting wild fruits, fiber, tree gum, resin, oil-bearing plants, firewood, wild medicinal herbs, fungus, and rural-household commodity industries.

(2) Forestry refers to planting trees of various kinds (excluding tea plantations, mulberry fields and orchards), collection of forestry products and cutting and felling of bamboo and trees by villages and other cooperative organizations under village level.

(3) Animal husbandry refers to raising and grazing of all kinds of farm animals except fishing and aquatic cultivating, and hunting and rising of wild animals.

(4) Fishery refers to cultivation and catching of fish and other aquatic products and cultivation and collection of seaweed and other aquatic plants.

(5) Service Industry for Farming, Forestry, Animal Husbandry and Fishery refers to all kinds of service activities that support farming, forestry, animal husbandry and fishery production, whereas activities of science, technology and professional service are not included.

In terms of ownership, China's agriculture includes specialized state farms (for farming, forestry, animal husbandry, fishery), farms managed by various government agencies, organizations, schools, research institutions, and army; farms managed by rural collective organizations at levels of the township, town, and village; farming, forestry, animal husbandry, fishery run by various rural collective organizations and farming run by collective family members' organizations of mining and industrial enterprises; farming, forestry, animal husbandry and fishery and some commodity industries run by individual farmers.

Gross output value of agriculture is obtained by first multiplying the output of products or by-products by their unit price. For a small number of products, annual output of which is not available or difficult to get due to the long production/growing process involved, the output value will be estimated through an indirect approach. The sum of output value of all products of farming, forestry, animal husbandry and fishery and output value of service activities will then and together to form gross output value of agriculture.

Before 1957, China's gross agricultural output value included the value of barnyard manure and handicraft products for self-consumption (clothes, shoes, stockings, and initial grain processing under-taken by peasants). After 1958, the output value of cutting and felling of bamboo and trees by villages and other cooperative organizations under villages have been included in forestry; value of barnyard manure has been excluded from animal husbandry; the value of self-consumed handicrafts has been excluded from sideline occupations, while output value of industries run by villages and cooperative organizations under village level has been included in sideline occupations and output value of fish catches by motor fishing boats has been added to fishery. Since 1980, the output value of handicraft products made for sale by farmer households has been added to sideline occupations, From 1984, industries run by villages and cooperative organizations under village level have been included in the sector of industry. After 1993, the category of sideline occupations has been canceled and hunting of wild animals has been classified into husbandry, and harvesting of wild vegetation and commodity industry run by rural households have been grouped into the category of agriculture. Since 2003, the output value of service industry for farming, forestry, animal husbandry and fishery is included in the gross output value of agriculture.

Current Prices

Current prices refer to the actual prices in the report period, for example, industrial producers prices, procurement prices of agricultural products, retail prices, and so on. Goods and services measured by the current prices, such as gross national product, gross output value of industry and agriculture, total retail sales, reflect the current-year actual activities. The various national economic indicators, such as current-year social economic efficiency, production, exchange, distribution and consumption could be understood and compared directly if they are measured by the current prices.

The indicators measured by the current prices can not exactly reflect the real change over different years, if the price level changes during the period of time. The comparable prices would be used in measuring growth rates, in order to deflate the price change.

Comparable Prices

Comparable Prices are applied when comparing indicators over time to reflect accurately the changes in real term. Two methods are used for calculating comparable prices: 1. output by constant price of certain year; 2. output in current prices divided by relevant price index.

Constant Price

Constant Price refers to the average price of a given product in certain year, which is used for comparison of output value over time. As the output value at constant prices removes the factor of price changes, it reflects the trend of production development over time. Since 1949, with the changes in general price level, National Bureau of Statistics has issued nationally unified constant prices five times: the 1952 constant prices for 1949 – 1957; the 1957 constant prices for 1957 – 1971; the 1970 constant prices for 1971 – 1981; the 1980 constant prices for 1981 – 1990; the 1990 constant prices for 1991 – 2000; and the 2000 constant prices have been used since 2001.

The Actual Area of Plowland at Year End

The Area of Plowland at Year End refers to the area of arable land and frequently-tended farm-fields at the beginning of a year. It includes cultivated land, the newly-reclaimed wasteland and inning land in the year, the farmland which has been laid idle for no more than three consecutive years, and land on fallow that year. It shall also include farmland with mulberry, tea, fruit and other trees but used mainly for growing crops as well as the reclaimed "beach-land" and "lake-land" along the sea coasts and the lake banks. However, it shall not include the land devoted especially for mulberry and the tea gardens, orchards, nurseries, woodlands, reed marches and natural grasslands. Ditches, pathways and ridges of field which are less than one meter wide are included in plowland.

Sown Area of Crops

Sown Area of Crops refers to area of land sown or transplanted with crops that have been harvested during report period, regardless of being in cultivated area or non-cultivated area. Area of land re-sown due to natural disasters is also included.

Grain Output

Grain Output refers to the total output in the whole country including grains produced by state farms, collective units, rural households, as well as by farms affiliated to industrial and mining enterprises and other production units. Grain includes rice, wheat, corn, sorghum, millet and other miscellaneous grains as well as tubers and bean. Output of beans refers to dry beans without pods. The output of tubers (sweet potatoes and potatoes, not including taros and cassava) was converted into that of grain at the ratio 4 : 1, i. e. 4 kilograms of fresh tubers was equivalent to 1 kilogram of grain up to 1963. Since 1964 the ratio for conversion has been 5:1. Tubers supplied as vegetables (such as potatoes) in cities and suburbs are calculated as fresh vegetables and their output is not included in the output of grain. Output of all other grains refers to husked grain. Data on grain production before 1989 were obtained through Comprehensive Statistical Reporting System. Since 1989, data from sample surveys are used.

Output of Aquatic Products

Output of Aquatic Products refers to catches of both artificially cultured and naturally grown aquatic products, including fish, shrimps, crabs and shellfish in sea and inland water as well as seaweed. Freshwater plants are not included. Data on output of aquatic products are reported by aquatic product and statistical agencies level by level. Before 1995, among the shellfish, the oyster was counted as fresh meat; 5 kilograms of ark shell, clams and frogs are equivalent to 1 kilogram of fresh aquatic products; they are all counted as fresh aquatic products since 1996.

Output of Pork, Beef, and Mutton

Output of Pork, Beef, and Mutton refers to the meat of slaughtered hogs, cattle, sheep and goats with head, feet, and offal taken away. Data refers to the production of the whole country. The first agriculture census of China in 1996 revealed some discrepancy between the production of animal products from the annual reports and that from the census. Efforts were made by the Rural Socio-economic Survey Organization of NBS to adjust the output value of animal husbandry to make the figures from the annual reports consistent with the census data. Since 1999, NBS conducted sample survey for the major animal husbandry products, such as hogs, cattle, sheep and goats and fowls, and the data from sample surveys are used as national finalized data. Those products, which are not covered by the sample survey, are still reported by statistical agencies level by level.

Total Power of Farm Machinery

Total Power of Farm Machinery refers to the total mechanical power of machinery used in farming, forestry animal husbandry and fishery, including machines used for ploughing, irrigation and drainage, crop growing, plant protection, harvesting, farm product processing, transport, stock breeding, fishery and water conservancy. Machinery employed for non-agricultural purposes such as township industry, capital construction, non-agricultural transport, scientific experiments and for teaching is excluded.

Major Indicators of Rural Income Distribution

Indicators of rural income distribution and efficiency are used for investigating the overall income distribution in rural area and for studying the rural economy in scale, development, multi-operation, commercialization, income distribution among state, collective units and individuals and economic efficiency. The statistical scope includes village enterprises, collective operations (collectively contracted operation), new economic unions and farmers family operations (family contracted operation).

(1) Gross income refers to current year operating revenue in farming, forestry, animal husbandry, fishery, industry, transportation, construction, commerce, catering, services and interest, rent, which can be used to compensate for current year's expenses and distributed among the state, collective units and farmers, but excludes the credit or actual revenue which can not be distributed, such as loan revenue, advance payments for purchases, state investment and farmers investment.

(2) Total expenses refers to current year expenses which realize current year's productive operating revenue, including production expenses, managerial expenses and other expenses.

(3) Total net income refers to current year's net gross revenue of total expenses.

(4) Net Income of Residents in Rural Area refers to the disposable portion of such residents after deduction of state tax and collective retention from net income, including cash and income in kind in money terms.

第六篇

CHAPTER 6

工 业

INDUSTRY

表6-1 主要年份工业总产值及其构成

单位:亿元

指 标	Indicators	1990	1995	1998	1999	2000	2001
总 计	**Total**	**176.85**	**968.03**	**1 414.99**	**1 450.81**	**1 625.77**	**1 888.74**
按隶属关系分	**By Subordination**						
中央工业	Central	42.48	225.99	331.21	323.62	381.41	386.40
市属工业	Municipal	88.44	491.63	640.62	610.35	599.57	779.48
非中央、市属工业	Local	45.93	250.41	443.16	516.84	644.79	722.86
按登记注册类型分	**By Type of Registration**						
国 有	State-owned	110.18	449.57	396.46	309.87	275.85	344.02
集 体	Collective-owned	49.09	122.54	105.85	90.04	70.91	57.02
港澳台及外商投资	Overseas Invested	7.07	231.94	695.25	851.48	1 012.34	1 242.91
其 他	Others	10.51	163.98	217.43	199.42	266.67	244.79
按轻、重工业分	**By Light/Heavy Industry**						
轻工业	Light Industry	72.08	424.42	575.55	533.52	514.58	535.06
重工业	Heavy Industry	104.77	543.61	839.44	917.29	1 111.19	1 353.68
按企业规模分	**By Scale of Enterprises**						
大型企业	Large	81.32	632.35	861.03	988.53	1 138.11	1 294.24
中型企业	Medium	21.40	96.37	163.34	163.48	187.00	239.26
小型企业	Small	74.13	239.31	390.62	298.80	300.66	355.24
构 成(%)	**Composition (%)**						
总 计	**Total**	**100.0**	**100.0**	**100.0**	**100.0**	**100.0**	**100.0**
按隶属关系分	**By Subordination**						
中央工业	Central	24.0	23.3	23.4	22.3	23.5	20.4
市属工业	Municipal	50.0	50.8	45.3	42.1	36.9	41.3
非中央、市属工业	Local	26.0	25.9	31.3	35.6	39.6	38.3
按登记注册类型分	**By Type of Registration**						
国 有	State-owned	62.3	46.4	28.0	21.4	17.0	18.2
集 体	Collective - owned	27.8	12.7	7.5	6.2	4.3	3.0
港澳台及外商投资	Overseas Invested	4.0	24.0	49.1	58.7	62.3	65.8
其 他	Others	5.9	16.9	15.4	13.7	16.4	13.0
按轻、重工业分	**By Light/Heavy Industry**						
轻工业	Light Industry	40.8	43.8	40.7	36.8	31.7	28.3
重工业	Heavy Industry	59.2	56.2	59.3	63.2	68.3	71.7
按企业规模分	**By Scale of Enterprises**						
大型企业	Large	46.0	65.3	60.9	68.1	70.0	68.5
中型企业	Medium	12.1	10.0	11.5	11.3	11.5	12.7
小型企业	Small	41.9	24.7	27.6	20.6	18.5	18.8

注：2011 年起，规模以上企业为年主营业务收入 2000 万元及以上。
Note: Above-scaled enterprises will be refered to those which have an annual main business income of 20 million yuan and above since 2011.

Gross Output Value of Industry and Its Composition in Main Years

(100 million yuan)

2002	2003	2004	2005	2006	2007	2008	2009	2010	2011	2012
2 193.82	**2 856.68**	**3 519.71**	**4 242.47**	**4 758.76**	**5 188.12**	**5 649.22**	**7 141.55**	**8 591.50**	**9 553.79**	**9 424.67**
431.13	549.05	677.04	1 321.05	1 538.42	1 663.26	1 999.48	1 653.93	2 216.69	2 278.33	2 235.91
805.98	1 082.55	1 254.17	1 135.29	1 249.74	1 373.81	1 289.49	2 010.76	2 043.34	2 284.38	1 986.87
956.71	1 225.08	1 588.50	1 786.13	1 970.60	2 151.05	2 360.25	3 476.86	4 331.47	4 991.08	5 201.89
241.56	290.97	358.04	550.18	573.84	662.21	679.71	729.56	885.71	927.97	960.60
49.57	46.02	49.09	38.67	36.87	34.89	31.60	47.87	34.70	34.67	33.63
1 522.31	1 985.30	2 461.66	2 632.70	2 980.46	3 001.98	3 088.54	4 008.58	5 047.75	5 899.02	5 846.88
380.38	534.39	650.92	1 020.92	1 167.59	1 489.04	1 849.37	2 355.54	2 623.34	2 692.13	2 583.56
541.28	647.92	764.94	825.40	878.66	952.26	1 070.62	1 402.71	1 535.63	1 677.47	1 638.43
1 652.54	2 208.76	2 754.77	3 417.07	3 880.10	4 235.86	4 578.60	5 738.84	7 055.87	7 876.32	7 786.24
1 564.20	1 229.85	1 426.29	1 989.45	1 976.08	2 309.39	2 731.96	3 318.52	4 097.63	6 154.87	6 105.36
209.92	862.86	1 083.29	1 173.99	1 725.62	1 841.13	1 822.86	2 022.62	2 593.18	1 477.88	1 580.14
419.70	763.97	1 010.13	1 079.03	1 057.06	1 037.60	1 094.40	1 800.41	1 900.69	1 921.04	1 739.17
100.0	**100.0**	**100.0**	**100.0**	**100.0**	**100.0**	**100.0**	**100.0**	**100.0**	**100.0**	**100.0**
19.7	19.2	19.3	31.1	32.3	32.0	35.4	23.2	25.8	23.8	23.7
36.7	37.9	35.6	26.8	26.3	26.5	22.8	28.1	23.8	23.9	21.1
43.6	42.9	45.1	42.1	41.4	41.5	41.8	48.7	50.4	52.3	55.2
11.0	10.2	10.2	13.0	12.1	12.8	12.0	10.2	10.3	9.7	10.2
2.3	1.6	1.4	0.9	0.8	0.7	0.6	0.7	0.4	0.4	0.4
69.4	69.5	69.9	62.0	62.6	57.8	54.7	56.1	58.8	61.7	62.0
17.3	18.7	18.5	24.1	24.5	28.7	32.7	33.0	30.5	28.2	27.4
24.7	22.7	21.7	19.5	18.5	18.4	19.0	19.6	17.9	17.6	17.4
75.3	77.3	78.3	80.5	81.5	81.6	81.0	80.4	82.1	82.4	82.6
71.3	43.1	40.5	46.9	41.5	44.5	48.3	46.5	47.7	64.4	64.8
9.6	30.2	30.8	27.7	36.3	35.5	32.3	28.3	30.2	15.5	16.8
19.1	26.7	28.7	25.4	22.2	20.0	19.4	25.2	22.1	20.1	18.5

表6-2　工业总产值、销售产值和出口交货值
(2012)

单位:亿元

指　标　Indicators		工业总产值(按现行价格计算) Gross Output Value of Industry (at Current Price)
总　计	**Total**	**9 424.67**
按隶属关系分	**By Subordination**	
中央工业	Central	2 235.91
市属工业	Municipal	1 986.87
非中央、市属工业	Local	5 201.89
按登记注册类型分	**By Type of Registration**	
内　资	Domestic Funded	3 577.79
国　有	State-owned	960.60
集　体	Collective-owned	33.63
股份合作制	Share-holding	16.71
联　营	Jointly-operated	8.39
有限责任公司	Companies with Limited Liability	787.84
股份有限公司	Companies Limited by Shares	978.24
私　营	Private	786.39
其　他	Others	5.99
港澳台商投资	Hong Kong/Macao/Taiwan Invested	981.26
#港澳台商独资	Solely Hong Kong/Macao/Taiwan Funded	691.19
外商投资	Foreigner Invested	4 865.62
#外商独资	Solely Foreigner Funded	2 741.61
按轻、重工业分	**By Light/Heavy Industry**	
轻工业	Light Industry	1 638.43
重工业	Heavy Industry	7 786.24
按企业规模分	**By Scale of Enterprises**	
大型企业	Large	6 105.36
中型企业	Medium	1 580.14
小型企业	Small	1 739.17

Gross Output Value, Sales Value and Export Delivery Value

(100 million yuan)

#镇及镇以上 Town and Above	工业销售产值 Sales Value of Industry	#镇及镇以上 Town and Above	出口交货值 Export Delivery Value	#镇及镇以上 Town and Above
4 450.75	**9 349.23**	**4 443.79**	**2 553.26**	**585.32**
2 235.91	2 216.09	2 216.09	376.06	376.06
1 986.87	2 000.72	2 000.72	180.76	180.76
227.97	5 132.42	226.99	1 996.44	28.50
2 532.27	3 540.82	2 515.02	303.67	223.07
954.59	965.39	959.42	18.09	17.48
12.20	34.10	12.95	1.05	0.85
4.04	16.37	3.88	0.31	
3.77	8.20	4.03	0.05	
661.14	770.08	645.56	183.60	172.12
889.35	974.16	882.39	34.75	32.03
3.74	767.12	3.74	64.32	0.09
3.44	5.41	3.05	1.51	0.51
128.21	974.41	127.03	343.90	20.07
0.13	686.76	0.13	230.14	
1 790.27	4 834.00	1 801.75	1 905.68	342.18
0.25	2 703.87	0.25	1 459.09	0.08
538.18	1 617.00	530.11	318.62	134.46
3 912.57	7 732.23	3 913.68	2 234.64	450.86
3 621.72	6 082.77	3 626.98	1 987.41	496.62
531.27	1 544.93	517.56	320.96	56.40
297.76	1 721.53	299.26	244.89	32.30

表6-3　主要工业产品生产和销售量
Output and Sales Volume of Major Industrial Products
(2012)

产品名称	Products	单位 Unit	生产量 Output	销售量 Sales Volume	生产量占全市比重(%) PNA/ Shanghai(%)
原油加工量	Volume of Crude Oil Processing	万吨 10 000 tons	1 088.34	1 103.59	49.3
汽　油	Gasoline	万吨 10 000 tons	203.01	204.33	66.6
柴　油	Diesel Oil	万吨 10 000 tons	419.36	405.60	51.0
化学纤维	Chemical Fiber	万吨 10 000 tons	12.77	12.26	26.4
合成纤维聚合物	Synthetic Polymer	万吨 10 000 tons	47.64	46.83	35.2
化学药品原药	Original Chemical Drug	吨 ton	2 276.71	2 235.90	8.4
钢　材	Steel	万吨 10 000 tons	19.00	18.86	0.8
家用洗衣机	Household Washing Machine	万台 10 000 sets	168.58	169.34	85.5
房间空气调节器	Household Air-conditioner	万台 10 000 sets	338.76	339.38	58.0
数字程控交换机	Program-controlled Exchange	万线 10 000 lines	121.90	121.90	100.0
电话单机	Telephone Set	万部 10 000 sets	245.17	274.67	99.9
#笔记本计算机	Including Notebooks	万部 10 000 sets	2 705.14	2 701.01	37.1
移动通信手持机(手机)	Mobile Phone	万台 10 000 sets	4 036.96	4 006.16	98.8
彩色电视机	Color TV Set	万部 10 000 sets	99.78	99.83	69.8
气体压缩机	Gas Compressor	万台 10 000 sets	1 345.02	1 427.24	74.5
轿　车	Car	万辆 10 000 vehicles	67.23	70.56	33.2
#新能源汽车	in which new-energy-fueled car	辆 vehicle	558.00	753.00	3.5
集成电路	Integrated Circuit	亿块 100 million pieces	102.97	102.88	64.2
集成电路圆片	IC Wafer	万片 10 000 pieces	218.45	217.29	70.7

表 6－3 续表 Continued

产品名称 Products		单 位 Unit	生产量 Output	销售量 Sales Volume	生产量占全市比重(%) PNA/Shanghai(%)
民用钢质船	Civil Steel Ship	万载重吨 10 000 DWT	450.90	450.90	59.0
起重机	Crane	万吨 10000 tons	39.10	39.11	85.6
微波炉	Microwave Oven	万台 10 000 sets	397.94	398.16	100.0
发电量	Electricity	亿千瓦时 100 mil. kwh	299.53	283.67	33.8
电子元件	Electronic Component	亿只 100 million pieces	745.65	749.29	59.5
光电子器件	Optoelectronic Device	亿只 100 million units	90.26	95.71	93.9
电饭锅	Electric Rice Cooker	万个 10 000 units	31.90	31.89	7.8
原电池(折 R20 标准只)	Size D Battery (R20 standard)	亿只 100 million units	13.12	13.65	69.3
塑料制品	Plastic Product	万吨 10 000 tons	33.43	33.54	18.1
合成橡胶	Synthetic Rubber	万吨 10 000 tons	23.72	23.31	95.8
初级形态的塑料	Plastics in Primary Form	万吨 10 000 tons	46.76	46.41	14.8
涂 料	Paint	万吨 10 000 tons	42.71	42.27	27.7
化学农药原药	Original Chemicals of Chemical Pesticide	吨 ton	921.72	789.00	6.0
人造板	Man-made Board	万立方米 10 000 cu · m	2.56	2.60	12.1
服 装	Garment	亿件 100 million units	6 535.79	7 356.51	13.0
印染布	Printing & Dyeing Cloth	万米 10 000 meters	2 247.23	2 295.73	37.3
布	Cloth	万米 10 000 meters	751.90	771.00	4.4
乳制品	Dairy Products	万吨 10 000 tons	4.27	4.28	7.3
商品混凝土	Commercial Concrete	万立方米 10 000 cu · m	796.28	799.66	27.5

表6-4 按行业分的工业总产值、销售产值和出口交货值
Gross Output Value, Sales Value and Export Delivery Value by Sector
(2012)

单位:亿元 (100 million yuan)

指 标	Indicators	工业总产值(按现行价格计算) Gross Output Value of Industry (at Current Price)	工业销售产值 Sales Value of Industry	出口交货值 Export Delivery Value
总 计	**Total**	**9 424.67**	**9 349.23**	**2 553.26**
#农副食品加工业	Processing of Agricultural Side-line Food	113.74	113.18	0.71
食品制造业	Food Manufacturing	111.96	106.63	2.32
酒、饮料和精制茶制造业	Manufacturing of Liquor, Beverage and Refined Tea	33.42	34.53	4.05
烟草制品业	Tobacco Products	2.98	2.98	0.08
纺织业	Textile Industry	48.52	48.50	9.85
纺织服装、服饰业	Textile Clothes and Accessories	159.48	169.49	28.44
皮革、毛皮、羽毛及其制品和制鞋业	Leather, Fur, Feather and their Products and Shoe-making	14.13	14.12	2.54
木材加工及木、竹、藤、棕、草制品业	Timber-processing, Bamboo, Cane, Palm Fiber and Straw Products	9.24	9.37	1.09
家具制造业	Furniture Manufacturing	87.33	87.15	20.32
造纸及纸制品业	Paper-making and Paper Products	63.30	61.94	12.47
印刷业和记录媒介复制业	Printing and Record Pressing	54.78	54.64	4.78
文教、工美、体育和娱乐用品制造业	Manufacturing of Cultural, Educational, Arts, Sports and Leisure Products	45.64	43.02	17.13
石油加工、炼焦及核燃料加工业	Petroleum Processing, Coke Products and Processing of Nuclear Fuel	794.61	784.51	26.75
化学原料和化学制品制造业	Raw Chemical Materials and Chemical Products	520.14	507.14	82.84
医药制造业	Medicine Manufacturing	238.28	227.83	19.31

单位:亿元 表6－4 续表 Continued (100 million yuan)

指 标 Indicators		工业总产值（按现行价格计算）Gross Output Value of Industry (at Current Price)	工业销售产值 Sales Value of Industry	出口交货值 Export Delivery Value
化学纤维制造业	Chemical Fiber Manufacturing	0.89	0.89	
橡胶和塑料制品业	Rubber and Plastic Products	140.14	139.18	14.77
非金属矿物制品业	Nonmetal Mineral Products	106.93	103.95	15.29
黑色金属冶炼及压延加工业	Smelting and Pressing of Ferrous Metal	43.83	42.71	1.92
有色金属冶炼及压延加工业	Smelting and Pressing of Nonferrous Metal	74.40	75.92	7.76
金属制品业	Metal Products	188.95	183.32	44.28
通用设备制造业	General Purpose Equipment Manufacturing	647.80	644.95	212.63
专用设备制造业	Special Purpose Equipment Manufacturing	348.71	336.83	78.78
汽车制造业	Automobile Manunfacturing	1 311.15	1 340.52	64.02
铁路、船舶、航空航天和其他运输设备制造业	Manufacturing of Railway, Ships, Aeronautics & Astronautics, and Other Transportation Equipment	300.07	292.30	166.56
电气机械及器材制造业	Electric Equipment and Machinery	446.09	436.04	162.94
计算机、通信和其他电子设备制造业	Manufacturing of Computers, Telecommunications and Other Electronic Equipment	2 492.10	2 456.90	1 505.73
仪器仪表制造业	Manufacturing of Instruments and Apparatuses	95.35	96.75	42.12
其他制造业	Other Manufacturing	24.97	25.26	1.47
废弃资源综合利用业	Comprehensive Reutilization of Discarded Resources	1.28	1.32	
金属制品、机械和设备修理业	Repairing of Metal Products, Machineries and Equipment	21.96	26.21	2.30
电力、热力的生产和供应业	Production and Supply of Electricity and Heating Power	841.19	841.09	
燃气生产和供应业	Production and Supply of Gas	30.87	31.29	
水的生产和供应业	Production and Supply of Tap Water	10.45	8.80	

表6-5 工业重点发展行业主要指标
(2012)

单位:万元

指 标	Indicators	企业单位数(个) Enterprises (unit)	从业人数(人) Employed Persons (person)	工业总产值 Gross Output Value of Industry
总 计	**Total**	**1 837**	**439 769**	**67 221 786**
按登记注册类型分	**By Type of Registration**			
内 资	Domestic Funded	1 289	144 451	19 770 286
国 有	State-owned	14	15 559	2 045 677
集 体	Collective-owned	38	3 052	132 458
股份合作制	Share-holding	28	1 957	77 875
联 营	Jointly-operated	11	858	46 047
有限责任公司	Companies with Limited Liability	117	39 617	5 064 650
股份有限公司	Companies Limited by Shares	24	18 621	8 852 559
私 营	Private	1 052	63 974	3 521 797
其 他	Others	5	813	29 224
港澳台商投资	Hong Kong/Macao/Taiwan Invested	114	40 795	7 843 580
#港澳台商独资	Solely Hong Kong/Macao/Taiwan Funded	77	26 319	6 272 466
外商投资	Foreigner Invested	434	254 523	39 607 919
#外商独资	Solely Foreigner Funded	304	183 456	22 579 427
按轻、重工业分	**By Light/Heavy Industry**			
轻工业	Light Industry	269	52 229	5 880 014
重工业	Heavy Industry	1 568	387 540	61 341 772
按企业规模分	**By Scale of Enterprises**			
大型企业	Large	66	244 302	48 394 750
中型企业	Medium	170	92 154	10 280 590
小型企业	Small	1 601	103 313	8 546 446
按行业分	**By Industry**			
电子信息产品制造业	Manufacturing of Electronic and Information Technology Products	564	209 693	26 945 727
汽车制造业	Auto Manufacturing	225	74 797	13 102 557
石油化工及精细化工制造业	Manufacturing of Petrochemical and Fine Chemicals	228	28 270	12 739 384
精品钢材制造业	Manufacturing of High Quality Steel Products	47	3 487	342 494
成套设备制造业	Manufacturing of Complete Equipment	621	87 998	10 783 104
生物医药制造业	Manufacturing of Biological Medicine	152	35 524	3 308 520

Major Indicators of PNA Pillar Industries

(10 000 yuan)

工业销售产值 Sales Value of Industry	固定资产原价 Original Value of Fixed Assets	资产总计 Total Assets	负债总计 Total Liabilities	实收资本 Paid-in Capital	主营业务收入 Revenue of Primary Operations	税金 Tax	利润总额 Total Profits
66 522 822	**25 418 926**	**68 889 539**	**34 452 633**	**17 016 908**	**78 234 252**	**2 970 941**	**5 584 847**
19 432 223	7 299 145	30 877 946	11 359 523	6 891 754	20 467 689	1 409 839	2 190 785
2 059 179	1 177 858	2 267 412	1 019 785	1 116 568	2 050 809	62 530	110 834
139 492	21 271	95 540	58 478	11 849	132 142	5 809	7 221
75 669	22 470	60 868	36 633	5 483	75 667	2 224	1 163
44 029	11 828	36 504	22 391	6 972	44 522	1 421	2 982
4 888 395	2 495 944	7 941 846	4 584 338	1 728 082	4 952 075	109 688	225 975
8 766 623	2 456 915	16 632 999	3 449 873	2 331 759	9 693 434	1 106 570	1 628 895
3 433 564	1 091 090	3 808 097	2 181 031	1 683 596	3 493 811	120 715	210 956
25 273	21 771	34 680	6 993	7 445	25 229	884	2 759
7 771 176	3 437 886	5 372 848	3 002 803	2 202 783	7 914 241	61 272	343 188
6 229 631	3 018 388	3 941 823	2 366 339	1 898 210	6 343 033	26 655	205 943
39 319 424	14 681 894	32 638 745	20 090 307	7 922 371	49 852 323	1 499 830	3 050 874
22 238 055	7 399 848	14 314 734	8 765 317	4 025 501	24 025 301	290 871	718 384
5 699 700	1 891 823	5 976 561	2 670 915	1 545 317	5 872 480	290 208	609 197
60 823 122	23 527 103	62 912 979	31 781 718	15 471 591	72 361 772	2 680 733	4 975 650
48 106 029	18 825 533	49 698 246	24 964 233	10 935 958	58 924 984	2 396 317	4 256 898
9 967 517	3 626 620	10 039 630	4 955 038	2 697 207	10 517 684	295 207	712 848
8 449 276	2 966 773	9 151 664	4 533 362	3 383 743	8 791 584	279 417	615 101
26 571 823	10 213 092	18 331 846	11 330 859	7 014 748	28 365 932	202 444	507 601
13 396 325	4 568 184	23 729 626	8 147 302	2 996 593	22 918 307	1 146 155	4 080 404
12 496 344	3 519 135	5 942 398	2 756 530	2 409 221	12 781 840	1 161 054	300 089
335 223	327 078	443 828	278 626	366 398	358 186	34 089	167
10 529 492	5 651 867	16 579 255	10 144 888	3 206 434	10 511 767	220 686	307 212
3 193 616	1 139 570	3 862 586	1 794 428	1 023 515	3 298 221	206 513	389 375

表6-6 高技术工业主要指标
(2012)

单位:万元

指 标	Indicators	企业单位数(个) Enterprises (unit)	从业人数(人) Employed Persons (person)	工业总产值 Gross Output Value of Industry
总 计	**Total**	**426**	**227 847**	**29 135 162**
按登记注册类型分	**By Type of Registration**			
内 资	Domestic Funded	211	32 561	1 976 453
国 有	State-owned	3	4 784	315 595
集 体	Collective-owned	1	60	1 230
股份合作制	Share-holding	2	63	867
联 营	Jointly-operated	3	293	15 258
有限责任公司	Companies with Limited Liability	38	9 858	658 909
股份有限公司	Companies Limited by Shares	6	3 174	191 884
私 营	Private	155	13 542	764 646
其 他	Others	3	787	28 066
港澳台商投资	Hong Kong/Macao/Taiwan Invested	46	25 482	6 526 066
#港澳台商独资	Solely Hong Kong/Macao/Taiwan Funded	34	18 219	5 555 239
外商投资	Foreigner Invested	169	169 804	20 632 643
#外商独资	Solely Foreigner Funded	129	142 227	16 441 378
按轻、重工业分	**By Light/Heavy Industry**			
轻工业	Light Industry	150	38 381	3 810 110
重工业	Heavy Industry	276	189 466	25 325 052
按企业规模分	**By Scale of Enterprises**			
大型企业	Large	38	168 346	23 469 796
中型企业	Medium	57	32 823	3 708 965
小型企业	Small	331	26 678	1 956 401
按工业行业分	**By Sector**			
信息化学品制造	Manufacturing of Information Chemicals	3	95	10 074
医药制造业	Manufacturing of Medicine	87	26 023	2 386 192
航空航天器制造	Manufacturing of Aviation and Space Vehicles	12	1 434	83 570
电子及通信设备制造业	Manufacturing of Electronics and Telecommunications Equipment	170	92 352	9 674 803
电子计算机及办公设备制造业	Manufacturing of Electronic Computers and Office Equipment	18	87 903	15 486 777
医疗设备及仪器仪表制造业	Manufacturing of Medical Equipment and Instrument	136	20 040	1 493 747

Major Indicators of PNA High-Tech Enterprises

(10 000 yuan)

工业销售产值 Sales Value of Industry	固定资产原价 Original Value of Fixed Assets	资产总计 Total Assets	负债总计 Total Liabilities	实收资本 Paid-in Capital	主营业务收入 Revenue of of Floating Assets	税金 Tax	利润总额 Total Profits
28 690 956	**10 832 484**	**21 059 158**	**12 490 066**	**6 820 161**	**30 442 380**	**364 706**	**828 993**
1 898 581	978 773	2 567 764	1 275 535	684 911	1 920 573	82 945	153 616
312 622	339 940	555 110	310 921	185 500	289 499	5 037	20 147
1 230	2 007	1 844	147	1 150	1 230	66	30
867	263	847	434	310	867	44	-6
17 844	2 846	5 065	3 456	1 477	17 845	358	134
631 171	271 472	885 034	397 683	230 231	657 512	36 043	61 447
181 259	83 403	295 392	90 814	75 953	182 353	10 536	26 551
729 472	257 206	790 253	465 391	182 954	747 196	30 055	42 785
24 114	21 637	34 219	6 688	7 337	24 071	808	2 527
6 475 346	2 953 943	4 015 230	2 251 211	1 926 033	6 520 486	31 016	254 610
5 526 791	2 741 101	3 147 098	1 956 934	1 733 110	5 566 106	14 386	159 091
20 317 030	6 899 768	14 476 165	8 963 321	4 209 216	22 001 322	250 744	420 767
16 293 552	5 596 405	9 374 344	6 097 461	2 832 925	17 849 529	161 850	324 368
3 698 807	1 145 815	4 200 439	1 847 077	1 089 423	3 782 447	206 613	388 543
24 992 149	9 686 670	16 858 720	10 642 989	5 730 738	26 659 933	158 093	440 450
23 207 865	9 078 338	15 799 519	10 166 134	5 285 406	24 824 608	217 920	403 238
3 553 532	990 282	2 942 239	1 376 796	782 502	3 595 027	74 017	217 122
1 929 559	763 864	2 317 400	947 136	752 253	2 022 745	72 770	208 634
11 687	1 114	3 619	1 338	851	11 687	845	399
2 281 669	878 715	2 910 486	1 394 196	827 404	2 344 893	172 003	252 890
82 407	83 241	136 253	93 530	87 536	82 214	2 970	- 111
9 483 919	8 836 160	11 047 704	5 604 602	5 209 397	9 741 066	66 940	278 373
15 321 369	651 441	5 563 585	4 875 140	358 259	16 717 822	85 417	121 015
1 509 906	381 813	1 397 511	521 260	336 714	1 544 698	36 532	176 427

表6-7　独立核算工业企业主要财务指标(规模以上)
(2012)

单位:万元

指　标	Indicators	企业单位数(个) Enterprises (unit)	从业人数(人) Employed Persons (person)	工业总产值 Gross Output Value of Industry
总　计	**Total**	**1 885**	**657 854**	**91 997 649**
按隶属关系分	**By Subordination**			
中央工业	Central	48	61 981	22 353 581
市属工业	Municipal	141	107 812	19 857 740
非中央、市属工业	Local	1 696	488 061	49 786 328
按登记注册类型分	**By Type of Registration**			
内　资	Domestic Funded	1 053	240 341	33 810 624
国　有	State-owned	36	36 576	9 601 207
集　体	Collective-owned	24	2 616	261 801
股份合作制	Share-holding	19	2 705	119 001
联　营	Jointly-operated	10	1 288	74 315
有限责任公司	Companies with Limited Liability	186	64 834	7 801 108
股份有限公司	Companies Limited by Shares	29	22 874	9 773 041
私　营	Private	741	107 850	6 125 041
其　他	Others	8	1 598	55 110
港澳台商投资	Hong Kong/Macao/Taiwan Invested	191	68 276	9 742 108
#港澳台商独资	Solely Hong Kong/Macao/Taiwan Funded	113	35 225	6 867 376
外商投资	Foreigner Invested	641	349 237	48 444 917
#外商独资	Solely Foreigner Funded	438	237 390	27 272 308
按轻、重工业分	**By Light/Heavy Industry**			
轻工业	Light Industry	597	179 988	15 420 120
重工业	Heavy Industry	1 288	477 866	76 577 529
按企业规模分	**By Scale of Enterprises**			
大型企业	Large	96	324 167	61 053 587
中型企业	Medium	307	166 721	15 801 382
小型企业	Small	1 482	166 966	15 142 680

Major Indicators of Industrial Enterprises with Independent Accounting Systems (Above-Certain-Scaled Enterprises)

(10 000 yuan)

工业销售产值 Sales Value of Industry	实收资本 Paid-in Capital	资产总计 Total Assets	流动资产合计 Total Circulating Assets	固定资产合计 Total Fixed Assets	固定资产原价 Original Value of Fixed Assets
91 243 290	**21 703 247**	**100 579 964**	**41 209 306**	**29 330 142**	**55 999 103**
22 155 373	5 636 038	30 779 270	11 418 090	16 060 364	28 772 868
19 996 231	5 771 290	31 260 447	9 896 415	5 170 658	9 686 143
49 091 686	10 295 919	38 540 247	19 894 801	8 099 120	17 540 092
33 440 918	8 942 744	52 828 829	15 864 295	18 976 163	33 139 778
9 649 135	2 431 958	17 495 360	4 618 498	12 808 851	22 688 206
266 562	11 817	182 078	125 322	21 416	46 292
115 647	10 461	100 005	46 973	26 951	46 478
72 404	14 322	63 424	35 909	9 949	22 875
7 623 537	2 984 685	11 482 220	5 037 948	3 402 553	5 941 101
9 732 155	2 507 695	17 639 485	2 828 581	1 463 221	2 594 209
5 932 252	969 119	5 792 363	3 139 825	1 223 462	1 762 846
49 228	12 687	73 894	31 241	19 759	37 771
9 673 579	2 717 789	7 225 643	3 550 912	1 504 448	4 381 203
6 823 109	2 107 393	4 528 455	2 279 969	1 009 751	3 447 686
48 128 793	10 042 713	40 525 492	21 794 099	8 849 531	18 478 122
26 894 925	4 969 197	18 118 975	10 019 633	3 992 751	9 050 568
15 205 791	3 447 260	14 186 843	6 147 243	3 301 980	5 739 660
76 037 500	18 255 987	86 393 121	35 062 063	26 028 161	50 259 443
60 827 727	13 120 476	68 914 973	26 958 923	21 436 341	42 209 124
15 449 312	4 313 974	16 016 183	7 295 677	4 111 889	7 377 971
14 966 251	4 268 797	15 648 808	6 954 706	3 781 912	6 412 008

单位:万元 表6-7 续表 Continued

指 标	Indicators	本年折旧 Depreciation of the Current Year	负债合计 Total Liabilities	所有者权益 Owner's Equity
总 计	**Total**	**3 175 437**	**47 113 085**	**53 286 685**
按隶属关系分	**By Subordination**			
中央工业	Central	1 574 231	13 589 808	17 189 461
市属工业	Municipal	562 506	11 934 870	19 183 410
非中央、市属工业	Local	1 038 701	21 588 406	16 913 814
按登记注册类型分	**By Type of Registration**			
内 资	Domestic Funded	1 837 397	19 036 177	33 776 405
国 有	State-owned	1 266 206	5 146 977	12 344 773
集 体	Collective-owned	2 382	125 322	56 756
股份合作制	Share-holding	2 808	49 951	50 054
联 营	Jointly-operated	896	39 033	24 391
有限责任公司	Companies with Limited Liability	290 122	6 452 418	5 028 223
股份有限公司	Companies Limited by Shares	147 802	3 889 256	13 750 228
私 营	Private	124 828	3 301 208	2 480 328
其 他	Others	2 353	32 012	41 651
港澳台商投资	Hong Kong/Macao/Taiwan Invested	196 319	4 003 129	3 217 799
#港澳台商独资	Solely Hong Kong/Macao/Taiwan Funded	149 960	2 623 415	1 902 644
外商投资	Foreigner Invested	1 141 722	24 073 778	16 292 482
#外商独资	Solely Foreigner Funded	576 711	10 700 035	7 410 903
按轻、重工业分	**By Light/Heavy Industry**			
轻工业	Light Industry	313 527	6 785 908	7 248 147
重工业	Heavy Industry	2 861 911	40 327 176	46 038 538
按企业规模分	**By Scale of Entrerprises**			
大型企业	Large	2 375 197	31 195 950	37 710 621
中型企业	Medium	411 030	8 044 211	7 963 545
小型企业	Small	389 211	7 872 924	7 612 519

(10 000 yuan)

主营业务收入 Revenue of Primary Operations	税金 Tax	#本年应交增值税 Current Year Value-Added Tax Payable	营业利润 Operation Profits	利润总额 Total Profits	应付职工薪酬 Wage/Fringe Benefits
104 009 601	**3 899 206**	**2 492 660**	**6 681 680**	**7 048 335**	**5 483 338**
22 267 868	1 496 015	668 644	- 20 335	15 822	1 173 845
29 959 558	1 418 466	904 629	4 540 737	4 642 229	1 232 053
51 782 175	984 724	919 387	2 161 279	2 390 285	3 077 441
34 991 359	1 999 209	1 089 428	2 576 456	2 771 745	2 044 760
9 796 052	408 904	375 912	265 542	267 369	607 408
263 125	7 721	7 255	5 663	10 533	10 282
117 471	3 329	3 083	1 403	3 396	9 904
73 083	2 185	2 001	2 984	3 207	5 267
7 757 644	243 433	222 208	364 275	436 235	619 777
10 921 638	1 151 462	310 520	1 651 845	1 709 272	328 980
6 014 453	180 352	166 730	282 940	338 775	456 042
47 893	1 822	1 720	1 803	2 957	7 100
9 826 611	117 924	112 530	524 009	576 986	493 485
6 937 637	44 166	41 965	228 698	255 894	295 751
59 191 632	1 782 073	1 290 702	3 581 215	3 699 604	2 945 094
29 022 743	470 484	446 939	990 716	1 056 076	1 606 405
16 036 540	626 989	580 985	1 321 956	1 412 135	1 238 501
87 973 061	3 272 216	1 911 676	5 359 724	5 636 200	4 244 838
71 967 950	2 966 533	1 626 780	4 682 251	4 892 262	3 216 569
16 313 429	470 971	436 739	1 013 263	1 075 980	1 219 088
15 728 223	461 701	429 142	986 167	1 080 093	1 047 681

表6-8 独立核算工业企业经济效益指标(规模以上)
(2012)

指 标	Indicators	工业经济效益综合指数 Composite Index of Industry Economic Results	总资产贡献率(%) Total Assets Contribution Ratio(%)
总 计	**Total**	**276.3**	**12.6**
按隶属关系分	**By Subordination**		
中央工业	Central	472.8	5.6
市属工业	Municipal	482.3	21.6
非中央、市属工业	Local	199.0	10.7
按登记注册类型分	**By Registration Categories**		
内 资	Domestic Funded	123.0	10.0
国 有	State-owned	131.2	4.2
集 体	Collective-owned	105.0	12.2
股份合作制	Share-holding	88.0	8.0
联 营	Jointly-operated	97.9	9.9
有限责任公司	Companies with Limited Liability	102.7	7.6
股份有限公司	Companies Limited by Shares	181.1	17.0
私 营	Private	104.8	10.9
其 他	Others	91.9	7.5
港澳台商投资	Hong Kong/Macao/Taiwan Invested	116.8	11.3
#港澳台商独资	Solely Hong Kong/Macao/Taiwan Funded	103.7	8.1
外商投资	Foreigner Invested	133.6	16.2
#外商独资	Solely Foreigner Funded	107.3	10.4
按轻、重工业分	**By Light/Heavy Industry**		
轻工业	Light Industry	136.0	17.0
重工业	Heavy Industry	125.9	11.8
按企业规模分	**By Scale of Enterprises**		
大型企业	Large	135.5	12.8
中型企业	Medium	116.4	12.0
小型企业	Small	115.0	12.1

Economic Results Indicators of Industrial Enterprise with Independent Accounting Systems (Above-Certain-Scaled Enterprises)

资本保值增值率(%) Ratio of Capital Holding and Adding(%)	资产负债率(%) Ratio of Capital to Liabilities(%)	流动资产周转率(次) Turnover Period of Circulating Assets(time)	成本费用利润率(%) After-tax Profit/Cost(%)	工业全员劳动生产率(元/人) Overall Industrial Labor Productivity (yuan/person)	工业产品销售率(%) Sales Rate of Industrial Products(%)
111.6	**46.8**	**1.9**	**7.2**	**274 664**	**99.2**
105.2	44.2	2.0	0.1	664 192	99.1
119.6	38.2	1.8	17.0	525 160	100.7
110.2	56.0	1.9	4.8	167 466	98.6
115.3	36.0	1.6	8.3	26 954	98.9
107.1	29.4	3.3	2.8	67 054	100.5
112.8	68.8	1.7	4.1	14 423	101.8
111.4	49.9	1.7	2.9	9 470	97.2
115.9	61.5	1.4	4.5	12 804	97.4
106.8	56.2	1.2	6.1	23 501	97.7
127.9	22.0	1.4	16.3	51 815	99.6
115.4	57.0	1.5	5.9	11 191	96.9
104.2	43.3	1.0	6.4	9 598	89.3
114.2	55.4	2.0	6.1	19 744	99.3
107.8	57.9	2.2	3.8	20 194	99.4
104.3	59.4	2.1	6.7	29 498	99.3
108.2	59.1	2.3	3.8	18 971	98.6
108.1	47.8	1.7	9.4	19 879	98.6
112.2	46.7	2.0	6.8	30 461	99.3
112.5	45.3	2.2	7.2	37 434	99.6
108.9	50.2	1.6	7.0	19 652	97.8
110.1	50.3	1.5	7.3	17 526	98.8

表6-9　独立核算大中型工业企业主要指标
(2012)

单位:万元

指　标	Indicators	企业单位数(个) Enterprises (unit)	从业人数(人) Average Number of Employed Persons (person)	工业总产值 Gross Output Value of Industry
总　计	**Total**	**403**	**490 888**	**76 854 969**
按隶属关系分	**By Subordination**			
中央工业	Central	26	58 415	22 143 500
市属工业	Municipal	67	98 044	18 051 220
非中央、市属工业	Local	310	334 429	36 660 249
按登记注册类型分	**Type of Registration**			
内　资	Domstic Funded	159	146 111	26 899 740
国　有	State-owned	17	33 850	9 427 414
集　体	Collective-owned	1	333	40 529
股份合作制	Share-holding	3	985	23 992
联　营	Jointly-operated	1	332	4 706
有限责任公司	Companies with Limited Liability	54	48 270	5 910 893
股份有限公司	Companies Limited by Shares	15	20 750	9 509 794
私　营	Private	66	40 809	1 954 404
其他内资	Other Domestic Investment	2	782	28 010
港澳台商投资	Hong Kong/Macao/Taiwan Invested	58	51 194	8 341 414
#港澳台商独资	Solely Hong Kong/Macao/Taiwan Funded	33	24 871	5 969 291
外商投资	Foreigner Invested	186	293 583	41 613 815
#外商独资	Solely Foreigner Funded	113	198 163	22 604 003
按轻、重工业分	**By Light/Heavy Industry**			
轻工业	Light Industry	96	324 167	61 053 587
重工业	Heavy Industry	307	166 721	15 801 382
按从业人数分	**By Number of Employees**			
5 000 人及以上	≥5 000 persons	15	165 289	32 244 883
3 000 ~ 4 999 人	3 000 ~ 4 999 persons	12	46 378	9 791 484
1 000 ~ 2 999 人	1 000 ~ 2 999 persons	78	128 534	19 254 834
999 及以下	≤ 999 persons	298	150 687	15 563 768
按工业总产值分	**By Gross Output Value of Industry**			
5 亿元及以上	≥500 million yuan	169	362 488	71 865 847
10000 ~ 49999 万元	100 ~ 499.99 million yuan	176	106 559	4 583 938
5 000 ~ 9 999 万元	50 ~ 99.99 million yuan	46	17 349	360 586
5 000 万元以下	<50 million yuan	12	4 492	44 598
按固定资产原价分	**By Original Value of Fixed Assets**			
5 亿元及以上	≥500 million yuan	80	260 632	55 261 172
10 000 ~ 49 999 万元	100 ~ 499.99 million yuan	147	137 015	12 471 198
5 000 ~ 9 999 万元	50 ~ 99.99 million yuan	79	45 056	7 080 511
1 000 ~ 4 999 万元	10 ~ 49.99 milion yuan	82	35 855	1 844 292
1 000 万元以下	<10 million yuan	15	12 330	197 797
按利税总额分	**By Profits and Taxes**			
1 亿元及以上	≥100 million yuan	30	161 017	42 068 858
5 000 ~ 9 999 万元	50 ~ 99.99 milion yuan	34	47 517	6 000 933
1 000 ~ 4 999 万元	10 ~ 49.99 milion yuan	85	64 866	5 650 674
1 000 万元以下	<10 million yuan	254	217 488	23 134 505

Major Indicators of Large and Medium Industrial Enterprises with Independent Accounting Systems

(10 000 yuan)

工业销售产值 Sales Value of Industry	固定资产原价 Original Value of Fixed Assets	资产总计 Total Assets	固定资产合计 Total Fixed Assets	流动资产合计 Total Floating Assets	主营业务收入 Revenue of of Floating Assets	利润总额 Total Profits
76 277 039	**49 587 096**	**84 931 156**	**25 548 230**	**43 418 738**	**88 281 379**	**5 968 241**
21 945 337	28 686 258	30 546 718	16 011 318	10 851 228	22 056 104	14 981
18 195 246	7 890 368	28 876 722	4 093 682	15 328 390	28 110 272	4 493 241
36 136 456	13 010 470	25 507 716	5 443 230	17 239 120	38 115 003	1 460 019
26 691 345	29 931 459	45 747 431	16 911 929	17 156 932	27 866 698	2 401 064
9 474 807	22 617 315	17 302 810	12 756 456	2 849 966	9 619 950	269 337
38 969	384	16 489	210	16 278	38 969	356
23 061	14 711	26 700	9 121	16 299	23 061	1 159
4 706	9 164	5 535	996	3 753	5 697	3
5 737 500	4 211 109	9 261 489	2 340 637	5 471 988	5 863 403	294 228
9 466 585	2 493 056	17 326 331	1 402 628	7 587 340	10 393 213	1 693 692
1 921 660	564 146	1 773 947	391 138	1 188 505	1 898 392	139 769
24 058	21 575	34 131	10 743	22 803	24 015	2 520
8 267 656	3 615 109	5 644 817	1 078 055	3 819 644	8 389 259	450 169
5 927 666	2 953 085	3 511 792	701 923	2 442 192	6 023 641	170 823
41 318 038	16 040 528	33 538 908	7 558 246	22 442 161	52 025 423	3 117 010
22 223 372	7 469 133	13 710 925	3 133 576	9 431 435	24 093 720	704 643
60 827 727	42 209 124	68 914 973	21 436 341	33 312 862	71 967 950	4 892 262
15 449 312	7 377 971	16 016 183	4 111 889	10 105 876	16 313 429	1 075 980
32 353 998	28 829 233	43 967 046	14 417 330	18 867 714	42 844 660	3 938 528
9 674 196	3 723 476	4 290 783	1 969 392	1 933 415	9 753 301	87 005
19 026 360	9 794 732	20 886 880	5 119 795	12 660 294	19 596 293	876 090
15 222 486	7 239 655	15 786 448	4 041 714	9 957 314	16 087 125	1 066 620
71 353 807	46 455 114	76 959 355	23 685 536	38 773 112	83 071 017	5 756 360
4 520 424	2 789 909	7 331 632	1 713 987	4 257 146	4 754 699	213 200
358 890	297 279	556 054	131 775	327 579	397 339	- 1 357
43 918	44 793	84 116	16 932	60 900	58 323	39
55 102 645	45 263 565	68 686 139	23 152 263	31 586 910	65 952 094	4 710 972
12 181 336	3 482 996	11 110 739	1 928 762	7 534 266	13 228 768	902 162
7 018 112	573 380	3 514 057	309 455	2 964 363	7 074 340	240 142
1 778 498	259 537	1 488 179	153 857	1 208 663	1 816 946	107 172
196 449	7 619	132 042	3 893	124 537	209 232	7 795
42 173 383	32 533 608	49 550 494	17 427 182	20 798 362	51 999 829	4 444 237
5 872 807	2 681 865	5 022 725	1 317 097	3 317 350	6 680 630	635 842
5 398 858	2 917 582	6 562 076	1 757 159	4 206 589	5 607 070	356 824
22 831 991	11 454 041	23 795 861	5 046 793	15 096 437	23 993 849	531 339

表6-10 港澳台及外商投资工业企业主要指标
(2012)

单位:万元

指 标	Indicators	企业单位数(个) Enterprises (unit)	从业人数(人) Employed Persons (person)	工业总产值 Gross Output Value of Industry
总 计	**Total**	**1 124**	**431 430**	**58 468 788**
按登记注册类型分	**By Type of Registration**			
与港澳台商合资经营企业	China-Hong Kong/Macao/Taiwan Joint Venture	91	25 115	1 881 617
与港澳台商合作经营企业	China-Hong Kong/Macao/Taiwan Cooperative	11	3 573	153 456
港澳台商独资企业	Solely Hong Kong/Macao/Taiwan Funded	165	38 025	6 911 909
港澳台商投资股份有限公司	Hong Kong/Macao/Taiwan Investment Companies Limited by Shares	3	5 620	862 913
其他港澳台商投资	Other HongKong/Macao/Taiwan Investment	1	125	2 694
中外合资经营企业	Sino-Foreign Jointly-operated	245	93 694	17 099 175
中外合作经营企业	Sino-Foreign Cooperative	20	7 514	554 504
外商独资企业	Solely Foreigner Funded	581	243 567	27 416 093
外商投资股份有限公司	Foreign Investment Company Limited by Shares	6	14 182	3 583 211
其他外商投资	Other Foreign Investment	1	15	3 217
按行业分	**By Sector**			
农副食品加工业	Processing of Agricultural Side-line Food	12	2 054	905 068
食品制造业	Food Manufacturing	18	4 830	974 282
酒、饮料和精制茶制造业	Manufacturing of Liquor, Beverage and Refined Tea	6	5 113	312 733
烟草制品业	Tobacco Products			
纺织业	Textile Industry	23	2 440	141 404
纺织服装、服饰业	Textile Clothes and Accessories	78	23 939	338 274
皮革、毛皮、羽毛及其制品和制鞋业	Leather, Fur, Feather and their Products and Shoe-making	13	1 358	31 326
木材加工及木、竹、藤、棕、草制品业	Timber-Processing, Bamboo, Cane, Palm Fiber and Straw Products	4	665	24 467
家具制造业	Furniture Manufacturing	9	8 502	810 325
造纸及纸制品业	Paper-making and Paper Products	19	4 340	387 503

Major Indicators of HK/Macao/Taiwan & Overseas Invested Industrial Enterprises

(10 000 yuan)

工业销售产值 Sales Value of Industry	固定资产原价 Original Value of Fixed Assets	资产总计 Total Assets	负债总计 Total Liabilities	实收资本 Paid-in Capital	主营业务收入 Revenue of of Floating Assets	税金 Tax	利润总额 Total Profits
58 084 135	**23 144 121**	**48 274 080**	**28 314 227**	**13 051 467**	**69 300 005**	**1 911 620**	**4 273 014**
1 874 537	764 454	2 079 312	1 096 902	477 134	1 910 466	66 448	270 429
152 570	84 839	123 563	99 568	47 305	149 522	4 782	2 355
6 867 641	3 498 041	4 646 625	2 677 140	2 191 462	6 982 170	46 083	250 952
846 618	142 014	543 094	200 424	114 272	852 240	3 902	48 572
2 694	2 664	3 441	2 545	291	2 694		358
17 229 542	6 254 440	14 274 160	8 127 030	3 619 559	26 155 308	1 262 809	2 729 945
538 154	295 217	566 065	313 782	229 253	673 891	23 865	35 458
27 038 710	9 173 756	18 342 547	10 814 138	5 088 574	29 166 528	475 501	1 058 750
3 530 452	2 928 654	7 692 730	4 981 682	1 283 520	3 403 970	27 819	- 125 548
3 217	42	2 543	1 017	96	3 217	412	1 743
898 893	109 719	653 313	273 835	78 806	996 024	3 472	104 450
919 003	182 998	631 587	405 231	114 016	949 251	84 954	131 948
322 505	268 771	269 748	184 778	142 353	381 443	11 473	14 131
140 681	47 117	126 743	62 622	48 107	140 072	1 653	8 542
402 050	113 563	334 011	216 701	76 226	422 799	21 836	170
30 361	11 700	23 381	19 417	9 785	30 361	246	- 915
25 387	10 123	41 920	22 053	9 527	34 050	1 125	1 622
809 563	137 803	635 784	367 161	75 854	810 648	21 899	170 060
375 552	363 972	463 509	215 387	194 750	380 998	9 264	23 307

单位:万元

表 6－10　续表　Continued

指　标	Indicators	企业单位数（个）Enterprises (unit)	从业人数（人）Employed Persons (person)	工业总产值 Gross Output Value of Industry
印刷业、记录媒介的复制	Printing and Record Medium Reproduction	16	2 667	134 494
文教、工美、体育和娱乐用品制造业	Manufacturing of Cultural, Educational, Arts, Sports and Leisure Products	31	4 677	178 133
石油加工、炼焦及核燃料加工业	Petroleum Processing, Coke Products and Processing of Nuclear Fuel	6	1 152	258 343
化学原料及化学制品制造业	Raw Chemical Materials and Chemical Products	75	14 691	3 906 689
医药制造业	Medicine Manufacturing	35	14 314	1 508 732
化学纤维制造业	Chemical Fiber	1	18	130
橡胶和塑料制品业	Rubber and Plastic Products	78	12 366	532 429
非金属矿物制品业	Nonmetal Mineral Products	39	7 087	545 413
黑色金属冶炼及压延加工业	Smelting and Pressing of Ferrous Metal	6	1 724	237 032
有色金属冶炼及压延加工业	Smelting and Pressing of Nonferrous Metal	9	1 440	383 316
金属制品业	Metal Products	57	10 108	861 519
通用设备制造业	General Purpose Equipment Manufacturing	141	32 898	5 044 872
专用设备制造业	Specialized Equipment Manufacturing	99	20 397	2 513 063
汽车制造业	Automobile Manufacturing	62	38 104	9 821 481
铁路、船舶、航空航天和其他运输设备制造业	Manufacturing of Railway, Ships, Aeronautics &Astronautics, and Other Transportation Equipment	25	4 150	368 840
电气机械及器材制造业	Electric Equipment and Machinery	88	31 216	2 977 969
计算机、通信和其他电子设备制造业	Manufacturing of Computers, Telecommunication and other Electronic Equipment	115	164 314	24 022 354
仪器仪表制造业	Manufacturing of Instrument and Apparatus	40	10 372	866 503
工艺品及其他制造业	Handicrafts and Other Production	11	4 029	223 517
金属制品、机械和设备修理业	Repairing of Metal Products, Machine and Equipment	5	915	65 024
电力、热力生产和供应业	Production and Supply of Electricity and Heating Power	2	234	23 480
水的生产和供应业	Production and Supply of Tap Water	1	1 316	70 076

(10 000 yuan)

工业销售产值 Sales Value of Industry	固定资产原价 Original Value of Fixed Assets	资产总计 Total Assets	负债总计 Total Liabilities	实收资本 Paid-in Capital	主营业务收入 Revenue of of Floating Assets	税金 Tax	利润总额 Total Profits
131 842	149 543	155 269	71 069	48 300	131 300	8 089	12 294
175 636	44 171	141 444	77 019	34 172	164 888	1 327	7 470
261 184	40 175	266 022	78 800	36 903	262 009	8 153	18 311
3 789 154	1 417 181	2 996 918	1 471 060	927 443	3 912 347	103 236	277 887
1 439 514	518 259	1 763 453	903 864	460 222	1 515 586	121 477	168 789
130	1 497	1 259	152	934	130	8	- 19
535 203	337 274	500 855	191 701	194 754	546 900	10 631	19 691
532 252	620 427	896 351	338 491	399 385	559 888	18 477	42 922
232 071	283 093	316 976	195 281	344 893	253 633	32 853	184
398 053	129 564	387 355	281 719	91 441	384 038	3 620	5 851
833 418	318 787	811 455	430 891	225 681	878 575	18 287	80 288
5 052 420	3 215 863	7 630 188	4 815 962	1 176 727	5 136 227	129 612	83 454
2 441 388	665 585	2 296 299	1 185 464	472 803	2 516 578	75 272	214 635
10 064 043	3 117 973	7 550 328	4 855 150	1 372 275	18 802 219	1 006 563	2 275 917
369 766	106 484	331 691	155 143	95 980	379 965	4 363	20 169
2 940 831	824 146	2 124 336	1 054 319	613 653	3 059 036	53 898	151 180
23 709 423	8 933 874	15 220 821	9 715 025	5 307 718	25 374 746	127 481	327 543
879 987	196 261	724 852	292 174	164 660	892 690	10 365	73 090
226 402	254 498	308 190	55 563	72 097	226 649	14 377	27 041
65 024	76 470	108 337	79 026	80 202	64 909	2 000	- 1 369
23 480	98 488	102 090	5 662	29 800	33 126	1 435	13 054
58 917	548 747	459 596	293 507	152 000	58 921	4 175	1 320

表6-11　私营工业企业主要指标
(2012)

单位:万元

指　标	Indicators	企业单位数(个) Enterprises (unit)	从业人数(人) Average Number of Employed Persons (person)	工业总产值 Gross Output Value of Industry
总　计	**Total**	**4 132**	**197 890**	**7 863 948**
按轻、重工业分	**By Light/Heavy Industry**			
轻工业	Light Industry	1 719	83 242	2 695 264
重工业	Heavy Industry	2 413	114 648	5 168 684
按主要工业行业分	**By Main Sector**			
#农副食品加工业	Processing of Agricultural Side-line Food	30	4 956	222 302
食品制造业	Food Producing	29	1 191	46 255
酒、饮料和精制茶制造业	Manufacturing of Liquor, Beverage and Refined Tea	6	146	5 491
纺织业	Textile Industry	223	7 171	214 161
纺织服装、鞋、帽制造业	Manufacturing of Textile Clothes, Shoes and Hats	418	23 816	467 812
皮革、毛皮、羽毛及其制品和制鞋业	Leather, Fur, Feather and their Products and Shoe-making	88	5 605	98 155
木材加工及木、竹、藤、棕、草制品业	Timber-processing, Bamboo, Cane, Palm Fiber and Straw Products	86	1 941	59 832
家具制造业	Furniture Making	85	2 935	59 265
造纸及纸制品业	Paper-making and Paper Products	158	5 377	182 345
印刷业和记录媒介的复制	Printing and Record Medium Reproduction	153	7 450	236 535
文教、工美、体育和娱乐用品制造业	Manufacturing of Cultural, Educational, Arts, Sports and Leisure Products	76	2 897	236 855
石油加工、炼焦及核燃料加工业	Petroleum Processing, Coke Products and Processing of Nuclear Fuel	12	486	50 670
化学原料及化学制品制造业	Raw Chemical Material and Chemical Products	155	8 501	307 939
医药制造业	Medicine Manufacturing	30	4 030	340 816
化学纤维制造业	Chemical Fiber Manufacturing	6	216	8 734
橡胶和塑料制品业	Rubber and Plastic Products	404	15 374	590 858
非金属矿物制品业	Nonmetal Mineral Products	134	4 731	200 009
黑色金属冶炼及压延加工业	Smelting and Pressing of Ferrous Metal	65	3 099	164 118
有色金属冶炼及压延加工业	Smelting and Pressing of Nonferrous Metal	50	1 535	133 510
金属制品业	Metal Products	606	21 773	751 042
通用设备制造业	Manufacturing of General Purpose Equipment	482	19 738	846 724
专用设备制造业	Manufacturing of Specialized Equipment	229	9 687	382 320
汽车制造业	Automobile Manufacturing	128	13 179	544 687
铁路、船舶、航空航天和其他运输设备制造业	Manufacturing of Railway, Ship, Aviation and Aerospace, and other Transportation Equipment	59	5 655	161 660
电气机械及器材制造业	Manufacturing of Electrical Machinery and Equipment	283	15 527	1 127 903
计算机、通信和其他电子设备制造业	Manufacturing of Computers, Telecommunications and Other Electronic Equipment	51	5 443	291 091
仪器仪表制造业	Manufacturing of Instrument and Meters	39	1 567	53 803
其他制造业	Other Manufacturings	26	754	25 937
金属制品、机械和设备修理业	Repairing of Metal Products, Machineries and Equipment	13	2 819	27 362

Major Indicators of PNA Private Industrial Enterprises

(10 000 yuan)

工业销售产值 Sales Value of Industry	固定资产原价 Original Value of Fixed Assets	资产总计 Total Assets	负债总计 Total Liabilities	实收资本 Paid-in Capital	主营业务收入 Revenue of of Floating Assets	税金 Tax	利润总额 Total Profits
7 671 158	**2 580 507**	**7 863 699**	**4 639 335**	**2 441 401**	**7 753 359**	**280 395**	**383 273**
2 641 767	997 804	2 469 038	1 492 926	477 699	2 639 414	104 510	107 409
5 029 392	1 582 704	5 394 660	3 146 409	1 963 702	5 113 945	175 885	275 864
222 953	43 444	91 929	48 829	18 091	200 802	3 821	4 976
46 470	15 882	39 545	21 750	8 479	46 221	1 175	1 481
5 491	2 604	14 440	9 734	5 550	5 491	795	806
216 371	81 953	322 825	253 045	46 047	224 500	22 601	- 7 028
463 927	152 993	343 928	231 022	56 950	463 131	15 303	8 509
98 997	26 289	60 581	39 255	9 777	99 368	4 154	2 702
60 163	14 457	50 458	33 095	11 855	59 175	1 824	564
58 235	18 399	60 736	35 535	15 597	58 416	1 749	1 899
179 701	74 115	148 789	87 046	20 769	179 115	5 685	3 685
233 192	130 870	214 727	119 480	44 158	234 314	9 819	15 469
212 718	40 608	142 328	83 446	27 496	212 678	3 616	13 852
47 100	11 335	102 890	37 651	25 613	77 186	910	-1 233
302 590	96 942	331 946	115 681	63 221	304 442	12 947	26 000
322 852	156 471	412 192	233 191	120 442	329 732	12 233	24 974
8 734	2 151	4 027	2 091	808	8 734	298	510
586 997	216 665	552 234	302 624	95 693	572 262	21 654	32 798
194 918	84 855	233 730	153 496	51 800	195 989	7 426	8 752
156 892	60 936	162 803	105 732	25 811	157 647	3 287	4 999
132 636	25 775	144 333	110 537	17 317	139 799	2 127	650
714 609	258 747	745 780	466 393	157 719	758 208	25 933	34 843
819 785	288 035	909 034	485 579	165 277	822 300	31 285	58 697
371 377	118 796	489 046	285 107	1 082 046	375 020	16 531	18 226
558 812	220 889	573 559	354 677	88 759	549 624	16 798	46 342
159 483	76 721	222 047	143 511	41 489	156 589	7 339	6 265
1 085 601	246 168	1 106 614	638 668	185 479	1 101 877	32 292	57 852
277 466	63 361	229 879	140 598	31 281	278 920	10 895	10 970
54 107	13 221	74 419	48 832	10 984	63 545	3 465	3 084
25 862	8 434	23 163	16 895	3 060	25 777	793	576
27 362	3 039	22 997	17 041	1 387	27 362	2 479	621

表6-12 工业企业单位数和从业人员平均人数的各种分组
Classification of Industrial Enterprises and Average Number of Persons Employed

指 标	Indicators	企业单位数(个) Enterprises (unit)		从业人员平均人数(人) Average Number of Persons Employed (person)	
		2011	2012	2011	2012
总 计	**Total**	**6 469**	**5 948**	**794 901**	**759 416**
按隶属关系分	**By Subordination**				
中央工业	Central	55	53	60 265	62 029
市属工业	Municipal	174	152	119 672	107 123
非中央、市属工业	Local	6 240	5 743	614 964	590 264
按登记注册类型分	**By Type of Registration**				
内 资	Domestic Funded	5 223	4 824	367 428	344 809
国 有	State-owned	50	41	36 321	37 455
集 体	Collective-owned	177	166	9 048	7 750
股份合作	Share-holding	108	93	6 665	5 525
联 营	Jointly Operated	30	24	1 803	1 573
有限责任公司	Companies with Limited Liabilities	304	300	70 958	70 215
股份有限公司	Companies Limited by Shares	52	49	26 381	23 283
私 营	Private	4 489	4 132	215 443	197 226
其 他	Others	13	19	809	1 782
港澳台商投资	HK/Macao/Taiwan Invested	298	271	79 672	74 771
#港澳台商独资	Solely HK/Macao/Taiwan Funded	176	165	41 780	39 915
外商投资	Foreigner Invested	948	853	347 801	339 836
#外商独资	Solely Foreigner Funded	647	581	227 246	224 798
按轻、重工业分	**By Light/Heavy Industry**				
轻工业	Light Industry	2 679	2 366	261 073	239 134
重工业	Heavy Industry	3 790	3 582	533 828	520 282
按企业规模分	**By Scale of Enterprises**				
大型企业	Large	92	96	298 999	302 842
中型企业	Medium	324	307	183 134	168 165
小型企业	Small	6 053	5 545	312 768	288 409

注：表中没有注明的即为全社会统计口径,后续各表相同。
Note: The fields that have not been specified in this table have been counted with the total statistical approuch. The tables followed are the same.

表6-13 规模以上工业企业分行业能源消费情况

Energy Consumption of Above-scaled Industrial Enterprises by Sector (2012)

指 标 Indicators		企业单位数（个）Enterprises (in Number)	综合能源消费量（吨标准煤）Comprehensive Energy Consumption (tons of standard coal)	产值能耗（吨标准煤/万元）Energy Consumption of Production Value (tons of standard coal/10 000 yuan
总 计	**Total**	**1 797**	**8 592 296**	**0.094**
农副食品加工业	Processing of Agricultural Side-line Food	18	69 851	0.063
食品制造业	Food Manufacturing	20	44 996	0.041
酒、饮料和精制茶制造业	Manufacturing of Liquor, Beverage and Refined Tea	6	33 891	0.105
烟草制品业	Tobacco Products	1	3 797	0.128
纺织业	Textile Industry	33	44 150	0.154
纺织服装、服饰业	Textile Clothes and Accessories	98	39 250	0.028
皮革、毛皮、羽毛及其制品和制鞋业	Leather, Fur, Feather and their Products and Shoe-making	17	5 550	0.065
木材加工及木、竹、藤、棕、草制品业	Timber-processing, Bamboo, Cane, Palm Fiber and Straw Products	6	1 675	0.033
家具制造业	Furniture Manufacturing	15	20 087	0.024
造纸及纸制品业	Paper-making and Paper Products	37	175 953	0.320
印刷业和记录媒介复制业	Printing and Record Pressing	43	35 777	0.079
文教、工美、体育和娱乐用品制造业	Manufacturing of Cultural, Educational, Arts, Sports and Leisure Products	32	12 850	0.032
石油加工、炼焦及核燃料加工业	Petroleum Processing, Coke Products and Processing of Nuclear Fuel	14	2 254 079	0.285
化学原料和化学制品制造业	Raw Chemical Materials and Chemical Products	109	654 432	0.128
医药制造业	Medicine Manufacturing	53	114 725	0.049
化学纤维制造业	Chemical Fiber Manufacturing	1	56	0.012
橡胶和塑料制品业	Rubber and Plastic Products	142	176 405	0.154
非金属矿物制品业	Nonmetal Mineral Products	78	181 997	0.192
黑色金属冶炼及压延加工业	Smelting and Pressing of Ferrous Metal	29	101 638	0.251
有色金属冶炼及压延加工业	Smelting and Pressing of Nonferrous Metal	31	61 458	0.092
金属制品业	Metal Products	129	92 607	0.062
通用设备制造业	Manufacturing of General Purpose Equipment	214	231 122	0.037
专用设备制造业	Manufacturing of Special Purpose Equipment	123	80 176	0.025
汽车制造业	Automobile Manunfacturing	127	420 304	0.032
铁路、船舶、航空航天和其他运输设备制造业	Manufacturing of Railway, Ships, Aviation and Aerospace, and Other Transportation Equipment	63	164 182	0.056
电气机械及器材制造业	Manufacturing of Electric Machinery and Equipment	170	118 691	0.029
计算机、通信和其他电子设备制造业	Manufacturing of Computers, Telecommunications and Other Electronic Equipment	112	668 328	0.027
仪器仪表制造业	Manufacturing of Instruments and Apparatuses	38	20 248	0.024
其他制造业	Other Manufacturings	10	32 455	0.103
废弃资源综合利用业	Comprehensive Reutilization of Discarded Resources	1	144	0.025
金属制品、机械和设备修理业	Repairing of Metal Products, Machineries and Equipment	13	15 795	0.082
电力、热力的生产和供应业	Production and Supply of Electricity and Thermal Power	9	2 544 575	0.303
燃气生产和供应业	Production and Supply of Gas	2	129 553	0.422
水的生产和供应业	Production and Supply of Tap Water	3	41 497	0.411

表6-14 规模以上工业企业分行业主要能源品种消费情况
(2012)

指标 Indicators		原 煤(吨) Raw Coal (tons)	洗精煤(吨) Cleaned Coal (tons)	其他洗煤(吨) Other Washed Coals(tons)
总 计	**Total**	**11 700 539**	**638 848**	**36 096**
农副食品加工业	Processing of Agricultural Side-line Food	42 448	868	
食品制造业	Food Manufacturing	4 653	6 490	
酒、饮料和精制茶制造业	Manufacturing of Liquor, Beverage and Refined Tea			
烟草制品业	Tobacco Products			
纺织业	Textile Industry	29 754	3 000	
纺织服装、服饰业	Textile Clothes and Accessories	14 783	18	
皮革、毛皮、羽毛及其制品和制鞋业	Leather, Fur, Feather and their Products and Shoe-making	1 241	24	24
木材加工及木、竹、藤、棕、草制品业	Timber-processing, Bamboo, Cane, Palm Fiber and Straw Products	27		
家具制造业	Furniture Manufacturing	1 418		
造纸及纸制品业	Paper-making and Paper Products	154 646	9 694	4 371
印刷业和记录媒介复制业	Printing and Record Pressing			753
文教、工美、体育和娱乐用品制造业	Manufacturing of Cultural, Educational, Arts, Sports and Leisure Products			
石油加工、炼焦及核燃料加工业	Petroleum Processing, Coke Products and Processing of Nuclear Fuel			
化学原料和化学制品制造业	Raw Chemical Materials and Chemical Products	1 017 416		2 470
医药制造业	Medicine Manufacturing	32 092		
化学纤维制造业	Chemical Fiber Manufacturing			
橡胶和塑料制品业	Rubber and Plastic Products	2 675	19 941	25 986
非金属矿物制品业	Nonmetal Mineral Products	8 569		697
黑色金属冶炼及压延加工业	Smelting and Pressing of Ferrous Metal	5 015	6 134	1 131
有色金属冶炼及压延加工业	melting and Pressing of Nonferrous Metal	23 985		
金属制品业	Metal Products	4 986	2 243	665
通用设备制造业	Manufacturing of General Purpose Equipment	759	181	
专用设备制造业	Manufacturing of Special Purpose Equipment			
汽车制造业	Automobile Manunfacturing	5 622	20	
铁路、船舶、航空航天和其他运输设备制造业	Manufacturing of Railway, Ships, Aviation and Aerospace, and Other Transportation Equipment			
电气机械及器材制造业	Electric Equipment and Machinery	5 171		
计算机、通信和其他电子设备制造业	Manufacturing of Computers, Telecommunications and Other Electronic Equipment			
仪器仪表制造业	Manufacturing of Instruments and Apparatuses	10		
其他制造业	Other Manufacturings	2 451		
废弃资源综合利用业	Comprehensive Reutilization of Discarded Resources			
金属制品、机械和设备修理业	Repairing of Metal Products, Machineries and Equipment	1 092		
电力、热力的生产和供应业	Production and Supply of Electricity and Thermal Power	10 341 733		
燃气生产和供应业	Production and Supply of Gas		590 235	
水的生产和供应业	Production and Supply of Tap Water			

Consumption of Main Kinds of Engery in Above-scaled Industrial Enterprises by Sector

煤制品(吨) Coal Products (tons)	焦 炭(吨) Coke (tons)	焦炉煤气(万立方米) Coke Oven Gas (10 000 cu · m)	发生炉煤气(万立方米) Generator Gas (10 000 cu · m)	天然气(气态)(万立方米) Natural Gas (gas state) (10 000 cu · m)	液化天然气(液态)(吨) LNG(liquid state) (tons)	原油(吨) Crude Oil (tons)
28 966	**4 792**	**14 630**	**7 982**	**68 176**	**2 039**	**10 908 080**
				164		
				442		
				5		
				3		
				96		
				34	5	
				6		
	88			147		
				176		
				47		
				4 591		10 908 080
274 70				890		
			30	270		
				8		
301				3 940		
885	3 115			2 435		
	1 095		2 686	16		
	284			867		
	210			348	1 536	
				388	2	
310			5 172	3 055	333	
				550	163	
				223		
			6	2 323		
				12		
				240		
				27		
			88	39 813		
		14 630		7 060		

表 6－14　续表　Continued

指标	Indicators	汽油(吨) Gasoline (tons)	煤油(吨) Kerosene (tons)	柴油(吨) Diesel Oil (tons)	燃料油(吨) Fuel Oil (tons)
总　计	**Total**	**44 192**	**3 789**	**74 979**	**93 100**
农副食品加工业	Processing of Agricultural Side-line Food	291		3 126	780
食品制造业	Food Manufacturing	197		823	84
酒、饮料和精制茶制造业	Manufacturing of Liquor, Beverage and Refined Tea	59		1 701	2 129
烟草制品业	Tobacco Products				
纺织业	Textile Industry	590		149	
纺织服装、服饰业	Textile Clothes and Accessories	1 977		1 960	89
皮革、毛皮、羽毛及其制品和制鞋业	Leather, Fur, Feather and their Products and Shoe-making	267		34	
木材加工及木、竹、藤、棕、草制品业	Timber-processing, Bamboo, Cane, Palm Fiber and Straw Products	88		96	
家具制造业	Furniture Manufacturing	207		297	
造纸及纸制品业	Paper-making and Paper Products	655	8	1 734	366
印刷业和记录媒介复制业	Printing and Record Pressing	1 258	1	1 617	501
文教、工美、体育和娱乐用品制造业	Manufacturing of Cultural, Educational, Arts, Sports and Leisure Products	782		152	
石油加工、炼焦及核燃料加工业	Petroleum Processing, Coke Products and Processing of Nuclear Fuel	700		276	28 038
化学原料和化学制品制造业	Raw Chemical Materials and Chemical Products	3 948	2 899	5 653	21 878
医药制造业	Medicine Manufacturing	800		1 215	75
化学纤维制造业	Chemical Fiber Manufacturing	5			
橡胶和塑料制品业	Rubber and Plastic Products	2 744	240	2 522	79
非金属矿物制品业	Nonmetal Mineral Products	1 012		7 606	1 210
黑色金属冶炼及压延加工业	Smelting and Pressing of Ferrous Metal	437	2	810	214
有色金属冶炼及压延加工业	melting and Pressing of Nonferrous Metal	366	334	2 242	2 163
金属制品业	Metal Products	2 303	47	2 368	884
通用设备制造业	Manufacturing of General Purpose Equipment	3 875	141	14 639	176
专用设备制造业	Manufacturing of Special Purpose Equipment	1 880	31	590	115
汽车制造业	Automobile Manunfacturing	7 868	76	3 925	241
铁路、船舶、航空航天和其他运输设备制造业	Manufacturing of Railway, Ships, Aviation and Aerospace, and Other Transportation Equipment	1 558	10	12 895	14 165
电气机械及器材制造业	Electric Equipment and Machinery	2 762		1 098	
计算机、通信和其他电子设备制造业	Manufacturing of Computers, Telecommunications and Other Electronic Equipment	1 517		605	
仪器仪表制造业	Manufacturing of Instruments and Apparatuses	361		117	
其他制造业	Other Manufacturings	216		2 611	
废弃资源综合利用业	Comprehensive Reutilization of Discarded Resources				
金属制品、机械和设备修理业	Repairing of Metal Products, Machineries and Equipment	350		877	
电力、热力的生产和供应业	Production and Supply of Electricity and Thermal Power	4 447		2 344	19 913
燃气生产和供应业	Production and Supply of Gas	459		878	
水的生产和供应业	Production and Supply of Tap Water	210		18	

液化石油气（吨）LPG (tons)	炼厂干气（吨）Dry Gas from Refineries (tons)	其他石油制品（吨）Other Petrolium Products (tons)	热　力（百万千焦）Heating Power (1 million KJ)	电　力（万千瓦时）Electric Power (10 000 KWH)	其他燃料（吨标准煤）Other Fuels (tons/standard coal)
44 662	**297 968**	**961 733**	**15 709 032**	**1 816 754**	**75 574**
1			122 003	8 728	
44			166 891	7 571	
301			102 296	8 071	
1			31 339	895	
5		1	2 673	5 753	500
15			4 812	7 352	89
		69		1 334	
				463	
90		2	8 400	4 710	1 771
41			47 761	13 208	
239			65 549	9 073	
7			23 318	3 557	
13 977	280 994	922 178	9 633 186	103 620	
27 590	16 974	30 373	2 649 142	122 069	
8		7	520 926	22 411	
				16	
495		21	90 641	43 766	
44		13		36 589	
4				18 228	
91				14 548	
507		124	25 535	21 544	383
92		1 444	66 957	63 600	53
6		316	56 266	23 070	
163		7 092	661 159	105 348	
70		26	231 908	35 775	
556			46 669	34 628	
307		30	650 197	204 082	
		35		6 446	
1		2		7 818	
				48	
		1		4 290	
		1	139 684	858 699	72 778
			361 720	5 727	
6				13 717	

表6-15　规模以上工业企业能源消费分组情况

Energy Consumption of Above-scaled Industrial Enterprises by Group (2012)

指标	Indicators	综合能源消费量（吨标准煤）Comprehensive Energy Consumption (tons of standard coal)	单位产值能耗（吨标准煤/万元）Energy Consumption of Production Value (tons of standard coal/10 000 yuan)
按轻、重工业分	**By Light/Heavy Industry**		
轻工业	Light Industry	918 378	0.060
重工业	Heavy Industry	7 673 918	0.101
按企业规模分	**By Scale of Enterprises**		
大型企业	Large	6 177 920	0.101
中型企业	Medium	1 025 426	0.072
小型企业	Small	1 388 950	0.088
按高载能行业分	**By High Engery Bearing**		
石油加工、炼焦及核燃料加工业	Petroleum Processing, Coke Products and Processing of Nuclear Fuel	2 254 079	0.285
非金属矿物制品业	Nonmetal Mineral Products	181 997	0.192
化学原料及化学制品制造业	Raw Chemical Materials and Chemical Products	654 432	0.128
黑色金属冶炼及压延加工业	Smelting and Pressing of Ferrous Metal	101 638	0.251
电力、热力的生产和供应业	Production and Supply of Electricity and Thermal Power	2 544 575	0.303
按重点行业分	**By Key Industry**		
电子信息产品制造业	Manufacturing of Electronic and Information Products	767 638	0.029
汽车制造业	Automobile Industry	420 298	0.032
石油化工及精细化工制造业	Petrochemical and Refining Industry	2 816 304	0.223
精品钢材制造业	Manufacturing of Refined Steel Products	78 780	0.243
成套设备制造业	Manufacturing of Complete Equipment	393 876	0.038
生物医药制造业	Manufacturing of Biological Medicine	146 034	0.045
按高技术行业分	**By High-tech Industry**		
信息化学品制造	Manufacturing of Information Chemicals	298	0.033
医药制造业	Manufacturing of Medicines	114 725	0.049
航空航天器制造	Manufacturing of Aviation and Space Vehicles	3 294	0.041
电子及通信设备制造业	Manufacuring of Electronic and Communication Equipment	610 790	0.063
电子计算机及办公设备制造业	Manufacturing of Electronic Computer and Office Equipment	57 270	0.004
医疗设备及仪器仪表制造业	Manufacturing of Medical Equipment, Instrument and Meters	31 328	0.022

主要统计指标解释

工　业

指从事自然资源的开采，对采掘品和农产品进行加工和再加工的物质生产部门。具体包括：(1)对自然资源的开采，如采矿、晒盐等(但不包括禽兽捕猎和水产捕捞)；(2)对农副产品的加工、再加工，如粮油加工、食品加工、缫丝、纺织、制革等；(3)对采掘品的加工、再加工，如炼铁、炼钢、化工生产、石油加工、机器制造、木材加工等，以及电力、自来水、煤气的生产和供应等；(4)对工业品的修理、翻新，如机器设备的修理、交通运输工具(包括小卧车)的修理等。

1984年以前农村的村及村以下办工业归属农业，1984年以后划归工业。

工业统计调查单位为独立核算法人工业企业。

独立核算法人工业企业指从事工业生产经营活动的单位。独立核算法人工业企业应同时具备以下条件：①依法成立，有自己的名称、组织机构和场所，能够承担民事责任；②独立拥有和使用资产，承担负债，有权与其他单位签订合同；③独立核算盈亏，并能够编制资产负债表。

轻工业

指主要提供生活消费品和制作手工工具的工业。按其所使用的原料不同，可分为两大类：(1)以农产品为原料的轻工业，是指直接或间接以农产品为基本原料的轻工业。主要包括食品制造、饮料制造、烟草加工、纺织、缝纫、皮革和毛皮制作、造纸以及印刷等工业；(2)以非农产品为原料的轻工业，是指以工业品为原料的轻工业。主要包括文教体育用品、化学药品制造、合成纤维制造、日用化学制品、日用玻璃制品、日用金属制品、手工工具制造、医疗器械制造、文化和办公用机械制造等工业。

重工业

指为国民经济各部门提供物质技术基础的主要生产资料的工业。按其生产性质和产品用途，可以分为下列三类：(1)采掘(伐)工业，是指对自然资源的开采，包括石油开采、煤炭开采、金属矿开采、非金属矿开采等工业；(2)原材料工业，指向国民经济各部门提供基本材料、动力和燃料的工业。包括金属冶炼及加工、炼焦及焦炭、化学、化工原料、水泥、人造板以及电力、石油和煤炭加工等工业；(3)加工工业，是指对工业原材料进行再加工制造的工业。包括装备国民经济各部门的机械设备制造工业、金属结构、水泥制品等工业，以及为农业提供的生产资料如化肥、农药等工业。

根据上述划分原则，修理业中以重工业产品为修理作业对象的划为重工业，反之划为轻工业。

工业总产值

(1)定义：工业总产值是以货币形式表现的，工业企业在一定时期内生产的工业最终产品或提供工业性劳务活动的总价值量。它反映一定时间内工业生产的总规模和总水平。

(2)计算原则：工业生产的原则，即凡是企业在报告期生产的经检验合格的产品，不管是否在报告期销售，均包括在内。

最终产品的原则，即凡是计入工业总产值的产品，必须是本企业生产的经检验合格的，不需要再进行任何加工的最终产品。如果企业有中间产品(半成品)对外销售，则对外销售的中间产品应视为企业的最终产品。

工厂法原则，即工业总产值是以工业企业作为基本计算(核算)单位，即按企业的最终产品计算工业总产值。按这种方法计算的工业总产值，不允许同一产品价值在企业内部重复计算，不能把企业内部各个车间(分厂)生产的成果相加，但允许企业间的重复计算。

(3)内容及计算方法：1995年全国工业普查对工业总产值(原规定)的内容及计算原则和方法做了某些修订，修订后的工业总产值(新规定)包括三项内容：即本期生产成品价值、对外加工费收入、在制品半成品期末期初差额价值三部分。

本期生产成品价值：指企业本期生产，并在报告期内不再进行加工，经检验、包装入库的全部工业成品(半产品)价值合计，包括企业生产的自制设备及提供给本企业在建工程、其他非工业部门和福利部门等单位使用的成品价值。本期生产成品价值为按自备原材料生产的产品的数量乘以本期不含增值税(销项税额)的产品实际销售平均单价计算；会计核算中按成本价格转帐的自制设备和自产自用的成品，按成本价格计算生产成品价值。生产成品价值中不包括用定货者来料加工的成品(半产品)价值。

对外加工费收入：指企业在报告期内完成的对外承接的工业品加工(包括用定货者来料加工产品)的加工费收入和对外工业修理作业所取得的加工费收入。对外加工费收入按不含增值税(销项税额)的价格计算，可根据会计“产品销售收入”科目的有关资料取得。

对于本企业对内非工业部门提供的加工修理、设备安装的劳务收入，如果企业会计核算基础较好，能取得这部分资料，而且这部分价值所占比重较大，应包括在对外加工费收入中。

自制半成品在制品期末期初差额价值：指企业报告期在制品期末减期初的差额价值，本指标一般可以从会计核算资料中取得。如果会计产品成本核算中不计算半成品、在制品的成本，则总产值中也不包括这部分价值，反之则包括。

(4)工业总产值统计范围变化和计算方法修订情况：1984年以前工业总产值不包括村办工业，村办工业总产值划归农业。1984年以后工业总产值包括村办工业。

1995年工业普查对工业总产值计算方法做了修订，即从1995年始按新修订(新规定)方法计算工业总产值。新规定与原规定的区别如下：

全价与加工费的计算原则不同：新规定为凡自备原材料，不论其生产繁简程度如何，一律按全价计算工业总产值；凡来料加工，允许按加工费计算工业总产值。原规定则视生产加工的繁简程度不同，规定哪些行业按全价，哪些行业按加工费计算工业总产值。

自制半成品、在产品期末期初差额价值的计算原则不同：新规定要求，凡会计产品成本核算时计算了成本的差额价值，总产值中就应包括，否则可不包括；原规定则按生产周期六个月的界限区分，凡生产周期六个月以上的企业，总产值计算中应包括这部分差额价值，否则可不包括。

计算价格不同：新规定按不含增值税（销项税额）的价格计算；原规定则按含增值税（销项税额）的价格计算。

工业销售产值

是以货币表现的工业企业在一定时期内销售的、本企业生产的工业产品总量。包括已销售的成品、半成品价值，对外提供的工业性作业价值和对本单位基本建设部门、生活福利部门等提供的产品和工业性作业及自制设备的价值。工业销售产值依循的是以产品所有权转移为计算原则，因此，已销售的成品、半成品不论是本期生产的、还是上期生产的，只要是本期销售出去的均包括在内。对外提供的工业性作业是指企业按合同对外提供的工业性劳务。

工业销售产值的计算范围、计算价格和计算方法与工业总产值一致，但两者计算的基础不同，工业销售产值计算的基础是产品销售总量，工业总产值计算的基础是工业产品生产总量。

出口交货值

是指工业企业交给外贸部门或自营（委托）出口（包括销往香港、澳门地区、台湾省）的产品价值；批量销于国内或在过境批量出口等但用外汇价格结算的产品价值；外商来样、来料加工，来件装配和补偿贸易等生产，分别参照计算总产值的规定要求按全价或加工费计算的价值。

大、中、小型企业

根据工业和信息化部、国家统计局、国家发展改革委、财政部《关于印发中小企业划型标准规定的通知》（工信部联企业【2011】300号），依据从业人员、营业收入、资产总额等指标或替代指标，将我国的企业划分为大型、中型、小型、微型等四种类型，原划分办法废止。工业企业划型标准见下表：

指标名称	计量单位	大　型	中　型	小　型	微　型
从业人员（X）	人	X≥1000	300≤X＜1000	20≤X＜300	X＜20
主营业务收入（Y）	万元	Y≥40000	2000≤Y＜40000	300≤Y＜2000	Y＜300

说明：大型、中型和小型企业必须同时满足所列指标下限，否则下划一档；微型企业只须满足所列指标中的一项即可。

独立核算工业企业、非独立核算工业生产单位

工业企业按其行政和财务是否独立，分为独立核算工业企业和非独立核算工业生产单位。

独立核算工业企业应同时具备下列三个条件：（1）行政上有独立的组织形式；（2）经济上独立核算，自负盈亏，编制独立的资金平衡表（或资产负债表）；（3）有权与其他单位签订合同，并在银行设有独立帐户。独立核算工业企业不论是单一性生产或联合性生产的企业，均以整个企业作为一个基层单位进行统计，而不按分厂、车间统计。

非独立核算工业生产单位是指不同时具备独立核算工业企业三个条件，附设于其他企业、事业、机关、团体、学校、科研机构、部队等单位的工业生产单位。非独立核算工业生产单位必须同时具备下列三个条件，才可列入工业统计范围，即：（1）有固定的生产场所和生产设备；（2）有固定的生产工人和学徒在10人以上；（3）一般单位常年生产，季节性生产的单位全年开工时间在三个月以上。

资产总计

资产是指企业拥有或者控制的能以货币计量的经济资源，包括各种财产、债权和其他权利。资产按其流动性（即资产的变现能力和支付能力）划分为：流动资产、长期投资、固定资产、无形资产、递延资产和其他资产。该指标根据企业会计“资产负债表”中“资产总计”项目的期末数增列。

流动资产合计

指可以在一年或者超过一年的一个营业周期内变现或者耗用的资产，包括现金及各种存款、短期投资、应收及预付货款、存款等。

流动资产平均余额

指企业在报告期内全部流动资产的平均余额。

固定资产净值年平均余额

指固定资产净值在报告期内余额的平均数。计算公式为：

固定资产净值年平均余额＝1至12月各月月初、月末固定资产净值之和/24

该指标根据“资产负债表”中“固定资产原价”、“累计折旧”指标的期初、期末数计算填列。

固定资产净值指固定资产原价减去历年已提折旧额后的净额。计算公式为：

固定资产净值＝固定资产原价－累计折旧

负债合计

负债合计是指企业所承担的能以货币计量，将以资产或劳务偿付的债务总计。负债一般按偿还期长短分为流动负债和长期负债。流动负债合计是指企业在一年内或超过一年的一个营业周期内偿还的债务；长期负债合计是指偿还期在一年以上或者超过一年的一个营业周期内偿还债

务。

所有者权益

指企业投资人对企业净资产的所有权。企业净资产等于企业全部资产减去全部负债后的余额，包括企业投资人对企业的最初投入的实际到位的资产及资本公积金、盈余公积金和未分配利润。所有者权益合计数小于零，表示企业资不抵债。

利润总额

指企业生产经营活动的最终成果，是企业在一定时期内实现的盈亏相抵后的利润总额（亏损以"－"号表示），它等于营业利润加上补贴收入加上投资收益加上营业外净收入再加上以前年度损益调整。

总资产贡献率

反映企业全部资产的获利能力，是企业经营业绩和管理水平的集中体现，是评价和考核企业盈利能力的核心指标。计算公式为：

总资产贡献率（%）＝利润总额＋税金总额＋利息支出/平均资金总额×100%

公式中：税金总额为产品销售税金及附加与应缴增值税之和；平均资产总额为期初期末资产之和的算术平均值。

资产负债率

该指标既反映企业经营风险的大小，也反映企业利用债权人提供的资金从事经营活动的能力。计算公式为：

资产负债率（%）＝负债总额/资产总额×100%

资产与负债均为报告期期末数。

流动资产周转次数

指一定时期内流动资产完成的周转次数，反映投入工业企业流动资金的周转速度。计算公式为：

流动资产周转次数＝产品销售收入/全部流动资产平均余额

公式中：全部流动资产平均余额为期初和期末的流动资产之和的算术平均值。

产品销售率

该指标反映工业产品已实现销售的程度，是分析工业产销衔接情况、研究工业产品满足社会需求的指标。计算公式为：

产品销售率（%）＝工业销售产值/工业总产值（现价）×100%

资本保值增值率

该指标反映企业净资产的变动状况，是企业发展能力的集中体现。计算公式为：

资本保值增值率＝报告期期末所有者权益/上年同期期末所有者权益

所有者权益等于资产总计减负债总计。

成本费用利润率

反映企业投入的生产成本及费用的经济效益，同时也反映企业降低成本所取得的经济效益。计算公式为：

成本费用利润（%）＝利润总额/成本费用总额×100%

公式中：成本费用总额为产品销售成本、销售费用、管理费用、财务费用之和。

全员劳动生产率

该指标反映企业的生产效率和劳动投入的经济效益。计算公式为：

$$全员劳动生产率（元/人）=\frac{工业增加值}{全部从业人员平均人数}$$

EXPLANATORY NOTES TO MAJOR STATISTICAL INDICATORS

Industry

Industry refers to the material production sector which is engaged in extraction of natural resources and processing and reprocessing of minerals and agricultural products, including (1) extraction of natural resources, such as mining, salt production (but not including hunting and fishing); (2) processing and reprocessing of farm and sideline produces, such as rice husking, flour milling, wine making, oil pressing, silk reeling, spinning and weaving, and leather making; (3) manufacture of industrial products, such as steel making, iron smelting, chemicals manufacturing, petroleum processing, machine building, timber processing; water and gas production and electricity generation and supply; (4) repairing of industrial products such as the repairing of machinery and means of transport (including cars).

Prior to 1984, the rural industry run by villages and cooperative organizations under village was classified into agriculture. Since 1984, it has been grouped into industry.

Units of industrial statistics survey corporate industrial enterprises with independent accounting system.

Corporate industrial enterprises with independent accounting system refer to enterprises engaging in industrial production activities, which meet the following requirements: ①They are established legally, having their own names, organizations, location, able to take civil liability; ②They possess and use their assets independently, assume liabilities, and are entitled to sign contracts with other units; ③They are financially independent and compile their own balance sheets.

Light Industry

refers to the industry that produces consumer goods and hand tools. It consists of two categories, depending on the materials used:

(1) Industries using farm products as raw materials. These are branches of light industry which directly or indirectly use farm products as basic raw materials, including the manufacture of food and beverages, tobacco processing, textile, clothing, fur and leather manufacturing, paper making, printing, etc.

(2) Industries using non farm products as raw materials. These are branches of light industry which use manufactured goods as raw materials, including the manufacture of cultural, educational articles and sports goods, chemicals, synthetic fiber, chemical products for daily use, glass products for daily use, metal products for daily use, hand tools, medical apparatus and instruments, and the manufacture of cultural and clerical machinery.

Heavy Industry

refers to the industry which produces capital goods, and provides various sectors of the national economy with necessary material and technical basis. It consists of the following three branches according to the purpose of production or the use of products:

(1) Mining, quarrying and logging industry refers to the industry that extracts natural resources, including extraction of petroleum, coal, metal and non-metal ores.

(2) Raw materials industry refers to the industry that provides various sectors of the national economy with raw materials, fuels and power. It includes smelting and processing of metals, coking and coke chemistry, chemical materials and building materials such as cement, plywood, and power, petroleum refining and coal dressing.

(3) Manufacturing industry refers to the industry that processes raw materials. It includes machine building industry which equips sectors of the national economy, industries of metal structure and cement products, industries producing means of agricultural production, such as chemical fertilizers and pesticides. According to the above principle of classification, the repairing trades which are engaged primarily in repairing products of heavy industry are classified into heavy industry while these engaged in repairing products of light industry are classified into light industry.

Gross Output Value of Industry

(1) Definition: Gross industrial output value is the total volume of final industrial products produced and industrial services provided during a given period. It reflects the total achievements and overall scale of industrial production during a given period.

(2) Principles for calculation: Statistics on industrial production follow the principle that all products produced by the enterprises and accepted during the reference period are to be included no matter whether they are sold or not during the reference period.

Determination of final products follow the principle that all products that are included in the calculation of grow industrial output value are the final products of the enterprise which have been accepted through quality check and require no further processing. If an enterprise has intermediate (semi-finished) products to sell, these intermediate products are considered as the final products of the enterprise.

Gross industrial output value is calculated following the principle of factory approach, i. e. industrial enterprise is used as the basic accounting unit in calculating the gross industrial output value. By this approach, value of the same product is not to be double counted, and the output value of different workshops (branch factories) should not be added. However, this approach does not exclude the possibility of double counting between enterprises.

(3) Content and calculation method: The old definition of gross industrial output value was modified duringthe national industrial census in 1995. The revised (new) definition of gross industrial output value consists of 3 components: value of the finished products during the reference period, income from external processing, and value of change in semi-finished products at the end and at the beginning of the reference period.

Value of the finished products during the reference period: refers to the value of all finished (semi-finished) industrial products that are produced during the reference period without the need for further processing, checked for acceptance, packed and put into the warehouse of the enterprise, including the value of own-produced equipment and the value of products provided to the projects under construction of the enterprise, and to other non-industrial or welfare units. Value of finished products during the reference period is calculated by the quantity of products produced using own materials multiplied by the average unit prices at which products are sold (excluding value-added tax). Own-produced equipment and products produced for own use are value at cost prices as in the case of enterprise accounting. Value of finished products does not include the value of finished products (semi-finished products) that are produced using the materials from the clients who make the orders.

Income from external processing: refers to income from contracted external processing of industrial products (including processing of industrial products using materials from the clients), and the income from industrial repairing work provided to other units. Income from external processing is calculated using information from the item "products sales income" in the enterprise accounting at the prices excluding value-added tax.

For income from services such as processing, repairing and installation of equipment provided to non-industrial units within the enterprise, if the accounting work of the enterprise is good enough to separate it from other records, and the share of such services is significant, it should also be included in the income from external processing.

Value of change in semi-finished products at the end and at the beginning of the reference period: refers to the value of change in semi-finished products at the end and at the beginning of the reference period, which generally can be obtained from accounting records of enterprises. If the enterprise accounting excludes the cost of semi-finished products, then it should not be included in the gross industrial output value, and vice versa.

(4) Changes in the coverage and method of calculation of gross industrial output value: Prior to 1984, the value of rural industry run by villages was classified into agriculture instead of industry. Since 1984, it has been included in the gross industrial output value.

Method of calculation for the gross industrial output value was modified in the industrial census in 1995. The difference in the new method as compared with the old one is outlined below:

Principle in using full value vs. processing fee: The new method stipulates that all products produced using own materials are to be calculated with full value in reporting the gross industrial output value irrespective of sophistication of production, and for external processing, it allows calculation using processing fee. In the old method, however, the use of full value or processing fee was determined by the degree of sophistication of production in different branches of industries.

Principle in determining the value of change in semi-finished products: The new method requires that value of the change in semi-finished products should be included in the gross industrial output value if it is included in the accounting record of the enterprise, otherwise it should not be included. By the old method, it is determined by the type of enterprises in terms of production cycle. If the production cycle is over 6 months, the value of change in semi-finished products is included in the gross industrial output value, otherwise it is excluded.

Difference in prices: The new method uses prices excluding value-added tax in the calculation of gross industrial output value, while the old method used prices including value-added tax.

Sales Output Value of Industry

refers to total sales value of products produced by industrial enterprises during a given period, including sales of finished goods, value of semi-products, value of industrial services provided to other units, value of products provided for capital construction sector, welfare sector and value of industrial services provided and self produced equipment within enterprises. Sales of finished goods and semi-products in current period are taken into account regardless of their production period.

The coverage, pricing, and calculation method for sales output value of industry are the same as for gross output value of industry except that the former is based on sales of products and the latter is based on the output of products.

Export Delivery Value of Industry

refers to the product value which industrial enterprises deliver to Foreign Trade Department, or value of products which are exported directly from producers (including the sales to Hong Kong, Macao and Taiwan); the product value, (at foreign exchange rate,) of domestic batch sale or transit batch export; full price or processing fee of the production with design, materials, assembling parts supplied by foreign businessmen and compensation trade.

Large, Medium and Small Enterprises

According to the Notice of the Ministry of Industry and Information Technology, National Bureau of Statistics, National Development and Reform Commission and the Ministry of Finance on printing and distributing the classification standard for middle and small enterprises (<2011 > No. 300), we will divide our national enterprises into four kinds that are large, middle, small and mini in accordance with the indicators or substitute indicators such as employed persons, operation income and total assets. The former method for classification will be discarded. The classification standard for industrial enterprises are shown as followed.

Indicators	Unit	Large	Middle	Small	Mini
Employed Persons(X)	Persons	X≥1000	300≤X<1000	20≤X<300	X<20
Main Operation Income(Y)	10 000 yuan	Y≥40000	2000≤Y<40000	300≤Y<2000	Y<300

Note: Large, middle and small enterprises must meet all of the lowest limit of the listed indicators, or they will be classified into the lower kind, respectively. Mini enterprises can meet only one of the listed indicators.

Industrial Enterprises with Independent Accounting

Systems and Industrial Production Units with Non-Independent Accounting Systems.

Depending on whether they have independent administration and accounting, industrial enterprises can be divided into industrial enterprises with independent accounting system and industrial production units with non-independent accounting system. An industrial enterprise with independent accounting system shall operate simultaneously under the following three conditions: (1) having an independent organization in terms of administration; (2) economically having independent accounting, taking care of its own profits and losses, and filing independent balance sheets; and (3) enjoying the right to sign contracts with other units and to open independent bank accounts. An industrial enterprise with independent accounting system, no matter under a unitary management or cooperative operation, shall be counted as single grassroots unit in statistics and its branch factories and workshops shall not be calculated separately.

An industrial production unit with non-independent accounting system is an industrial production unit which does not operate simultaneously under the above mentioned three conditions of industrial enterprises with independent accounting systems and is attached to an enterprise, institution, government department, organization, school, scientific research institution, or army unit. An industrial production with non-independent accounting system unit can be included into the industrial statistics only when it operates simultaneously under the following three conditions: (1) having fixed production sites and production equipment; (2) having more than 10 permanent workers and apprentices; and (3) operating all year round if it's a normal production unit or operating more than three months a year if it's a seasonal production unit.

Aggregate Assets

Total Assets refer to all economic resources, in monetary terms, that is owned or controlled by enterprises, including properties, creditors equity and other economic rights of all forms. Classified by the degree of equitability, total assets include circulating assets, long-term investment, fixed assets, intangible assets and deferred assets, and other assets. Data on this indicator can be obtained by the year-end figures of total assets in the Assets and Liability Table of accounting records of enterprises.

Total of Working Capitals

Total of Working Capitals refer to capitals which can be cashed in or spent or consumed in an operating cycle of one year or over one year, including cash, all kinds of deposits, short term investment, receivable and payable payment for goods or deposits.

Average Value of Working Capitals

Average Value of Working Capitals refers to the average value of all working capitals of the enterprise during the reference period.

Annual Average of Net Value of Fixed Assets

refer to average of the net value of fixed assets during the reference period, calculated with the following formula:

Annual Average of Net Value of Fixed Assets = sum of net value of fixed assets at the beginning and at the end of each month from January to December / 24.

Information on this indicator can be obtained from the beginning and ending figures of the original value of fixed assets and cumulative depreciation from the Assets and Liability Table of enterprises.

Net value of fixed assets refers to the original value of fixed assets minus depreciation over the years, i. e. :

Net value of fixed assets = original value of fixed assets-cumulative depreciation

Aggregate Liabilities

Aggregate liabilities refer to the total debts of an enterprise which can be calculated in monetary term and will be repaid in the forms of assets or service. Usually, the debts are divided into liquid liability and long-term debt according to the length of the payback period. The liquid liability is the debt that an enterprise will pay back during an operation cycle which is either shorter or longer than a year. The long-term debt refers to a debt whose payback period is longer than a year or which will be repaid during an operation cycle that is longer than a year.

Creditors' Equity

Creditors' Equity refers to investors ownership of net assets of the enterprise, which is equal to the total assets of the enterprise minus its total liabilities, including the primary input actually received at the enterprise from investors, capital accumulation fund, surplus accumulation fund and undistributed profit. When the total of creditors' equity is less than zero, that indicates the liability of the enterprise is larger that its assets.

Total Profits

Total Profits refer to the final achievements of production and operation of the enterprises, represented by the total profits after deducting losses (loss is expressed by the negative figure). It is the sum of profits from operation, income from subsidies, investment earnings, net income from activities other than operation, and adjustment of profits and losses of previous years.

Ratio of Profits, Taxes and Interests to Average Assets

Ratio of Profits, Taxes and Interests to Average Assets reflects the profit-making capability of all assets of the enterprise and is a key indicator manifesting the performance and management and evaluating the profit-making potential of the enterprise. It is calculated as follows:

Ratio of Profits, Taxes and Interests to Average Assets (%) = [(total profits + total taxes + interest payment) / average assets] ×100%

In the above formula, total taxes is the sum of tax and extra charges on the sales of products and value-added tax payable; and average assets is the arithmetic mean of the sum of beginning assets and ending assets.

Ratio of Debts to Asset

Ratio of Debts to Assets reflect both the operation risk and the capability of the enterprise in making use of the capital from the creditors. It is calculated as follows:

Ratio of Debts to Assets (%) = (total debts / total assets) × 100%

Both assets and debts are figures at the end of the reference period.

Turnover of Working Capital

Turnover of Working Capital refers to the number of times of turnover of working capital in a given period of time, which reflects the speed of the turnover of working capital of industrial enterprises, and is calculated as follows:

Turnover of Working Capital = (sales revenue of products) / (average balance of total working capital)

In the above formula, average balance of total working capital refers to the arithmetic mean of the sum of working capital at the beginning and at the end of the reference period.

Ratio of Sales to Gross Output Value

Ratio of Sales to Gross Output Value reflects the degree at which industrial products are sold. It helps to analyze the linkage between production and sales and the extent of the needs of the society that has been met by the supply of industrial products. It is calculated as follows:

Ratio of Sales to Gross Output Value = (Industrial sales / Gross industrial output value at current prices) ×100%

Capital Maintenance and Appreciation Rate

Capital Maintenance and Appreciation Rate reflects the changes of an enterprise's net assets. It epitomizes the growth capability of an enterprise. Its calculating formula is:

Capital maintenance and appreciation rate = Ownership equity at the end of the reporting period/Ownership equity at the same period of the previous year. Ownership equity is the result of total assets minus total liabilities.

Ratio of Profits to Total Industrial Costs

Ratio of Profits to Total Industrial Costs refers to the ratio of profits realized in a given period to the total costs in the same period, which reflects the economic efficiency of input cost and is calculated as follows:

Ratio of Profits to Total Industrial Cost(%) = (total profits/ total costs) ×100%

Total costs in the above formula is the sum of cost of products sold, marketing cost, management cost and financial cost.

Overall Labour Productivity

Overall Labour Productivity is an indicator reflecting the production efficiency of an enterprise and the economic efficiency of its labour input, calculated by the formula:

Overall Labour Productivity (yuan/person) = industrial value-added/average of all persons engaged.

第七篇

CHAPTER 7

建筑业

CONSTRUCTION

表7－1　主要年份建筑业企业主要指标

指　标 Indicators		单　位 Unit	1995
施工企业单位数	Number of Construction Enterprises	个 unit	243
年末从业人员数	Employed Persons (Year End)	人 person	125 627
全年从业人员平均数	Annual Average Employed Persons	人 person	140 994
建筑业总产值	Gross Output Value of Construction	万元 10 000 yuan	1 045 601
#建筑工程	Construction Projects	万元 10 000 yuan	905 848
安装工程	Installation Projects	万元 10 000 yuan	110 763
竣工产值	Output Value of Construction Projects Completed	万元 10 000 yuan	446 202
房屋建筑面积	Floor Space of Buildings		
施工面积	Floor Space Under Construction	万平方米 10 000 sq·m	1 042.05
#本年新开工	New Start in Current Year	万平方米 10 000 sq·m	285.02
竣工面积	Floor Space Completed	万平方米 10 000 sq·m	290.25
#住　宅	Housing	万平方米 10 000 sq·m	150.63
全员劳动生产率	Overall Labor Productivity	元/人 yuan/person	74 159
房屋建筑面积竣工率	Ratio of Floor Space Completed over That under Construction	%	27.9
平均每个职工竣工房屋面积	Floor Space Completed Per Staff Member	平方米/人 sq·m/person	20.59

注：建筑业总产值为建筑业企业自行完成的施工产值。
Note: Gross output value of construction refers to the output value of construction completed by construction enterprises themselves.

Major Indicators of Construction Industry in Main Years

2000	2005	2007	2008	2009	2010	2011	2012
367	398	469	522	680	699	720	651
93 753	159 099	123 957	181 687	293 496	253 822	259 056	268 981
116 722	208 807	273 887	203 498	408 349	361 140	424 530	358 750
935 731	3 353 790	5 416 041	6 607 274	8 938 091	9 801 257	11 353 474	12 231 885
886 356	2 599 981	4 655 203	5 421 540	7 323 235	8 001 415	9 746 424	10 415 352
115 164	643 346	611 949	1 020 528	760 443	1 526 037	1 440 514	1 602 576
786 808	2 322 347	3 319 285	3 507 229	5 335 389	6 858 981	5 650 019	6 128 065
1 149.25	3 009.91	3 798.19	4 324.58	6 237.41	6 886.55	8 451.28	9 976.65
426.18	1 291.18	1 430.47	1 569.64	2 153.29	2 501.17	2 675.90	3 040.28
520.61	903.45	1 066.82	877.13	1 611.78	1 641.86	1 520.70	1 619.20
350.65	523.94	469.87	477.70	724.81	695.52	677.63	843.41
80 167	160 617	197 747	324 685	218 884	271 398	267 436	340 961
45.3	30.0	28.1	20.3	25.8	23.8	18.0	16.2
44.60	43.27	38.95	43.10	39.47	45.46	35.82	45.13

表7-2 建筑业企业主要指标
(2012)

指 标	Indicators	企业单位数(个) Number of Enterprises (unit)	年末从业人员数(人) Employed Persons at Year-end (person)	年从业人员平均数(人) Annual Average Employed Persons (person)	建筑业总产值(万元) Gross Output Value of Construction (10 000 yuan)	竣工产值(万元) Output Value of Completed Construction Projects (10 000 yuan)
合 计	**Total**	**651**	**268 981**	**358 750**	**12 231 885**	**6 128 065**
#外省市	Non-Shanghai	27	12 581	12 922	261 305	40 627
按注册登记类型分	**By Type of Registration**					
内 资	Domestic Investment	619	256 685	341 761	11 222 919	5 604 265
国 有	State-owned	26	11 727	26 538	1 083 092	356 957
集 体	Collective-owned	11	1 017	1 348	44 275	50 753
股份合作	Share-holding	4	402	324	6 599	482
联 营	Jointly Operated	4	516	502	13 573	15 051
国有独资公司	Wholly state-owned Companies	8	16 193	20 579	587 007	429 992
责任有限公司	Companies with Limited Liabilities	87	128 231	122 220	5 853 087	2 483 628
股份有限公司	Companies Limited by Shares	13	11 541	31 060	741 169	611 272
私 营	Private	466	87 058	139 190	2 894 117	1 656 130
港澳台商投资	HK/Macao/Taiwan Invested	13	2 601	3 817	457 064	101 331
外商投资	Foreigner Invested	19	9 695	13 172	551 902	422 469
按行业分	**By Sector**					
房屋和土木工程建筑业	Housing and Civil Engineering Construction	184	197 342	253 615	7 758 119	4 092 333
建筑安装业	Installation	165	34 138	57 918	2 256 475	890 942
建筑装饰业	Decoration	142	16 050	27 918	1 129 898	598 698
其他建筑业	Other Constructions	160	21 451	19 299	1 087 393	546 092
按建筑业资质等级分	**By Qualification of Construction Industry**					
#特 级	Special Grade	6	105 425	114 375	4 958 202	2 249 177
一 级	Grade Ⅰ	98	78 992	107 534	4 138 389	1 895 796
二 级	Grade Ⅱ	185	52 994	65 226	2 146 757	1 320 152
三 级	Grade Ⅲ	354	31 117	71 615	944 400	635 343

注：建筑业总产值为建筑业企业自行完成的施工产值；建筑业资质等级为新标准资质。

Note: Gross Output Value of Construction refers to the output value of construction completed by construction enterprises themselves. Qualification of construction industry refers to the qualification under new standards.

Major Indicators of Construction Enterprises

房屋建筑施工面积（万平方米）Floor Space Under Construction (10 000 sq·m)	#本年新开工 New Start in Current Year	房屋竣工面积（万平方米）Floor Space Completed (10 000 sq·m)	#住宅 Residential Housing	全员劳动生产率（元/人）Overall Labor Productivity (yuan/person)	平均每个职工竣工房屋面积（平方米/人）Floor Space Completed Per Staff Member (sq·m/person)	房屋建筑面积竣工率（%）Ratio of Floor Space Completed (%)
9 976.65	**3 040.28**	**1 619.20**	**843.41**	**340 961**	**45.13**	**16.2**
198.32	56.89	5.51	1.97	202 217	4.26	2.8
9 793.77	2 964.62	1526.03	843.41	328 385	44.65	15.6
133.70	31.69	13.77	5.39	408 129	5.19	10.3
18.09	9.06	10.74	4.37	328 450	79.67	59.4
				203 672		
1.87	1.87	1.87		270 378	37.25	100.0
329.17	139.65	100.26	78.22	285 246	48.72	30.5
7 025.63	2 129.96	737.62	429.33	478 898	60.35	10.5
981.07	232.94	205.05	84.45	238 625	66.02	20.9
1 304.24	419.45	456.72	241.65	207 926	32.81	35.0
				1 197 443		
182.88	75.66	93.17		418 996	70.73	50.9
9 818.61	2 962.98	1 559.87	824.89	305 901	61.51	15.9
83.71	23.75	38.66	12.28	389 598	6.67	46.2
37.59	25.76	17.40	6.24	404 720	6.23	46.3
36.74	27.79	3.27		563 445	1.69	8.9
7 595.40	2 244.24	807.35	438.34	433 504	70.59	10.6
1 282.27	456.97	386.03	246.50	384 845	35.90	30.1
888.12	232.40	306.89	125.87	329 126	47.05	34.6
210.86	106.66	118.93	32.70	131 872	16.61	56.4

表7－3　建筑业财务报表
(2012)

单位:万元

指　标	Indicators	合　计 Total	内　资 Domestic Investment
企业单位数(个)	**Number of Enterprises (unit)**	**613**	**582**
年末资产负债	**Balance Sheet at Year-end**		
资产总计	Total Assets	16 461 010	14 661 764
#流动资产	Floating Assets	12 442 174	10 816 252
固定资产	Fixed Assets	1 318 564	1 171 123
固定资产原价	Initial Value of Fixed Assets	1 917 504	1 793 528
累计折旧	Accumulated Depreciation	732 390	693 721
#本年折旧	Depreciation This Year	111 048	95 664
负债总计	Total Liabilities	12 246 332	10 732 081
流动负债	Current Liabilities	11 333 727	9 893 531
非流动负债	Non-current Liabilities	912 605	838 550
所有者权益总计	Total Rights and Interests of Owners	4 214 678	3 929 683
损益及分配	**Profit and Loss and Their Distribution**		
主营业务收入	Income of Main Operations	14 178 421	12 866 363
主营业务成本	Cost of Main Operations	12 594 831	11 500 974
主营业务税金及附加	Taxes and Additional Taxes of Main Operations	378 067	362 476
管理费用	Administrative Expenses	496 492	420 860
#税　金	Taxes	8 767	8 059
财务费用	Financial Expenses	111 808	102 233
营业利润	Operation Profits	438 870	367 647
利润总额	Total Profits	505 021	398 785

注：以上财务数据不包含外省市进沪建筑业企业。
Note: The above-mentioned financial data exclude construction enterprises from other provinces and cities that enter the construction market in Shanghai.

Financial Statements of Construction Industry

(10 000yuan)

国有 State-owned	集体 Collective-owned	股份合作 Share-holding	联营 Jointly-operated	国有独资公司 Wholly state-owned company	责任有限公司 Companies with Limited Liability	股份有限公司 Companies Limited by Shares	私营 Private	港澳台商投资 Hong kong/ Macao/ Taiwan Investment	外商投资 FIE
19	**10**	**4**	**4**	**7**	**78**	**8**	**452**	**12**	**19**
2 629 733	58 793	22 013	24 293	1 013 407	6 291 415	1 406 154	3 215 956	732 660	1 066 586
1 578 977	50 067	18 720	15 608	418 504	4 911 952	1 023 306	2 799 118	615 503	1 010 419
74 679	1 898	3 237	2 560	491 221	311 560	52 452	233 516	102 114	45 327
136 682	6 115	4 397	3 524	694 511	498 244	65 461	384 594	54 136	69 840
65 771	4 264	1 160	1 177	203 526	215 136	27 177	175 510	14 078	24 591
4 647	445	20	136	22 393	36 015	3 644	28 364	1 938	13 446
2 075 293	33 628	12 292	12 173	460 820	5 158 070	1 051 391	1 928 414	597 213	917 038
1 579 539	33 473	12 292	12 173	417 620	5 135 509	871 984	1 830 941	562 110	878 086
495 754	155			43 200	22 561	179 407	97 473	35 103	38 952
554 440	25 165	9 721	12 120	552 587	1 133 345	354 763	1 287 542	135 447	149 548
1 344 324	48 278	5 254	11 571	671 385	6 369 467	1 431 030	2 985 054	618 723	693 335
939 964	40 255	4 950	10 575	595 213	5 841 181	1 390 464	2 678 372	493 228	600 629
34 852	1 348	153	315	10 469	198 215	32 140	84 984	4 512	11 079
47 833	3 597	603	1 206	11 995	173 085	25 315	157 226	28 747	46 885
682	58		15	223	2 371	1 378	3 332	288	420
43 218	32	107	35	2 983	30 933	7 582	17 343	8 381	1 194
49 453	3 476	558	450	53 826	185 096	31 395	43 393	44 502	26 721
52 063	3 634	544	99	55 548	197 107	36 240	53 550	79 259	26 977

主要统计指标解释

建筑业总产值

建筑业总产值是以货币形式表现的建筑业企业在一定时期内生产的建筑业产品和提供的服务的总和。建筑业总产值包括：

（1）建筑工程产值：指列入建筑工程预算内的各种工程价值。

（2）安装工程产值：指设备安装工程价值，不包括被安装设备本身价值。

（3）其他产值：建筑业总产值中除建筑工程、安装工程以外的产值。包括房屋构筑物修理产值、非标准设备制造产值、总包企业向分包企业收取的管理费以及不能明确划分的施工活动所完成的产值。

a. 房屋构筑物修理产值：指房屋和构筑物修理所完成的产值，但不包括被修理房屋、构筑物本身价值和生产设备的修理产值。

b. 非标准设备制造产值：指加工制造没有定型的非标准生产设备的加工费和原材料价值（如化工厂、炼油厂用的各种罐、槽，矿井生产统一使用的各种漏斗、三角槽、阀门等）以及附属加工厂为本企业承建工程制作的非标准设备的价值。

房屋建筑施工面积

房屋建筑施工面积指在报告期内施过工的全部房屋建筑面积，包括本期新开工的房屋面积、上期施工跨入本期继续施工的房屋面积、上期停缓建在本期恢复施工的房屋面积、本期竣工的房屋面积及本期施工后又停缓建的房屋面积。

房屋建筑竣工面积

房屋建筑竣工面积 指在报告期内房屋建筑按照设计要求全部完工，达到了使用条件，经验收鉴定合格的房屋建筑面积。

房屋建筑面积竣工率

指一定时期内房屋竣工面积占同期房屋施工面积的比率。该指标从房屋建筑施工速度的角度反映投资效果的指标。

EXPLANATORY NOTES TO MAJOR STATISTICAL INDICATORS

Gross Output Value of Construction

Gross Output Value of Construction refers to total of construction products and services, expressed in money terms, produced or rendered by (completed by) construction enterprises during a given period of time. It includes:

(1) Output value of construction projects, that is the value of projects covered by the project budgets;

(2) Output value of installation projects, that is the value of the installation of equipment, (excluding the value of the equipment to be installed);

(3) Output value of other projects refers to other output value of gross output value of construction industry besides construction and installation projects. It includes the output value of building repairing, nonstandard equipment manufacturing, the management fees going from subcontractor to original contractor and other construction output value which can not be measure off definitely.

a. Output value of repair of buildings and structures, that is the value created through the repairs of buildings or structures, but does not include the value of buildings or structures being repaired and the value of the repair of production equipment;

b. Output value of manufactured non - standard equipment that is the value of non - standard production equipment (including raw materials and manufacturing cost) made for the construction project, irrespective of whether the equipment is manufactured on the construction site or by subsidiary workshops.

Floor Space of Buildings under Construction

Floor Space of Buildings under Construction refers to floor space of buildings under construction during the reference period, including newly started buildings, buildings started earlier and continued during the reference period, and buildings suspended earlier but restarted during the reference period, buildings completed during the reference period, and buildings under construction and then suspended during the reference period.

Floor Space of Buildings Completed

Floor Space of Buildings Completed refers to the floor space of buildings that are completed in the reference period in accordance with the requirements of the design, up to the standard for putting them into use, and have been checked and accepted by concerned departments as qualified ones.

Completion Rate of Floor Space of Buildings

Completion Rate of Floor Space of Buildings refers to the ratio of the floor space of buildings completed in certain period of time to the floor space of buildings under construction in the same period. This indicator reflects the investment result from the perspective of the speed of construction.

第八篇

CHAPTER 8

金融业及要素市场

FINANCE AND BANKING,
AND FACTOR MARKETS

表8-1　各类金融机构数
Statistics of all Kinds of Financial Institutions

单位:个　　(unit)

指　标	Indicators	2010	2011	2012
总　计	**Total**	**649**	**692**	**737**
银行类机构合计	**Subtotal of Banks**	**211**	**221**	**230**
中资银行	Chinese Banks	29	32	34
外资银行法人行	Foreign Banks and Corporate Banks	18	18	18
外资银行分行	Branches of Foreign Banks	57	61	61
外资银行代表处	Representative Offices of Foreign Banks	60	63	68
银行营运中心	Bank Operation Centers	23	24	24
非银行金融机构	Non-banking Financial Institutions	24	23	25
证券类机构合计	**Subtotal of Securities Institutions**	**261**	**276**	**290**
中资证券(包括中介机构)	Chinese Securities Institutions (including intermediary organs)	68	75	80
外资证券(包括代表处)	Foreign Securities Institutions (including representative offices)	53	55	55
基金公司	Fund Companies	46	49	54
期货公司	Futures Companies	81	83	85
非证券金融机构	Non-securities Financial Institutions	13	14	16
保险机构合计	**Subtotal of Insurance Companies**	**177**	**195**	**217**
中资保险(集团)	Chinese Insurance Companies (Groups)	46	49	52
外资保险	Foreign Insurance Companies	27	29	31
外资保险代表处	Representative Offices of Foreign Insurance Companies	23	27	31
保险中介	Agencies of Insurance Companies	76	84	94
保险营运中心	Insurance Operation Centers	5	6	9

表8-2 主要年份中资银行人民币存贷款年末余额
Chinese Banks' Year-end RMB Balance of Deposits and Loans in Main Years

单位:亿元 (100 million yuan)

指 标	Indicators	1990	2000	2005	2010	2011	2012
存款余额合计	**Total Deposit Balance**	**36.48**	**1 046.81**	**2 915.41**	**8 848.87**	**10 243.30**	**11 357.76**
#企业存款	Enterprise Deposits	9.67	644.79	1 530.99	5 239.12	5 923.46	6 417.20
居民储蓄存款	Resident Savings Deposits	20.62	360.99	1 105.96	2 943.49	3 375.71	3 886.60
其他存款	Others	1.66	10.61	166.38	427.38	667.37	748.29
贷款余额合计	**Total Loan Balance**	**28.19**	**891.59**	**2 674.76**	**6 434.95**	**7 238.06**	**7 901.57**
#企业贷款	Enterprise Loans			2 014.23	5 343.68	5 929.33	6 373.57
#短期贷款	Short Term Loans			716.01	1 504.28	1 615.62	1 996.58
中长期贷款	Medium and Long Term Loans			1 298.22	3 839.40	4 313.71	4 376.99
票据融资	Securities Financing			193.73	82.59	157.07	286.51
个人贷款	Individual Loans			464.40	1 007.62	1 150.64	1 233.31
#住房按揭贷款	Housing Mortgage Loans			431.28	888.58	935.71	977.59
汽车消费贷款	Car Loans			4.08	14.76	25.60	29.50

表8-3　外资银行主要指标
(2012)

指标	Indicators	单位数(个) Enterprises (unit)	从业人数(人) Employed Persons (person)	普通贷款(万美元) Ordinary Loans (USD 10 000)
总　计	**Total**	**80**	**17 498**	**2 006 713**
按各大洲分	**By Continent**			
亚洲地区	Asia	41	10 883	1 387 075
欧洲地区	Europe	25	4 254	326 278
美洲地区	America	9	2 033	208 382
大洋洲地区	Oceania Region	4	312	84 883
非洲地区	Africa	1	16	95
按进驻各大厦分	**By Mansion Where Enterprises Handle Their Businesses**			
环球金融中心大厦	Shanghai World Financial Center	13	2 128	351 574
汇亚大厦	Azia Center	7	1 551	341 553
金茂大厦	Jinmao Building	7	449	222 883
中银大厦	Bank of China Tower	3	101	23 069
恒生银行大厦	Hangseng Bank Tower	4	462	104 386
证券大厦	Shanghai Stock Exchange Building	1	661	
花旗大厦	Citigroup Mansion	4	1 495	97 677
星展银行大厦	DBS Tower	3	904	128 246
船舶大厦	Marine Tower	3	109	32 532
东亚银行大厦	Global Financial Tower	4	1 298	65 047
国金中心	Shanghai International Financial Center	5	540	95 630
其他大厦	Other Buildings	26	7 800	544 116
按普通贷款分	**By Regular Loans**			
7亿美元以上	> USD 700 million	10	6 457	1 307 302
5~7亿美元	USD 500~700 million	2	839	118 147
3~5亿美元	USD 300~500 million	6	1 155	221 774
1~3亿美元	USD 100~300 million	14	1 386	241 812
1亿美元以下	< USD 100 million	48	7 661	117 678
按普通存款分	**By Regular Deposit**			
10亿美元以上	> USD 1 000 million	6	5 002	851 762
3~10亿美元	USD 300~1 000 million	9	3 446	457 060
1~3亿美元	USD 100~300 million	5	764	147 138
1千万~1亿美元	USD 10~100 million	15	975	195 359
1千万美元以下	< USD 10 million	45	7 311	355 394
按资产总额分	**By Total Assets**			
10亿美元以上	> USD 1 000 million	21	12 183	1 479 587
5~10亿美元	USD 500~1 000 million	13	2 919	256 423
3~5亿美元	USD 300~500 million	8	1 023	119 644
1~3亿美元	USD 100~300 million	22	1 138	137 799
1亿美元以下	< USD 100 million	16	235	13 260
按税金分	**By Tax**			
2000万元以上	≥20 million yuan	25	11 922	1 577 915
500~2000万元	5~20 million yuan	25	4 204	340 435
100~500万元	1~5 million yuan	8	306	46 149
100万元以下	< 1 million yuan	22	1 066	42 214

Major Indicators of Foreign Banks

普通存款（万美元） Ordinary Deposits (USD 10 000)	人民币贷款（万元） RMB Loans (10 000 yuan)	人民币存款（万元） RMB Deposits (10 000 yuan)	资产总额（万美元） Total Assets (USD 10 000)	利润总额（万元） Operation Profit (10 000 yuan)	拆入同业（万元） Borrowing from Correspondence Banks (10 000 yuan)	拆放同业（万元） Banker Call Loans (10 000 yuan)
1 684 898	**20 174 188**	**39 860 967**	**8 968 379**	**641 942**	**2 060 313**	**6 725 969**
1 171 567	12 810 387	26 314 363	5 556 985	373 872	1 535 000	4 921 215
286 076	5 176 459	7 699 229	1 976 658	118 864	279 232	1 408 655
185 922	1 929 567	5 192 269	1 200 079	109 533	170 739	142 176
40 974	257 775	655 106	229 057	38 951	75 342	253 923
359			5 600	722		
296 649	2 832 783	4 585 041	1 626 473	149 160	247 732	643 100
288 533	2 049 895	4 567 012	1 148 212	53 242	127 139	755 593
20 041	710 589	729 505	406 608	50 857	176 900	121 582
9 845	69 351	227 313	41 157	7 335		
55 669	951 832	1 526 724	207 260	51 831	10 000	12 450
545		23 000	307 562	-47 390	210 000	10 500
159 890	1 474 903	4 023 259	919 449	80 003	63 200	67 484
79 819	1 018 112	2 867 338	247 754	-1 798	325 000	955 368
1 908	297 703	57 791	70 180	14 775	51 000	14 000
35 647	1 416 218	2 071 877	454 405	9 041	502 000	50 000
66 766	452 449	1 730 701	311 957	65 907	6 000	45 568
669 586	8 900 353	17 451 406	3 227 362	208 979	341 342	4 050 324
1 196 224	11 041 798	25 613 098	3 797 385	610 998	834 739	3 070 476
94 619	1 645 174	3 621 157	297 302	83 484		28 000
83 817	1 725 664	2 968 667	596 525	95 191	183 000	574 021
186 285	3 376 184	4 651 880	768 168	127 950	143 732	262 429
123 953	2 385 368	3 006 165	3 508 999	-275 681	898 842	2 791 043
1 040 316	8 783 097	20 235 164	3 111 212	541 581	284 500	2 027 158
478 160	6 417 315	13 921 295	1 116 054	216 198	447 000	3 550 708
90 055	1 318 327	2 691 184	569 082	88 307	194 971	264 100
70 202	1 963 918	2 275 104	670 121	93 481	65 000	330 707
6 165	1 691 531	738 220	3 501 910	-297 625	1 068 842	553 296
1 368 173	12 809 001	29 905 245	7 229 079	520 908	1 733 471	3 968 237
104 331	3 667 037	4 954 663	947 288	-38 656	107 000	2 505 930
152 632	2 480 792	3 923 000	298 093	93 596	74 000	126 290
58 458	1 081 116	1 072 328	402 609	55 855	120 042	121 012
1 304	136 242	5 731	91 310	10 239	25 800	4 500
1 589 029	17 979 659	38 347 700	6 579 282	866 157	1 487 471	6 400 105
78 914	2 112 408	1 354 621	1 817 917	-208 686	493 800	224 039
12 240	64 183	130 820	225 088	33 857	20 000	6 813
4 715	17 938	27 826	346 092	-49 386	59 042	95 012

表8－4　外资银行存贷款年末余额
Foreign Banks' Year-end Balance of Deposits and Loans

指　标	Indicators	单　位	Unit	2005	2010	2011	2012
外汇存贷款	**Deposits and Loans of Foreign Exchange**	**亿美元**	**USD 100 million**	**197.19**	**327.45**	**378.44**	**369.12**
客户存款	Deposits of Customers	亿美元	USD 100 million	59.43	132.06	171.63	168.49
#短　期	Short Term	亿美元	USD 100 million	22.35	52.96	82.26	78.61
同业存款	Inter-bank Deposits	亿美元	USD 100 million	4.13	33.73	22.23	67.37
拆入同业	Deposits From Other Banks	亿美元	USD 100 million	29.30	128.33	102.37	101.38
普通贷款	Ordinary Loans	亿美元	USD 100 million	137.76	195.39	206.81	200.67
#短　期	Short Term	亿美元	USD 100 million	67.05	93.98	97.63	89.70
投　资	Investment	亿美元	USD 100 million	8.21	9.51	2.58	0.84
拆放同业	Deposits to Other Banks	亿美元	USD 100 million	15.64	101.07	77.52	109.72
人民币存贷款	**RMB Deposits and Loans**	**亿元**	**100 million yuan**	**1 203.72**	**4 910.27**	**5 725.50**	**6 003.52**
客户存款	Deposits of Customers	亿元	100 million yuan	615.44	3 000.91	3 714.54	3 986.10
拆入同业	Deposits From Other Banks	亿元	100 million yuan	53.76	157.13	138.82	206.03
普通贷款	Ordinary Loans	亿元	100 million yuan	588.28	1 909.36	2 010.99	2 017.42
投　资	Investment	亿元	100 million yuan	115.83	1 657.37	2 370.55	2 043.79
拆放同业	Deposits to Other Banks	亿元	100 million yuan	5.63	449.44	443.19	672.60

表8-5 历年中资保险机构原保险保费收入和赔款支出

Former Premium Income and Indemnity Expenditure of Chinese Insurance Business in Main Years (1992～2012)

单位:亿元 (100 million yuan)

年 份 Year	原保险保费收入 Former Premium Income	财产险 Property Insurance	人身险 Life Insurance	原保险赔款支出 Former Indemnity Expenditure	财产险 Property Insurance	人身险 Life Insurance	赔款率(%) Rate of Indemnity(%)	财产险 Property Insurance	人身险 Life Insurance
1992	1.13	0.75	0.38	0.69	0.20	0.49	61.1	26.7	128.9
1993	2.51	1.42	1.09	0.30	0.06	0.24	12.0	4.2	25.9
1994	5.37	3.30	2.07	1.77	1.63	0.14	33.0	49.4	6.8
1995	13.63	10.42	3.21	3.12	2.97	0.15	22.9	28.5	4.7
1996	22.02	7.70	14.32	3.83	3.41	0.42	17.4	44.3	2.9
1997	38.34	9.19	29.15	4.91	4.71	0.20	12.8	51.3	0.7
1998	44.09	9.93	34.16	6.28	4.48	1.80	14.2	45.1	5.3
1999	51.42	10.84	40.58	7.76	5.71	2.05	15.1	52.7	5.1
2000	63.31	13.40	49.91	7.06	3.87	3.19	11.2	28.9	6.4
2001	99.36	13.73	85.63	9.08	4.92	4.16	9.1	35.8	4.9
2002	118.31	16.55	101.76	10.12	7.17	2.95	8.6	43.3	2.9
2003	129.83	21.88	107.95	20.73	9.04	11.69	16.0	41.3	10.8
2004	118.09	29.52	88.57	19.59	11.62	7.97	16.6	39.4	9.0
2005	140.63	40.03	100.60	23.16	20.09	3.07	16.5	50.2	3.1
2006	171.47	45.51	125.96	26.17	22.16	4.01	15.3	48.7	3.2
2007	182.33	52.47	129.86	29.29	24.54	4.75	16.1	46.8	3.7
2008	230.84	55.25	175.59	37.01	30.99	6.02	16.0	56.1	3.4
2009	221.20	68.75	152.45	43.54	36.26	7.28	19.7	52.7	4.8
2010	329.82	100.41	229.41	45.65	39.93	5.72	13.8	39.8	2.5
2011	295.18	120.53	174.65	61.74	56.19	5.52	20.9	46.6	3.2
2012	319.56	130.38	189.18	80.74	72.11	8.63	25.3	55.3	4.6

表8-6　中资保险机构主要险种的原保险保费收入和赔款支出
Former Premium Income and Indemnity Expenditure of Major Types of Chinese Funded Insurance Business
(2012)

单位:亿元　　(100 million yuan)

指　标	Indicators	原保险保费收入 Former Premium Income	原保险赔款支出 Former Indemnity Expenditure	赔款率(%) Rate of Indemnity(%)
总　计	**Total**	**319.56**	**80.74**	**25.3**
财产险小计	Subtotal of Property Insurance	130.38	72.11	55.3
企业财产险	Enterprise Property Insurance	12.90	5.59	43.3
机动车辆险	Motor Vehicle Insurance	100.19	60.29	60.2
其　他	Others	17.29	6.23	36.0
人身险小计	Subtotal of Life Insurance	189.18	8.63	4.6
个　险	Individual Insurance	149.31	1.09	0.7
团　险	Team Insurance	39.87	7.54	18.9

表8-7　外资保险机构主要险种的原保险保费收入和赔款支出
Former Premium Income and Indemnity Expenditure of Major Types of Foreign Funded Insurance Business
(2012)

单位:亿元　　(100 million yuan)

指　标	Indicators	原保险保费收入 Former Premium Income	原保险赔款支出 Former Indemnity Expenditure	赔款率(%) Rate of Indemnity(%)
总　计	**Total**	**111.65**	**9.95**	**8.9**
财产保险小计	Subtotal of Property Insurance	17.76	5.99	33.7
#企业财产险	Enterprise Property Insurance	5.04	1.79	35.5
货运险	Cargo Transportation Insurance	4.65	2.25	48.4
家财险	Household Property Insurance	0.10		3.0
责任保险	Liability Insurance	5.22	1.06	20.3
人身险	Life Insurance	93.89	3.96	4.2

表8-8 上海证券交易所市场交易主要指标
Statistics of Shanghai Stock Exchange

指 标	Indicators	单 位 Unit	2005	2010	2011	2012
交易天数	**Trading Days**	**天 day**	**242**	**242**	**244**	**243**
上市证券数	**Number of Securities Traded**	**个 unit**	**1 073**	**1 500**	**1 691**	**2 098**
股 票	Stocks	个 unit	878	938	975	998
A 股	A Share	个 unit	824	884	921	944
B 股	B Share	个 unit	54	54	54	54
债 券	Bonds	个 unit	165	536	680	1 059
政府债	Government Bonds	个 unit	43	199	213	191
公司债	Corporate Bonds	个 unit	65	284	417	830
回 购	Repurchase	个 unit	57	53	50	38
证券投资基金	Funds of Securities Investment	个 unit	25	13	13	12
ETF	Exchange Traded Funds	个 unit	1	12	23	29
权 证	Warrant	个 unit	4	1		
股票市价总值	**Total Value of Stock Price**	**亿元 100 million yuan**	**38 067.81**	**179 007.24**	**148 376.22**	**158 698.44**
成交金额	**Turnover Value**	**亿元 100 million yuan**	**49 775.61**	**398 395.73**	**454 651.56**	**547 535.22**
股 票	Stocks	亿元 100 million yuan	19 240.21	304 312.01	237 560.46	164 545.01
A 股	A Share	亿元 100 million yuan	19 061.49	303 215.93	236 814.27	164 047.38
B 股	B Share	亿元 100 million yuan	178.72	1 096.08	746.18	413.48
债 券	Bonds	亿元 100 million yuan	28 138.41	74 914.42	210 714.87	379 818.85
政府债	Government Bonds	亿元 100 million yuan	2 772.79	1 590.04	1 243.11	905.56
公司债	Corporate Bonds	亿元 100 million yuan	446.56	3 306.79	4 850.47	7 537.43
回 购	Repurchase	亿元 100 million yuan	24 919.06	70 017.59	204 621.29	371 375.86
基 金	Funds	亿元 100 million yuan	576.78	4 771.71	2 901.41	3 171.36
权 证	Warrant	亿元 100 million yuan	1 763.07	14 397.58	3 474.82	
其 他	Others	亿元 100 million yuan	57.14			
成交数量	**Volume Turnover**					
股 票	Stocks	亿手 100 million contracts	3 986.59	25 964.43	21 193.87	18 948.94
A 股	A Share	亿手 100 million contracts	3 926.89	25 812.40	21 079.68	18 850.54
B 股	B Share	亿手 100 million contracts	59.70	152.03	114.19	77.89
债 券	Bonds	亿手 100 million contracts	28.15	74.81	210.69	379.76
政府债	Government Bonds	亿手 100 million contracts	2.81	1.57	1.25	0.90
公司债	Corporate Bonds	亿手 100 million contracts	0.42	3.22	4.82	7.48
回 购	Repurchase	亿手 100 million contracts	24.92	70.02	204.62	371.38
基 金	Funds	亿手 100 million contracts	778.73	3 580.37	2 370.84	2 541.17
权 证	Warrant	亿手 100 million contracts	1 274.79	10 735.99	1 395.94	
其 他	Others	亿手 100 million contracts	0.12			

注：2010 年起，上交所统计口径有调整，原表中"国债现货"和"地方政府债"数据，现合并为"政府债"；原表中"公司债"和"可转债"数据，现合并统称为"公司债"。

Note: Shanghai Stock Exchange has changed its statistical approach for its data since 2010. The data in the fields of "National Debts on Spots" and "Local Government Bonds" in the former table have been merged as those of "Government Bonds" and the fields of "Corporate Debts" and "Convertible Bonds" have been merged as "Corporate Bonds".

表8-9 上海证券交易所市盈率和换手率
P/E Ratio & Turnover Rate of Shanghai Stock Exchange

指 标	Indicators	2005	2010	2011	2012
市盈率(%)	**P/E Rate**	**16.3**	**21.6**	**13.4**	**12.3**
A 股	A Share	16.4	21.6	13.4	12.3
B 股	B Share	12.4	23.9	12.3	13.2
换手率(%)	**Turnover Rate**	**274.4**	**198.5**	**124.8**	**101.6**
A 股	A Share	290.7	199.3	125.1	101.9
B 股	B Share	58.5	119.0	86.8	57.5

表8-10 上海证券交易所市场筹集资金
Capital Raising of Shanghai Stock Exchang

单位:亿元 (100 million yuan)

指 标	Indicators	2005	2010	2011	2012
A 股小计	**Subtotal of A Shares**	**308.75**	**5 532.14**	**3 199.69**	**2 890.31**
A 股首次发行	IPO of A Shares	28.55	1 891.51	1 014.01	333.57
A 股再次发行	Second Issuing of A Shares	280.20	3 640.62	2 185.68	2 556.74
#A 股增发	Additional Issuing of A Shares	278.78	2 102.90	1 774.07	2 416.59
A 股配股	Rights Issuing of A Shares	1.42	1 415.73	378.37	110.77
A 股行权	Rights Claiming of A Shares		84.28	29.49	

表8-11 浦东新区上市公司分行业汇总情况
Listed Companies in PNA by Sector
(2012)

指 标	Indicators	单 位 Unit	地产类 Real Estate	工业类 Industry	公用事业类 Public Utilities	商业类 Commerce	综合类 Comprehens-ive
发行股数	Number of Stocks Issued	亿股 100 million in number	77.71	210.18	388.95	34.70	814.06
流通股数	Number of Stocks Circulated	亿股 100 million in number	77.71	196.72	346.31	32.12	669.72
成交额	Volume	亿元 100 million yuan	904.79	2 967.90	900.18	607.00	4 211.28
成交股数	Number of Stock Transacted	亿股 100 million in number	140.08	298.51	148.92	69.07	581.19
市盈率	P/E Ratio	%	18.1	20.5	12.2	22.6	8.4
换手率	Turnover Rate	%	182.0	162.9	47.8	220.0	88.2
市价总值	Total Market Value	亿元 100 million yuan	606.12	1 527.62	1 531.35	265.72	5 028.50
流通市值	Circulating Market Value	亿元 100 million yuan	606.12	1 390.48	1 294.12	243.79	4 099.19

注:1. 浦东新区上市公司指公司注册地含"浦东"的公司。
2. 数据包含 A 股和 B 股。
3. "成交额"、"成交股数"、"换手率"为2012年整年数据。
4. "发行股数"、"流通股数"、"市盈率"、"市值总值"、"流通市值"为2012年12月31日数据。

Note: 1. Newly listed companies in PNA refer to those companies that registered in Pudong.
2. The data include both A shares and B shares.
3. The items of Business Volume, Number of Transacted Stocks and Turnover Rate are data in the whole year of 2012.
4. The items of Number of Issued Stocks, Number of Circulated Stocks, P/E Ratio, Total Market Value and Circulating Market Value are data of December 31, 2012.

表8-12 上海联合产权交易所基本情况
Shanghai United Assets and Equity Exchange

指 标	Indicators	单 位 Unit	2005	2010	2011	2012
成交企业数	**Number of Enterprises Acquired /Merged**	**户 unit**	**3 395**	**1 981**	**1 749**	**1 424**
按企业产权出让分	By Property Rights Transferring Out					
#国有企业	State-owned Enterprises	户 unit	1 457	1 099	1 039	799
集体企业	Collective-owned Enterprises	户 unit	488	136	123	175
有限责任	Limited Liability	户 unit	659	211	191	117
按企业产权受让分	By Property Rights Transferring In					
#国有企业	State-owned Enterprises	户 unit	777	766	557	453
集体企业	Collective-owned Enterprises	户 unit	76	38	75	66
有限责任	Limited Liability	户 unit	567	233	178	113
外商独资	Solely Foreigner Funded	户 unit	231	62	63	48
私营企业	Private Enterprises	户 unit	385	270	307	314
自然人	Natural Person	户 unit	1 329	563	520	386
交易额合计	**Total Volume of Trade**	**亿元 100 million yuan**	**4 002.80**	**2 325.35**	**1 016.91**	**1 256.48**
按企业产权出让分	By Property Rights Transferring Out					
#国有企业	State-owned Enterprises	亿元 100 million yuan	1 489.64	1 807.25	788.43	1 079.20
集体企业	Collective-owned Enterprises	亿元 100 million yuan	46.78	7.69	13.89	26.30
有限责任	Limited Liability	亿元 100 million yuan	225.29	47.01	93.61	58.50
按企业产权受让分	By Property Rights Transferring In					
#国有企业	State-owned Enterprises	亿元 100 million yuan	690.52	1702.79	569.88	984.00
集体企业	Collective-owned Enterprises	亿元 100 million yuan	11.95	32.67	9.48	30.66
有限责任	Limited Liability	亿元 100 million yuan	835.91	99.21	169.90	65.82
外商独资	Solely Foreigner Funded	亿元 100 million yuan	116.72	31.68	62.11	22.94
私营企业	Private Enterprises	亿元 100 million yuan	96.07	87.72	130.05	124.53
自然人	Natural Person	亿元 100 million yuan	154.86	12.19	19.66	14.61

注：交易额，原指"产权交易标的对应总资产金额"，2010 年起调整为"产权交易合同价款金额"。
Note: Total Volume of Trade, formerly referred to "Total Capital Corresponding to Transacted Object of Property Rights", has been readjusted as "Contracted Value of Transacted Property Rights" since 2010.

表8-13　上海期货交易所市场交易主要指标
Major Indicators of Shanghai Futures Exchange

指　标	Indicators	单　位　Unit	2005	2010	2011	2012
会员单位	**Membership**	**户 unit**	**215**	**209**	**208**	**208**
经纪单位	Broking	户 unit	175	164	163	161
非经纪单位	Non-Broking	户 unit	40	45	45	47
交易天数	Business Days in the Year	天 day	242	242	244	243
上市交易品种	Business Lines	个 unit	4	8	9	10
成交量	**Total Volume of Business**	**万手 10 000 contracts**	**6 757.95**	**124 379.64**	**61 647.84**	**73 065.88**
铜	Copper	万手 10 000 contracts	2 470.41	10 157.71	9 792.23	11 456.97
铝	Aluminum	万手 10 000 contracts	425.00	3 452.40	1 990.78	788.54
锌	Zinc	万手 10 000 contracts		29 317.87	10 732.70	4 220.18
铅	Lead	万手 10 000 contracts			58.66	13.73
黄　金	Gold	万手 10 000 contracts		679.41	1 444.35	1 183.35
白　银	Silver	万手 10 000 contracts				4 252.99
天然橡胶	Natural Rubber	万手 10 000 contracts	1 900.63	33 482.98	20 857.28	15 035.25
燃料油	Fuel Oil	万手 10 000 contracts	1 961.91	2 136.44	394.23	1.83
螺纹钢	Rebar	万手 10 000 contracts		45 122.48	16 376.96	36 112.50
线　材	Wire Rod	万手 10 000 contracts		30.35	0.65	0.54
成交金额	**Total Value of Business**	**亿元 100 million yuan**	**65 402.03**	**1234 794.76**	**869 068.72**	**891 953.72**
铜	Copper	亿元 100 million yuan	40 463.23	296 437.54	299 334.19	327 489.41
铝	Aluminum	亿元 100 million yuan	3 714.46	28 342.48	17 070.34	6 189.80
锌	Zinc	亿元 100 million yuan		255 725.62	92 365.50	32 263.76
铅	Lead	亿元 100 million yuan			2 561.59	530.01
黄　金	Gold	亿元 100 million yuan		18 291.92	50 976.08	40 364.37
白　银	Silver	亿元 100 million yuan				41 308.60
天然橡胶	Natural Rubber	亿元 100 million yuan	15 601.79	426 464.81	330 474.23	308 986.96
燃料油	Fuel Oil	亿元 100 million yuan	5 622.55	9 886.37	1 928.77	47.42
螺纹钢	Rebar	亿元 100 million yuan		199 517.15	74 355.03	134 771.25
线　材	Wire Rod	亿元 100 million yuan		128.87	2.99	2.13
年末持仓量	**Year End Contracts**	**万手 10 000 contracts**	**30.95**	**206.46**	**214.00**	**248.43**
铜	Copper	万手 10 000 contracts	10.58	37.31	42.96	37.90
铝	Aluminum	万手 10 000 contracts	7.89	23.73	24.99	16.75
锌	Zinc	万手 10 000 contracts		40.24	37.37	22.49
铅	Lead	万手 10 000 contracts			0.26	0.57
黄　金	Gold	万手 10 000 contracts		7.88	10.23	11.14
白　银	Silver	万手 10 000 contracts				24.44
天然橡胶	Natural Rubber	万手 10 000 contracts	5.70	21.46	29.93	17.57

表 8－13 续表 Continued

指 标	Indicators	单 位 Unit	2005	2010	2011	2012
燃料油	Fuel Oil	万手 10 000 contracts	6.78	10.44	0.09	0.01
螺纹钢	Rebar	万手 10 000 contracts		65.40	68.17	117.56
线材	Wire Rod	万手 10 000 contracts		0.01	0.01	…
交割量	**Volume of Transaction**	**万手 10 000 contracts**	**8.73**	**37.69**	**27.75**	**26.29**
铜	Copper	万手 10 000 contracts	3.07	3.84	3.17	6.42
铝	Aluminum	万手 10 000 contracts	2.18	11.52	12.16	8.70
锌	Zinc	万手 10 000 contracts		6.15	6.71	5.04
铅	Lead	万手 10 000 contracts			0.13	0.25
黄 金	Gold	万手 10 000 contracts		0.05	0.07	0.26
白 银	Silver	万手 10 000 contracts				2.80
天然橡胶	Natural Rubber	万手 10 000 contracts	1.52	2.57	1.01	0.91
燃料油	Fuel Oil	万手 10 000 contracts	1.96	6.90	4.18	0.05
螺纹钢	Rebar	万手 10 000 contracts		6.00	0.32	1.86
线 材	Wire Rod	万手 10 000 contracts		0.66	…	…
交割金额	**Value of Transaction**	**亿元 100 million yuan**	**88.29**	**349.06**	**312.44**	**360.81**
铜	Copper	亿元 100 million yuan	54.54	113.40	106.24	184.57
铝	Aluminum	亿元 100 million yuan	18.07	90.41	102.86	67.95
锌	Zinc	亿元 100 million yuan		53.77	57.57	38.10
铅	Lead	亿元 100 million yuan			4.89	9.68
黄 金	Gold	亿元 100 million yuan		1.46	2.30	8.75
白 银	Silver	亿元 100 million yuan				28.65
天然橡胶	Natural Rubber	亿元 100 million yuan	10.79	32.21	17.12	14.50
燃料油	Fuel Oil	亿元 100 million yuan	4.89	30.28	19.92	1.41
螺纹钢	Rebar	亿元 100 million yuan		24.89	1.54	7.20
线 材	Wire Rod	亿元 100 million yuan		2.64	…	…
交割率	**Rate of Transaction**					
铜	Copper	%	0.2	0.1	0.1	0.1
铝	Aluminum	%	1.0	0.7	1.0	1.8
锌	Zinc	%		0.1	0.1	0.2
铅	Lead	%			0.5	3.5
黄 金	Gold	%		…	…	…
白 银	Silver	%				0.2
天然橡胶	Natural Rubber	%	0.3	…	…	…
燃料油	Fuel Oil	%	0.2	0.5	0.7	4.9
螺纹钢	Rebar	%		…		…
线 材	Wire Rod	%		2.0	…	…

表8-14 上海钻石交易所市场交易主要指标
Major Indicators of Shanghai Diamond Exchange

指标	Indicators	单位 Unit	2010	2011	2012
会员单位	**Membership**	**户 Unit**	**283**	**326**	**345**
外资会员	Foreign Member	户 Unit	193	215	229
中资会员	Chinese Member	户 Unit	90	111	116
成交量	**Total Volume of Business**	**万克拉 10 000 carat**	**19 762.53**	**14 821.08**	**7 511.54**
钻石进境量	Volume of Diamond Coming in Border	万克拉 10 000 carat	92.60	78.62	319.27
钻石出境量	Volume of Diamond Leaving our Country	万克拉 10 000 carat	24.03	20.54	23.87
钻石进口量	Volume of Imports	万克拉 10 000 carat	118.53	140.35	118.76
钻石出口量	Volume of Exports	万克拉 10 000 carat	19 518.03	14 573.90	7 043.08
钻石保税交易量	Volume of Bonded Transactions	万克拉 10 000 carat	7.54	6.06	5.86
钻石加工贸易量	Volume of Processing Trade	万克拉 10 000 carat	1.80	1.61	0.70
成交金额	**Total Value of Transactions**	**万美元 10 000 USD**	**288 568.49**	**470 669.41**	**386 779.31**
钻石进境额	Amount of Diamond Coming in Border	万美元 10 000 USD	104 620.22	171 616.92	150 452.62
钻石出境额	Amount of Diamond Leaving our Country	万美元 10 000 USD	38 044.48	78 816.94	64 878.73
钻石进口额	Amount of Imports	万美元 10 000 USD	131 092.79	204 010.28	158 439.26
钻石出口额	Amount of Exports	万美元 10 000 USD	1 281.58	1 809.73	778.87
钻石保税交易额	Amount of Bonded Transactions	万美元 10 000 USD	13 042.58	13 334.89	11 820.68
钻石加工贸易额	Amount of Processing Trade	万美元 10 000 USD	486.84	1 080.65	409.15

表8-15　新区属人才交流市场基本情况
Basic Statistics of PNA Professional Resources Market(PPRM)

指　标	Indicators	单位　Unit	2005	2010	2011	2012
全年举办交流活动	Number of Exchange Activites in the Year	场 in number	133	193	214	212
参与人才招聘单位	Number of Participating Organizations	个 unit	3 859	7 462	7 220	6 738
接待咨询服务人次	Job-seeking Visitors Received	万人次 10 000 person-times	19.67	37.00	35.00	40.50
办理择业登记人数	Job-seeking Visitors Registered	人次 person-time	90 452	211 000	205 000	216 000
达成意向人数	Number of Job-seekers Who Have Signed Letters of Intent	人 person	37 302	39 949	34 433	33 742
获得上海市居住证人数	Number of Persons Who Have Obtained Shanghai Residence Permits	人 person	7 158	30 985	43 606	50 349
后续服务	**Follow-up Services**					
档案保管	File-keeping	件 file	5 691	13 489	13 561	13 083
户籍挂靠(迁入)	Domiciling(immigration)	户 unit	1 605	1 175	2 278	2 507

主要统计指标解释

存　款

是企业、机关、团体或居民等根据资金必须收回的原则,把货币资金存入银行或其他信用机构保管并取得一定利息的一种信用活动形式。根据存款对象的不同可划分为企业存款、财政存款、机关团体存款、储蓄存款等科目。它是银行信贷资金的主要来源。

贷　款

是银行或其他信用机构根据资金必须归还的原则,按一定利率,为企业、个人等提供资金的一种信用活动形式。我国银行贷款分为短期贷款、中期流动资金贷款、中长期贷款、信托贷款以及工业贷款、商业贷款等科目。

居民储蓄存款年末余额

居民和农民个人在银行、信用社等金融机构储蓄存款年末余额。不包括居民的手存现金和企事业单位、部队、机关团体等的集体存款。

保险金额

指保险人承担赔偿或者给付保险金责任的最高限额。

保险费

保险费是指投保人根据保险合同的有关规定,为保险受益人取得因保险事故发生所造成的经济损失予以补偿(或给付)权利,付给保险人的代价。包括财产险和人身险储金类支出。

保险赔款及给付

保险赔款及给付指保险事故发生后,经查证确属保险责任范围以内的保险标的损失,保险人根据保险合同的规定履行赔偿义务,给予被保险人(或投保人指定的受益人)的款项。

市价总值

市价总值即全部股份乘上市场价格。

流通市值

流通市值指在某特定时间内当时可交易的流通股股数乘以当时股价得出的流通股票总价值。

市盈率

市盈率是某种股票每股市价与每股盈利的比率。

市盈率 = 普通股每股市场价格 ÷ 普通股每年每股盈利

换手率

换手率是指在一定时间内市场中股票转手买卖的频率。

金融债券

金融债券,是指银行和非银行金融机构为筹集资金而发行的债券。其债务人为发行债券的金融机构。

企业债券

企业债券通常又称为公司债券,是企业依照法定程序发行,约定在一定期限内还本付息的债券。企业债券代表着发债企业和投资者之间的一种债权债务关系。债券持有人是企业的债权人,不是所有者,无权参与或干涉企业经营管理,但债券持有人有权按期收回本息。企业债券与股票一样,同属有价证券,可以自由转让。

可转换债券

可转换债券,又译可换股债券,是债券的一种,它可以转换为债券发行公司的股票,其转换比率一般会在发行时确定。可转换债券通常具有较低的票面利率,因为可以转换成股票的权利是对债券持有人的一种补偿。另外,将可转换债券转换为普通股时,所换得的股票价值一般远大于原债券价值。可转换债券是在发行公司债券的基础上,附加了一份期权,并允许购买人在规定的时间范围内将其购买的债券转换成指定公司的股票。

持仓量

持仓量指的是在交易所市场上未平仓的期权合约的数量,也指某一种类或系列中未平仓的期权合约的数量。

成交量

成交量指当天成交的股票数量。

交　割

交割概念来源于期货,分为:实物交割和现金交割。

实物交割,是指期货合约的买卖双方于合约到期时,根据交易所制订的规则和程序,通过期货合约标的物的所有权转移,将到期未平仓合约进行了结的行为。商品期货交易一般采用实物交割的方式。

现金交割,是指到期末平仓期货合约进行交割时,用结算价格来计算未平仓合约的盈亏,以现金支付的方式最终了结期货合约的交割方式。这种交割方式主要用于金融期货等期货标的物无法进行实物交割的期货合约。

EXPLANATORY NOTES TO MAJOR STATISTICAL INDICATORS

Deposits

Deposits are a form of credit by which enterprises, institutions, organizations or residents put money into banks and other credit institutions for safekeeping and earn interests under the principle of free withdrawal. According to different depositors, deposits are divided into enterprise deposits, treasury deposits, deposits of institutions and organizations, urban savings deposits and other deposits. Deposits constitute a major source of bank credit funds.

Loans

Loans are a form of credit by which banks and other credit institutions provide funds with a specified interest to enterprises and individuals under the principle of free repayment. Loans from Chinese banks include short term loans, medium term circulating capital loans, long term loans, trust loans, industrial loans and commercial loans.

Savings Deposit Balance of Urban and Rural Residents

refers to year-end savings deposit balance of urban residents and farmers at banks, credit unions and other financial institutions, excluding cash held by residents and collective savings of enterprises, institutions, military units and government agencies.

Amount Insured

Amount Insured refers to the maximum that the insurant will get for the claim of the case insured .

Premium

Premium is the fee paid by the insurant to the insurer to obtain the obligation of compensation from the insurance within the agreed terms. It includes saving payment for property and life insurance.

Insurance Indemnity

Insurance Indemnity is the compensation paid by the insurer to the insurant or the beneficiary, when an accident has happened to the insured property or life and the loss has been investigated and verified to be within the insurance obligation.

Total Market Value

Total Market Value means all of the stock shares multiplied by their relevant market price.

Circulation Value on the Market

Circulation Value on the Market means the tradable circulation shares multiplied by their relevant share prices during a certain period of time.

P/E Ratio

P/E Ratio refers to the ratio between the price of a certain share and its earnings per year. The P/E ratio is the price of a traded common share divided by its annual earnings.

Exchange Rate

Exchange Rate means the trading frequency of certain stock shares on the market during a certain period of time.

Financial Bonds

Financial Bonds refer to those that banks and non-banking financial institutions issue to raise funds. Their debtors are the financial institutions that issue the bonds.

Corporate Bonds

Corporate Bonds usually refer to business bonds, which will be issued in accordance with the statutory procedures of the business and repay the original investment plus agreed interest within a certain period of time. Corporate bonds represent a kind of debtor-creditor relationship between the issuing enterprises and the investors. Bondholders are creditors of the certain enterprise, not the owners, and they do not have the right to participate or interfere with the business management. However, the bondholders have the right to claim the principal and interest on time. Like the stock shares, corporate bonds belong to marketable securities and can be freely transferable.

Convertible Bonds

Convertible Bonds, also translated into convertible exchangeable bonds, can be converted into the stock shares of the enterprise that issue the bonds. The conversion rate will usually be determined at the time of distribution. Convertible bonds generally have lower nominal interest rates, because the right of being converted into stock shares is a kind of compensation to the bondholders. In addition, when the bonds are converted into ordinary shares, the prices of these shares usually are far higher than the original value of the bonds. In essence, the convertible bonds have an additional option on the basis of the business bonds, and these bondholders are allowed to convert the convertible bonds they have purchased into the stock shares of specific companies during the specific period.

Open Interest

Open Interest refers to the number of open option contracts in the exchange market, also refers to the number of one or series of open option contracts.

Turnover

Turnover refers to the transaction volume of stock shares traded on that certain day.

Delivery

Delivery, its concept comes from futures, can be divided into physical delivery and cash delivery.

Physical delivery refers to the behavior that the vendor and the purchaser finish the open contracts at the end of the term by means of the ownership transfer of the object of futures contracts in accordance with rules and procedures of the stock exchange when the contract expires. The transaction of commodity futures usually adopts the physical delivery.

Cash delivery refers to the way that the two sides finally close their futures contracts by means of cash, with the settlement price used to calculate earnings or loss of the open contracts when the open futures contracts are delivered at the end of term. This kind of delivery is mainly used for futures contracts that their objects can not be dealt with physical delivery such as the financial futures.

第九篇

CHAPTER 9

房地产

REAL ESTATE

表9-1　房地产开发投资
(2012)

单位:亿元

指　标	Indicators	企业个数(个) Enterprises (unit)	本年完成投资 Current Year Investment Completed	建筑工程 Construction Project
总　计	**Total**	**716**	**600.30**	**350.91**
按登记注册类型分	**By Type of Registration**			
内　资	Domestic Investment	608	524.51	297.90
国　有	State-owned	73	48.47	36.03
集　体	Collective-owned	12	8.42	4.76
股份合作	Share-holding			
联　营	Jointly-operated	6	10.64	4.93
有限责任公司	Companies with Limited Liabilities	230	296.55	156.68
股份有限公司	Companies Limited by Shares	50	16.94	16.93
私　营	Private	234	143.13	78.23
其　他	Others	3	0.36	0.34
港澳台商投资	Hong Kong/Macao/Taiwan Investment	67	32.16	28.22
#港澳台商独资	Solely Hong Kong/Macao/Taiwan Funded	28	13.04	10.87
外商投资	FIE	41	43.64	24.79
#外商独资	Solely Foreign Funded	24	23.29	16.53
按隶属关系分	**By Subordination**			
中央属	Central Government	16	39.77	18.04
市(局)属	Municipality/Bureau	57	86.44	47.75
区　属	PNA	169	111.83	71.47
其他属	Others	474	362.27	213.65
按企业资质等级分	**By Qualifications of Enterprises**			
一　级	Grade 1	49	25.52	7.85
二　级	Grade 2	166	83.61	72.22
三　级	Grade 3	117	51.63	26.56
无　级	No Grade	384	439.54	244.28

Investment in Real Estate Development

(100 million yuan)

完成投资按构成分 By Composition of Completed Investment			完成投资按工程用途分 By Project Use of Completed Investment			
安装工程 Installation	设备工器具购置 Equipment Purchasing	其他费用 Other Cost	住　宅 Residential Housing	办公楼 Office Buildings	商业营业用房 Commerce/ Operation	其　他 Others
46.02	**1.38**	**201.99**	**370.85**	**51.99**	**84.43**	**93.03**
43.54	1.37	181.70	339.50	41.26	63.35	80.41
3.21	0.29	8.93	36.18	3.57	2.98	5.74
0.85		2.82	7.58	0.01	0.22	0.61
		5.71	9.08		0.11	1.45
29.91	0.38	109.58	211.62	13.77	22.23	48.93
		0.01	2.59	7.55	2.89	3.91
9.57	0.70	54.63	72.44	16.36	34.57	19.76
		0.02			0.36	
0.68		3.25	13.62	6.04	10.14	2.36
		2.17	8.96	2.89	1.01	0.17
1.79	0.01	17.04	17.73	4.70	10.94	10.27
0.99		5.77	7.81	4.39	7.35	3.73
0.51		21.22	36.09	3.46	0.15	0.07
12.20	0.10	26.39	48.55	8.74	14.07	15.08
11.25	0.35	28.76	71.85	9.04	9.12	21.82
22.06	0.93	125.63	214.36	30.75	61.09	56.07
4.41	0.16	13.11	18.37	0.08	1.10	5.97
2.84	0.20	8.35	55.34	9.02	7.04	12.21
2.82		22.25	37.27	4.12	4.72	5.53
35.95	1.03	158.28	259.87	38.78	71.57	69.32

表9-2 房地产开发企业投资资金来源

(2012)

单位:亿元

指 标	Indicators	本年资金来源合计 Total Sources of Funds	上年末结余资本 Remnant Capital of Previous Year	本年资金来源小计 Subtotal of Current Year
总 计	**Total**	**1 307.56**	**330.04**	**977.51**
按登记注册类型分	**By Type of Registration**			
内 资	Domestic Investment	1 054.87	232.47	822.40
国 有	State-owned	103.70	18.35	85.35
集 体	Collective-owned	11.30	0.06	11.24
股份合作	Share-holding			
联 营	Jointly-operated	16.45	0.51	15.94
有限责任公司	Companies with Limited Liabilities	581.25	126.21	455.04
股份有限公司	Companies Limited by Shares	17.86	0.30	17.56
私 营	Private	323.23	86.31	236.91
其 他	Others	1.08	0.72	0.36
港澳台商投资	Hong Kong/Macao/Taiwan Investment	136.59	73.31	63.27
#港澳台商独资	Solely Hong Kong/Macao/Taiwan Funded	48.20	16.08	32.12
外商投资	FIE	116.10	24.26	91.84
#外商独资	Solely Foreign Funded	76.40	20.07	56.34
按隶属关系分	**By Subordination**			
中央属	Central Government	47.80	12.48	35.32
市(局)属	Municipality/Bureau	221.22	65.45	155.76
区 属	PNA	172.16	26.14	146.01
其他属	Others	866.38	225.96	640.42
按企业资质等级分	**By Qualifications of Enterprises**			
一 级	Grade 1	29.72	0.52	29.20
二 级	Grade 2	166.70	38.62	128.07
三 级	Grade 3	129.14	19.58	109.56
无 级	No Grade	982.00	271.31	710.69

Sources of Funds of Investment in Real Estate Development

(100 million yuan)

国内贷款 Domestic Loans	利用外资 Foreign Funds	自筹资金 Self-raised Funds	#自有资金 Self-owned	其他资金来源 Other Funds	本年各项应付款合计 Current Year Total Amount Payable	#工程款 Project Funds
220.98	**1.96**	**382.23**	**194.68**	**372.35**	**116.84**	**71.56**
176.86		354.71	180.95	290.82	106.70	65.97
33.81		15.27	11.25	36.28	12.73	10.09
		9.08	5.50	2.16		
1.83		14.11	1.57			
76.22		234.85	116.17	143.97	62.55	38.46
3.99		13.51	13.51	0.05		
61.01		67.53	32.58	108.37	31.42	17.42
		0.36	0.36			
7.27		10.55	9.10	45.45	5.73	3.40
7.26		3.83	2.99	21.03	2.61	1.27
36.84	1.96	16.96	4.63	36.08	4.42	2.19
16.40	1.96	7.28	4.33	30.69	1.75	1.57
5.08		26.71	1.00	3.52	1.08	1.08
24.52		95.37	59.78	35.87	8.72	5.06
43.42		60.40	51.40	42.20	43.99	27.00
147.95	1.96	199.74	82.50	290.76	63.05	38.42
1.70		22.83	21.95	4.67	23.19	10.33
39.23		46.16	40.07	42.68	7.01	5.05
21.55		48.27	15.47	39.74	21.74	15.33
158.50	1.96	264.97	117.19	285.26	64.92	40.86

表9-3　房地产开发企业房屋施工面积、竣工面积和销售面积 (2012)

单位:万平方米

指　标	Indicators	施工面积 Floor Area Under Construction	#新开工面积 Floor Area of New Starts	竣工面积 Floor Area Completed
总　计	**Total**	**3 527.25**	**596.61**	**626.96**
按登记注册类型分	**By Type of Registration**			
内　资	Domestic Investment	3 133.72	576.80	534.89
国　有	State-owned	401.37	41.29	169.33
集　体	Collective-owned	66.46	24.92	8.92
股份合作	Share-holding			
联　营	Jointly-operated	87.63	15.12	68.27
有限责任公司	Companies with Limited Liabilities	1 538.73	307.54	128.33
股份有限公司	Companies Limited by Shares	218.01	62.55	32.13
私　营	Private	815.60	125.38	127.91
其　他	Others	5.91		
港澳台商投资	Hong Kong/Macao/Taiwan Invested	204.61	1.04	75.38
#港澳台商独资	Solely Hong Kong/Macao/Taiwan Funded	42.15		
外商投资	FIE	188.92	18.77	16.69
#外商独资	Solely Foreign Funded	136.16	3.70	7.88
按隶属关系分	**By Subordination**			
中央属	Central Government	152.41		16.81
市(局)属	Municipality/Bureau	424.47	76.69	95.45
区　属	PNA	947.26	213.41	236.22
其他属	Others	2 003.11	306.51	278.48
按企业资质等级分	**By Qualifications of Enterprises**			
一　级	Grade 1	173.17	49.46	23.83
二　级	Grade 2	773.48	155.50	159.77
三　级	Grade 3	278.49	78.26	42.12
无　级	No Grade	2 302.10	313.39	401.25

Floor Space Under Construction, Completed and Sold in Real Estate Development in Real Estate Development

(10 000 sq · m)

#住　宅 Housing	办公楼 Office Building	商业营业用房 Commerce/ Operation	竣工价值(亿元) Completion Value (100 million yuan)	现房销售面积 Sold Floor Space for Completed Housing	期房销售面积 Area of Forward Sale of Future Marketable Housing
433.38	**80.95**	**36.17**	**283.77**	**206.36**	**334.43**
414.10	27.76	22.38	210.37	199.04	307.26
136.31	11.24	3.97	61.36	91.73	35.44
7.50		0.08	1.65	9.14	
56.37		0.30	25.68	0.11	51.92
107.03	0.18	2.85	52.38	59.25	123.05
21.60	7.22	1.07	12.44	2.26	
85.30	9.12	14.12	56.87	36.22	96.85
				0.33	
19.29	49.07	2.03	51.40	6.07	16.17
				1.91	3.70
	4.13	11.75	21.99	1.24	11.00
	4.13	2.93	9.80	1.06	8.42
16.81			7.36	23.87	
80.27	1.47	0.30	31.57	27.37	90.78
171.83	17.26	15.09	104.04	74.93	21.36
164.48	62.22	20.77	140.81	80.19	222.29
18.03		2.64	2.86	17.73	1.08
128.94	11.71	3.70	56.67	72.38	55.72
30.00	1.47	2.57	12.87	29.01	32.33
256.41	67.76	27.26	211.38	87.24	245.30

表9-4 历年全社会房屋施工面积、竣工面积
Total Floor Space Under Construction and Completed in Main Years (1992~2012)

年 份 Year	施工面积（万平方米）Floor Space Under Construction (10 000 sq·m)	#住 宅 Residential Housing	竣工面积（万平方米）Floor Space Completed (10 000 sq·m)	#住 宅 Residential Housing	房屋建筑面积竣工率（%）Construction Completion Rate(%)	#住 宅 Residential Housing
1992	312.15	123.00	104.70	69.27	33.5	56.3
1993	764.36	285.34	169.44	76.68	22.2	26.9
1994	1 158.24	450.03	458.33	113.92	39.6	25.3
1995	1 577.21	583.96	404.58	199.84	25.7	34.2
1996	2 226.58	904.18	674.49	355.31	30.3	39.3
1997	1 954.70	768.15	581.03	271.64	29.7	35.4
1998	2 014.17	911.68	578.31	301.41	28.7	33.1
1999	1 766.88	856.25	573.20	268.27	32.4	31.3
2000	1 549.57	711.80	544.22	255.21	35.1	35.9
2001	1 526.45	879.01	469.53	249.96	30.8	28.4
2002	2 328.47	1 737.98	611.48	512.11	26.3	29.5
2003	2 242.65	1 607.68	671.70	498.85	29.9	31.0
2004	2 250.62	1 569.76	632.76	453.83	28.1	28.9
2005	2 390.79	1 695.24	684.96	512.42	28.6	30.2
2006	2 204.65	1 589.11	779.65	597.52	35.4	37.6
2007	1 983.86	1 255.32	516.59	419.29	26.0	33.4
2008	1 964.30	1 058.98	477.85	255.77	24.3	24.2
2009	2 977.23	1 792.12	742.28	505.70	24.9	28.2
2010	3 211.12	2 085.07	424.90	296.70	13.2	14.2
2011	3 511.82	2 296.52	487.81	286.14	13.9	12.5
2012	3 527.25	2 280.68	626.96	433.38	17.8	19.0

表9-5 主要年份房地产开发企业房屋建筑面积和造价

Floor Space and Cost of Constructions Developed by Real Estate Companies in Main years

指 标	Indicators	1998	2000	2005	2010	2011	2012
房屋施工面积（万平方米）	**Floor Space Under Construction (10 000 sq · m)**	**1 458.94**	**1 119.67**	**2 390.79**	**3 211.12**	**3 511.82**	**3 527.25**
住 宅	Residential Housing	789.35	712.17	1 695.24	2 085.07	2 296.52	2 280.68
#别墅、高档公寓	Villas and Flats	77.46	72.64	490.51	394.58	389.13	361.28
办公楼	Office Buildings	404.07	199.39	196.68	300.14	355.28	320.66
商业营业用房	Commercial Buildings	155.58	106.63	222.13	389.62	374.73	387.60
其 他	Others	109.94	101.48	276.74	436.30	485.29	538.30
房屋竣工面积（万平方米）	**Floor Space Completed (10 000 sq · m)**	**360.36**	**384.03**	**684.96**	**424.90**	**487.81**	**626.96**
住 宅	Residential Housing	231.94	264.91	512.42	296.70	286.14	433.38
#别墅、高档公寓	Villas and Flats	26.10	23.59	168.59	85.58	82.00	32.74
办公楼	Office Buildings	71.15	54.62	54.08	31.61	56.76	80.95
商业营业用房	Commercial Buildings	41.16	28.10	32.85	35.85	73.01	36.17
其 他	Others	16.11	36.40	85.61	60.74	71.90	76.46
房屋竣工价值（亿元）	**Value of Buildings Completed (100 million yuan)**	**141.19**	**110.16**	**204.11**	**173.20**	**253.25**	**283.77**
住 宅	Residential Housing	61.74	55.36	147.55	127.76	137.29	162.55
#别墅、高档公寓	Villas and Flats	16.91	9.86	61.51	71.53	61.26	16.71
办公楼	Office Buildings	53.89	35.25	26.18	13.98	36.45	65.87
商业营业用房	Commercial Buildings	20.61	11.02	10.09	12.98	53.16	24.99
其 他	Others	4.95	8.53	20.29	18.47	26.35	30.36
竣工房屋平均造价（元/平方米）	**Average Construction Cost (yuan/sq · m)**	**3 918**	**2 869**	**2 980**	**4 076**	**5 192**	**4 526**
住 宅	Residential Housing	2 662	2 090	2 879	4 306	4 798	3 751
#别墅、高档公寓	Villas and Flats	6 481	4 179	3 648	8 358	7 471	5 104
办公楼	Office Buildings	7 575	6 454	4 841	4 423	6 421	8 137
商业营业用房	Commercial Buildings	5 007	3 921	3 075	3 622	7 281	6 910
其 他	Others	3 078	2 345	2 371	3 042	3 666	3 971

表9－6　浦东房地产交易中心交易情况
Transactions in Pudong Real Estate Trading Center

指　标	Indicators	单　位 Unit	2010	2011	2012
商品房交易登记	**Registered Transactions of Commodity Housing**				
#商品房出售套数	Number of Commodity Housing Sold	套 set	73 892	50 670	40 683
商品房出售面积	Floor Space of Commodity Housing Sold	平方米 sq·m	7 197 092	5 096 893	3 973 445
商品房出售金额	Value of Commodity Housing Sold	万元 10 000 yuan	6 799 748	6 015 128	4 391 072
商品房预售套数	Number of Forward Sale of Commodity Housing	套 set	14 905	10 726	23 919
商品房预售面积	Floor Space of Forward Sale of Commodity Housing	平方米 sq·m	1 629 081	1 238 582	2 151 384
商品房预售金额	Value of Forward Sale of Commodity Housing	万元 10 000 yuan	3 283 668	2 810 003	3 967 502
存量房交易登记	**Registered Transactions of Housing at Stock**				
存量房交易过户套数	Trading Number of Housing at Stock	套 set	43 162	30 890	34 196
存量房交易过户面积	Trading Floor Space of Housing at Stock	平方米 sq·m	4 537 343	2 893 805	3 345 306
存量房交易过户金额	Trading Value of Housing at Stock	万元 10 000 yuan	6 277 733	4 765 762	5 348 412

主要统计指标解释

房地产开发投资

指各种登记注册类型的房地产开发公司、商品房建设公司及其他房地产开发法人单位和附属于其他法人单位实际从事房地产开发或经营活动的单位统一开发的包括统代建、拆迁还建的住宅、厂房、仓库、饭店、宾馆、度假村、写字楼、办公楼等房屋建筑物和配套的服务设施，土地开发工程（如道路、给水、排水、供电、供热、通讯、平整场地等基础设施工程）的投资；不包括单纯的土地交易活动。

施工面积

指报告期内施工的全部房屋建筑面积。包括本期新开工的面积和上期开工跨入本期继续施工的房屋面积，以及上期已停建在本期恢复施工的房屋面积。本期竣工和本期施工后又停缓建的房屋，其建筑面积仍计入本期房屋施工面积中。

竣工面积

指在报告期内房屋建筑按照设计要求已经全部完工，达到住人和使用条件，经验收鉴定合格（或达到竣工验收标准），正式移交使用单位的各栋房屋建筑面积的总和。

房屋建筑面积竣工率

指一定时期内房屋竣工面积占同期房屋施工面积的比率。该指标从房屋建筑施工速度的角度反映投资效果的指标。

别墅、高档公寓

指建筑造价和销售价格明显高于一般商品住宅的商品住宅。别墅一般指地处郊区，独立成栋的商品住宅；高档公寓一般指地处市内高尚社区，高层或多层的商品住宅。别墅、高档公寓的确定标准：一是经有房地产投资计划审批权的主管部门审批建设的别墅、高档公寓开发项目；二是销售价格高于当地同等地段商品住宅平均销售价格一倍以上的别墅、公寓开发项目。该指标可以分析房地产投资结构，反映高收入家庭商品住宅的供求平衡情况。

EXPLANATORY NOTES TO MAJOR STATISTICAL INDICATORS

Investment in Real Estate Development

It includes the investment by the real estate development companies, commercial buildings construction companies and other real estate development units of various types of ownership in the construction of house buildings, such as residential buildings, factory buildings, warehouses, hotels, guesthouses, holiday villages, office buildings, and the complementary service facilities and land development projects, such as roads, water supply, water drainage, power supply, heating, telecommunications, land leveling and other projects of infrastructure. It excludes the activities in simple land transactions.

Floor Space under Construction

Floor Space under Construction refers to total floor space of all buildings under construction during the reference period, including floor space of newly started buildings during the reference period, floor space of construction extended from the previous period to the current period, and floor space of construction suspended during the previous period and resumed in the current period. Floor space of construction completed in the current period, and floor space of construction started and then suspended in the current period are also included in the floor space under construction of the current year.

Floor Space of Buildings Completed

Floor Space of Buildings Completed refers to the floor space of all buildings completed in the reference period, which have been appraised and accepted (or come up to the designed standards) and have been transferred to the owners for use.

Completion Rate of Floor Space of Buildings

Completion Rate of Floor Space of Buildings refers to the ratio of the floor space of buildings completed in certain period of time to the floor space of buildings under construction in the same period. This indicator reflects the investment result from the perspective of the speed of construction.

Villas, High-Grade Apartments

Villas, High-Grade Apartments refers to commercial houses whose construction costs and marketing prices are significantly higher than ordinary housing. Villas are independent structures generally located in the suburbs; high-grade apartments are multi-story buildings located in elegant urban neighborhoods. Criteria for villas and high-grade apartments include: 1) projects for the construction of villas or high-grade apartments have to be approved by competent departments in charge of real estate development and investment plans, and 2) prices for projects on villas or high-grade apartments are higher by over 100% compared with the average prices of ordinary commercial housing projects in similar location. This indicator helps to analyze the investment structure of the real estate industry and the demand and supply of housing for high-income households.

第十篇

CHAPTER 10

国内外贸易

DOMESTIC AND FOREIGN TRADES

表 10-1 历年商品销售总额

Total Sales of Commercial Goods in Main Years (1994 ~2012)

单位:亿元 (100 million yuan)

年 份 Year	商品购进总额 Total Value of Goods Purchased	商品销售总额 Total Value of Goods Sold	期末库存 Inventory at Year-End
1994	150.11	171.46	10.40
1995	186.38	200.05	17.03
1996	202.48	242.39	15.90
1997	278.41	274.26	37.23
1998	260.70	306.12	26.75
1999	517.13	593.37	57.62
2000	686.44	752.94	62.63
2001	891.30	1 004.89	64.55
2002	1 152.32	1 787.51	51.08
2003	2 366.49	2 422.87	187.75
2004	2 788.95	2 932.10	258.35
2005	2 499.25	2 807.47	224.16
2006	2 638.45	2 944.96	220.71
2007	3 337.31	3 613.46	245.43
2008	4 174.85	4 646.70	376.29
2009	4 913.26	5 905.20	495.57
2010	8 386.78	8 263.56	1 509.06
2011	12 866.04	10 502.98	2 303.33
2012	12 463.17	14 546.69	1 169.08

表10-2 历年社会消费品零售总额

Total Retail Sales of Social Consumer Goods in Main Years (1993～2012)

单位:亿元 (100 million yuan)

年份 Year	消费品零售总额 Total Retail Sales of Consumer Goods	#餐饮 Catering	按商品用途分 By Use 食品 Food	衣着 Clothing	用品 Articles	燃料 Fuel	商品销售总额 Total Sales of Retail Goods
1993	41.92		14.04	4.74	22.80	0.34	
1994	82.74	3.18	39.58	6.47	36.08	0.61	171.46
1995	110.00	4.07	49.50	8.36	51.59	0.55	200.05
1996	140.21	4.03	53.13	12.17	74.01	0.90	242.39
1997	162.23	5.41	62.89	12.54	84.72	2.08	274.26
1998	178.97	4.78	65.06	16.61	96.27	1.03	306.12
1999	198.31	19.02	74.17	15.26	104.17	4.71	593.37
2000	215.17	25.80	81.55	13.65	117.94	2.03	752.94
2001	233.02	28.50	81.27	13.99	135.28	2.48	1 004.89
2002	284.24	25.19	75.12	14.08	190.61	4.43	1 787.51
2003	313.24	24.50	72.53	14.49	220.21	6.01	2 422.87
2004	358.21	31.49	83.73	17.84	251.42	5.22	2 932.10
2005	353.69	43.80	111.00	27.53	213.52	1.64	2 807.47
2006	400.02	51.55	125.88	32.24	240.83	1.07	2 944.96
2007	456.04	60.52	128.66	35.63	283.45	8.30	3 613.46
2008	526.89	68.16	167.23	45.39	306.53	7.74	4 646.70
2009	859.63	102.74	256.11	77.78	498.41	27.33	5 905.20
2010	1 036.88	138.03	268.69	92.32	604.08	71.79	8 263.56
2011	1 204.04	152.43	309.09	114.46	650.35	130.14	10 502.98
2012	1 349.73	166.78	341.95	124.25	728.03	155.50	14 546.69

表10-3　连锁商业零售额
Retail Sales of Commercial Chains

单位:万元　(10 000 yuan)

指　标	Indicators	2010	2011	2012
连锁商业零售总额	**Total Retail Sales of Commercial Chains**	**2 259 603**	**2 439 773**	**2 441 670**
超市及大型超市	Supermarkets and Shopping Malls	934 491	917 676	960 829
便利店	Convenience Stores	136 299	167 699	201 500
家居建材商店	Stores of Building Materials for House Decorations	35 972	35 233	33 591
家电连锁店	House Appliance Chain Stores	438 901	439 006	290 255
连锁餐饮	Catering Chains	127 810	114 881	136 099
医药连锁	Pharmcy Chains	13 377	14 101	12 941
成品油连锁	Refined Oil Chains	518 197	694 528	747 923
其他连锁	Other Chains	54 556	56 649	58 531

表10-4　社会商业商品购、销、存总额
Total Values of Social Products on Purchase, Sales and Inventory

单位:亿元　(100 million yuan)

指　标	Indicators	2010	2011	2012
商品购进总额	**Total Goods Purchased**	**8 386.78**	**12 866.04**	**12 463.17**
#进　口	Imports	1 632.04	2 568.25	2 745.53
商品销售总额	**Total Goods Sold**	**8 263.56**	**10 502.98**	**14 546.69**
商品零售总额	Total Sales of Retail Goods	1 036.88	1 204.04	1 349.73
商品批发销售总额	Total Sales of Wholesale Goods	7 226.68	9 298.94	13 196.96
#出　口	Exports	663.82	941.75	1 032.06
年末库存总额	**Total Inventory at Year-end**	**1 509.06**	**2 303.33**	**1 169.08**

表10-5 社会消费品零售总额
Total Retail Sales of Consumer Goods

单位:万元 (10 000 yuan)

指 标	Indicators	2010	2011	2012
社会消费品零售总额	**Total Retail Sales of Consumer Goods**	**10 368 802**	**12 040 411**	**13 497 288**
按登记注册类型分	**By Type of Registration**			
内 资	Domestic Funded	6 947 927	8 086 101	8 865 668
国 有	State-owned	697 711	838 801	810 426
集 体	Collective-owned	552 532	321 702	313 290
股份有限公司	Companies with Limited Liability	1 151 463	1 248 803	1 429 636
私 营	Private	2 157 908	2 980 805	3 403 931
其 他	Others	2 388 313	2 695 990	2 908 386
港澳台商投资	Hong Kong/Macao/Taiwan Invested	1 243 829	1 573 804	1 728 556
外商投资	Foreigner Invested	2 177 046	2 380 506	2 903 064
按行业分	**By Sector**			
商业零售额	Commerce	8 988 464	10 516 109	11 829 502
餐饮业零售额	Catering	1 380 338	1 524 302	1 667 786
按商品用途分	**By Use**			
食品类	Food	2 686 915	3 090 903	3 419 502
衣着类	Clothing	923 241	1 144 602	1 242 501
用品类	Articles	6 040 820	6 503 501	7 280 295
燃料类	Fuel	717 826	1 301 405	1 554 990
构 成（%）	**Composition (%)**			
总 计	**Total**	**100.0**	**100.0**	**100.0**
按登记注册类型分	**By Type of Registration**			
内 资	Domestic Funded	67.0	67.2	65.7
国 有	State-owned	6.7	7.0	6.0
集 体	Collective-owned	5.3	2.7	2.3
股份有限公司	Company with Limited Liability	11.1	10.4	10.6
私 营	Private	20.8	24.7	25.2
其 他	Others	23.1	22.4	21.5
港澳台商投资	Hong Kong/Macao/Taiwan Invested	12.0	13.0	12.8
外商投资	Foreigner Invested	21.0	19.8	21.5
按行业分	**By Sector**			
商业零售额	Commerce	86.7	87.3	87.6
餐饮业零售额	Catering	13.3	12.7	12.4
按商品用途分	**By Use**			
食品类	Food	25.9	25.7	25.3
衣着类	Clothing	8.9	9.5	9.2
用品类	Articles	58.3	54.0	53.9
燃料类	Fuel	6.9	10.8	11.5

表10－6 限额以上商业企业主要财务指标
Major Financial Indicators of Above-Quota Commercial Enterprises

单位:万元 (10 000 yuan)

指 标	Indicators	2010	2011	2012
企业单位数(个)	**Number of Enterprises (unit)**	**1 524**	**1 746**	**1 713**
年末资产负债	**Assets and Liabilities at Year－end**			
资产总计	Total Assets	35 132 544	50 081 988	57 265 727
#流动资产合计	Total Circulating Assets	28 436 799	41 362 051	45 081 173
#存 货	Goods in Stock	6 637 479	10 044 123	10 360 824
固定资产合计	Total Fixed Assets	1 936 378	2 445 981	2 361 754
固定资产原价	Original Value of Fixed Assets	2 713 858	3 462 058	3 781 717
累计折旧	Accumulated Depreciation	962 398	1 272 434	1 463 248
#本年提取折旧	Depreciation in Current Year	177 580	181 675	289 909
负债总计	Total Liabilities	24 413 996	35 211 001	41 100 479
所有者权益总计	Owner's Equity	10 718 548	14 870 987	16 165 248
#实收资本	Paid-up Capital	4 116 682	5 507 911	6 435 951
#国家资本	State-owned Capital Assets	1 470 542	1 023 164	902 734
港澳台商资本	Hong Kong/Macao/Taiwan Capital Assets	414 141	777 974	632 318
外商资本	Foreign Capital Assets	811 726	1 139 568	1 711 170
法人资本	Legal Person Capital Assets	726 655	1 590 981	1 740 710
损益及分配(限批发零售贸易业填)	**Profit, Loss and Distribution (Only for Wholesale and Retails)**			
营业收入	Operating Revenue	833 143 406	128 133 473	141 457 065
#主营业务收入	Main Operation Revenue	828 879 416	127 666 389	139 929 966
主营业务成本	Main Operation Cost	770 844 602	117 854 883	126 412 558
营业费用	Operating Expenses	23 609 805	4 253 014	5 867 483
业务税金及附加	Operation Tax & Surtax	1 115 249	157 597	160 951
主营业务利润	Profit From Main Business	56 919 565	9 653 909	13 365 515
其他业务利润	Other Earnings	3 319 656	502 260	521 658

表10-7 商品交易市场基本情况
Commodity Market Transactions
(2012)

指 标	Indicators	市场数(个) Number of Markets(unit)	营业面积(平方米) Business Space(sq·m)	成交额(万元) Transaction Value (10 000 yuan)
合 计	**Total**	**176**	**1 061 578**	**19 957 147**
综合市场	**Integrated Markets**	**57**	**264 031**	**1 138 665**
生产资料综合市场	Integrated Market for Productive Materials	1	10 000	1 730
农产品综合市场	Integrated Market for Agricultural Products	46	183 125	1 057 039
其他综合市场	Other Integrated Markets	10	70 906	79 896
专业市场	**Professional Markets**	**119**	**797 547**	**18 818 482**
生产资料市场	Market for Productive Materials	7	85 231	14 303 734
农产品市场	Market for Agricultural Products	63	210 768	711 891
食品饮料烟酒市场	Market of Food, Beverage, Tobacco and Liquor	6	17 791	14 258
纺织品服装鞋帽市场	Market of Textiles, Clothes, Shoes and Hats	10	35 114	13 867
日用品及文化用品市场	Market of Commodities and Stationers' Goods	2	7 312	3 084 867
家俱、五金装饰材料市场	Market of Furniture, Hardware and Decoration Materials	19	302 900	295 093
汽车及零配件市场	Market of Automobiles and Spare and Accessory Parts	2	35 360	276 020
电器、通讯器材市场	Market of Electric Appliances and Communication Equipment	2	8 534	99 029
花、鸟、鱼、虫市场	Market of Flowers, Birds, Fishes and Insects	2	16 700	12 279
其他专业市场	Other Professional Markets	6	77 837	7 444

表10-8　商品交易市场摊位数量及成交额
Number of Stalls and Transaction Value in Commodity Market
(2012)

指　标	Indicators	数　量（个）Stalls (unit)	成交额（万元）Transaction Value (10000 yuan)
已出租摊位总计	**Total Stalls Leased**	**27 189**	**19 957 147**
食品、饮料、烟酒类	Food, Beverage, Tobacco and Liquor	17 508	1 768 091
服装、鞋帽、针、纺织品类	Garments, Shoes, Hats and Knitwear	2 934	22 904
化妆品类	Cosmetics	13	103
金银珠宝类	Gold, Silver and Jewelry	9	88
日用品类	Articles for Daily Use	349	3 100 694
五金电料类	Hardware Materials	212	6 734
体育、娱乐用品类	Sports and Recreation Articles	9	55
书报杂志类	Books and Newspapers	3	33
电子出版物及音像制品	Electronic Publications and Audio-Video Products	3	14
家用电器和音像器材类	Household Appliances and Audio-Video Equipment	15	226
中西药品	Western and Traditional Chinese Medicine	8	126
文化办公用品类	Culture and Office Articles	482	108 593
通讯器材类	Telecommunications Equipment	13	221
家具类	Furniture	462	15 111
木材及制品类	Timber and Its Products	56	3 097
石油及制品类	Petroleum and its products	550	14 069 446
金属材料及制品类	Metal Materials and Products	165	125 000
建筑及装潢材料类	Building and Decoration Materials	2 595	301 316
汽车类	Automobiles	54	276 020
种子饲料类	Seeds and Feeding Stuff	2	15
其他类	Others	1 747	159 260

表10-9 限额以上主要商品销售量
Sales Amount of Main Above-quota Goods

指 标	Indicators	单 位 Unit	2012
电脑(微型计算机)	Computer (PC)	台 set	2 054 370
煤 炭	Coal	吨 ton	42 694 634
汽 油	Gasoline	吨 ton	2 326 786
柴 油	Diesel Oil	吨 ton	1 769 560
钢 材	Steel Products	吨 ton	7 935 549
铜	Copper	吨 ton	1 222 566
铝	Aluminium	吨 ton	1 790 590
水 泥	Cement	吨 ton	2 912 356
汽 车	Motor Vehicles	辆 unit	1 707 118
#轿 车	Cars	辆 unit	1 455 350

表10-10 电子商务交易情况
Transactions of E-businesses

单位:亿元 (100 million yuan)

指 标	Indicators	2010	2011	2012
商品类电子商务交易额	**E-business Trading Volume for Commodities**	**2 324.95**	**3 106.63**	**3 511.00**
提供交易平台发生的电子商务交易额	E-business Trading Volume by Providing Platforms	2 065.27	2 745.25	3 030.00
B2B	B to B	2 059.59	2 724.51	3 001.00
B2C	B to C	3.82	16.25	22.50
C2C	C to C	1.85	4.48	6.50
企业自营发生的电子商务销售额	E-business Trading Volume by Enterprises	59.72	104.64	141.00
B2B	B to B	41.32	69.37	87.00
B2C	B to C	18.40	35.27	54.00
企业自营发生的电子商务采购额	E-business Purchasing Volume by Enterprises	199.97	256.74	340.00
服务类电子商务交易额	**E-business Trading Volume for Services**	**5 223.24**	**14 907.87**	**27 500.00**

表 10－11　历年进出口货物总值

Total Value of Imports and Exports in Main Years
(1993～2012)

单位:亿美元　　　　(USD 100 million)

年　份 Year	进出口总值 Total Value of Imports and Exports	出口总值 Total Export Value	#一般贸易 Ordinary Trade	加工贸易 Processing Trade	海关特殊监管区域物流货物 Goods for Logistics within Special Supervision of the Customs	进口总值 Total Import Value	#一般贸易 Ordinary Trade	加工贸易 Processing Trade	海关特殊监管区域物流货物 Goods for Logistics within Special Supervision of the Customs
1993	25.92	12.02	6.67			13.90	5.26		
1994	47.35	23.21	13.73			24.14	5.60		
1995	71.96	39.63	24.40			32.34	11.72		
1996	80.78	38.75	21.31			42.03	14.12		
1997	99.01	45.86	23.06			53.15	17.00		
1998	119.82	52.80	25.14			67.02	21.74		
1999	153.65	66.67	28.58			86.98	35.90		
2000	254.86	95.80	44.21			159.06	71.91		
2001	297.83	110.22	49.56			187.61	87.74		
2002	368.98	136.02	62.96			232.96	98.94		
2003	581.33	211.92	102.80			369.41	156.60		
2004	808.07	323.78	145.55			484.29	185.68		
2005	894.75	372.12	175.38			522.63	186.52		
2006	1 073.10	444.71	212.50			628.39	198.72		
2007	1 280.52	528.10	257.50			752.42	248.66		
2008	1 449.59	604.23	300.42			845.36	286.70		
2009	1 389.89	576.50	241.40			813.39	332.19		
2010	1 865.62	738.79	306.50	286.05	127.51	1 126.83	430.70	123.24	506.01
2011	2 260.00	888.98	356.82	339.00	167.03	1 371.02	537.42	152.78	600.65
2012	2 398.93	939.83	361.39	359.28	189.68	1 459.10	542.57	145.04	696.28

表10-12 重要商品的出口货物总值
Total Value of Important Exported Goods

单位:万美元 (USD 10 000)

指 标	Indicators	2011	2012
总 计	**Total**	**8 889 777**	**9 398 286**
#机电产品	**Mechanic and Electric Products**	**5 819 091**	**6 291 299**
#高新技术产品	**Hi-tech Products**	**3 410 823**	**3 848 800**
自动数据处理设备及其部件	Automatic Data Processing Equipment and its Parts	934 617	1 289 478
服装及衣着附件	Clothing and its Accessories	801 968	752 922
电话机	Telephone Sets	491 137	718 108
集成电路	Integrated Circuits	650 302	675 118
船 舶	Ships	565 330	454 624
纺织纱线、织物及制品	Textile Yarns, Fabrics and their Products	342 867	331 972
成品油	Refined Oils	143 432	188 922
医药品	Medicines	128 447	175 002
未锻造的铜及铜材	Unwrought Copper and its Bar	107 407	171 433
汽车零件	Automobile Parts	146 386	170 469
液晶显示板	LCDs	279 722	165 152
自动数据处理设备的零件	Parts of Automatic Data Processing Equipment	167 403	135 752
通断保护电路装置及零件	Protection Circuit Devices and their Parts	121 695	126 824
家具及其零件	Furniture and its Parts	89 646	93 186
箱包及类似容器	Boxes and Similar Containers	94 040	93 079
二极管及类似半导体器件	Diodes and Similar Semiconductor Devices	78 752	87 448
汽车(包括整套散件)	Automobiles (including CKD parts)	32 967	83 163
农产品	Agricultural Products	78 347	76 284
塑料制品	Plastic Products	67 703	71 870
钢 材	Steel	74 582	68 999
珍珠、钻石、宝石及半宝石	Pearls, Diamonds, Precious Stones and Half - precious Stones	82 604	67 203
未锻造的铝及铝材	Unwrought Aluminium and its Bar	56 913	66 405

表10-13 重要商品的进口货物总值
Total Value of Important Imported Goods

单位:万美元 (USD 10 000)

指 标	Indicators	2011	2012
总 计	**Total**	**13 710 166**	**14 590 981**
#机电产品	**Mechanic and Electric Products**	**8 010 976**	**8 623 071**
#高新技术产品	**Hi-tech Products**	**4 844 576**	**5 739 420**
集成电路	Integrated Circuits	2 111 820	2 621 233
未锻造的铜及铜材	Unwrought Copper and its Bar	816 420	1 138 302
汽车(包括整套散件)	Cars (including CKD parts)	688 467	834 414
自动数据处理设备及其部件	Automatic Data Processing Equipment and its Parts	614 323	701 689
农产品	Agricultural Products	568 841	629 992
初级形状的塑料	Primarily-formed Plastics	584 947	533 149
医药品	Medicines	352 572	449 406
计量检测分析自控仪器及器具	Automatically-controlled Equipment and Devices for Measuring and Checking Analysis	363 290	399 560
成品油	Refined Oils	321 223	303 486
飞 机	Aeroplanes	136 762	297 169
通断保护电路装置及零件	Protection Circuit Devices and their Parts	298 636	277 619
医疗仪器及器械	Medical Instrument and Appliances	157 661	198 296
钻 石	Diamonds	251 453	192 780
自动数据处理设备的零件	Parts of Automatic Data Processing Equipment	204 880	151 492
手 表	Wrist Watches	150 648	143 952
汽车零件	Automobile Parts	140 933	141 811
印刷、装订机械及零件	Printing and Binding Machineries and their Parts	142 529	135 404
酒 类	Alcohols	112 936	128 891
纺织纱线、织物及制品	Textile Yarns, Fabrics and their Products	122 377	117 369
二甲苯	Xylene	55 428	110 519
变压、整流、电感器及零件	Tranformers, Rectifiers, Inductors and their Parts	127 450	103 189
服装及衣着附件	Clothes and their Parts	78 144	90 276

表10-14 主要年份按国别(地区)分的出口货物总值
Total Value of Exports by Country/Region in Main Years

单位:万美元 (USD 10 000)

国别(地区)	Country/Region	2005	2010	2011	2012
总 计	**Total**	**3 721 174**	**7 387 919**	**8 889 777**	**9 398 286**
#亚 洲	**Asia**	**1 697 530**	**3 340 974**	**4 008 927**	**4 250 789**
#中国香港	Hong Kong, China	468 087	717 639	894 808	926 930
中国澳门	Macao, China	1 789	5 557	2 538	3 819
中国台湾	Taiwan, China	130 197	271 421	252 646	229 610
印 度	India	35 233	133 175	172 209	207 384
孟加拉国	Bangladesh	13 023	24 808	23 996	30 266
印度尼西亚	Indonesia	26 669	71 303	106 161	113 966
日 本	Japan	451 176	774 154	941 837	976 183
马来西亚	Malaysia	66 363	244 468	239 705	228 808
巴基斯坦	Pakistan	10 116	15 838	19 206	21 754
菲律宾	Philippines	64 628	71 219	52 081	60 828
沙特阿拉伯	Saudi Arabia	14 897	31 085	39 014	60 202
新加坡	Singapore	109 379	305 192	358 309	406 605
韩 国	Republic of Korea	136 003	260 049	345 273	360 928
斯里兰卡	Sri Lanka	4 348	5 962	19 966	12 718
泰 国	Thailand	33 224	96 554	121 400	135 386
阿拉伯联合酋长国	United Arab Emirates	46 529	100 559	128 450	172 789
欧 洲	**Europe**	**843 460**	**1 893 937**	**2 078 237**	**2 019 811**
#欧 盟	European Union	785 409	1 701 505	1 876 080	1 778 648
#比利时	Belgium	61 105	101 144	108 887	75 966
英 国	United Kingdom	114 380	178 263	205 468	186 359
德 国	Germany	187 924	380 488	402 674	549 783
法 国	France	63 802	166 625	195 189	156 655
爱尔兰	Ireland	15 151	16 467	16 139	17 474
意大利	Italy	51 163	184 868	128 924	102 934
荷 兰	Netherlands	108 070	225 709	286 581	270 525
西班牙	Spain	42 824	78 986	91 665	81 725
波 兰	Poland	12 284	44 788	46 238	40 464
瑞 典	Sweden	22 954	39 060	37 447	33 836
瑞 士	Switzerland	11 441	26 010	31 282	25 754
俄罗斯	Russia	25 442	126 041	135 989	179 644
拉丁美洲	**Latin America**	**144 120**	**384 886**	**481 649**	**469 966**
#阿根廷	Argentina	5 739	24 892	30 188	25 645
巴 西	Brazil	34 310	120 169	131 689	126 637
智 利	Chile	11 408	23 641	34 166	35 206
墨西哥	Mexico	28 773	99 863	131 568	107 366
巴拿马	Panama	19 659	17 688	35 555	51 733
北美洲	**North America**	**863 433**	**1 279 355**	**1 691 715**	**2 083 853**
#加拿大	Canada	92 621	97 013	114 692	154 688
美 国	United States of America	770 807	1 182 329	1 576 981	1 929 155

表10-15 主要年份按国别(地区)分的进口货物总值
Total Value of Imports by Country/Region in Main Years

单位:万美元 (USD 10 000)

国别(地区)	Country/Region	2005	2010	2011	2012
总 计	**Total**	**5 226 325**	**11 268 269**	**13 710 166**	**14 590 981**
#亚 洲	**Asia**	**3 046 147**	**6 234 946**	**7 380 567**	**7 634 781**
#中国香港	Hong Kong, China	46 910	38 575	37 730	51 324
中国台湾	Taiwan, China	379 850	762 696	739 051	740 398
印 度	India	58 457	184 487	228 127	227 179
印度尼西亚	Indonesia	76 588	84 572	142 256	124 589
日 本	Japan	919 062	1 738 090	1 873 155	1 775 284
马来西亚	Malaysia	220 785	736 065	1 085 857	1 285 543
新加坡	Singapore	199 594	251 998	311 494	328 612
韩 国	Repubic of Korea	511 641	949 805	1 194 667	1 085 306
泰 国	Thailand	148 120	330 108	361 610	293 449
非 洲	**Africa**	**39 824**	**214 711**	**205 600**	**211 715**
欧 洲	**Europe**	**1 122 993**	**2 515 255**	**3 599 233**	**4 021 579**
#欧 盟	European Union	998 473	2 092 754	3 001 599	3 485 468
#比利时	Belgium	52 002	200 446	309 580	266 263
英 国	United Kingdom	72 078	113 428	290 432	453 809
德 国	Germany	385 695	797 961	1 074 889	1 243 157
法 国	France	159 106	293 253	395 971	520 329
意大利	Italy	102 266	192 625	250 713	223 494
荷 兰	Netherlands	44 876	77 545	120 438	137 847
西班牙	Spain	19 596	50 883	67 389	77 827
波 兰	Poland	4 920	18 727	33 896	35 934
瑞 典	Sweden	34 688	114 719	136 830	136 065
瑞 士	Switzerland	68 211	214 630	318 329	308 041
俄罗斯	Russia	31 450	144 899	197 925	143 864
拉丁美洲	**Latin America**	**127 155**	**645 571**	**748 629**	**925 345**
#巴 西	Brazil	26 441	107 078	125 129	105 155
智 利	Chile	35 236	299 182	340 495	435 567
墨西哥	Mexico	26 439	103 963	148 394	150 876
北美洲	**North America**	**820 607**	**1 420 899**	**1 513 938**	**1 441 074**
#加拿大	Canada	61 936	129 762	155 054	127 875
美 国	United States of America	758 389	1 291 123	1 358 874	1 313 199
大洋洲	**Oceania**	**69 599**	**235 546**	**259 117**	**354 518**
#澳大利亚	Australia	56 073	173 509	202 708	302 304
新西兰	New Zealand	9 197	52 040	51 641	49 263

主要统计指标解释

社会消费品零售总额

指批发和零售业、餐饮业、新闻出版业、邮政业和其他服务业等,售予城乡居民用于生活消费的商品和社会集团用于公共消费的商品之总量。社会消费品零售总额包括:

(1) 批发和零售业企业(单位):

①售予城乡居民的各种生活消费品;

②售予入境旅游的外国人、华侨、港澳台同胞的各类商品;

③售予行政事业单位、社会团体、军队和武警等机构的商品,以及以零售方式售予各类企业的商品。具体包括:用于非生产和社会交往的办公用品,如通讯设备、计算器具和设备、电讯网络设备、文印设备、音像视听器材和设备、纸张、本册、文具及装订文印材料、家具、日用电器、针纺织品、清洁卫生用品、文体用品、奖品、纪念品、礼品等;供内部人员乘坐的交通工具和燃料;用于办公设施修缮的各类配件、材料、工具等;用于取暖和防暑降温的设备、燃料、材料及食品等;专用于教学的用品和设备;非营利医疗机构的中、西药品、中药材和医疗设备器材;非专用的劳动保护用品;不对外营业的内部食堂用的餐具、炊具、设备、清洁卫生工具和食品、燃料等;军队、武警用于其人员生活的衣着品和个人用品;其他各类非生产性设备和用品。

(2) 餐饮业出售的主食、菜肴、烟酒饮料和其他商品。

(3) 新闻出版业、邮政业售予城乡居民、企事业单位、军队和武警等机构的书报杂志、音像制品、邮品等。

(4) 其他服务业出售的食品、烟酒饮料、服装鞋帽、日常生活用品、医药保健用品、艺术品、工艺美术品、玩具、殡葬用品以及其他消费品。

批发零售贸易业商品购、销、存总额

指各种登记注册类型的批发、零售贸易企业(单位)以本企业(单位)为总体的,从上海、上海以外市场购进的商品总量、销售和出口的商品总量、库存商品总量等情况。该指标对促进工农业生产发展、活跃市场、平抑物价、保障供给、满足需求具有举足轻重的作用。该指标可以反映商品流转过程中商品的购进、销售、库存之间的比例关系和存在的问题。

商品购进总额

指从本企业(单位)以外的单位和个人购进(包括从境外直接进口)作为转卖或加工后转卖的商品总额。它反映批发零售贸易业从国内、国外市场上购进商品的总量。商品购进总额包括:①从工农业生产者购进的商品;②从出版社、报社的出版发行部门购进的图书、杂志和报纸;③从各种登记注册类型的批发零售贸易企业(单位)购进的商品;④从其他单位购进的商品,如从机关、团体、企业等单位购进的剩余物资,从餐饮业、服务业购进的商品,从海关、市场管理部门购进的缉私和没收的商品,从居民手中收购的废旧商品等;⑤从国(境)外直接进口的商品。不包括企业(单位)为自身经营用和未通过买卖行为而收入的商品以及销售退回、商品升溢等。

商品销售总额

商品销售总额指对本企业以外的单位和个人出售(包括对国(境)外直接出口)的商品。这个指标反映批发零售贸易业在上海市场以及上海以外市场上销售商品的总量。商品销售总额包括:①售给城乡居民和社会集团消费用的商品;②售给工业、农业、建筑业、运输邮电业、批发零售贸易业、餐饮业、服务业等作为生产、经营使用的商品;③售给批发零售贸易业作为转卖或加工后转卖的商品;④对国(境)外直接出口的商品。不包括:出售本企业自用的废旧包装用品,未通过买卖行为付出的商品,经本单位介绍,由买卖双方直接结算,本单位只收取手续费的业务,购货退出的商品以及商品损耗和损失等。

批发零售贸易业年末库存

是指年末各种经济类型的批发零售贸易企业(单位)已取得所有权的商品,它反映各地区、各批发零售贸易企业的商品库存情况和对市场商品供应的保证程度。期末库存包括;①存放在批发零售贸易业经营单位(如门市部、批发站、经营处)仓库、货场、货柜和货架中的商品;②挑选、整理、包装中的商品;③已记入购进而尚未运到本单位的商品,即发货单或银行承兑凭证已到而货未到部份;④寄放他处的商品,如因购货方拒绝承付而暂存放在购货方的商品和已办完加工成品收回手续而未提回的商品;⑤委托其他单位代销(未作销售或调出)尚未售出的商品;⑥代其他单位购进尚未交付的商品。不包括所有权不属于本单位的商品、拨付除批发零售贸易业以外的其他行业所属独立核算加工厂等加工生产尚未收回成品的商品,代国家物资储备部门保管的商品等。期末库存总额计算方法是:农副产品采购单位按购进价计算;批发单位按进货价计算;零售单位按什么价格核算就按什么价格计算。

主营业务收入

指企业在销售商品、提供劳务等日常活动中所产生的收入总额。

主营业务成本

指企业已销商品应负担的进货原价和商品进价成本。

营业费用

指批发零售贸易企业在购、销、存过程中发生的各项经

营费用。包括运输费、装卸费、包装费、保险费、展览费、差旅费、广告费、商品损耗、进出口商品累计佣金、经营人员的工资及福利费等。

外贸进出口总额

外贸进出口总额是指海关统计中按经营单位即进出口企业在海关注册地的行政区域口径统计的数据，它反映的是上海浦东新区行政辖区内各类具有进出口经营权企业（外贸企业）的进出口。它不包含外省市外贸企业途经上海浦东新区口岸由上海海关结关放行及统计的进出口商品，但包含上海浦东新区外贸企业经由非上海口岸进出口结关放行及统计的商品。

商品类电子商务交易额

指借助网络订单且实际交割的商品总额，借助网络订单指通过网络发送订单。付款可以是网上，也可以是网下进行。

提供交易平台发生的电子商务交易额

指为电子商务交易双方提供的平台中实现的商品类电子商务交易额。

企业自营发生的电子商务销售额

指企业在自己的电子商务平台上借助网络订单实际销售的商品总额。

企业自营发生的电子商务采购额

指企业在自己的电子商务平台上借助网络订单实际采购的商品总额。

服务类电子商务交易额

指服务类电子商务产生的交易额，非实物商品交易。包含金融服务、住宿旅游服务、交通仓储服务以及通信服务等等。

B2B

指企业对企业的电子商务交易。

B2C

指企业对个人的电子商务交易。

C2C

指个人对个人的电子商务交易。

EXPLANATORY NOTES TO MAJOR STATISTICAL INDICATORS

Total Retail Sales of Consumer Goods

Total Retail Sales of Consumer Goods refers to the sum of retail sales of commodities sold by wholesale, retail, catering, publishing, post and telecommunications and other service industries to urban and rural households for private consumption and to social institutions for public consumption. Retail sales of consumer goods include:

(1) Sales by wholesale and retail units:

①of consumer goods sold to urban and rural households

②of commodities sold to foreigners, overseas Chinese and Chinese compatriots from Hong Kong, Macau and Taiwan visiting in China

③of commodities sold to government agencies, institutions, social organizations, military and armed police units, and commodities sold to enterprises in the form of retail sales. More specifically, they include: office facilities and articles for non – production purposes such as communications equipment, computing equipment and instruments, TV and network equipment, printing and copying equipment, audio – visual equipment and instruments, paper, notebooks, stationeries, furniture, electric appliances, knitwear, sanitation and cleaning articles, cultural and sport articles, articles for prizes, souvenirs, etc.; transport vehicles and fuels for employees; materials, spare parts and tools for the maintenance of office facilities; equipment, fuels, materials and food for winter heating or summer cooling purposes; articles and equipment for teaching purpose; Chinese and western medicines and medical equipment and facilities purchased by non profit – making medical institutes; non – specialized work safety articles; cooking utensils, tableware, equipment, cleaning articles, food and fuels purchased by internal cafeterias; clothes and personal articles purchased by military or armed police units for their officials and soldiers; and other equipment and articles for non – production purposes.

(2) Sales of stable food, cooked dishes, beverages, tobaccos and other articles by catering units.

(3) Sales of books, newspapers, magazines, audio – visual products and post products by publishing, post and telecommunications departments to urban and rural households and to enterprises, institutions, military and armed police units.

(4) Sales of food, beverages, tobaccos, clothing, hats, footwear, articles for daily use, medicines, medical and health articles, work of art, handicrafts, toys, funeral articles and other articles by other service industries.

Purchase, Sales and Stock of Commodities by Wholesale and Retail Trades

Purchase, Sales and Stock of Commodities by Wholesale and Retail Trades refer to the total volume of commodities purchased, total volume of sales and exports, and the stock of commodities by wholesale and retail enterprises (establishments) of different status of registration from Shanghai and out – of – Shanghai markets. This indicator plays an important role in promoting industrial and agricultural production, thriving market, stabilizing prices, ensuring market supply and meeting the needs of consumers. It also reflects the relationship among purchase, sales and stock of commodities in the circulation of goods and reveals the existing problems.

Total Purchase of Commodities

Total purchase of commodities refers to purchase of commodities from other establishments or individuals (including direct import abroad) for the purpose of reselling, either with or without further processing of the commodities purchased. This indicator shows the total value of purchases of commodities by wholesale and retail establishments from domestic and overseas markets, they include: ① agricultural and industrial products purchased from producers; ② books, magazines and newspapers purchased from distribution departments of the publishers; ③commodities purchased from wholesale and retail establishments; ④commodities purchased from other units, such as surplus materials purchased from government agencies, enterprises or institutions, commodities purchased from catering and service establishments, confiscated goods purchased from customs authorities or market management agencies, second hand goods and reusable stuff purchased from residents; ⑤commodities directly imported abroad. Excluded are commodities purchased by establishments for their own business operation, commodities obtained without buying or selling procedures, rejected commodities, etc.

Total Sales of Commodities

Total Sales of Commodities refer to the selling of commodities to other establishments and individuals (including direct export). Reflecting the total value of sales of commodities at Shanghai markets and out - of - Shanghai markets, this indicator includes: ① commodities sold to urban and rural households and institutions for their consumption; ② commodities sold to establishments in industry, agriculture, construction, transportation, post and telecommunications, wholesale and retail trade, catering and service trade and public utility for their production and operation; ③ commodities sold to wholesale and retail establishments for re - selling, with or without further processing; and ④commodities for direct export to other countries. Excluded are selling of waste packaging materials used by enterprises themselves commodities transferred without buying or selling procedures, commission income from brokerage in transactions whose settlement is directly handled by buyers and sellers, rejected commodities in the purchase, loss in commodities, etc.

Commodities Stock of Wholesale and Retail Enterprises at Year-end

refers to total commodities possessed by wholesale and retail enterprises (units of various ownership, which reflects the commodity stock level of various wholesale and retail enterprises and the potential for market supply. This indicator includes; ①commodities located in storage, rooms, garages, counters, and shelves of operating units(such as sales stores, wholesale stations, and operating offices) of wholesale and retail enterprises; ② commodities in the process of selecting, sorting, and packing; ③commodities not arrived but recorded as purchase in the account, i. e. commodities have not arrived but payment receipts for the commodities from the sellers or the banks have arrived; ④commodities deposited in other places rather than places mentioned above, for instance; commodities in the hold of purchasers temporarily due to the refusal of payment and commodities not taken back after going through processing procedures; ⑤ commodities entrusted to other units to sell but not sold out yet; ⑥ commodities purchased for other units but not delivered yet. Commodities not included as stock are those not owned by enterprises, those allocated to financially independent factories rather than wholesale and retail enterprises for processing but not taken back yet, and finally those put in stock by wholesale and retail enterprises on behalf of the state material reserves units. The value of commodities stock at the end of period, the value is calculated at purchasing price of agricultural goods purchasing units and wholesale units and retail units at accounting prices.

Prime Operating Revenue

Prime Operating Revenue refers to the earnings a corporation receives in daily activity such as selling goods and offering labor service.

Operating Cost

Operating Cost refers to the cost a corporation paid to buy and deliver the commodities.

Operating Expenses

Operating Expenses refer to the spending that a wholesaler or retailer pays in buying, selling or stocking goods. It includes fees incurred in transport, loading and unloading, packaging, insurance, exhibition, business trip, advertisement, commodity wastage, commissions in import and export, salaries and bonus paid to workers involved.

The Volume of Foreign Trade

The Volume of Foreign Trade is offered by Customs authorities, covering the operation units, or the enterprises involved in import and export, that have registered in the administrative regions where the Customs operate. It reflects the import and export of all the enterprises with import and export rights (foreign trade enterprises) under the administration of Shanghai Pudong New Area Municipality. It excludes those commodities of foreign trade enterprises from out of town that underwent customs clearance at Shanghai Pudong New Area ports but includes commodities of foreign trade enterprises of Shanghai Pudong New Area that underwent customs clearance in non-Shanghai ports.

E-business Trading Volume for Commodities

refers to the total volume of commodities that have been ordered and actually transacted through the network, and the term of "through the network" means sending orders via the internet. Payment can be made both online and offline.

E-business Trading Volume by Providing Platforms

refers to the E-business trading volume for commodities that certain platforms are provided for the two parties for E-businesses.

E-business Trading Volume by Enterprises

refers to the total volume that enterprises make actual sales by means of orders through the network under their own E-business platforms.

E-business Purchasing Volume by Enterprises

refers to the total volume that enterprises make actual purchases by means of orders through the network under their own E – business platforms.

E-business Trading Volume for Services

refers to the trading volume provided by Service E-business, which is not commodity E-business. It includes services such as finance, accommodations, tourism, transportation, warehousing and communications.

B2B

refers to E-business transactions between business to business.

B2C

refers to E-business transactions between business to consumer.

C2C

refers to E-business transactions between consumer to consumer.

第十一篇

CHAPTER 11

服务、旅游和住宿业

SERVICES, TOURISM AND HOTELS

表11-1 社会服务业经济总量(营业收入)
Total Economics of Social Services (Operating Revenue)
(2010~2012)

单位:亿元 (100 million yuan)

指 标	Indicators	2010	2011	2012
总 计	**Total**	**2 515.23**	**2 762.27**	**3 020.11**
装卸搬运和运输代理业、仓储业	Handling, Other Transportation Services and Warehousing	322.92	329.29	379.51
信息传输、软件和信息技术服务业	Information Transmission, Computer Services and Software	881.51	1 004.49	1 131.14
#软件开发	Software	321.01	344.27	341.74
租赁和商务服务业	Leasing and Business Services	931.83	964.56	1 020.26
#商务服务业	Commercial Services	886.33	892.44	930.21
#企业管理服务	Business Management Services	480.49	524.07	560.14
咨询与调查	Consulting and Surveys	111.09	161.88	128.35
广告业	Advertising	66.28	69.54	76.55
科学研究和技术服务业	Scientific Researches and Technology Service	266.04	341.26	350.46
水利、环境和公共设施管理业	Water Conservancy, Environment and Public Facilities Management	35.32	27.72	37.89
居民服务、修理和其他服务业	Resident Services, Repair and Other Services	40.54	45.77	43.48
教 育	Education	12.43	15.71	18.38
卫生和社会工作	Health and Social Work	6.16	8.13	9.72
文化、体育和娱乐业	Culture, Sports and Entertainment	18.49	25.34	29.26

注:本篇社会服务业相关表式自2012年起,采用国民经济行业分类(GB/T 4754-2011),部分行业中类及小类的数据范围有所变化,但增幅的计算基数仍采用2011年年鉴公布数。

Note: The relavant forms in this chapter of social services have been classified by the national economical trades (GB/T 4754-2011) since 2012. Some changes happen in the data scope of the middle and small sorts of certain trades, but the calculation base for the increase rate will adopt the released data as in the Yearbook of 2011.

表11－2 社会服务业经济总量
Total Economics of Social Services
(2012)

单位:亿元 (100 million yuan)

指 标	Indicators	营业收入 Operating Revenue	增 幅(%) Increased by	比 重(%) Percentage
总 计	**Total**	**3 020.11**	**9.3**	**100.0**
装卸搬运和运输代理业、仓储业	Handling, Other Transportation Services and Warehousing	379.51	15.3	12.6
信息传输、软件和信息技术服务业	Information Transmission, Computer Services and Software	1 131.14	12.6	37.5
#软件开发	Software	341.74	-0.7	11.3
租赁和商务服务业	Leasing and Business Services	1 020.26	5.8	33.8
#商务服务业	Commercial Services	930.21	4.2	30.8
#企业管理服务	Business Management Services	560.14	6.9	18.5
咨询与调查	Consulting and Surveys	128.35	-20.7	4.2
广告业	Advertising	76.55	10.1	2.5
科学研究和技术服务业	Scientific Researches and Technology Service	350.46	2.7	11.6
水利、环境和公共设施管理业	Water Conservancy, Environment and Public Facilities Management	37.89	36.7	1.3
居民服务、修理和其他服务业	Resident Services and Other Services	43.48	-5.0	1.4
教 育	Education	18.38	17.0	0.6
卫生和社会工作	Health and Social Work	9.72	19.6	0.3
文化、体育和娱乐业	Culture, Sports and Entertainment	29.26	15.5	1.0

表11－3　社会服务业从业人员数

Number of Employees of Social Services
(2010～2012)

单位:万人　(10 000 persons)

指　标	Indicators	2010	2011	2012
总　计	**Total**	**38.35**	**39.88**	**45.33**
装卸搬运和运输代理业、仓储业	Handling, Other Transportation Services and Warehousing	3.41	3.53	4.07
信息传输、软件和信息技术服务业	Information Transmission, Computer Services and Software	9.83	10.78	11.89
#软件开发	Software	5.47	6.05	6.12
租赁和商务服务业	Leasing and Business Services	14.77	14.42	17.45
#商务服务业	Commercial Services	14.37	14.05	16.79
#企业管理服务	Business Management Services	4.67	4.45	6.78
咨询与调查	Consulting and Surveys	2.69	2.76	2.71
广告业	Advertising	0.47	0.50	0.51
科学研究和技术服务业	Scientific Researches and Technology Service	5.20	5.89	6.33
水利、环境和公共设施管理业	Water Conservancy, Environment and Public Facilities Management	0.98	0.89	1.25
居民服务、修理和其他服务业	Resident Services and Other Services	2.91	2.99	2.68
教　育	Education	0.44	0.55	0.61
卫生和社会工作	Health and Social Work	0.31	0.32	0.39
文化、体育和娱乐业	Culture, Sports and Entertainment	0.49	0.51	0.67

表11－4 社会服务业从业人员数
Number of Employees of Social Services
(2012)

单位:万人 (10 000 persons)

指 标	Indicators	从业人员数 Number of Employees	增 幅(%) Increased by	比 重(%) Percentage
总 计	**Total**	**45.33**	**13.7**	**100.0**
装卸搬运和运输代理业、仓储业	Handling, Other Transportation Services and Warehousing	4.07	15.3	9.0
信息传输、软件和信息技术服务业	Information Transmission, Computer Services and Software	11.89	10.3	26.2
#软件开发	Software	6.12	1.2	13.5
租赁和商务服务业	Leasing and Business Services	17.45	21.0	38.5
#商务服务业	Commercial Services	16.79	19.5	37.0
#企业管理服务	Business Management Services	6.78	52.4	15.0
咨询与调查	Consulting and Surveys	2.71	-1.8	6.0
广告业	Advertising	0.51	2.0	1.1
科学研究和技术服务业	Scientific Researches and Technology Service	6.33	7.5	14.0
水利、环境和公共设施管理业	Water Conservancy, Environment and Public Facilities Management	1.25	40.4	2.8
居民服务、修理和其他服务业	Resident Services and Other Services	2.68	-10.4	5.9
教 育	Education	0.61	10.9	1.3
卫生和社会工作	Health and Social Work	0.39	21.9	0.9
文化、体育和娱乐业	Culture, Sports and Entertainment	0.67	31.4	1.5

表11－5 主要年份接待国内外游客情况
Foreign and Domestic Tourists Received in Main Years

单位:万人次 (10 000 persons)

指 标	Indicators	2005	2010	2011	2012
接待游客总数	**Total Tourists Received**	**1 660**	**3 215**	**3 133**	**2 780**
国内游客数	Domestic	1 566	3 085	3 033	2 680
国外游客数	Foreign	94	130	100	100
按接待单位分	By Receiving Agency				
#宾馆接待游客	Hotels	164	278	255	284
旅行社接待游客	Tourist Agencies	111	185	180	213
景点接待游客	Tourist Attractions	1 385	2 752	2 698	2 283
平均每天接待旅游人数(人次/天)	Average Number of Tourists Received Everyday (person-time/day)	45 474	88 094	85 836	76 164

表11－6 旅馆、旅行社经营情况
Operation of Hotels and Travel Agencies

指 标	Indicators	单 位 Unit	2005	2010	2011	2012
旅馆业	**Hotel Industry**					
接待能力状况	**Receiving Capacity**					
客房数	Rooms	间 room	12 692	15 780	17 755	19 024
客房床位数	Beds	张 bed	20 245	22 652	26 129	28 322
实际住宿人次数	Actual Staying Guests	万人次 10 000 person-times	163.84	278.33	254.82	283.67
#境外来沪住宿人次数	Overseas Guests	万人次 10 000 person-times	73.03	99.21	99.66	100.24
实际住宿人天数	Actual Staying Days	万人天 10 000 person · days	371.18	491.33	429.30	469.67
#境外来沪住宿人天数	Staying Days of Overseas Guests	万人天 10 000 person · days	195.58	187.84	180.16	179.21
财务经营状况	**Financial Operation**					
固定资产原值	Original Value of Fixed Assets	亿元 100 million yuan	82.35	119.19	137.17	112.60
营业收入	Operation Earning	亿元 100 million yuan	37.09	55.85	51.56	55.18
#客房收入	Hotel Room Earning	亿元 100 million yuan	21.77	31.87	26.82	27.44
餐饮收入	Catering Earning	亿元 100 million yuan	15.32	19.22	21.84	22.68
旅行社	**Travel Agency**					
旅行社接待人次数	Persons Received by PNA Travel Agencies	万人次 10 000 person-times	110.69	185.25	180.27	213.50
国内旅行社	Domestic Travel Agencies	万人次 10 000 person-times	89.86	154.52	152.61	186.16
国际旅行社	International Travel Agencies	万人次 10 000 person-times	20.83	30.73	27.66	27.34
旅行社营业收入	Operation Earnings of PNA Travel Agencies	亿元 100 million yuan	14.68	30.00	33.50	53.12
国内旅行社	Domestic Travel Agencies	亿元 100 million yuan	8.44	16.08	23.00	29.17
国际旅行社	International Travel Agencies	亿元 100 million yuan	6.24	13.92	10.50	23.95

表 11-7 旅游景点经营情况
Operation of Tourist Attractions

指 标 Indicators		单 位 Unit	2005	2010	2011	2012
主要景点营业情况	**Business in Major Tourist Attractions**					
主要景点个数	Main Tourist Attractions	个 in number	23	25	27	32
接待参观人次	Visitors Received	万人次 10 000 person-times	1 908	2 752	2 698	2 342
营业收入	Operation Earnings	万元 10 000 yuan	87 500	144 781	121 532	129 355

表 11-8 会议、展览情况
Conferences and Fairs

指 标 Indicators		单 位 Unit	2005	2010	2011	2012
举办展览(博览)	**Number of Exhibitions Hosted**	**次 time**	**114**	**120**	**156**	**184**
#国际性	International	次 time	91	100	135	160
#三万平方米及以上	≥30 000 sq · m	次 time	29	38	54	70
#五万平方米及以上	≥50 000 sq · m	次 time	15	28	37	43
展览面积	Display Area	万平方米 10 000 sq · m	238	400	551	709
参展客商	Exhibition-Attending Investors	个 unit	48 412	69 713	90 670	135 791
接待(参观)人数	Visitors Received	万人次 10 000 person-times	266.90	309.70	444.70	579.73
召开会议	Conferences Hosted	次 time	1 583	1 504	13 486	19 400
#跨省市	Trans-provincial	次 time	61	112		
国际性	International	次 time	199	26	1 949	2 930
参加会议人员	Number of Participants	万人次 10 000 person-times	16.69	17.03	132.34	152.01
#海外与会人员	Overseas Participants	万人次 10 000 person-times	3.00	1.34	16.31	24.28

注：2011 年起会议统计的范围为浦东四星级以上宾馆。
Note: The statistical scope for the conferences since the year of 2011 refers to the hotels with four stars or more in Pudong.

主要统计指标解释

接待国外游客人数

指来上海浦东新区参观、访问、旅行、探亲、访友、休养、考察、参加会议和从事经济、科技、文化、教育、体育、宗教等活动的外国人、华侨、港澳和台湾同胞的人数。不包括来上海浦东新区常住1年以上的外国专家、留学生等。上海浦东新区入境的境外旅游人数包括从上海浦东新区口岸入境的境外旅游人数和从我国其他口岸入境的境外旅游人数。

EXPLANATORY NOTES TO MAJOR STATISTICAL INDICATORS

Number of Overseas Tourists Through Shanghai Customs

Number of Overseas Tourists through Shanghai Pudong New Area Customs refers to the number of foreigners, overseas Chinese, and compatriots from Hong Kong, Macao and Taiwan coming to Shanghai Pudong New Area for sightseeing, visits, tours, family reunions, meeting friends, vacations, study tours, attending meetings and other activities of an economic, scientific and technological, cultural, physical culture and religious nature. This does not include foreign experts and students residing in Shanghai Pudong New Area for over 1 year. The number of overseas tourists to Shanghai Pudong New Area includes those overseas tourists entering China through Shanghai Pudong New Area customs and through customs other than Shanghai.

第十二篇

CHAPTER 12

科学技术

SCIENCE AND TECHNOLOGY

表 12－1　历年科技成果

Achievements in Scientific & Technological Research in Main Years (1995～2012)

单位:项　　(item)

年　份 Year	获上海市高新技术成果转化百佳项目 Top 100 Projects Which Have Successfully Commercialized Achievements in Scientific & Technological Research	获上海市以上科技进步奖 Shanghai and Above Level Achievement Awards in Science and Technology	按奖项分 Award Grade					
			一等奖 First Prize	#国家级 National Grade	二等奖 Second Prize	#国家级 National Grade	三等奖 Third Prize	青年科技杰出贡献奖 Youth Science and Technology Outstanding Contribution Award
1995		2			1		1	
1996								
1997		2			1		1	
1998		14			3		11	
1999		12	2		3		7	
2000		11			5		6	
2001		16			5		11	
2002		37	8		13		16	
2003	11	34	8		10		16	
2004	11	45	10		16		19	
2005	25	35	5	1	10	3	20	
2006	17	48	11	1	23	5	14	
2007		73	11	2	31	11	31	
2008		66	10		27	6	29	
2009		50	5		23	5	22	
2010		63	8		29	10	26	
2011		92	15		43	12	34	
2012		69	19	1	25	3	24	1

注：上海市高新技术成果转化百佳项目从 2001 年起评比。
Note: We started to appraise the above-mentioned Top 100 Projects since 2001.

表12-2 历年各类技术合同项目
All Kinds of Technical Contracts in Main Years (1994~2012)

单位:项 (item)

年份 Year	各类合同项目 Item of Contracts	技术开发 Technical Development	技术转让 Technology Tranfer	技术咨询 Technical Consultation	技术服务 Technical Service
1994	595	25	43	98	429
1995	924	42	33	147	702
1996	1 525	12	16	215	1 282
1997	1 742	23	56	291	1 372
1998	1 659	57	49	282	1 271
1999	1 998	85	21	406	1 486
2000	1 940	79	24	458	1 379
2001	2 253	260	86	405	1 502
2002	2 281	372	116	465	1 328
2003	2 406	500	284	422	1 200
2004	2 362	580	148	406	1 228
2005	3 034	1 155	225	353	1 301
2006	2 636	1 448	100	204	884
2007	2 545	1 326	118	86	1 015
2008	2 294	1 448	94	262	490
2009	2 518	1 757	112	194	455
2010	2 550	1 774	139	100	537
2011	2 932	2 269	137	181	345
2012	2 722	2 133	124	116	349

表 12-3　历年各类技术合同成交金额

Business Volume of All Kinds of Technical Contracts in Main Years (1994~2012)

单位:万元　　(10 000 yuan)

年　份 Year	成交金额 Business Volume	技术开发 Technical Development	技术转让 Technology Tranfer	技术咨询 Technical Consultation	技术服务 Technical Service
1994	6 225	284	404	492	5 045
1995	12 514	3 863	2 105	936	5 610
1996	21 255	599	573	1 772	18 311
1997	15 644	749	1 286	2 386	11 223
1998	21 286	3 924	2 106	2 098	13 158
1999	24 788	7 194	1 509	2 929	13 156
2000	39 707	7 969	15 893	2 524	13 321
2001	62 892	30 778	8 709	3 317	20 088
2002	86 786	51 233	12 303	4 585	18 665
2003	112 355	79 274	12 978	5 217	14 886
2004	221 295	185 897	13 881	4 030	17 487
2005	386 406	335 848	33 096	3 087	14 375
2006	641 015	525 942	96 628	2 952	15 493
2007	839 052	694 197	125 175	2 586	17 094
2008	957 346	870 937	69 244	3 512	13 653
2009	1 299 693	1 145 384	137 907	2 111	14 291
2010	1 210 256	1 023 716	96 063	16 254	74 224
2011	1 269 191	1 125 001	66 825	2 508	74 857
2012	1 578 060	1 247 899	136 211	2 749	191 201

表 12－4 历年专利申请情况
Statistics of Patent Claiming in Main Years
(1999～2012)

单位:项 (item)

年 份 Year	专利申请 总 量 Total Patent Claimings	发 明 Inventions	实用新型 Utility Models	外观设计 Design in Appearance
1999	386	67	216	103
2000	718	209	241	268
2001	1 103	222	453	428
2002	2 397	467	591	1 339
2003	2 580	1 064	852	664
2004	2 871	1 676	719	476
2005	3 141	1 794	863	484
2006	6 767	2 557	1 224	2 986
2007	8 435	3 054	1 386	3 995
2008	8 980	3 065	1 893	4 022
2009	14 645	5 372	3 936	5 337
2010	17 587	6 576	4 902	6 109
2011	18 819	9 218	6 973	2 628
2012	21 972	12 902	7 158	1 912

表 12－5 历年专利授权情况
Statistics of Patents Authorized in Main Years
(2001～2012)

单位:项 (item)

年 份 Year	专利授权 总 量 Total Patents Authorized	发 明 Inventions	实用新型 Utility Models	外观设计 Design in Appearance
2001	519			
2002	668			
2003	1 542			
2004	1 066	95	528	443
2005	1 204	329	576	299
2006	1 432	375	655	402
2007	4 086	409	1 152	2 525
2008	3 677	841	1 442	1 394
2009	8 046	1 557	2 266	4 223
2010	12 764	1 503	3 950	7 311
2011	12 685	2 149	5 423	5 113
2012	11 226	2 789	6 653	1 784

表 12-6 区属企业、事业单位各类专业技术人员(2012 年末)

Professional Personnel Working in Enterprises and Institutions in PNA (Total by the End of 2012)

单位:人 (person)

指 标	Indicators	合 计 Total	# 女 性 Female	按学历分 By Education Level 研究生 Post Graduate	大学本科 University	高等专科 Junior University	中等专科 Specialized Secondary School	高中及以下 Senior High School and Below
总 计	**Total**	**41 802**	**30 512**	**1 536**	**27 857**	**9 880**	**2 146**	**383**
工程技术人员	Engineering	1 037	358	106	687	197	40	7
农业技术人员	Agricultural	397	109	24	177	106	69	21
科学研究人员	Research	173	85	12	84	57	11	9
卫生技术人员	Healthcare	11 412	8 183	729	5 412	3 577	1 506	188
教学人员	Teaching	26 523	20 395	593	20 504	5 109	299	18
经济人员	Economic	510	208	24	186	210	50	40
会计人员	Financial/Accounting	905	644	16	383	339	122	45
统计人员	Statistical	136	93	2	81	37	8	8
翻译人员	Interpreter/Translator	3	2	1	1			1
图书档案文博人员	Librarian/Archivist/Museum Staff	444	325	19	187	180	28	30
新闻、出版人员	News-Reporting/Publishing	77	31	6	61	10		
律师、公证人员	Lawyer/Notary	25	14	2	23			
播音人员	Radio Crew Member							
工艺美术人员	Artisan	2			1		1	
体育人员	Sports	66	27		44	20		2
艺术人员	Actor/Actress	45	22	1	11	16	5	12
政工人员	Political	47	16	1	15	22	7	2

表12-7 区属企业、事业单位各年龄组专业技术职务及专业技术人员(2012年末)
Technical Professions and Technicians Grouped by Ages in PNA Enterprises and Institutions (Total by the End of 2012)

单位:人 (person)

指 标	Indicators	合 计 Total	按年龄分 By Age 35岁及以下 35 Years Old and Below	36至40岁 36~40 Years Old	41至45岁 41~45 Yeas Old	46至50岁 46~50 Years Old	51至54岁 51~54 Years Old	55岁以上 55 Years Old and Above
总 计	**Total**	**41 802**	**16 380**	**8 126**	**8 450**	**5 086**	**2 160**	**1 600**
按专业技术职务分	**By Professional Position**							
高级职务	Senior	3 718	23	511	1 189	1 253	398	344
中级职务	Intermediate	18 374	3 109	5 044	5 542	2 918	1 022	739
初级职务	Junior	18 402	12 029	2 533	1 693	903	733	511
未聘职务	Laid-off	1 308	1 219	38	26	12	7	6
按专业技术类别分	**By Profession**							
工程技术人员	Engineering	1 037	399	189	198	126	59	66
农业技术人员	Agricultural	397	76	42	58	94	45	82
科学研究人员	Scientific	173	58	26	20	31	18	20
卫生技术人员	Healthcare	11 412	4 699	2 337	1 801	1 150	826	599
教学人员	Teaching	26 523	10 637	5 106	5 966	3 304	888	622
经济人员	Economic	510	82	69	94	77	108	80
会计人员	Financial/Accounting	905	206	216	164	160	108	51
统计人员	Statistical	136	46	33	25	17	9	6
图书档案文博人员	Librarian/Archivist/Museum Staff	444	126	53	83	84	53	45
政工人员	Political	47	5	5	6	10	15	6
其他专业技术人员	Others	218	46	50	35	33	31	23

表12-8 大中型工业企业科技活动人员情况
Scientific and Technical Personnel of Large and Medium Industrial Enterprises (2012)

指标	Indicators	有科技活动企业数(个) Number of Enterprises with Scientific Technical Activities (unit)	从事科技活动人员(人) Total Number of Personnel Undertaking Scientific Technical Activities (person)	#高中级技术职称人员(人) People with Senior and Intermediate Technical Titles (person)
总计	**Total**	**176**	**52 519**	**16 107**
按注册登记大类分组	**Grouped by Type of Registration**			
国有	State-owned	11	5 486	2 984
集体	Collective-owned			
股份制及其他有限公司	Share-holding	47	10 630	3 505
私营	Private	27	3 307	462
外商及港澳台投资	Overseas Invested Enterprises	90	33 042	9 149
其他	Others	1	54	7
按隶属关系分组	**Grouped by Subordination**			
中央工业	Central	20	13 884	6 065
地方工业	Local	156	38 635	10 042
按企业规模分组	**Grouped by Enterprise Scale**			
大型企业	Large	63	41 475	13 729
中型企业	Medium	113	11 044	2 378
按工业行业大类分组	**Grouped by Sector**			
农副食品加工业	Farm and Sideline Products Processing	1	245	11
烟草制品业	Tobacco Manufacturing	1	28	12
纺织业	Textile Industry	2	121	10
家具制造业	Furniture Manufacturing	1	936	71
造纸和纸制品业	Papermaking and Paper Products	2	183	3
印刷和记录媒介复制业	Printing and Record Medium Reproduction Industry	5	593	139
文教、工美、体育和娱乐用品制造业	Culture, Art, Sports and Recreation Supplies Manufacturing	2	69	42
石油加工、炼焦和核燃料加工业	Oil Processing, Coking and Nuclear Fuel Processing	2	169	70
化学原料和化学制品制造业	Raw Chemical Materials and Chemical Products	5	780	248
医药制造业	Medicine Manufacture	15	2 672	1 004
橡胶和塑料制品业	Rubber and Plastic Products Industry	2	211	24
非金属矿物制品业	Nonmetal Mineral Products	7	570	184
有色金属冶炼和压延加工业	Smelting and Rolling of Nonferrous Metals	1	77	30
金属制品业	Metal Products	9	1 038	107
通用设备制造业	General Equipment Manufacture	17	3 587	1 304
专用设备制造业	Special Purpose Equipment Manufacturing	19	3 416	1 212
汽车制造业	Automobile Manufacturing	26	11 261	2 672
铁路、船舶、航空航天和其他运输设备制造业	Railroad, Ship, Aviation and Other Transportation Equipment Manufacturing	3	1 794	804
电气机械和器材制造业	Electric Equipment and Machinery Manufacturing	21	3 235	460
计算机、通信和其他电子设备制造业	Computer, Communications and Other Electronic Equipment Manufacturing	26	17 472	5 296
仪器仪表制造业	Instrument Manufacturing	3	567	129
电力、热力生产和供应业	Production and Supply of Electricity and Thermal Power	3	3 429	2 231
燃气生产和供应业	Production and Supply of Fuel Gas	2	42	26
水的生产和供应业	Production and Supply of Water	1	24	18

表12-9 大中型工业企业技术开发项目和人员情况
Technical Development Projects and Personnel of Large and Medium Industrial Enterprises (2012)

指标	Indicators	项目数(项) Number of Projects (item)	从事技术开发人数(人) Number of Technical Development Personnel (person)	科技项目经费内部支出(千元) Internal Expenditure for Projects of Science and Technology (1 000 yuan)
总计	**Total**	**3 651**	**43 741**	**15 334 972**
按注册登记大类分组	**Grouped by Type of Registration**			
国有	State-owned	353	5 103	1 077 363
集体	Collective-owned			
股份制及其他有限公司	Share-holding	752	9 087	3 824 826
私营	Private	254	2 484	406 881
外商及港澳台投资	Overseas Invested Enterprises	2 262	27 020	10 019 426
其他	Others	30	47	6 476
按隶属关系分组	**Grouped by Subordination**			
中央工业	Central	898	10 958	3 810 097
地方工业	Local	2 753	32 783	11 524 875
按企业规模分组	**Grouped by Enterprise Scale**			
大型企业	Large	2 417	34 710	13 018 552
中型企业	Medium	1 234	9 031	2 316 420
按工业行业大类分组	**Grouped by Sector**			
农副食品加工业	Farm and Sideline Products Processing	8	200	15 735
烟草制品业	Tobacco Manufacturing	6	24	4 390
纺织业	Textile Industry	8	78	16 785
家具制造业	Furniture Manufacturing	166	771	185 309
造纸和纸制品业	Papermaking and Paper Products	11	167	35 995
印刷和记录媒介复制业	Printing and Record Medium Reproduction Industry	27	522	74 385
文教、工美、体育和娱乐用品制造业	Culture, Art, Sports and Recreation Supplies Manufacturing	24	58	15 596
石油加工、炼焦和核燃料加工业	Oil Processing, Coking and Nuclear Fuel Processing	55	139	21 052
化学原料和化学制品制造业	Raw Chemical Materials and Chemical Products	131	641	264 858
医药制造业	Medicine Manufacture	370	2 337	757 835
橡胶和塑料制品业	Rubber and Plastic Products Industry	14	202	17 255
非金属矿物制品业	Nonmetal Mineral Products	52	416	133 727
有色金属冶炼和压延加工业	Smelting and Rolling of Nonferrous Metals	8	67	12 901
金属制品业	Metal Products	38	924	122 964
通用设备制造业	General Equipment Manufacture	326	2 537	1 145 050
专用设备制造业	Special Purpose Equipment Manufacturing	202	2 879	847 791
汽车制造业	Automobile Manufacturing Industry	869	9 585	5 058 367
铁路、船舶、航空航天和其他运输设备制造业	Railroad, Marine, Aviation and Other Transportation Equipment Manufacturing	106	1 602	711 904
电气机械和器材制造业	Electric Equipment and Machinery Manufacturing	297	2 523	783 832
计算机、通信和其他电子设备制造业	Computer, Communications and Other Electronic Equipment Manufacturing	669	14 130	4 491 035
仪器仪表制造业	Instrument Manufacturing	25	561	112 575
电力、热力生产和供应业	Production and Supply of Electricity and Thermal Power	231	3 316	504 449
燃气生产和供应业	Production and Supply of Fuel Gas	7	41	532
水的生产和供应业	Production and Supply of Water	1	21	650

表 12-10　大中型工业科技活动经费支出情况（2012）

单位：千元

指　标	Indicators	企业内部科技活动支出合计 Total Expenditures of Scientific and Technological Activities Within Enterprises
总　计	**Total**	**17 626 051**
按注册登记大类分组	**Grouped by Type of Registration**	
国　有	State-owned	1 094 630
集　体	Collective-owned	
股份制及其他有限公司	Share-holding	4 485 991
私　营	Private	505 969
外商及港澳台投资	Overseas Invested Enterprises	11 532 245
其　他	Others	7 216
按隶属关系分组	**Grouped by Subordination**	
中央工业	Central	4 110 098
地方工业	Local	13 515 953
按企业规模分组	**Grouped by Enterprise Scale**	
大型企业	Large	14 814 186
中型企业	Medium	2 811 865
按工业行业大类分组	**Grouped by Sector**	
农副食品加工业	Farm and Sideline Products Processing	20 723
烟草制品业	Tobacco Manufacturing	5 886
纺织业	Textile Industry	18 552
家具制造业	Furniture Manufacturing	237 383
造纸和纸制品业	Papermaking and Paper Products	41 230
印刷和记录媒介复制业	Printing and Record Medium Reproduction Industry	76 675
文教、工美、体育和娱乐用品制造业	Culture, Art, Sports and Recreation Supplies Manufacturing	16 395
石油加工、炼焦和核燃料加工业	Oil Processing, Coking and Nuclear Fuel Processing	23 578
化学原料和化学制品制造业	Raw Chemical Materials and Chemical Products	338 652
医药制造业	Medicine Manufacture	979 865
橡胶和塑料制品业	Rubber and Plastic Products Industry	17 256
非金属矿物制品业	Nonmetal Mineral Products	139 780
有色金属冶炼和压延加工业	Smelting and Rolling of Nonferrous Metals	82 901
金属制品业	Metal Products	148 209
通用设备制造业	General Equipment Manufacture	1 231 755
专用设备制造业	Special Purpose Equipment Manufacturing	994 049
汽车制造业	Automobile Manufacturing Industry	6 008 232
铁路、船舶、航空航天和其他运输设备制造业	Railroad, Marine, Aviation and Other Transportation Equipment Manufacturing	826 758
电气机械和器材制造业	Electric Equipment and Machinery Manufacturing	940 363
计算机、通信和其他电子设备制造业	Computer, Communications and Other Electronic Equipment Manufacturing	4 845 611
仪器仪表制造业	Instrument Manufacturing	122 157
电力、热力生产和供应业	Production and Supply of Electricity and Thermal Power	508 409
燃气生产和供应业	Production and Supply of Fuel Gas	532
水的生产和供应业	Production and Supply of Water	1 100

Expenditures of Large and Medium-sized Industrial Science and Technology Activities

(1 000 yuan)

委托外单位科技活动支出合计 Total Expenditures of Scientific and Technological Activities Organized by Other Enterprises	其他技术活动费用支出 Expenses of Other Technological Activities			
	技术改造经费支出 Expenditures on Technical Transformation	技术引进经费支出 Expenditures on Technical Introdnction	消化吸收经费支出 Expenditures on Technical Digestion and Absorption	购买国内技术经费支出 Expenditure in Buying Domestic Technology
1 815 192	**3 347 896**	**2 771 592**	**1 334 685**	**103 210**
156 099	129 547			
826 329	1 389 704	585 527	48 197	103 015
840	10 190		1 537	
831 490	1 818 455	2 186 065	1 284 951	195
434				
492 403	817 215	279 658	36 608	41 360
1 322 789	2 530 681	2 491 934	1 298 077	61 850
1 649 261	2 831 610	2 689 996	1 313 147	102 640
165 931	516 286	81 596	21 538	570
500	500			
40 951				
	4 014			
196				
5 764	314 690			
5 920	172 622		14 480	375
11 231	65 340	32		2 680
	7 200			
2 311	9 450			
	22 151			
12 012	176 373	246 718	9 585	
15 858	89 887	10 862	31 467	
841 774	1 639 875	2 208 114	1 123 751	11 100
78 611	295 810	41 200	913	41 360
206 716	69 023	154 394	153 812	
406 565	212 830	110 272	677	47 695
3 172	6 290			
181 281	188 880			
1 330	61 015			
1 000	11 946			

表 12-11 大中型工业企业技术开发机构情况
Technical Development Institutions of Large and Medium Industrial Enterprises (2012)

指 标	Indicators	企业办技术开发机构数（个）Technical Development Institutions in Enterprises (unit)	技术开发机构科技活动人数（人）Technical Development Personnel (person)	技术开发机构科技经费内部支出（千元）Expenditure of Technical Development (1 000 yuan)
总 计	**Total**	**178**	**30 990**	**12 790 432**
按注册登记大类分组	**Grouped by Type of Registration**			
国 有	State-owned	8	1 234	445 615
股份制及其他有限公司	Share-holding	40	7 083	2 890 869
私 营	Private	25	1 814	325 424
外商及港澳台投资	Overseas Invested Enterprises	104	20 805	9 122 048
其 他	Others	1	54	6 476
按隶属关系分组	**Grouped by Subordination**			
中央工业	Central	13	7 972	3 006 666
地方工业	Local	165	23 018	9 783 766
按企业规模分组	**Grouped by Enterprise Scale**			
大型企业	Large	72	24 857	11 092 041
中型企业	Medium	106	6 133	1 698 391
按工业行业大类分组	**Grouped by Sector**			
农副食品加工业	Farm and Sideline Products Processing	1	120	800
纺织业	Textile Industry	2	66	15 481
家具制造业	Furniture Manufacturing	1	496	237 383
造纸和纸制品业	Papermaking and Paper Products	1	9	1 150
印刷和记录媒介复制业	Printing and Record Medium Reproduction Industry	3	164	55 541
文教、工美、体育和娱乐用品制造业	Culture, Art, Sports and Recreation Supplies Manufacturing	1	41	12 672
石油加工、炼焦和核燃料加工业	Oil Processing, Coking and Nuclear Fuel Processing	1	76	10 136
化学原料和化学制品制造业	Raw Chemical Materials and Chemical Products	23	528	189 018
医药制造业	Medicine Manufacture	18	2 053	724 184
橡胶和塑料制品业	Rubber and Plastic Products Industry	1	94	2 932
非金属矿物制品业	Nonmetal Mineral Products	4	259	46 835
有色金属冶炼和压延加工业	Smelting and Rolling of Nonferrous Metals	1	20	82 607
金属制品业	Metal Products	5	224	54 141
通用设备制造业	General Equipment Manufacture	16	2 166	978 437
专用设备制造业	Special Purpose Equipment Manufacturing	20	2 234	565 984
汽车制造业	Automobile Manufacturing Industry	26	9 042	5 079 070
铁路、船舶、航空航天和其他运输设备制造业	Railroad, Marine, Aviation and Other Transportation Equipment Manufacturing	2	1 647	451 241
电气机械和器材制造业	Electric Equipment and Machinery Manufacturing	24	1 567	385 323
计算机、通信和其他电子设备制造业	Computer, Communications and Other Electronic Equipment Manufacturing	26	9 193	3 534 261
仪器仪表制造业	Instrument Manufacturing	1	452	103 236
电力、热力生产和供应业	Production and Supply of Electricity and Thermal Power	1	539	260 000

表12-12 大中型工业企业专利情况
Patents Utilized by Large and Medium-sized Industrial Enterprises (2012)

单位:件 (item)

指标	Indicators	专利申请数 Patent Applications	#发明专利数 Patents of Creations and Inventions	有效发明专利数 Number of Effective Patents	#境外授权 Authorized Overseas
总计	**Total**	**6 419**	**3 596**	**3 594**	**160**
按注册登记大类分组	**Grouped by Type of Registration**				
国有	State-owned	1 479	560	373	5
集体	Collective-owned				
股份制及其他有限公司	Share-holding	1 221	516	530	4
私营	Private	247	102	163	2
外商及港澳台投资	Overseas Invested Enterprises	3 459	2 405	2 528	149
其他	Others	13	13		
按隶属关系分组	**Grouped by Subordination**				
中央工业	Central	1 787	826	935	15
地方工业	Local	4 632	2 770	2 659	145
按企业规模分组	**Grouped by Enterprise Scale**				
大型企业	Large	5 228	3 180	2 914	133
中型企业	Medium	1 191	416	680	27
按工业行业大类分组	**Grouped by Sector**				
农副食品加工业	Farm and Sideline Products Processing	41	24	3	
烟草制品业	Tobacco Manufacturing	4	1		
纺织业	Textile Industry	68		2	
家具制造业	Furniture Manufacturing	29	14	16	
印刷和记录媒介复制业	Printing and Record Medium Reproduction Industry	21	6	16	
文教、工美、体育和娱乐用品制造业	Culture, Art, Sports and Recreation Supplies Manufacturing	161	4	7	1
石油加工、炼焦和核燃料加工业	Oil Processing, Coking and Nuclear Fuel Processing			1	
化学原料和化学制品制造业	Raw Chemical Materials and Chemical Products	27	27	112	6
医药制造业	Medicine Manufacture	123	85	149	10
橡胶和塑料制品业	Rubber and Plastic Products Industry	9	6	23	
非金属矿物制品业	Nonmetal Mineral Products	78	60	53	9
有色金属冶炼和压延加工业	Smelting and Rolling of Nonferrous Metals	25	5	5	
金属制品业	Metal Products	92	17	91	
通用设备制造业	General Equipment Manufacture	398	73	208	17
专用设备制造业	Special Purpose Equipment Manufacturing	344	165	104	8
汽车制造业	Automobile Manufacturing Industry	922	258	161	3
铁路、船舶、航空航天和其他运输设备制造业	Railroad, Marine, Aviation and Other Transportation Equipment Manufacturing	86	21	93	
电气机械和器材制造业	Electric Equipment and Machinery Manufacturing	174	39	81	
计算机、通信和其他电子设备制造业	Computer, Communications and Other Electronic Equipment Manufacturing	2 749	2 477	2 376	106
仪器仪表制造业	Instrument Manufacturing	17	2	15	
电力、热力生产和供应业	Production and Supply of Electricity and Thermal Power	1 049	310	76	
燃气生产和供应业	Production and Supply of Fuel Gas	2	2		
水的生产和供应业	Production and Supply of Water			2	

表12-13 大中型工业企业新产品产出情况
Output of New Products of Large and Medium Industrial Enterprises (2012)

单位:千元 (1 000 yuan)

指 标	Indicators	新产品产值 Output of New Products	新产品销售收入 Sales Revenue	#出口 Export
总 计	**Total**	**194 410 681**	**267 050 925**	**50 466 364**
按注册登记大类分组	**Grouped by Type of Registration**			
国 有	State-owned	13 261 834	12 710 288	1 079 949
集 体	Collective-owned			
股份制及其他有限公司	Share-holding	32 731 882	34 524 905	14 785 684
私 营	Private	4 145 849	3 938 813	624 297
外商及港澳台投资	Overseas Invested Enterprises	144 271 116	215 876 908	33 976 434
其 他	Others		11	
按隶属关系分组	**Grouped by Subordination**			
中央工业	Central	41 926 155	43 430 239	26 077 196
地方工业	Local	152 484 526	223 620 686	24 389 168
按企业规模分组	**Grouped by Enterprise Scale**			
大型企业	Large	172 504 704	244 162 857	48 003 347
中型企业	Medium	21 905 977	22 888 068	2 463 017
按工业行业大类分组	**Grouped by Sector**			
农副食品加工业	Farm and Sideline Products Processing	329 861	329 861	
纺织业	Textile Industry	64 998	64 198	
家具制造业	Furniture Manufacturing	2 610 330	2 610 330	
造纸和纸制品业	Papermaking and Paper Products	1 047 885	747 657	635 508
印刷和记录媒介复制业	Printing and Record Medium Reproduction Industry	585 183	970 842	18 659
文教、工美、体育和娱乐用品制造业	Culture, Art, Sports and Recreation Supplies Manufacturing	167 867	265 800	113 783
石油加工、炼焦和核燃料加工业	Oil Processing, Coking and Nuclear Fuel Processing	361 720	349 760	15 427
化学原料和化学制品制造业	Raw Chemical Materials and Chemical Products	3 958 927	3 794 464	467 569
医药制造业	Medicine Manufacture	7 627 777	8 886 751	375 020
橡胶和塑料制品业	Rubber and Plastic Products Industry	22 558	21 529	
非金属矿物制品业	Nonmetal Mineral Products	628 834	766 972	68 781
有色金属冶炼和压延加工业	Smelting and Rolling of Nonferrous Metals	1 025 307	989 767	13 390
金属制品业	Metal Products	1 169 206	1 048 747	286 523
通用设备制造业	General Equipment Manufacture	17 936 990	18 752 153	7 764 082
专用设备制造业	Special Purpose Equipment Manufacturing	4 992 791	5 060 300	279 585
汽车制造业	Automobile Manufacturing Industry	86 183 263	158 484 596	3 586 913
铁路、船舶、航空航天和其他运输设备制造业	Railroad, Marine, Aviation and Other Transportation Equipment Manufacturing	19 353 989	18 991 428	13 450 933
电气机械和器材制造业	Electric Equipment and Machinery Manufacturing	13 064 822	13 056 250	7 164 121
计算机、通信和其他电子设备制造业	Computer, Communications and Other Electronic Equipment Manufacturing	33 278 373	31 859 520	16 226 070

表 12-14 主要年份科技企业主要经济指标
Major Economic Indicators of Technical Research Enterprises Run by Entrepreneurs in Main Years

指 标	Indicators	单位 Unit	1998	2000	2005	2010	2011	2012
企业单位数	Number of Enterprises	个 unit	592	828	700	2 525	3 768	4 083
企业专利总数	Number of Enterprise Patents	项 item				4 918	3 829	2 572
职工人数	Number of Employees	万人 10 000 persons	2.43	3.04	5.76	9.47	34.21	26.63
从事科技活动人员	Persons Employed in Science and Technology	万人 10 000 persons				1.59	9.01	6.39
资产总额	Total Assets	亿元 100 million yuan	69.10	122.40	575.47	766.56	4 896.10	3 854.86
技工贸销售总额	Total Sales	亿元 100 million yuan	38.99	82.01	521.45	858.06	3 707.86	2 071.63
产品销售收入	Income for Selling Products	亿元 100 million yuan				770.89	3 530.08	1 976.35
利润总额	Total Profits	亿元 100 million yuan	0.43	4.64	35.58	64.99	482.79	169.5
上交税收	Tax Payable	亿元 100 million yuan	1.37	2.70	18.22	44.66	195.93	117.58
创汇总额	Total Foreign Exchange	亿美元 USD 100 million	0.43	0.95	12.65	25.67	108.63	88.38
投入科研开发费	Investment in Research and Development	亿元 100 million yuan	2.35	4.18	34.72	26.56	223.77	155.77

注：2011 年起数据含 2000 万以上科技企业。
Note: The data include technology enterprises that have the output value of more than 20 million yuan since the year of 2011.

主要统计指标解释

专　利

是专利权的简称，是对发明人的发明创造经审查合格后，由专利局依据专利法授予发明人和设计人对该项发明创造享有的专有权。包括发明、实用新型和外观设计。反映拥有自主知识产权的科技和设计成果情况。

发　明

指对产品、方法或者其改进所提出的新的技术方案。是国际通行的反映拥有自主知识产权技术的核心指标。

实用新型

指对产品的形状、构造或者其结合所提出的适于实用的新的技术方案。反映具有一定技术含量的技术成果情况。

外观设计

指对产品的形状、图案、色彩或者其结合所作出的富有美感并适于工业上应用的新设计。反映拥有自主知识产权的外观设计成果情况。

专业技术人员

专业技术人员指事业、企业单位中已被聘任专业技术职务的从事专业技术工作和专业技术管理的人员，以及虽未被聘任专业技术职务，但现在专业技术岗位上工作的人员。

国有企业

指企业全部资产归国家所有，并按《中华人民共和国企业法人登记管理条例》规定登记注册的非公司制的经济组织。不包括有限责任公司中的国有独资公司。

集体企业

集体企业指企业资产归集体所有，并按《中华人民共和国企业法人登记管理条例》规定登记注册的经济组织。

科技活动

指在自然科学、农业科学、医药科学、工程与技术科学、人文与社会科学领域（简称科学技术领域）中，与科技知识的产生、发展、传播和应用密切相关的有组织的活动。可分为研究与试验发展（R&D）、研究与试验发展成果应用及相关的科技服务三类活动。该定义是联合国教科文组织考虑成员国特别是发展中国家开展科技统计工作的需要，而对科技活动所作的统计界定。

科技活动人员

指直接从事科技活动、以及专门从事科技活动管理和为科技活动提供直接服务，累计从事科技活动的时间占全年制度工作时间10%及以上的人员。（1）直接从事科技活动的人员，包括：在独立核算的科学研究与技术开发机构、高等学校、各类企业及其他事业单位内设的研究室、实验室、技术开发中心及中试车间（基地）等机构中从事科技活动的研究人员、工程技术人员、技术工人及其它人员；虽不在上述机构工作，但编入科技活动项目（课题）组的人员；科技信息与文献机构中的专业技术人员；从事论文设计的研究生等。（2）专门从事科技活动管理和为科技活动提供直接服务的人员包括：独立核算的科学研究与技术开发机构、科技信息与文献机构、高等学校、各类企业及其他事业单位主管科技工作的负责人，专门从事科技活动的计划、行政、人事、财务、物资供应、设备维护、图书资料管理等工作的各类人员，但不包括保卫、医疗保健人员、司机、食堂人员、茶炉工、水暖工、清洁工等为科技活动提供间接服务的人员。该指标用来反映投入科技活动人力的规模。

科学家和工程师

科学家与工程师指科技活动人员中具有高、中级技术职称（职务）的人员和不具有高、中级技术职称（职务）的大学本科及以上学历人员。

科技活动经费筹集

指从各种渠道筹集到的计划用于科技活动的经费，包括政府资金、事业资金、企业资金、银行贷款和其他收入等。反映各社会经济主体对促进科技进步所作的努力。

政府资金

指从各级政府部门获得的计划用于科技活动的经费，包括科学事业费、科技三项费、科研基建费、科学基金、教育等部门事业费中计划用于科技活动的经费以及政府部门预算外资金中计划用于科技活动的经费等。

新产品

指采用新技术原理、新设计构思研制、生产的全新产品，或在结构、材质、工艺等某一方面比原有产品有明显改进，从而显著提高了产品性能或扩大了使用功能的产品。既包括政府有关部门认定并在有效期内的新产品，也包括企业自行研制开发、在统计规定的新产品跟踪期限内的产品。跟踪期限规定如下：装备类跟踪五年，消费品类跟踪二年，其他类跟踪三年。用来反映科技产出及对经济增长的直接贡献。

R&D

是"科学研究与试验发展"(Research and Development)的英文缩写。其含义是指在科学技术领域,为增加知识总量,以及运用这些知识去创造新的应用进行的系统的创造性的活动。R&D 包括基础研究、应用研究、试验发展三类活动。

EXPLANATORY NOTES TO MAJOR STATISTICAL INDICATORS

Patent

Patent is an abbreviation for the patent right and refers to the exclusive right of ownership by the inventors or designers for the creation or inventions, given from the patent offices after due process of assessment and approval in accordance with the Patent Law. Patents are granted for inventions, utility models and designs. This indicator reflects the achievements of S&T and design with independent intellectual property.

Invention

Inventions refer to the new technical proposals to the products or methods or their modifications. This is universal core indicator reflecting the technologies with independent intellectual property.

Utility Models

Utility Models refer to the practical and new technical proposals on the shape and structure of the product or the combination of both. This indicator reflects the condition of technological results with certain technical content.

Exterior Design

Designs refer to the aesthetics and industrially applicable new designs for the shape, pattern and color of the product, or their combinations. This indicator reflects the appearance design achievements with independent intellectual property.

Professional and Technical Personnel

Professional and Technical Personnel refer to professional, technical and managerial staff members in institutions or enterprises who not only have professional and technical titles but also hold professional and technical posts. They also include those who work on professional and technical posts but do not have professional and technical titles.

State-owned Enterprises

State-owned Enterprises refer to non-corporation economic units where the entire assets are owned by the state and which have registered in accordance with the Regulation of the People's Republic of China on the Management of Registration of Corporate Enterprises. Excluded from this category are sole state-funded corporations in the limited liability corporations.

Collective-owned Enterprises

Collective-owned Enterprises refer to economic units where the assets are owned collectively and which have registered in accordance with the Regulation of the People's Republic of China on the Management of Registration of Corporate Enterprises.

Scientific and Technological Activities (S&T Activities)

Scientific and Technological Activities (S&T Activities) refer to organized activities which are closely related with the creation, development, dissemination and application of the scientific and technical knowledge in the fields of natural sciences, agricultural sciences, medical sciences, engineering and technological sciences, humanities and social sciences (referred to as scientific and technological fields). S&T activities can be classified into 3 categories: research and development (R&D) activities, application of R&D results, and related S&T services. This statistical definition is made by UNICHIEF for scientific and technological activities to meet the need of carrying out statistical work in this field for its member countries in particular those developing countries.

Personnel Engaged in S&T Activities

Personnel Engaged in S&T Activities refer to personnel directly engaged in S&T activities, in the management of S&T activities, and in providing direct service to S&T activities, who spend over 10% of the total working hours in a year in S&T activities. (1) Personnel directly engaged in S&T activities include researchers, engineers, technicians and other related personnel engaged in S&T activities in independent-accounting R&D institutions, institutions of higher learning, and in research institutes, laboratories, technology development centers and central experiment workshops under enterprises and institutions. Also included are people working in S&T information archiving institutes, and graduate students working on the design of their thesis. (2) Personnel engaged in the management of S&T activities and in providing direct service to S&T activities include senior management people responsible for S&T activities in independent-accounting R&D institutions, S&T information archiving institutes, institutions of higher learning, and in enterprises and institutions where S&T activities are undertaken. Also included are people responsible for the planning, administration, personnel management, financial management, logistics supply, equipment maintenance, information and library management that are related with S&T activities. People providing indirect services are excluded, such as security, medical service, drivers, plumbers, cleaners and those providing catering and related service. This indicator reflects the size of personnel engaged in S&T activities.

Scientists and Engineers

Scientists and Engineers refer to persons engaged in S&T activities who have obtained titles of senior and middle level professional positions, and those without such position but have completed university or higher education.

Funding for S&T Activities

Funding for S&T Activities refers to funds obtained from various sources for S&T activities, including government funds, self-raised funds by institutions, self-raised funds by enterprises, loans from banks and other funds. This indicator reflects the efforts made by various social economic entities in promoting the development of S&T.

Government Funds

Government Funds refer to funds obtained from government agencies at all levels to be used for S&T activities, including fund for scientific undertakings, 3 kinds of fund for S&T activities, fund for capital construction for scientific researches, science fund, funds from education expenditures by education departments for S&T activities, and extra-budget fund from government agencies for S&T activities.

New Products

New Products refer to new products produced with new technology and new design, or products that represent noticeable improvement in terms of structure, material, or production process so as to improve significantly the character or function of the older versions. They include new products certified by relevant government agencies within the period of certification, as well as new products designed and produced by enterprises within the new product track time limit prescribed by the statistical regulations. The new product track time limit is prescribed as following: equipment products 5 years, consumption products 2 years, other products 3 years. This indictor reflects the direct contribution of S&T output to economic growth.

R&D

R&D is an abbreviation which stands for 'Science Research and Experimental Development', which means systematic and creative endeavors aimed at expanding the overall volume of knowledge and applying the knowledge in systematic creation. R&D includes basic studies, application research and experimental development.

第十三篇

CHAPTER 13

人民生活

PEOPLE'S LIVELIHOOD

表13-1　从业人员报酬
Wages of Employed Persons
(2012)

单位:亿元　　(100 million yuan)

指　标	Indicators	合　计 Total	国有单位 State-owned Enterprises	集体单位 Collective-owned Enterprises	港澳台及外商投资单位 Overseas Invested Enterprises	其他单位 Others
总　计	**Total**	**1 447.60**	**245.84**	**7.90**	**762.50**	**431.36**
农、林、牧、渔业	Farming, Forestry, Animal Husbandry and Fishery	0.75	0.43			0.32
采矿业	Mining	0.39				0.39
制造业	Manufacturing	418.84	23.96	1.45	311.71	81.72
电力、热力、燃气及水生产和供应业	Production and Supply of Electricity, Heat, Gas and Water	13.65	9.76	0.02	1.58	2.29
建筑业	Construction	108.71	7.65	0.89	13.05	87.11
批发和零售业	Wholesale and Retail	269.12	5.13	0.84	231.92	31.23
交通运输、仓储和邮政业	Transportation, Warehousing and Post Service	68.98	21.10	0.01	8.44	39.42
住宿和餐饮业	Hotel and Catering	14.39	2.07	0.39	9.29	2.64
信息传输、软件和信息技术服务业	Information Transmission, Software and Information Technology Services	70.43	25.02		38.56	6.85
#软件和信息技术服务业	Software and Information Technology Services	41.93	0.50		34.94	6.49
金融业	Banking	275.82	41.13	0.02	84.09	150.58
房地产业	Real Estate	30.62	5.20	0.17	12.78	12.47
租赁和商务服务业	Leasing and Business Service	40.19	7.93	0.19	25.62	6.45
科学研究和技术服务业	Scientific Research and Technology Services	38.47	11.54		23.64	3.29
水利、环境和公共设施管理业	Water Conservancy, Environment and Public Facilities Administration	4.47	3.09	0.01	0.05	1.32
#公共设施管理业	Public Facilities Administration	3.35	2.36	0.01	0.05	0.93
居民服务、修理和其他服务业	Residents Service, Repair and other Services	1.20	0.30		0.65	0.25
教　育	Education	38.73	34.92	0.39		3.42
卫生和社会工作	Healthcare and Social Work	26.21	23.02	3.19		
卫　生	Healthcare	25.83	22.67	3.16		
社会工作	Social Work	0.38	0.34	0.04		
文化、体育和娱乐业	Culture, Sports and Entertainment	5.37	2.64	0.08	1.12	1.53
#文化艺术业	Culture and Arts	1.35	0.94	0.08		0.33
体　育	Sports	2.34	1.09		0.54	0.70
娱乐业	Entertainment	1.17	0.51		0.48	0.18
公共管理、社会保障和社会组织	Public Management, Social Guarantee and Social Organizations	21.28	20.96	0.25		0.07

表13-2 从业人员平均报酬
Average Wages of Employed Persons
(2012)

单位:元 (yuan)

指 标	Indicators	合 计 Total	国有单位 State-owned Enterprises	集体单位 Collective-owned Enterprises	港澳台及外商投资单位 Overseas Invested Enterprises	其他单位 Others
总平均	**Annual Average Wages**	**91 645**	**98 773**	**56 292**	**105 056**	**90 675**
农、林、牧、渔业	Farming, Forestry, Animal Husbandry and Fishery	64 464	70 187			58 084
采矿业	Mining	223 630				223 630
制造业	Manufacturing	76 151	71 807	43 120	76 937	75 570
电力、热力、燃气及水生产和供应业	Production and Supply of Electricity, Heat, Gas and Water	110 158	109 400	56 211	87 259	140 996
建筑业	Construction	48 416	86 587	55 092	92 689	43 558
批发和零售业	Wholesale and Retail	133 112	114 827	47 836	149 753	76 017
交通运输、仓储和邮政业	Transportation, Warehousing and Post Service	78 574	89 620	85 235	90 425	71 819
住宿和餐饮业	Hotel and Catering	41 578	53 501	30 778	38 204	51 167
信息传输、软件和信息技术服务业业	Information Transmission, Software and Information Technology Services	144 640	153 947		140 076	139 434
#软件和信息技术服务业	Software and Information Technology Services	142 986	114 020		144 013	140 349
金融业	Banking	141 922	199 723	113 762	236 529	108 973
房地产业	Real Estate	71 201	95 336	43 479	58 254	81 888
租赁和商务服务业	Leasing and Business Service	105 179	61 663	36 781	164 144	69 883
科学研究和技术服务业	Scientific Research and Technology Services	146 611	96 997	37 667	203 234	121 767
水利、环境和公共设施管理业	Water Conservancy, Environment and Public Facilities Administration	64 725	57 795	58 583	31 156	95 793
#公共设施管理业	Public Facilities Administration	65 265	56 308	58 583	31 156	123 228
居民服务、修理和其他服务业	Residents Service, Repair and other Services	64 330	104 700		54 812	63 406
教 育	Education	84 345	84 747	82 791		80 618
卫生和社会工作	Healthcare and Social Work	99 740	103 653	78 410		
卫 生	Healthcare	100 434	104 223	79 641		
社会工作	Social Work	67 993	76 228	34 459		
文化、体育和娱乐业	Culture, Sports and Entertainment	58 578	74 702	68 932	42 492	53 095
#文化艺术业	Culture and Arts	77 913	68 110	68 932		138 371
体 育	Sports	38 531	63 499		23 126	35 167
娱乐业	Entertainment	187 377	157 669		259 525	157 308
公共管理、社会保障和社会组织	Public Management, Social Guarantee and Social Organizations	81 456	81 721	62 486		90 973

表13-3　历年职工工资总额
Total Wages of Staff and Workers in Main Years
(1990~2012)

单位:亿元　　(100 million yuan)

年　份 Year	总　计 Total	国有单位 State-owned Enterprises	集体单位 Collective-owned Enterprises	其他单位 Others	#港澳台及外商投资单位 Overseas Invested Enterprises
1990	11.52	9.05	2.24	0.23	
1991	13.69	10.55	2.77	0.37	
1992	23.17	19.01	3.52	0.64	
1993	47.26	35.49	4.24	7.53	
1994	60.75	44.77	5.02	10.96	
1995	80.29	58.22	5.88	16.19	
1996	83.37	55.98	6.35	21.04	
1997	84.18	52.32	6.23	25.63	
1998	89.70	47.13	4.63	37.94	
1999	106.67	53.08	4.95	48.64	
2000	120.59	54.98	4.25	61.36	
2001	140.36	53.14	3.47	83.75	
2002	160.37	54.79	3.29	102.29	
2003	170.99	56.99	2.83	111.17	49.99
2004	184.02	66.16	2.85	115.01	48.92
2005	235.03	66.55	2.70	165.78	64.67
2006	278.91	63.83	2.81	212.27	97.78
2007	354.32	94.30	3.28	256.74	124.93
2008	480.32	88.50	3.43	388.39	174.64
2009	627.92	129.68	5.07	493.17	265.16
2010	765.95	139.43	5.13	621.39	277.86
2011	1 243.20	234.78	6.84	1 001.58	532.74
2012	1 331.81	238.70	7.46	1 085.65	699.59

表13-4 职工工资总额
Total Wages of Staff and Workers
(2012)

单位:亿元 (100 million yuan)

指标 Indicators	合计 Total	国有单位 State-owned Enterprises	集体单位 Collective-owned Enterprises	港澳台及外商投资单位 Overseas Invested Enterprises	其他单位 Others
总计 Total	**1 331.81**	**238.69**	**7.49**	**699.59**	**386.06**
农、林、牧、渔业 Farming, Forestry, Animal Husbandry and Fishery	0.74	0.42			0.32
采矿业 Mining	0.39				0.39
制造业 Manufacturing	400.90	23.31	1.35	298.40	77.84
电力、热力、燃气及水生产和供应业 Production and Supply of Electricity, Heat, Gas and Water	13.62	9.74	0.02	1.57	2.29
建筑业 Construction	65.92	5.30	0.88	8.95	50.79
批发和零售业 Wholesale and Retail	245.66	5.05	0.81	209.10	30.70
交通运输、仓储和邮政业 Transportation, Warehousing and Post Service	67.40	20.73	0.02	7.98	38.67
住宿和餐饮业 Hotel and Catering	11.54	1.89	0.32	7.00	2.33
信息传输、软件和信息技术服务业业 Information Transmission, Software and Information Technology Services	69.45	24.97		37.69	6.79
#软件和信息技术服务业 Software and Information Technology Services	41.02	0.50		34.09	6.43
金融业 Banking	263.48	40.99	0.02	72.71	149.76
房地产业 Real Estate	27.91	4.97	0.15	11.30	11.49
租赁和商务服务业 Leasing and Business Service	34.85	6.82	0.17	21.57	6.29
科学研究和技术服务务业 Scientific Research and Technology Services	36.16	11.35	0.01	21.57	3.23
水利、环境和公共设施管理业 Water Conservancy, Environment and Public Facilities Administration	4.13	2.79	0.01	0.05	1.28
#公共设施管理业 Public Facilities Administration	3.05	2.11	0.01	0.05	0.88
居民服务、修理和其他服务业 Residents Service, Repair and other Services	1.07	0.28		0.60	0.19
教育 Education	37.07	34.44	0.39		2.24
卫生和社会工作 Healthcare and Social Work	25.28	22.29	3.00		
卫生 Healthcare	24.97	21.98	2.99		
社会工作 Social Work	0.32	0.31	0.01		
文化、体育和娱乐业 Culture, Sports and Entertainment	5.03	2.47	0.08	1.09	1.39
#文化艺术业 Culture and Arts	1.29	0.88	0.08		0.33
体育 Sports	2.08	0.99		0.51	0.58
娱乐业 Entertainment	1.17	0.51		0.48	0.18
公共管理、社会保障和社会组织 Public Management, Social Guarantee and Social Organizations	21.21	20.88	0.26		0.07

表 13-5　历年职工平均工资

Average Wages of Staff and Workers in Main Years (1990～2012)

单位:元　　　　(yuan)

年　份 Year	年平均工资 Annual Average Wages	国有单位 State-owned Enterprises	集体单位 Collective-owned Enterprises	其他单位 Others	#港澳台及外商投资单位 Overseas Invested Enterprises
1990	2 939	3 069	2 466	3 665	
1991	3 363	3 479	2 906	4 305	
1992	4 350	4 532	3 468	5 506	
1993	5 999	5 927	4 984	7 241	
1994	7 906	7 616	6 584	10 514	
1995	9 995	10 087	6 749	11 651	
1996	11 351	11 623	7 445	12 559	
1997	12 425	12 463	7 863	14 359	
1998	13 417	12 977	7 421	15 615	
1999	15 563	14 561	8 659	18 443	22 911
2000	17 607	15 721	9 243	21 216	24 656
2001	20 349	17 503	9 092	24 066	29 710
2002	22 740	19 410	9 863	26 255	32 342
2003	25 620	22 655	10 748	28 543	38 753
2004	29 512	26 863	11 727	32 585	41 812
2005	33 186	27 707	12 390	37 153	50 779
2006	41 725	36 065	16 953	44 698	68 658
2007	56 878	49 004	20 656	59 710	68 674
2008	69 872	49 891	24 017	78 338	71 199
2009	76 026	63 747	23 419	82 074	74 376
2010	89 424	66 802	27 984	98 719	83 679
2011	90 721	85 168	48 915	92 679	85 597
2012	92 040	94 085	50 272	92 123	100 625

表13-6 职工平均工资
Average Wages of Staff and Workers
(2012)

单位:元 (yuan)

指 标	Indicators	合 计 Total	国有单位 State-owned Enterprises	集体单位 Collective-owned Enterprises	港澳台及外商投资单位 Overseas Invested Enterprises	其他单位 Others
总平均工资	**Annual Average Wages**	**92 040**	**94 085**	**50 272**	**100 625**	**79 943**
农、林、牧、渔业	Farming, Forestry, Animal Husbandry and Fishery	63 105	67 574			57 974
采矿业	Mining	227 970				227 970
制造业	Manufacturing	73 328	63 534	38 880	74 477	73 614
电力、热力、燃气及水生产和供应业	Production and Supply of Electricity, Heat, Gas and Water	110 449	109 850	58 348	86 239	141 696
建筑业	Construction	60 811	85 323	55 976	124 067	54 401
批发和零售业	Wholesale and Retail	122 267	97 528	29 884	137 575	74 965
交通运输、仓储和邮政业	Transportation, Warehousing and Post Service	77 490	88 228	54 469	86 041	71 391
住宿和餐饮业	Hotel and Catering	47 832	52 418	31 200	48 112	47 117
信息传输、软件和信息技术服务业	Information Transmission, Software and Information Technology Services	137 881	153 406		128 886	139 920
#软件和信息技术服务业	Software and Information Technology Services	132 192	113 615		131 050	140 463
金融业	Banking	137 635	188 864	83 267	226 652	108 693
房地产业	Real Estate	71 495	95 395	49 061	57 538	82 675
租赁和商务服务业	Leasing and Business Service	68 966	33 896	18 866	152 509	43 136
科学研究和技术服务业	Scientific Research and Technology Services	142 830	97 164	37 667	195 815	123 801
水利、环境和公共设施管理业	Water Conservancy, Environment and Public Facilities Administration	66 449	59 433	58 583	31 156	96 221
#公共设施管理业	Public Facilities Administration	66 875	57 494	58 583	31 156	125 847
居民服务、修理和其他服务业	Residents Service, Repair and other Services	67 529	104 754		57 646	69 882
教 育	Education	86 213	87 171	85 196		73 881
卫生和社会工作	Healthcare and Social Work	103 624	107 049	83 632		
卫 生	Healthcare	103 847	107 296	83 907		
社会工作	Social Work	88 439	91 724	41 304		
文化、体育和娱乐业	Culture, Sports and Entertainment	60 075	75 859	59 729	44 772	54 582
#文化艺术业	Culture and Arts	83 339	73 569	59 729		152 042
体 育	Sports	37 905	60 703		23 737	33 921
娱乐业	Entertainment	188 292	157 639		260 885	158 451
公共管理、社会保障和社会组织	Public Management, Social Guarantee and Social Organizations	82 527	82 783	63 929		90 973

表13-7　城镇居民家庭基本情况
Background of Urban Families

指　标	Indicators	单　位　Unit	2010	2011	2012
调查户数	Households Surveyed	户 household	600	600	600
调查户总人口	Total Population of Households Surveyed	人 person	1 704	1 692	1 668
调查户就业人口	Employed Persons in Households Surveyed	人 person	918	906	888
#国有单位就业人口	Employed by State - owned Enterprises	人 person	402	402	396
城镇集体单位就业人口	Employed by Collective-owned Enterprises	人 person	48	42	36
其他各类单位就业人口	Employed by Other Enterprises	人 person	222	222	228
平均每户常住人口	Average Number of Permanent Residents Per Household	人 person	2.84	2.82	2.78
平均每户就业人口	Average Number of Employed Persons Per Household	人 person	1.53	1.51	1.48
平均每户就业面	Average Employment Rate Per Household	%	53.9	53.5	53.2
平均每一就业者赡养人口	Number of Persons Supported by Each Employed Person	人 person	1.86	1.87	1.88
恩格尔系数	Engel's Coefficient	%	34.8	34.5	37.5
平均消费倾向	Average Propensity to Consumption	%	67.7	68.6	60.4
平均每人年实际收入	Annual Actual Income Per Capita	元 yuan	36 399	41 257	45 510
平均每人年可支配收入	Annual Disposable Income Per Capita	元 yuan	32 330	36 815	40 901
平均每人年消费性支出	Annual Consumption Spending Per Capita	元 yuan	21 897	25 239	24 723
平均每人住房建筑面积	Average Floor Space Per Capita	平方米 sq · m	39.26	36.30	36.50

注：本表至表13-16为住户调查资料，人均住房面积由建交委提供。
Note: The contents in from this table to Table 13-16 are the survey data of households in Pudong. The data of housing space per capita are provided by Pudong Construction and Transport Committee.

表 13-8 历年城乡居民收支情况
Income and Expenditure of Urban and Suburban Residents in Main Years (2006～2012)

单位:元 (yuan)

指 标	Indicators	2006	2007	2008	2009	2010	2011	2012
城镇居民收支状况	**Income and Expenditure of Urban Residents**							
人均总收入	Gross Income Per Capita	23 625	26 856	30 900	33 983	36 399	41 257	45 510
#可支配收入	Disposable Income	21 452	24 273	27 797	30 390	32 330	36 815	40 901
工薪收入	Wage Income	16 320	18 690	21 728	23 789	21 706	24 554	27 159
经营净收入	Operational Income	590	494	400	549	869	1 018	1 170
财产性收入	Property Income	391	544	597	648	715	891	1 073
转移性收入	Transferable Income	6 324	7 128	8 175	8 997	9 040	10 352	11 499
人均总支出	Total Expenses Per Capita	21 443	26 862	29 055	33 290	30 102	36 408	35 718
#消费支出	Consumption Expenses	14 349	17 802	19 579	22 379	21 897	25 239	24 723
#食 品	Foodstuff	5 299	6 272	6 921	7 757	7 631	8 696	9 278
医疗与保健	Medical Care	804	831	1 064	1 331	1 143	1 044	1 123
教育文化娱乐服务	Education, Culture and Amusement Services	2 362	2 861	3 027	3 326	3 324	3 528	3 936
社会保障支出	Social Security Expenses	1 758	2 018	2 248	2 679	2 941	3 329	3 665
农村居民收入状况	**Income and Expenditure of Suburban Residents**							
人均总收入	Gross Income Per Capita	11 715	13 157	14 869	16 080	14 759	17 191	19 033
#可支配收入	Disposable Income	10 911	12 246	13 778	14 963	13 898	15 861	17 641
工薪收入	Wage Income	8 223	9 117	10 179	10 751	10 223	11 362	12 543
经营净收入	Operational Income	320	298	249	260	743	823	555
财产性收入	Property Income	1 522	1 914	2 303	2 604	1 314	1 439	1 540
转移性收入	Transferable Income	1 650	1 828	2 138	2 465	1 618	2 237	3 003

注：2010 年起居民各项结构性收入改为可支配收入口径。
Note: All kinds of structural income of suburban residents since 2010 were changed to the item of disposable income.

表13－9　城镇居民家庭人均收入与支出状况（按收入水平分）

Average Income and Expenses of Urban Families（by income level）（2012）

单位：元　　　　　　　　　　　　　　　　　　　　　　　　　　　　（yuan）

指　标	Indicators	总平均 Overall Average	低收入户 Low-income Household	较低收入户 Lower-income Household	中等收入户 Medium-income Household	较高收入户 Medium Higher-income Household	高收入户 High-income Household
人均总收入	**Gross Income Per Capita**	**45 510**	**19 766**	**29 357**	**38 223**	**48 756**	**95 682**
#人均可支配收入	Disposable Income Per Capita	40 901	17 857	26 688	34 372	43 970	85 398
工资性收入	Wage Income	27 159	12 031	14 718	21 637	29 348	60 661
经营净收入	Operational Income	1 170	209	135	472	768	4 456
财产性收入	Property Income	1 073	84	407	296	662	4 103
转移性收入	Transferable Income	11 499	5 533	11 428	11 967	13 192	16 178
人均总支出	**Total Expenses Per Capita**	**35 718**	**17 752**	**24 798**	**29 521**	**34 327**	**75 239**
消费性支出	Consumption Expenses	24 723	14 245	19 108	23 257	25 297	43 389
食　品	Foodstuff	9 278	6 362	8 747	9 245	9 658	12 804
衣　着	Clothing	2 010	1 013	1 403	1 885	2 236	3 672
家庭设备用品及服务	Family Appliances and Services	1 716	885	1 240	1 216	1 779	3 601
医疗保健	Medical Care	1 123	831	756	799	1 262	2 021
交通和通信	Traffic and Communications	3 552	1 833	2 369	3 882	3 473	6 481
教育文化娱乐服务	Education, Culture and Amusement Services	3 936	1 939	2 354	3 380	3 712	8 644
居　住	Habitation	1 907	1 083	1 639	1 948	1 991	2 999
其他商品及服务	Miscellaneous Commodities and Services	1 201	301	600	902	1 187	3 167
财产性支出	Property Expenses	286	35	348	152	388	540
转移性支出	Transferable Expenses	5 275	1 545	3 036	2 732	4 456	15 272
社会保障支出	Social Security Expenses	3 665	1 667	2 306	3 353	4 019	7 307
购、建房支出	Expenses for Purchasing/Building Houses	1 769	260		27	168	8 731

注：收入水平根据居民家庭人均可支配收入由低到高排序，分别按家庭数量的20%分为5组。

Note: Income levels are sorted from the low to the high according to the disposable income per capita of urban families. They are divided into five groups from 20% of the total number of families respectively.

表13-10 每百户城镇居民家庭年末耐用消费品拥有量
Possession of Durable Consumer Goods Per 100 Urban Households at Year-End

指　标	Indicators	单　位 Unit	2010	2011	2012
摩托车	Mototrcycle	辆 in number	9	9	9
助力车	Scooter	辆 in number	22	25	27
家用汽车	Household Car	辆 in number	18	22	22
洗衣机	Washing Machine	台 set	100	100	100
电冰箱	Household Refrigerator	台 set	102	103	103
彩色电视机	Color TV Set	台 set	198	198	200
家用电脑	Personal Computer	台 set	116	125	127
组合音响	Stereo System	套 set	47	45	45
摄像机	Video Camera	架 set	15	17	17
照相机	Camera	架 set	72	75	75
钢　琴	Piano	架 set	5	5	5
微波炉	Microwave Oven	台 set	95	97	97
空调器	Air Conditioner	台 set	206	202	206
淋浴热水器	Water Heater	台 set	104	102	103
健身器材	Fitness Goods	套 set	9	9	9
普通电话	Fixed Telephone	部 set	96	94	94
移动电话	Mobile Phone	部 set	216	221	225

表 13－11 城镇居民家庭生活质量
Living Conditions of Urban Families

指 标	Indicators	单 位 Unit	2010	2011	2012
生活用水	**Tap Water for Residential Use**				
独用自来水	Private Tap Water	%	100.0	100.0	100.0
公用自来水	Shared Tap Water	%			
居室卫生设备	**Sanitary Equipment**				
无卫生设备	Without any Sanitary Equipment	%			
有厕所浴室	With Lavatory	%	98.2	97.5	97.9
有厕所无浴室	With Lavatory but no Bathroom	%	1.4	1.9	1.6
公 用	Shared Sanitary Equipment	%	0.4	0.6	0.5
居室取暖设备	**Heating Equipment**				
无取暖设备	Without any Heating	%	2.3	1.7	1.5
冷暖空调	Air Conditioner	%	97.1	98.1	98.4
暖 气	Heating	%			
其 他	Others	%	0.6	0.2	0.1
炊用燃气	**Gas for Cooking**				
天然气	Natural Gas	%	92.1	87.8	89.2
液化石油气	Liquefied Petroleum Gas	%	6.9	11.6	10.2
煤	Coal	%	0.6	0.3	0.3
其 他	Others	%	0.4	0.3	0.3
通信设备	**Telecommunications Equipment**				
无电话	Without Telephone	%			
固定电话	Fixed Telephone	部/百户 set / hundred households	95.7	94.0	94.3
移动电话	Mobile Telephone	部/百户 set / hundred households	216.2	221.4	224.8

表13-12 城镇居民家庭人均可支配收入
Annual Disposable Income Per Capita for Urban Families

按人均年可支配收入分组	Grouped by Annual Disposable Income Per Capita	比 重 Proportion	2010	2011	2012
总 计	**Total**	%	**100.0**	**100.0**	**100.0**
6 000 元以下	Below 6 000 yuan	%		2.0	0.2
6 000 ~ 12 000 元	6 000 ~ 12 000 yuan	%	4.7	6.0	1.5
1 2000 ~ 18 000 元	12 000 ~ 18 000 yuan	%	12.8	9.4	7.1
1 8000 ~ 24 000 元	18 000 ~ 24 000 yuan	%	20.5	14.4	13.8
2 4000 ~ 30 000 元	24 000 ~ 30 000 yuan	%	19.0	16.7	16.7
3 0000 ~ 36 000 元	30 000 ~ 36 000 yuan	%	11.2	14.8	15.7
3 6000 ~ 42 000 元	36 000 ~ 42 000 yuan	%	10.5	10.2	13.3
4 2000 ~ 48 000 元	42 000 ~ 48 000 yuan	%	5.8	6.5	8.0
4 8000 元以上	Above 48 000 yuan	%	15.5	20.0	23.7

表13-13 城镇居民家庭人均消费性支出
Annual Consumer Spending Per Capita for Urban Families

按人均年消费性支出分组	Grouped by Annual Nonproductive Expenditure Per Capita	比 重 Proportion	2010	2011	2012
总 计	**Total**	%	**100.0**	**100.0**	**100.0**
6 000 元以下	Below 6 000 yuan	%	1.7	5.6	0.8
6 000 ~ 12 000 元	6 000 ~ 12 000 yuan	%	19.3	14.3	13.4
12 000 ~ 18 000 元	12 000 ~ 18 000 yuan	%	28.6	25.9	27.0
18 000 ~ 24 000 元	18 000 ~ 24 000 yuan	%	21.7	20.6	21.0
24 000 ~ 30 000 元	24 000 ~ 30 000 yuan	%	11.7	13.5	14.3
30 000 ~ 36 000 元	30 000 ~ 36 000 yuan	%	4.3	5.2	7.0
36 000 ~ 42 000 元	36 000 ~ 42 000 yuan	%	3.0	3.3	4.4
42 000 ~ 48 000 元	42 000 ~ 48 000 yuan	%	3.0	3.5	3.8
48 000 元以上	Above 48 000 yuan	%	6.7	8.1	8.3

表 13-14 城镇居民家庭人均年消费支出状况
Annual Nonproductive Expenditure Per Capita for Urban Families

单位:元 (yuan)

指 标	Indicators	2010	2011	2012
总 计	**Total**	**21 897**	**25 239**	**24 723**
食 品	**Food**	**7 631**	**8 696**	**9 278**
#粮油类	Cereals & Oils	772	892	920
肉禽蛋水产品	Meat, Poultry, Eggs and Aquatic Products	2 018	2 401	2 621
蔬菜类	Vegetables	640	694	785
糖烟酒饮料类	Sugar, Tobacco, Alcoholic Drinks and Other Beverages	923	1 036	1 066
干鲜瓜果类	Dry and Fresh Fruits	654	785	830
糕点、奶及奶制品	Cakes, Milk and Dairy Products	599	693	761
衣 着	**Clothing**	**1 831**	**2 035**	**2 010**
#服 装	Clothes	1 350	1 492	1 492
鞋 类	Shoes	389	434	421
家庭设备用品及服务	**Household Appliances and Service**	**1 695**	**1 898**	**1 716**
#耐用消费品	Durable Consumer Goods	685	847	638
室内装饰品	Household Ornaments	55	33	33
家具材料	Furniture and Materials	4	3	6
家庭服务	Household Services	176	172	172
医疗保健	**Health Care**	**1 143**	**1 044**	**1 123**
#药品费	Medicines	424	394	414
滋补保健品	Nutritious Health Products	313	336	327
医疗费	Medical Treatment	330	252	344
交通和通信	**Transportation and Telecommunications**	**3 456**	**4 537**	**3 552**
交 通	Transportation	2 310	3 300	2 281
通 信	Telecommunications	1 146	1 237	1 271
教育文化娱乐服务	**Education, Culture, Entertainment Services**	**3 324**	**3 528**	**3 936**
文化娱乐用品	Cultural and Entertainment Products	968	926	857
文化娱乐服务	Cultural and Entertainment Services	1 429	1 550	2 007
教 育	Education	927	1 051	1 072
居 住	**Housing**	**1 649**	**2 162**	**1 907**
住 房	Accommodation	742	1 222	958
水电燃料及其他	Water, Electricity, Fuel and Others	727	749	777
居住服务费	Accommodation Services	180	190	173
杂项商品及服务	**Miscellancous Utensils and Services**	**1 167**	**1 339**	**1 201**

表13-15 农村居民家庭基本情况
Basic Information of Rural Families

指 标 Indicators		单 位 Unit	2010	2011	2012
调查户数	Households Surveyed	户 household	500	500	500
调查户总人口	Total Population of Households Surveyed	人 person	1 453	1 412	1 380
调查户总劳动力	Total Number of Laborers in the Household Surveyed	人 person	1 002	961	938
调查户就业人口	Employed Persons in Households Surveyed	人 person	897	883	857
#纯务农	Totally Engaged in Agriculture	人 person	48	92	87
本镇内企业	Employed by Enterprises in the Town	人 person	515	511	538
本镇外企业	Employed by Enterprises in Other Towns	人 person	277	224	205
平均每户人口	Average Number of Residents Per Household	人 person	2.91	2.82	2.76
平均每户劳动力	Average Number of Laborers Per Household	人 person	2.00	1.92	1.88
平均每户就业人口	Average Employed Persons Per Household	人 person	1.79	1.77	1.71
平均每户就业面	Average Employed Persons Per Household	%	61.7	62.5	62.1
平均每一就业者赡养人口	Number of Persons Supported by Each Employed Person	人 person	1.63	1.59	1.61

表13-16 农村居民收入情况
Incomes of Suburban Citizens

单位:元 (yuan)

指标	Indicators	2010	2011	2012
人均总收入	Total Income Per Capita	14 759	17 191	19 033
#可支配收入	Disposable Income	13 898	15 861	17 641
工资性收入	Wage Income	10 223	11 362	12 543
#非企业组织中劳动所得	Income from Other Sources	894	1 121	1 284
本镇企业中劳动所得	Income from Working in Enterprises in the Town	6 955	7 301	8 113
常住人口外出从业所得	Income from Working in Enterprises in Other Places	2 364	2 940	3 146
财产性收入	Unearned Income	1 314	1 439	1 540
#股息	Stock Dividend			
租金	Rent	1 014	972	1 110
红利	Dividend	34	77	
转移性收入	Transferable Income	1 618	2 237	3 003
#农村以外亲友赠送	Gifts from Relatives and Friends in Urban Area	23	24	40
救济金、保险年金	Relief and Life Annuity	13	18	10
退休金、抚恤金	Pension and Compensation	1 902	2 359	2 875
家庭经营所得	Income from Family-Run Operations	743	823	555
财产性支出	Property Expenditure	4		
转移性支出	Transfer Expenditure	1 060	1 341	1 766
#赠送农村以外亲友	Gifts to Relatives and Friends in Urban Area	82	117	100
缴纳保险金	Insurance Premium Payment	186	239	222

主要统计指标解释

从业人员报酬

从业人员报酬指各单位在一定时期内直接支付给本单位全部从业人员的劳动报酬总额。包括在岗职工工资总额和本单位其他从业人员劳动报酬两部分。

职工工资总额

工资总额指各单位在一定时期内直接支付给本单位全部职工的劳动报酬总额。工资总额的计算原则应以直接支付给职工的全部劳动报酬为根据。各单位支付给职工的劳动报酬以及其他根据有关规定支付的工资,不论是计入成本的还是不计入成本的,不论是按国家规定列入计征奖金税项目的,还是未列入计征奖金税项目的,不论是以货币形式支付的还是以实物形式支付的,均包括在工资总额内。

职工平均工资

平均工资指企业、事业、机关单位的职工在一定时期内平均每人所得的货币工资额。它表明一定时期职工工资收入的高低程度,是反映职工工资水平的主要指标。计算公式为:

平均工资=报告期实际支付的全部职工工资总额/报告期全部职工平均人数

城镇居民可支配收入

城镇居民可支配收入指居民可用于最终消费支出和其他非义务性支出以及储蓄的总和,即居民家庭可以用来自由支配的收入。它是家庭总收入扣除交纳的所得税、个人交纳的社会保障费以及调查户的记账补贴后的收入。不包括出售财物和借贷收入。

城镇居民家庭消费支出

指城镇居民家庭用于日常生活的全部支出,包括食品、衣着、家庭设备用品及服务、医疗保健、交通和通信、教育文化娱乐服务、居住、杂项商品和服务等八大类。

城镇居民家庭人均服务性消费支出

指调查户用于本家庭支付社会提供的各种文化和生活方面的非商品性服务费用。服务性消费的特点在于其劳动过程和消费过程在时间与空间上的统一。在居民家庭八大类消费中,服务消费支出包括:(1)食品类中加工服务费和部分在外饮食费用;(2)衣着类中衣着加工服务费;(3)家庭设备用品及服务类中家庭服务(如家政服务费用);(4)医疗保健类中医疗费(如诊疗费、上门出诊费、护工费用);(5)交通和通信类中交通工具服务费(如汽车使用、维修费用)、交通费中使用飞机、轮船、火车等交通工具费用、通信服务费(如电信费、邮费);(6)教育文化娱乐服务类中文化娱乐服务费(如参观、游览费用、健身活动费、团体旅游、其他文娱活动费)、文娱用品修理服务费、教育费(如义务、非义务教育支出)、成人教育支出、家教费、培训班费用、择校费;(7)居住类中租赁费用、部分房屋装潢费用(人工费用)、居住服务费(如物业管理、维修费用);(8)杂项商品和服务(如美容、洗澡、理发费用,旅馆住宿等费用)。

农村居民可支配收入

指一定时期内农村居民总收入中,扣除家庭经营费用支出、生产性固定资产折旧、交纳税金和上交承包金、公益性及转移支付后的(包括养老、失业、合作医疗、保险基金及罚款等支付),可用于生活消费、生产投资和储蓄的收入。它与纯收入的主要区别是扣除了转移性支付,加上实际得到的公益性及转移性收入后的余额。农村居民可支配收入包括:工资性收入、家庭经营净收入、财产性收入、转移性净收入。

农村居民家庭生活消费支出

指农村住户用于物质生活和精神生活方面的支出。包括食品,衣着,居住,家庭设备用品及服务,医疗保健,交通和通信,文化教育娱乐用品及服务,其他商品和服务等消费支出。

财产性收入

指金融资产或有形非生产性资产的所有者向其他机构单位提供资金或将有形非生产性资产供其支配,作为回报而从中获得的收入。

转移性收入

指农村住户和住户成员无须付出任何对应物而获得的货物、服务、资金或资产所有权等,不包括无偿提供的用于固定资本形成的资金。一般情况下,是指农村住户在二次分配中的所有收入。

基本养老保险

(1)参加保险人数:指报告期末按照国家法律、法规和有关政策规定参加基本养老保险的职工人数。包括不能正常缴费、已中断缴费但未终止保险关系的职工人数。

(2)社会统筹基金收入:指根据国家规定,由纳入基本养老保险范围的单位,按照国家规定的缴费基数和缴费比例缴纳的社会统筹基金,以及通过其他方式取得的形成基金来源的收入,包括:单位缴纳的社会统筹基金收入、财政补贴收入、利息收入、其他收入。

(3)社会统筹基金支出:指按照国家政策规定的开支范围和开支标准从社会统筹基金中支付给参加基本养老保险的离休、退休、退职人员个人的养老金、丧葬抚恤补助,以及由于保险关系转移、上下级之间调剂资金等原因而发生的支出。包括:基础性养老金、过渡性养老金、离休金、退休金、退职金、补贴、丧葬抚恤补助、其他支出。

(4)社会统筹基金结余:指截止报告期末基本养老保险的社会统筹基金结余金额。包括银行存款、财政专户、债券投资和其他。

城镇登记失业人员

城镇登记失业人员指有非农业户口,在一定的劳动年龄内(16 岁以上及男 50 岁以下、女 45 岁以下),有劳动能力,无业而要求就业,并在当地就业服务机构进行求职登记的人员。

EXPLANATORY NOTES TO MAJOR STATISTICAL INDICATORS

Labor Compensation

Labor Compensation refers to total payment by various units to their employees during a certain period of time, including wages to permanent staff and workers and payment to other employees.

Total Wages Bill

Total Wages Bill refers to the total remuneration payment to staff and workers in various units during a certain period of time. The calculation of total wages is based on the total remuneration payment to the staff and workers. Therefore, all the wages and salaries and other payments to staff and workers are included in the total wages regardless of their sources, category, and forms (in kind or cash). (Total wages of staff and workers in this yearbook include only total wages of fully employed staff and workers, excluding the living allowances distributed to those who have left their working units while keeping their labor contract/employment relation unchanged).

Average Wage

Average Wage refers to the average wage in money terms per person during a certain period of time for staff and workers in enterprises, institutions, and government agencies, which reflects the general level of wage income during a certain period of time and is calculated as follows: Average Wage = Total Wages of Staff and Workers at Reference Time / Average Number of Staff and Workers at Reference Time.

Disposable Income of Urban Households

Disposable Income of Urban Households refers to the actual income at the disposal of members of the households which can be used for final consumption, other non-compulsory expenditure and savings, which is part of the urban households' income that can be disposed by the urban households themselves. It is the income after deducting personal income tax, social insurance paid by individuals and investigation allowance from the total income of the households. The income from selling properties and borrowing are not included.

Consumption Expenditures of Urban Households

Consumption Expenditures of Urban Households refer to all the expenditures paid by urban households for consumption in daily life, including 8 categories as follows: food; clothing; household facilities, articles and services; medical care; traffic and telecommunication; education, culture and recreation services; housing; miscellaneous commodities and services.

Urbanities' per-capita Spending on Services

Urbanities' per-capita spending on services refers to urbanites pay for services rather than commodities. Services are offered and consumed at the same time and place. The service spending for an urban family falls into the following eight types: (1)Money paid for food processing and money spent while eating out; (2)Money paid for clothing processing; (3)Domestic services and services for home amenities; (4) Medical cost (including medical diagnosis and treatment, in-home medical services and nursing cost); (5)Transport tool service fees (such as for the use of a car and maintenance fee thereby arising), transport tools (plane, ship, train) fees, post and telecommunications fees; (6)Fees for culture and entertainment services (such as tour and fitness building), fees for repair of sports and entertainment items, education cost (spending on obligatory and non-obligatory education), adult education cost, tutor fees, training courses fees and extra money paid as sponsorship fee to a school a student outside his or her education community; (7)Housing rents, some interior decoration cost (for labor), residence service fees (such as for property management and repairs); (8)Fees for other services (such as at a beauty salon, bathhouse, hairdresser's and hotels).

Disposable Income of Rural Households

Disposable Income of Rural Households refers to the part of the rural households' income in a certain period after deducting family business expenditure, depreciation of productive fixed assets, taxes, contract expenditure, welfare funds and transferred expenditure, (including pensions, unemployment relief, cooperative medical funds, premiums and fines), which can be used for personal consumption, production investment and deposit. It differs from the net income in that it is the balance of the actual welfare and transferred income after deducting transferred expenditure. The disposable income includes: wages and salaries, net income from household business, property income, net transferred income.

Living Expenditures for Consumption of Rural Households

Living Expenditures for Consumption of Rural Households refer to expenditures of material and culture life of rural household, including expenses on food, clothing, housing, household appliances and service, medical and health care, traffic and communication items, cultural, education and recreation items and service and other commodities and service.

Income from Properties

Income from Properties refers to the income received as returns by owners of financial assets or tangible non-productive assets by providing capitals or tangible non-productive assets to other institutional units.

Income from Transfers

Income from Transfers refers to the receipt by rural households and their members of goods, services, capitals or rights of assets without giving or repaying accordingly, excluding capitals provided to them for the formation of fixed assets. In general, it refers to all income received by rural households through redistribution.

Basic Endowment Insurance

(1) Number of people participating in the insurance program: by the end of reference period, number of staff and workers participating in the insurance program in line with national laws, regulations and related policies, including those who can not make regular payment or interrupt payment but not terminate the insurance program.

(2) Revenue of social comprehensive funds: according to national provision, payments made by units covered in basic endowment insurance program, and income from other resources, including: income of social comprehensive funds paid by unites, financial subsidies, interest income and others.

(3) Expenditure of social comprehensive funds: refer to payment made to those retired and resigned people covered in endowment insurance program in terms of pension or compensation within the expenditure scope and standards according to related national policies, and the expenditure occurred due to shift of the insurance relationship or adjustment funds among agencies, including: basic pension, transitional pension, pension for resigned people, pension for retired people, pension for people quitting jobs, subsidies, funeral subsidies and other expenditure.

(4) Balance of social comprehensive funds: refer to the balance of basic endowment insurance of social comprehensive funds at the end of the reference period, including: bank savings, special fiscal account, investment in bonds and others.

Registered Urban Unemployment

Registered Urban Unemployment refers to those non-agricultural population within working age (16 – 50 years for male and 16 – 45 years for females) who are able and willing to work but unemployed and have registered for job in local employment service agencies.

第十四篇

CHAPTER 14

就业与社会保障

EMPLOYMENT AND SOCIAL SECURITY

表 14－1　历年从业人员数

Number of Employed Persons in Main Years

（1993～2012）

单位：人　　　　　（person）

年　份 Year	从业人员 Employed Persons	国有、集体、其他经济单位从业人员 Employed Persons in State-owned, Collective-owned and Other Economic Institutions	城镇个体劳动者 Urban Self-employed	农村集体和个体劳动者 Rural Collective and Self-employed Workers	其　他 Others
1993	1 043 985	788 821	18 146	237 018	
1994	1 049 985	767 146	35 696	247 143	
1995	1 079 744	798 884	38 243	242 617	
1996	1 039 692	759 936	44 516	235 240	
1997	981 826	703 890	49 878	228 058	
1998	963 211	638 707	68 252	256 252	
1999	983 401	645 583	43 284	294 534	
2000	1 040 411	636 923	61 000	316 063	26 425
2001	1 114 514	650 633	85 608	344 027	34 246
2002	1 199 864	686 637	107 590	361 881	43 756
2003	1 268 717	674 381	135 592	404 422	54 322
2004	1 302 723	643 628	162 251	436 504	60 340
2005	1 440 763	746 714	178 173	444 433	71 443
2006	1 467 145	720 105	200 638	461 395	85 007
2007	1 490 809	708 308	194 419	498 633	89 449
2008	1 507 631	749 400	232 209	440 184	85 838
2009	2 009 539	920 081		997 835	91 623
2010	2 351 115	1 004 078		1 140 203	206 834
2011	2 806 796	1 488 778		1 150 443	167 575
2012	2 970 091	1 584 025		1 136 420	249 646

注：自 2009 年起从业人员数中不包括城镇个体劳动者。
Note: The number of employed persons excludes that of individual workers in towns since the year of 2009.

表 14-2 各行业从业人员数
Number of Employed Persons by Sector
(2012)

单位:人 (person)

指 标	Indicators	从业人员 Employed Persons	#国有、集体、其他经济单位从业人员 Employed Persons in State-owned, Collective-owned and Other Economic Institutions	农村集体劳动者 Rural Collective Labors	其 他 Others
总 计	**Total**	**2 970 091**	**1 584 025**	**1 136 420**	**249 646**
按三次产业分	**By Industry**				
第一产业	Primary Industry	137 109	1 150	134 920	1 039
第二产业	Secondary Industry	1 669 882	795 373	691 652	182 857
第三产业	Tertiary Industry	1 163 100	787 502	309 848	65 750
按行业分	**By Sector**				
农、林、牧、渔业	Farming, Forestry, Animal Husbandry and Fishery	137 109	1 150	134 920	1 039
采矿业	Mining	163	163		
制造业	Manufacturing	1 255 085	561 884	581 024	112 177
电力、热力、燃气及水生产和供应业	Production and Supply of Electricity, Heat, Gas and Water	26 932	12 311	14 525	96
建筑业	Construction	387 702	221 015	96 103	70 584
批发和零售业	Wholesale and Retail	306 296	205 754	86 307	14 235
交通运输、仓储和邮政业	Transportation, Warehousing and Post Service	162 046	85 649	70 960	5 437
住宿和餐饮业	Hotel and Catering	58 268	35 321	8 295	14 652
信息传输、软件和信息技术服务业	Information Transmission, Software and Information Technology Services	56 737	48 440	5 197	3 100
#软件和信息技术服务业	Software and Information Technology Services	29 351	29 351		
金融业	Banking	190 550	190 352		198
房地产业	Real Estate	50 983	42 099		8 884
租赁和商务服务业	Leasing and Business Service	45 896	38 327		7 569
科学研究和技术服务业	Scientific Research and Technology Services	39 295	26 553	8 175	4 567
水利、环境和公共设施管理业	Water Conservancy, Environment and Public Facilities Administration	11 983	6 904	4 016	1 063
#公共设施管理业	Public Facilities Administration	5 143	5 143		
居民服务、修理和其他服务业	Residents Service, Repair and other Services	130 062	1 767	123 928	4 367
教 育	Education	46 133	45 393		740
卫生和社会工作	Healthcare and Social Work	28 576	26 341	1 403	832
文化、体育和娱乐业	Culture, Sports and Entertainment	10 531	8 914	1 567	50
公共管理、社会保障和社会组织	Public Management, Social Guarantee and Social Organizations	25 744	25 688		56

注：1. 国有、集体、其他经济单位从业人员包括职工中的在岗职工和其他从业人员。
2. 从业人员数中不包括城镇个体劳动者。

Note: 1. Employed staff and workers in state-owned, collective-owned and other business enterprises include those who are actually working in those companies.
2. The number of employed persons excludes that of private and individual workers in towns.

表 14-3　历年职工人数

Staff and Workers in Main Years

(1993～2012)

单位:人　　(person)

年　份 Year	合　计 Total	国有经济单位 State-owned Enterprises	集体经济单位 Collective-owned Enterprises	其他经济单位 Others	#港澳台及外商投资单位 Overseas Invested Enterprises
1993	788 821	597 417	84 811	106 593	
1994	767 146	582 477	76 023	108 646	
1995	798 884	571 398	85 955	141 531	
1996	719 634	469 966	85 030	164 638	
1997	663 163	405 349	77 072	180 742	52 405
1998	661 406	354 408	60 633	246 365	111 015
1999	677 348	355 607	56 824	264 917	126 897
2000	677 544	340 605	44 654	292 285	137 332
2001	687 694	299 186	37 756	350 752	134 732
2002	701 949	276 876	33 390	391 683	160 884
2003	671 434	249 461	25 549	396 424	136 212
2004	614 014	238 073	23 217	352 724	119 658
2005	701 553	233 350	20 431	447 772	129 890
2006	665 680	173 204	16 196	476 280	145 534
2007	631 720	188 892	16 278	426 550	186 480
2008	667 882	175 428	11 823	480 631	225 566
2009	797 302	193 246	20 408	583 648	297 093
2010	850 176	201 002	17 155	632 019	336 022
2011	1 385 342	275 135	13 728	1 096 479	627 996
2012	1 451 359	282 539	24 766	1 144 054	695 262

表 14-4 各行业职工人数
Staff and Workers by Sector
(2012)

单位:人 (person)

指标	Indicators	职工人数 Staff and Workers	国有经济单位 State-owned Enterprises	城镇集体经济单位 Collective-owned Enterprises	其他经济单位 Others	#港澳台及外商投资单位 Overseas Invested Enterprises
总 计	**Total**	**1 451 359**	**282 539**	**24 766**	**1 144 054**	**695 262**
按三次产业分	**By Industry**					
第一产业	Primary Industry	1 587	1 010		577	
第二产业	Secondary Industry	576 373	44 952	7 352	524 069	362 204
第三产业	Tertiary Industry	873 399	236 577	17 414	619 408	333 058
按行业分	**By Sector**					
农、林、牧、渔业	Farming, Forestry, Animal Husbandry and Fishery	1 587	1 010		577	
采矿业	Mining	229			229	
制造业	Manufacturing	485 476	28 870	5 090	451 516	349 470
电力、热力、燃气及水生产和供应业	Production and Supply of Electricity, Heat, Gas and Water	13 178	9 102	224	3 852	1 887
建筑业	Construction	77 490	6 980	2 038	68 472	10 847
批发和零售业	Wholesale and Retail	264 575	9 652	4 209	250 714	187 782
交通运输、仓储和邮政业	Transportation, Warehousing and Post Service	67 151	19 412	88	47 651	8 739
住宿和餐饮业	Hotel and Catering	31 313	5 388	1 587	24 338	17 331
信息传输、软件和信息技术服务业业	Information Transmission, Software and Information Technology Services	50 803	15 637		35 166	30 227
#软件和信息技术服务业	Software and Information Technology Services	32 146	1 013		31 133	26 730
金融业	Banking	169 067	19 248	159	149 660	35 441
房地产业	Real Estate	73 851	12 044	1 408	60 399	28 025
租赁和商务服务业	Leasing and Business Service	37 344	11 077	1 285	24 982	11 496
科学研究和技术服务业	Scientific Research and Technology Services	29 285	13 771	84	15 430	11 743
水利、环境和公共设施管理业	Water Conservancy, Environment and Public Facilities Administration	7 788	5 522	84	2 182	238
#公共设施管理业	Public Facilities Administration	5 975	4 106	84	1 785	238
居民服务、修理和其他服务业	Residents Service, Repair and other Services	1 844	677		1 167	474
教 育	Education	71 201	66 140	1 017	4 044	
卫生和社会工作	Healthcare and Social Work	23 975	19 180	4 795		
文化、体育和娱乐业	Culture, Sports and Entertainment	9 565	5 423	680	3 462	1 562
公共管理、社会保障和社会组织	Public Management, Social Guarantee and Social Organizations	35 637	33 406	2 018	213	

表 14-5 工业企业从业人员与职工人数

Employed Staff and Workers in Industrial Enterprises (2012)

单位:人 (person)

指 标	Indicators	从业人员人数 Employed Persons	职工人数 Staff and Workers
总 计	**Total**	**574 358**	**498 883**
按登记注册类型分	**By Type of Registration**		
国有经济单位	State-owned Enterprises	40 924	37 972
集体经济单位	Collective-owned Enterprises	3 321	5 314
其他经济单位	Others	530 113	455 597
#港澳台及外商投资单位	Overseas Invested Enterprises	422 733	351 357
按行业分	**By Sector**		
#石油和天然气开采业	Industry of Petroleum and Natural Gas Exploration	163	229
农副食品加工业	Processing of Agricultural Side - line Food	2 956	3 742
食品制造业	Food Manufacturing	10 073	7 989
酒、饮料和精制茶制造业	Manufacturing of Alcohol, Beverage and Refined Tea	5 876	4 216
烟草加工业	Tobacco Processing	520	450
纺织业	Textile Industry	534	350
纺织服装、服饰业	Textile, Clothing and Accessories	27 645	31 130
皮革、毛皮、羽毛及其制品和制鞋业	Leather, Fur, Plume and their Products and Shoes Making	1 377	1 977
木材加工及木、竹、藤、棕、草制品业	Timber Processing, Bamboo, Cane, Palm, Fiber and Straw Products	1 034	1 126
家具制造业	Furniture Manufacturing	2 877	2 859
造纸及纸制品业	Paper-making and Paper Products	6 863	5 550
印刷业和记录媒介的复制	Printing and Record Medium Reproduction	5 766	6 286
文教、工美、体育和娱乐用品制造业	Culture, Education, Arts, Crafts, Sports and Entertainment Products	5 040	6 359
石油加工,炼焦及核燃料加工业	Petroleum Processing and Coking Products	5 860	6 045
化学原料及化学制品制造业	Chemical Materials and Chemical Products	19 578	23 053
医药制造业	Medicine Manufacturing	21 660	23 076
化学纤维制造业	Chemical Fiber Manufacturing		
橡胶和塑料制品业	Rubber and Plastic Products	16 282	19 964
非金属矿物制品业	Nonmetal Mineral Products	12 082	13 744
黑色金属冶炼及压延加工业	Smelting and Pressing of Ferrous Metals	3 606	4 314
有色金属冶炼及压延加工业	Smelting and Pressing of Non - ferrous Metals	1 893	2 609
金属制品业	Metal Products	18 353	20 567
通用设备制造业	Manufacturing of Equipment for General Use	37 793	38 215
专用设备制造业	Manufacturing of Special Purpose Equipment	26 150	30 248
汽车制造业	Automobile Manufacturing	65 821	47 881
铁路、船舶、航空航天和其他运输设备制造业	Manufacturing of Railway, Ships, Aviation and other Transportion Equipment	29 433	20 339
电气机械和器材制造业	Manufacturing of Electric Equipment and Machinery	35 130	29 551
计算机、通信和其他电子设备制造业	Manufacturing of Computers, Telecommunications and other Electronic Equipment	172 865	107 350
仪器仪表制造业	Manufacturing of Instrument and Meters	11 342	11 137
其他制造业	Other Productions	3 974	3 459
废弃资源综合利用业	Recycling and Resuse of Discarded Resources	73	145
金属制品、机械和设备修理业	Metal Products, Mechineries and Equipment Repair	5 537	6 065
电力,热力的生产和供应业	Production and Supply of Electricity and Heat	2 889	3 575
燃气生产和供应业	Production and Supply of Gas	5 066	4 843
水的生产和供应业	Production and Supply of Tap Water	4 356	4 760

表14-6 应届毕业生构成及就业基本情况
Composition of Fresh Graduates and Their Employment

指 标	Indicators	单 位 Unit	2005	2010	2011	2012
毕业生按性别分	**By Sex of Graduates**					
男性比重	Proportion of Male Graduates	%	48.9	46.8	46.8	50.2
女性比重	Proportion of Female Graduates	%	51.1	53.2	53.2	49.8
毕业生按学历分	**By Educational Qualifications of Graduates**					
三校毕业生比重	Proportion of Graduates from Three Kinds of Colleges	%	37.0	17.0	15.6	16.7
大专毕业生比重	Proportion of Junior College Graduates	%	38.4	40.7	39.4	32.4
本科及以上毕业生比重	Proportion of University Graduates or Those with Higher Degrees	%	24.7	42.3	45.0	50.9
毕业生总体就业率	**Overall Employment Rate of Graduates**	**%**	**65.8**	**64.1**	**75.1**	**73.5**
就业率按性别分	**Employment Rate, By Sex of Graduates**					
男性就业率	Employment Rate of Male Graduates	%	62.6	61.8	72.9	71.3
女性就业率	Employment Rate of Female Graduates	%	68.7	66.2	77.1	75.8
就业率按学历分	**Employment Rate, by Educational Qualifications**					
三校生	Graduates from Three Kinds of Colleges	%	53.3	49.2	59.6	63.4
大专生	Graduates of Junior Colleges	%	69.1	60.6	71.3	68.3
本科生及以上	Graduates of Universities or those with Higher Degrees	%	74.8	72.4	83.0	79.4
就业率按毕业院校分	**Employment Rate, by Colleges**					
重点院校就业率	Employment Rate of Graduates from Key Universities	%	79.9	75.3	84.3	
普通院校就业率	Employment Rate of Graduates from Common Universities	%	70.0	65.4	78.1	
民办院校就业率	Employment Rate of Graduates from Colleges Run by Private Investment	%	64.2	61.0	70.1	
首份工作薪酬收入均值	**Average Monthly Salaries of First Jobs**	**元**	**1 617**	**2 370**	**2 724**	**3 441**
三校生	Graduates from Three Kinds of Colleges	元	1 101	1 773	2 012	2 580
大专生	Graduates of Junior Colleges	元	1 404	2 093	2 296	2 954
本科生及以上	Graduates of Universities or those with Higher Degrees	元	2 327	2 718	3 187	3 843

注：数据取自对新区各类应届毕业生进行的抽样调查。调查对象为常住人口口径，居住在抽中居(村)委会、应届毕业的大专院校毕业生和三校毕业生。自2010年起，调查抽样范围覆盖新浦东的城乡全部村居委，且调查时点改为当年7月1日零时。2012年起调查对象改为具有浦东户籍、应届毕业的大专院校毕业生和三校毕业生

Note: These data come from sample surveys to fresh graduates of different colleges and universities in PNA. The surveyed graduates are graduated from junior colleges and three kinds of colleges who are de jure population and live in the selected urban/rural residential committees. The area of survey sampling covered all of the village and neighborhood committees in new PNA since 2010 and the survey time changed to 0 : 00 of June 1 of that current year. Since 2012, the surveyed have been changed to those who graduated from junior colleges and three kinds of colleges registered in Pudong in current year.

表14-7　享受居民最低生活保障人数
Number of Residents Benefiting from Guarantee of Minimum Standard of Living (2012)

单位：人　　　　(person)

指　标	Indicators	保障对象 Residents to be Guaranteed	城镇低保 Guarantee of Minimum Standard of Living in Urban Area	农村贫困户 Poverty Households in Rural Area
总　计	**Total**	**37 598**	**34 777**	**2 821**
潍坊新村街道	Weifangxincun Subdistrict	713	713	
陆家嘴街道	Lujiazui Subdistrict	1 663	1 663	
周家渡街道	Zhoujiadu Subdistrict	2 600	2 600	
塘桥街道	Tangqiao Subdistrict	843	843	
上钢新村街道	Shanggangxincun Subdistrict	1 701	1 701	
南码头路街道	Nanmatoulu Subdistrict	833	833	
沪东新村街道	Hudongxincun Subdistrict	1 184	1 184	
金杨新村街道	Jinyangxincun Subdistrict	1 184	1 184	
洋泾街道	Yangjing Subdistrict	1 011	1 011	
浦兴路街道	Puxinglu Subdistrict	1 826	1 826	
东明路街道	Dongminglu Subdistrict	905	905	
花木街道	Huamu Subdistrict	2 167	2 167	
川沙新镇	Chuansha New Town	2 515	2 145	370
高桥镇	Gaoqiao Town	655	648	7
北蔡镇	Beicai Town	1 909	1 905	4
合庆镇	Heqing Town	552	487	65
唐　镇	Tangzhen Town	179	167	12
曹路镇	Caolu Town	1 496	1 466	30

单位:人　　　　表 14－7 续表 Continued　　　　(person)

指　标 Indicators		保障对象 Residents to be Guaranteed	城镇低保 Guarantee of Minimum Standard of Living in Urban Area	农村贫困户 Poverty Households in Rural Area
金桥镇	Jinqiao Town	195	195	
高行镇	Gaohang Town	757	757	
高东镇	Gaodong Town	802	740	62
张江镇	Zhangjiang Town	997	997	
三林镇	Sanlin Town	1 678	1 667	11
惠南镇	Huinan Town	1 272	1 030	242
周浦镇	Zhoupu Town	425	399	26
新场镇	Xinchang Town	664	510	154
大团镇	Datuan Town	755	482	273
康桥镇	Kangqiao Town	380	380	
航头镇	Hangtou Town	291	224	67
祝桥镇	Zhuqiao Town	3 276	2 572	704
泥城镇	Nicheng Town	706	500	206
宣桥镇	Xuanqiao Town	413	314	99
书院镇	Shuyuan Town	386	124	262
万祥镇	Wanxiang Town	204	139	65
老港镇	Laogang Town	306	144	162
南汇新城镇	Nanhui New Town	155	155	

表 14-8　劳动就业及社会保障
Employment and Social Security

指　标	Indicators	单　位　Unit	2010	2011	2012
劳动就业	**Employment**				
期末城镇登记失业人数	Actual Number of Those Registered as Unemployed at Year-end	人 person	43 453	44 848	45 331
招工录用总数	Total Recruitment	人 person	287 873	265 821	278 871
征地劳动力安置	Recruitment of Those Who Have Lost Jobs Because of Requisition of Land	人 person	29 310	5 313	7 272
新增就业岗位	Number of Newly Increased Employment	人 person	140 440	153 980	150 515
社会保险	**Social Security**				
失业保险金发放人次	Unemployment Insurance Payment Distribution	人次 person-time	294 180	250 161	264 834
失业保险金发放金额	Unemployment Insurance Payment	万元 10 000 yuan	17 156	15 540	17 683
农村社会养老保险期末参保人数	Number of Persons Who Joined Endowment Insurance Program in Rural Area at Year end	人 person	91 747	227 053	137 884
农村社会养老保险期末享受人数	Number of Persons Who Benefited from Endowment Insurance Program in Rural Area at Year end	人 person	58 432	68 444	69 465
社会救助	**Social Relief**				
城镇居民低保人数	Urban Residents Who Benefit from Subsistence Allowances from the State	人 person	72 424	66 289	41 121
城镇居民低保金额	Subsistence Allowances to Urban Residents	万元 10 000 yuan	24 902	26 143	25 293
农村居民低保人数	Number of Rural Population Benefiting from Subsistence Allowance	人 person	11 119	9 140	5 160
农村居民低保金额	Amount of Subsistence Allowance for Rural Population	万元 10 000 yuan	2 285	2 348	2 584

表14-9 收养性单位基本情况
Background of Welfare Facilities
(2012)

指 标	Indicators	单 位 Unit	合 计 Total	社会福利院 Welfare Homes	敬老院 Homes for Senior Citizens
单位数	**Total Number**	**个 unit**	**127**	**1**	**126**
年末职工人数	**Number of Staff and Workers (Year End)**	**人 person**	**5 225**	**145**	**5 080**
#医护人员	Medical Personnel and Nurses	人 person	3 700	97	3 603
年末床位数	**Number of Beds**	**张 bed**	**22 789**	**250**	**22 539**
年末在院人数	**Persons Housed (Year End)**	**人 person**	**14 935**	**207**	**14 728**
#女 性	Female	人 person	9 807	133	9 674
#自费人员	Those at Their Own Expenses	人 person	14 128	207	13 921
在院人员按年龄分	Persons Housed by Age				
老 人	Old People	人 person	14 537	207	14 330
青壮年	Young and Middle-aged People	人 person	398		398
儿 童	Children	人 person			

表14-10 残疾人事业及居家养老情况
Statistics of Disabled Persons & Life of Disabled Persons Including the Aged

指 标	Indicators	单 位 Unit	2010	2011	2012
残疾人事业	**Disabled Persons**				
白内障复明手术	Operations for Recovery from Cataract	例 in number	2 281	6 298	2 825
低视力配用助视器人数	Number of Bad Eyesighted Persons Equipped with Typoscope	人 person	153	78	692
低听力配用助听器人数	Number of Bad Auditioned Persons Equipped with Haudiphone	人 person	336	203	339
精神病人数	Number of Mental Patients	人 person	15 735	22 360	22 594
监护精神病人数	Number of Mental Patients Supervised	人 person	15 230	21 866	21 735
麻风畸残发放辅助用具	Auxiliary Appliances Dispensed for Persons Suffering from Leprosy, Malformation and Disability	件 piece	28	11	
城镇残疾人就业人数	Employed Disabled Persons in Towns and Subdistricts	人 person	125	994	857
居家养老	**Life of Disabled Persons Including the Aged**				
期末养老机构床位数	Number of Beds in Old-Aged Institutions at End of Term	张 bed	22 096	22 318	22 789
居家养老护理人员数	Number of Care Workers for the Old-Aged Living at Home	人 person	3 953	3 925	4 094
居家养老服务总数	Number of Services for the Old-Aged Living at Home	人 person	47 610	49 009	52 243
#补贴数	Number of the Old Disabled Persons	人 person	41 596	37 475	40 265
新增安康通安装数	Number of New Installations for Ankangtong SIM Cards	人次 persons-time	1 776	1 627	

表14-11 红十字会基本情况
Statistics of Red Cross in PNA

指 标 Indicators		单 位 Unit	2010	2011	2012
救 灾	**Providing Disaster Relief**				
捐赠款物	Donation of Money and Clothes	万元 10 000 yuan	2 790	1 765	1.03
救 助	**Salvage**				
救助款物	Salvation of Money and Clothes	万元 10 000 yuan	1 186	1 761	4 491
受益人次	Number of Persons Benefited	人次 person-time	14 031	38 251	54 000
救 护	**Rescue**				
师资培训	Teachers Trained	人 person	29	5	85
救护员培训	Rescue Workers Trained	人 person	4 501	13 152	4 084
救护防病知识普及	Popularization of Rescue and Disease Protection	人次 person-time	59 265	21 784	58 190
预防艾滋病	Protection of AIDS	人次 person-time	31 520	21 200	82 000
遗体捐献登记	Registration of Body Donations	例 in number	202	255	230
基层组织	Grassroot Organizations	个 in number	281	281	286
社区公益服务站点	Community Public Service Stations	个 in number	523	833	847
志愿者	Volunteers	人 in number	6 491	7 431	9 215

表14-12 廉租住房
Low Rent Housing in Main Years

指 标 Indicators		单位 Unit	2005	2010	2011	2012
廉租住房人均居住面积认定标准	Approved Standard for Living Space Per Capita in Low-Rent Housing	平方米 sq·m	7	≦7	≦7	≦7
廉租住房人均月收入认定标准	Approved Standard for Monthly Income Per Capita in Low-Rent Housing	元 yuan	300	≦1100	≦1100	≦1760
受理登记	Registration					
累计受理户数	Number of Households Registered	户 household	1 847	6 672	7 466	7 929
累计审核登记户数	Approved Number of Households Registered	户 household	1 730	6 512	7 316	7 929
累计实有登记户数	Actual Number of Households Registered	户 household	1 678	6 456	7 266	7 929
配租户数	Number of Households Assisted	户 household	1 670	6 450	7 147	7 929
配租金额	Total Rent of Assisted Households	万元 10 000 yuan	780	12 059	15 240	18 525

表 14-13 社会捐赠与帮困
Social Donations and Financial Aids

指 标 Indicators		单位 Unit	2010	2011	2012
社会捐赠	**Social Donations**				
捐赠款金额	Amount of Donations	万元 10 000 yuan	12 416	11 625	13 797
捐赠衣被	Clothes and Quilts for Donation	万件 10 000 unit	88	15	19
医疗救助	**Medical Assistance**				
医疗救助人次	Number of Medical Assistance	人次 person-time	13 096	55 571	42 584
医疗救助金额	Amount of Medical Assistance	万元 10 000 yuan	5 122	6 416	4 326
帮困助学	**Financial Aids for Students**				
帮困助学人次	Number of Financial Aids for Students	人次 person-time	18 136	29 020	15 910
帮困助学金额	Amount of Financial Aids for Students	万元 10 000 yuan	907	2 316	1 848

表 14-14 社会保障标准
Standard for Social Security

单位:元 (yuan)

指 标 Indicators		2010	2011	2012
职工月最低工资标准	Standard of Minimum Monthly Salary for Employees	1 120	1 280	1 450
城镇居民月最低生活保障标准	Standard of Minimum Monthly Living Expenses for Urban Residents	450	505	570
农村居民月最低生活保障标准	Standard of Minimum Monthly Living Expenses for Rural Residents	300	360	430
农村社会养老保险金月最低标准	Minimum Monthly Pension Insurance for Rural Residents in PNA		485	555

主要统计指标解释

从业人员

从业人员指从事一定社会劳动并取得劳动报酬或经营收入的人员，包括在岗职工、再就业的离退休人员、私营业主、个体户主、私营和个体从业人员、乡镇企业从业人员、农村从业人员、其他从业人员(包括民办教师、宗教职业者、现役军人等)。这一指标反映了一定时期内全部劳动力资源的实际利用情况，是研究我国基本国情国力的重要指标。

各单位的从业人员指在各级国家机关、政党机关、社会团体及企业、事业单位中工作，取得工资或其他形式的劳动报酬的全部人员。包括在岗职工、再就业的离退休人员、民办教师以及在各单位中工作的外方人员和港澳台方人员、兼职人员、借用的外单位人员和第二职业者。不包括离开本单位仍保留劳动关系的职工。各单位的就业人员反映了各单位实际参加生产或工作的全部劳动力。

职　工

职工指在国有、城镇集体、联营、股份制、外商和港、澳、台投资、其他单位及其附属机构工作，并由其支付工资的各类人员。不包括下列人员：(1)乡镇企业就业人员；(2)私营企业就业人员；(3)城镇个体劳动者；(4)离休、退休、退职人员；(5)再就业的离、退休人员；(6)民办教师；(7)在城镇单位中工作的外方及港、澳、台人员；(8)其他按有关规定不列入职工统计范围的人员。(1998 年及以后的数据均为在岗职工数据，其他相关指标如职工工资总额，职工平均工资等指标也从 1998 年按此口径进行了相应调整)。

登记注册类型

登记注册类型是以工商行政管理机关登记注册的具有法人资格的各类企业为划分对象。产业活动单位和行政机关、事业单位、社会团体及其他经济组织参照执行。

国有企业指企业全部资产归国家所有，并按《中华人民共和国企业法人登记管理条例》规定登记注册的非公司制的经济组织。不包括有限责任公司中的国有独资公司。

集体企业指企业资产归集体所有，并按《中华人民共和国企业法人登记管理条例》规定登记注册的经济组织。

股份合作企业指以合作制为基础，由企业职工共同出资入股，吸收一定比例的社会资产投资组建，实行自主经营，自负盈亏，共同劳动，民主管理，按劳动分配与按股份分红相结合的一种集体经济组织。

联营企业指两个及两个以上相同或不同所有制性质的企业法人或事业单位法人，按自愿、平等、互利的原则，共同投资组成的经济组织。联营企业包括国有联营企业、集体联营企业、国有与集体联营企业和其他联营企业。

有限责任公司指根据《中华人民共和国公司登记管理条例》规定登记注册，由 2 个以上，50 个以下的股东共同出资，每个股东以其所认缴的出资额对公司承担有限责任，公司以其全部资产对其债务承担责任的经济组织。有限责任公司包括国有独资公司以及其他有限责任公司。

股份有限公司指根据《中华人民共和国公司登记管理条例》规定登记注册，其全部注册资本由等额股份构成并通过发行股票筹集资本，股东以其认购的股份对公司承担有限责任，公司以其全部资产对其债务承担责任的经济组织。

私营企业指由自然人投资设立或由自然人控股，以雇佣劳动为基础的营利性经济组织。包括按照《公司法》、《合伙企业法》、《私营企业暂行条例》规定登记注册的私营有限责任公司、私营股份有限公司、私营合伙企业和私营独资企业。

与港澳台商投资合资经营企业指港澳台地区投资者与内地企业依照《中华人民共和国中外合资经营企业法》及有关法律的规定，按合同的比例投资设立、分享利润和分担风险的企业。

港澳台商投资合作经营企业指港澳台地区投资者与内地企业依照《中华人民共和国中外合资经营企业法》及有关法律的规定，依照合同的约定进行投资或提供条件设立、分享利润和分担风险的企业。

港澳台商独资经营企业指依照《中华人民共和国外资企业法》及有关法律的规定，在内地由港澳台商地区投资者全额投资设立的企业。

港澳台商投资股份有限公司指根据国家有关规定，经外经贸部依法批准设立，其中港、澳、台商的股本占公司注册资本的比例达 25% 以上的股份有限公司。凡其中港、澳、台商的股本占公司注册资本的比例小于 25% 的，属于内资企业中股份有限公司。

中外合资经营企业指外国企业或外国人与中国内地企业依照《中华人民共和国中外合资经营企业法》及有关法律的规定，按合同规定的比例投资设立、分享利润和分担风险的企业。

中外合作经营企业指外国企业或外国人与中国内地企业依照《中华人民共和国中外合作经营企业法》及有关法律的规定，依照合作合同的约定进行投资或提供条件设立、分享利润和分担风险的企业。

外资企业指依照《中华人民共和国外资企业法》及有关法律的规定，在中国内地由外国投资者全额投资设立的企业。

外商投资股份有限公司指根据国家有关规定，经外经贸部依法批准设立，其中外资的股本占公司注册资本的比例达 25% 以上的股份有限公司。凡其中外资股本占公司注册资本的比例小于 25% 的，属于内资企业中的股份有限公司。

国民经济行业分类

《国民经济行业分类》国家标准于1984年首次发布，1994年对其进行了第一次修订，2002年为第二次修订。

本年鉴的行业分类使用2002年修订的行业分类标准。

2002年新行业分类标准按照国际通行的经济活动同质性原则划分行业，进一步打破了部门管理界限，对原标准中不符合这一原则的分类进行了调整；根据我国社会经济活动的发展状况，重点加强了第三产业的分类，新增了大量服务业方面的活动类别；对新标准的每一个行业小类，全部与国际标准产业分类的最细一层分类建立了对应关系。新修订的《国民经济行业分类》主要目的之一是与联合国的《全部经济活动的国际标准产业分类》接轨，准确反映一定时期内国民经济行业的构成状况。

失业保险

①参加保险人数：指报告期末按照国家法律、法规和有关政策规定参加了失业保险的城镇企业事业单位的职工及地方政府规定参加失业保险的其他人员的人数。

②失业保险金：指为保障失业人员的基本生活而按规定支付的失业保险金金额。

社会福利事业单位

社会福利事业单位指集中收养社会孤老、残、幼的机构。包括由民政部门管理的社会福利院、儿童福利院、精神病人福利院和城镇集体办的福利院，以及农村集体办的敬老院。

优抚对象

优抚指政府对革命烈士家庭、病故残疾工作人员以及参战负伤致残的民兵、民工的抚恤和人民群众对其的优待。优抚对象包括革命烈士家属、因公牺牲和病故军人家属、革命伤残人员、现役军属、退伍红军老战士、红军失散人员、复员军人、退伍军人、在职退役军人、在乡退役军人、带病回乡退伍军人、复退军人精神病员、孤老优抚对象等。

EXPLANATORY NOTES TO MAJOR STATISTICAL INDICATORS

Employees

Employees refer to the persons who are engaged in social working and receive remuneration payment or earn business income, including total staff and workers, re – employed retirees, employers of private enterprises, self – employ ed workers, employees in private enterprises and individual economy, employees in township enterprises, employed persons in the rural areas , and other employed persons (including teachers in the schools run by the local people, people engaged in religious profession and t he servicemen, etc.). This indicator reflects the actual utilization of total labor force during a certain period of time and is often used for the research on China' s economic situation and national power.

Employees in Various Units refer to all the persons working in government agencies of various levels, political and party organizations, social organizations, enterprises and institutions, and receiving wages or other forms of payment. They include fully-employed staff and workers, re-employed retirees, teachers in schools run by the local people, foreigners and Chinese compatriots from Hong Kong, Macao, and Taiwan working in various units, part-time employees, employees of other units working temporarily at current post s, and employees holding the second job, but exclude staff and workers who have left their working units while keeping their labor contract (employment relation) unchanged. This indicator reflects the total number of laborers actually engaged in production or other operations in various units.

Staff and Workers

Staff and Workers refer to persons working in, and receive payment from units of state ownership, collective ownership, joint ownership, share holding ownership, foreign ownership, and ownership by entrepreneurs from Hong Kong, Macao, and Taiwan, and other types of ownership and their affiliated units. They do not include 1) persons employed in township enterprises, 2) persons employed in private enterprises, 3) urban self-employed persons, 4) retirees, 5) re-employed retirees, 6) teachers in the schools run by the local people, 7) foreigners and persons from Hong Kong, Macao and Taiwan who work in urban units, and 8) other persons not to be included by relevant regulations. (Data of 1998 and afterward refer to fully employed staff and workers. Other related statistics such as total wages and average wage are adjusted since 1998 accordingly).

Registration Categories

Registration Categories are used to classify all kinds of enterprises that have the legal person status and have registered with the industrial and commercial administrations. The classification of business units, administrative and public institutions, social organizations and other economical bodies may refer to it.

The state-owned enterprises are economic organizations whose assets are solely owned by the state and whose registrations are made according to "Regulations of the People's Republic of China for Controlling the Registration of Enterprises as Legal Persons" excluding the state-owned liability limited companies.

The collective-owned enterprises are economic organizations whose assets are owned by collecting and whose registration are made according to "Regulations of the People's Republic of China for Controlling the Registration of Enterprises as Legal Persons."

Share-holding cooperative enterprises are a kind of collective economic organizations based on a cooperative system. In addition to the shares bought by their workers and staff, the enterprises also absorb a certain percentage of social capital. They enjoy the autonomy in operation and are responsible for their own losses and profits. The share-holders work together, conduct democratic management, and combine labor-based distribution with share-based dividends.

Joint-owned enterprises refer to economic organizations set up with joint investment from legal persons of two or more enterprises of different ownerships or institutions according to principle of voluntary participation, equality and mutual benefit. They include state-owned joint operation enterprises, collective joint operation enterprises, state-collective joint operation enterprises and other types of joint operation enterprises.

A company with limited liability is a company registered in accordance with the "Regulations of the People's Republic of China on Administration of Company Registration." Its investment comes from more than 2 and less than 50 shareholders. Each shareholder assumes limited liability for the company according to his subscription to capital stock. The company assumes liabilities for its debts according to all its assets. Such economic organizations include solely state – invested companies and other types of companies with limited liability.

A share-holding company with limited liability refers to economic organizations registered in accordance with the "Regulations of the People's Republic of China on Administration of Company Registration". All its registered capital is composed of shares of equal value and its capital is collected through share issuing. The shareholders bear limited liability for the company according to the amount of shares they have bought from the company and the company assumes liabilities for its debts according all its assets.

A private enterprise refers to profit-making economic organizations set up with investment from natural persons or with controlling interest in the hands of natural persons who employ laborers for operation. Such enterprises include private companies with limited liability private joint stock companies limited private partnership enterprises and solely individual-invested enterprises, which are registered according to the "Company Law," "Partnership Enterprises Law" and "Interim Regulations of Private Enterprises."

The joint ventures with investment from Hong Kong, Macao and Taiwan refer to those established according to the "Law of the People's Republic of China on Chinese-foreign Joint Ventures" and regulations stipulated in relevant laws, by investors from those regions and the Chinese mainland enterprises with contracted share of investment and sharing profits and ventures between the parties.

Cooperative businesses with investment from Hong Kong, Macao and Taiwan refer to enterprises jointly set up by investors from Hong Kong, Macao and Taiwan and mainland enterprises according to the "Law of the People's Republic of China on Chinese-foreign Contractural Joint Ventures" and other relevant regulations. They invest or provide conditions for establishment, decide profit distribution, and share risks according to provisions prescribed in the cooperative venture contracts.

Solely Hong Kong, Macao and Taiwan Funded enterprises refer to enterprises set up on the mainland according to the "Law of the People's Republic of China on Foreign Capital Enterprises and solely invested by investors from Hong Kong, Macao and Taiwan."

A share-holding company with limited liability with investment from Hong Kong, Macao and Taiwan refers to any joint stock company limited that is set up according relevant state regulations and is approved by the Ministry of Foreign Economic Relations and Trade. The investment from Hong Kong, Macao and Taiwan investors must account more than 25 per-cent of the company's total capital. If such investment is less than 25 percent, it shall be classified as a joint stock company limited invested by domestic investors.

A Sino-foreign joint venture refers to any enterprise that is jointly set up by foreign enterprises or foreigners with Chinese enterprises in accordance with the "Law of the People's Republic of China on Joint Ventures with Chinese and Foreign Investment." The investors shall put in investment, share profits and risks according to the contract on the joint venture.

Sino-foreign cooperative Businesses refer to the enterprises set up by foreign enterprises or foreigners with Chinese enterprises as their partners, in line with "The Sino-foreign Cooperative Ventures Law of the People's Republic of China" and other relevant laws and regulations. The partners of the cooperative ventures will invest, take profits and share risks according to the requirements of stipulated in the contract.

A Solely Foreign-Funded enterprises refers to any enterprise that is set up on the Chinese mainland according to the "Law of the People's Republic of China on Foreign-Capital Enterprises" and with all its investment coming from foreign investors.

The foreign-invested joint stock company limited refers to any joint stock company limited that is set up according to relevant state regulations and is approved by the Ministry of Foreign Economic Relations and Trade. The foreign investment must account more than 25 per-cent of the company's total capital. If such investment is less than 25 percent, it shall be classified as a joint stock company limited invested by Chinese investors.

Classification of the Sectors of the National Economy

Classification of the Sectors of the National Economy was first published in 1984 and revisions were made into it in 1994 and 2002 respectively.

This Yearbook follows standards in the 2002 version of the Classification of the Sectors of the National Economy.

In the 2002 version, economic sectors are classified in accordance with the international categories of the economic activities, abolishing in definition between different administrative departments. Given the development of China's social and economic activities, more detailed classification is made of the service sector. The further breakdown of each economic sector in the latest version is geared to the most specific categorization in international practice. The latest version aims at, among others, an objective and precise presentation of the composition of the national economy in a certain period.

Unemployment Insurance

1. Number of people participated in unemployment insurance program: the number of staff and workers in urban enterprises or institutions and other people according to local government regulations participated in unemployment insurance program in line with national law, regulations and related policies by the end of the reference period.

2. Sum of Unemployment Insurance: refers to total amount of insurance paid to un-employees to guarantee their basic lives according to related regulations.

Social Welfare Institutions

Social Welfare Institutions refer to institutions taking care of old people without children, handicapped people and orphans. They include social welfare institutions run by civil affairs departments, children's welfare institutions, welfare institutions for mental patients, and collectively-run old people's homes in rural areas.

Special Care

Special Care is offered by the government to the family member of the martyrs, disabled or demobilized servicemen or laborers who were injured on duty. Entitled to the special care are family members of the revolutionary martyrs, family members of servicemen who dies on duty or died of an illness, disabled servicemen, family members of servicemen on active service, retired veteran Red Army soldiers, scattered Red Army soldiers, demobilized servicemen, ex-servicemen, servicemen who were demobilized while on duty, ex-servicemen back to their rural homes, ex-servicemen who were demobilized because of an illness and have gone back to their rural homes, ex-servicemen who suffer from mental illness and elderly persons with no family.

第十五篇

CHAPTER 15

教育、文化、体育、卫生

EDUCATION, CULTURE, SPORTS AND PUBLIC HEALTH

表 15-1　各级各类学校基本情况
Schools by Education Level and Type
(2012)

单位:人　　(person)

指　标	Indicators	学校(所) Schools (unit)	毕业生数 Graduates	招生数 Student Enrollment	在校学生数 Students Enrolled	教职员工数 Faculty and Staff	# 专任教师 Full-time Faculty
总　计	**Total**	**358**	**109 003**	**128 928**	**532 235**	**40 522**	**31 384**
高等学校	Institutions of Higher Education	27	34 579	35 379	177 954	12 492	7 771
中等技术学校	Secondary Technical Schools	7	3 592	2 946	11 698	1 066	446
普通中学	High Schools	149	34 504	40 919	139 722	13 696	11 329
职业中学	Vocational Schools	7	4 995	6 864	19 011	1 095	909
小　学	Primary Schools	165	31 230	42 718	183 060	11 971	10 755
特殊教育学校	Special Education Schools	3	103	102	790	202	174

注：高等学校招生数和毕业生数仅包含普通本、专科学生数。
Note: The number of enrolment and that of graduates from universities and colleges only include the number of students in ordinary universities and colleges.

表 15-2　各级各类学校占地面积和校舍建筑面积
Ground Space of Schools and Floor Space of School Buildings by Education Level and Type
(2012)

单位:万平方米　　(10 000 sq · m)

指　标	Indicators	学校(所) Schools (unit)	占地面积 Ground Space	校舍建筑面积 Floor Space of School Buildings
总　计	**Total**	**358**	**1 380.41**	**743.55**
高等学校	Institutions of Higher Education	27	615.20	294.09
中等技术学校	Secondary Technical Schools	7	22.59	21.15
普通中学	High Schools	149	488.57	280.41
职业中学	Vocational Schools	7	35.67	24.06
小　学	Primary Schools	165	213.68	120.46
特殊教育学校	Special Education Schools	3	4.70	3.38

表15-3 各级各类学校女学生和女教师
Female Students and Teachers by Education Level and Type (2012)

单位:人 (person)

指 标 Indicators		女学生 Female Students		女教师 Female Faculty	
		人 数 Students	占学生总数(%) of Students(%)	人 数 Teachers	占教师总数(%) of Teachers(%)
总 计	**Total**	**255 067**	**47.9**	**20 783**	**66.2**
高等学校	Institutions of Higher Education	87 009	48.9	3 689	47.5
中等专业学校	Secondary Specialized Schools	6 958	59.5	276	61.9
普通中学	High Schools	67 739	48.5	7 646	67.5
职业中学	Vocational Schools	8 906	46.8	608	66.9
小 学	Primary Schools	84 185	46.0	8 419	78.3
特殊教育学校	Special Education Schools	270	34.2	145	83.3

表15-4 主要年份各阶段教育实施情况
Basic Statisics of Various Phases of Education in Main Years

单位:% (%)

指 标 Indicators		2009	2010	2011	2012
小 学	**Primary Schools**				
小学学龄儿童净入学率	Net Enrollment Rate of School Children	100.0	100.0	100.0	100.0
初 中	**Junior Schools**				
初中学生净入学率	Net Enrollment Rate of Students In Junior Schools	100.0	100.0	100.0	100.0
高 中	**High Schools**				
初中毕业生升学率	Enrollment Quotas of Junior School Graduates	97.2	96.1	97.0	97.1

表15-5　市、区实验性示范性中学基本情况一览

(2012)

指　标	Indicators	班级数(个) Classes (in Number)	初　中 Junior Schools	高　中 High Schools
总　计	**Total**	**819**	**129**	**690**
市实验性示范性中学	**Experimental and Demonstrative High Schools in Shanghai**	**319**	**53**	**266**
华东师范大学第二附属中学	Second High School Affiliated to Huadong Normal University	29		29
上海市建平中学	Shanghai Jianping High School	36		36
上海市进才中学	Shanghai Jincai High School	38		38
上海市洋泾中学	Shanghai Yangjing High School	41		41
上海南汇中学	Shanghai Nanhui High School	61	3	58
上海市实验学校	Shanghai Municipal Experimental High School	33	15	18
上海外国语大学附属浦东外国语学校	Pudong Foreign Languages High School Affiliated to Shanghai Foreign Languages University	44	33	11
上海市川沙中学	Shanghai Chuansha High School	37	2	35
区实验性示范性中学	**Experimental and Demonstrative High Schools in Pudong**	**500**	**76**	**424**
华东师范大学附属东昌中学	Dongchang High School Affiliated to Huadong Normal University	36		36
上海市上南中学	Shanghai Shangnan High School	36		36
上海市高桥中学	Shanghai Gaoqiao High School	36		36
上海市三林中学	Shanghai Sanlin High School	30		30
上海市杨思高级中学	Shanghai Yangsi High School	24		24
上海海事大学附属北蔡高级中学	Beicai High School Affiliated to Shanghai Maritime University	14		14
上海市浦东中学	Shanghai Pudong High School	18		18
上海市陆行中学	Shanghai Luhang High School	24		24
上海市高行中学	Shanghai Gaohang High School	36	24	12
上海市香山中学	Shanghai Xiangshan High School	28	16	12
上海市建平世纪中学	Shanghai Jianping Century High School	18		18
上海市新川中学	Shanghai Xinchuan High School	24		24
上海市大团高级中学	Shanghai Datuan High School	30		30
上海市新场中学	Shanghai Xinchang High School	30		30
华东师范大学附属周浦中学	Zhoupu High School Affiliated to Huadong Normal University	36		36
上海市南汇第一中学	Shanghai Nanhui First High School	54	36	18
上海交通大学附属浦东实验高中	Pudong Experimental High School Affiliated to Shanghai Jiaotong University	26		26

Statistics of Municipal and PNA Experimental and Demonstrative High Schools

在校学生(人) Students Enrolled (Persons)	初中 Junior Schools	高中 High Schools	教职员工(人) Faculty (Persons)	专任教师(人) Full-time Teachers	高中 High Schools	初中 Junior Schools	占地面积(平方米) Ground Space (sq. m)	校舍建筑面积(平方米) Floor Space of School Buildings (sq. m)	运动场(馆)面积(平方米) Floor Space of Sports Grounds (Stadiums) (sq. m)
31 245	**4 783**	**26 462**	**3 532**	**2 849**	**2 505**	**344**	**1 423 239**	**779 845**	**370 684**
12 307	**1 960**	**10 347**	**1 458**	**1 126**	**982**	**144**	**753 609**	**417 778**	**162 321**
1 184		1 184	169	113	113		100 000	52 285	25 350
1 472		1 472	159	134	134		41 358	35 836	7 075
1 446		1 446	191	155	155		114 146	59 842	35 504
1 504		1 504	177	141	141		51 811	39 824	8 300
2 369	107	2 262	255	202	202		259 064	103 707	36 092
1 132	465	667	179	116	71	45	73 723	28 831	17 600
1 722	1 307	415	164	147	48	99	81 004	72 323	21 000
1 478	81	1 397	164	118	118		32 503	25 130	11 400
18 938	**2 823**	**16 115**	**2 074**	**1 723**	**1 523**	**200**	**669 630**	**362 067**	**208 363**
1 388		1 388	143	106	106		29 232	16 803	10 384
1 381		1 381	152	127	127		18 834	17 503	9 340
1 385		1 385	152	114	114		41 675	24 206	11 582
1 212		1 212	141	118	118		34 087	20 593	13 737
921		921	110	93	93		37 714	19 053	8 730
515		515	55	46	46		25 338	16 459	11 013
658		658	75	64	64		29 093	19 295	9 847
878		878	98	70	70		40 766	21 033	11 410
1 337	896	441	128	113	50	63	37 077	17 694	12 659
1 020	540	480	106	92	53	39	21 242	17 724	9 000
683		683	74	67	67		36 488	15 653	9 699
928		928	84	82	82		21 940	13 457	10 200
1 178		1 178	123	106	106		64 414	24 954	19 980
1 102		1 102	126	116	116		42 774	19 930	14 572
1 427		1 427	172	149	149		79 696	39 193	8 000
2 070	1 387	683	191	160	62	98	87 389	40 795	28 637
855		855	144	100	100		21 871	17 722	9 573

表 15-6 普通中学和小学专任教师学历情况
Education Level of Full - Time Teachers at Junior and High Schools and Primary Schools
(2012)

单位:人 (person)

指 标 Indicators		教师数 Faculty Contracts	大学本科毕业及以上 Graduated from University or Above	大学专科毕业 Graduated from Junior University	高中阶段毕业 Graduated from Senior High School	高中毕业以下 Below Senior High School or below
教师学历分布	**Education Level of Teachers**	**22 084**	**18 276**	**3 503**	**292**	**13**
高 中	High Schools	3 427	3 410	17		
初 中	Junior Schools	7 902	7 655	245	1	1
小 学	Primary Schools	10 755	7 211	3 241	291	12
教师学历构成(%)	**Education Level Composition of Teachers (%)**	**100.0**	**82.8**	**15.8**	**1.3**	**0.1**
高 中	High Schools	100.0	99.5	0.5		
初 中	Junior Schools	100.0	96.9	3.1	…	…
小 学	Primary Schools	100.0	67.0	30.1	2.7	0.1

表 15-7 幼儿园基本情况
Statistics of Kindergartens
(2012)

指 标 Indicators		幼儿园(所) Kindergartens (unit)	班级数(个) Classes (unit)	幼儿数(人) Children Enrolled (person)	教职员(人) Faculty and Staff (person)	#专任教师 Full-time Faculty
总 计	**Total**	**261**	**3 381**	**103 321**	**9 325**	**6 503**
教育部门办	Run by Government Education Department	175	2 612	82 466	6 053	4 921
民 办	Run by Entrepreneurs	85	765	20 735	3 252	1 571
其他部门办	Run by Other Organizations	1	4	120	20	11

表 15-8 民工子弟学校基本情况
Statistics of Schools for Children of Migrant Workers

指 标 Indicators		单 位 Unit	2009	2010	2011	2012
学校总计	**Total of Schools**	**所 in number**	**41**	**41**	**41**	**41**
小 学	Primary Schools	所 in number	41	41	41	41
混合型初中小学	Mixed Primary and Junior Schools	所 in number				
班级总计	**Total of Classes**	**个 in number**	**534**	**553**	**586**	**592**
小 学	Primary Schools	个 in number	534	553	586	592
初 中	Junior Schools	个 in number				
教职员工数	**Number of Teaching Staff**	**人 persons**	**1 647**	**1 526**	**1 646**	**1 621**
小 学	Primary Schools	人 persons	1 647	1 526	1 646	1 621
学生总计	**Total of Students**	**人 persons**	**25 311**	**25 768**	**28 259**	**27 900**
小 学	Primary Schools	人 persons	25 311	25 768	28 259	27 900
初 中	Junior Schools	人 persons				

表15-9 文化事业
Cultural Establishments

指 标	Indicators	单 位 Unit	2010	2011	2012
街道、镇社区文化活动中心	Culture and Activity Center for Sub-district and Town	个 unit	38	38	37
行政村(居委)综合文化活动室	Comprehensive Culture and Activity Room for Administrative Village (Neighborhood Committee)	个 unit	1 117	1 078	1 135
街镇图书馆藏书量	Number of Books Collected in Sub-district and Town Libraries	万册 10 000 Books	104.57	106.84	95.60
文化资源	**Cultural Resources**				
区属文化基层单位	PNA Grassroot Cultural Institutions	个 unit	16	15	15
公共文化设施数	Number of Public Cultural Facilities	个 unit	1 280	1 308	1 188
公益电影放映次数	Number of Welfare Films Screened	场次 in number	21 553	33 731	15 681
#外来务工人员公益电影放映	Number of Welfare Films Screened for Migrant Workers	场次 in number	225	430	150
业余文艺团队个数	Number of Amateur Literary and Artistic Teams	个 unit	3 261	2 996	3 680
文化交流	**Cultural Exchanges**				
赴境外演出、展览次数	Number of Performances and Exhibitions in Foreign Countries and Regions	次 time	1	4	1
境外艺术团来访个数	Number of Overseas Artist Teams Visited	个 unit	18	6	
境外艺术团演出场次	Number of Overseas Artist Teams Performed	场次 in number	54	30	
文艺创作演出情况	**Literary and Artistic Creations and Performances**				
群众文艺创作数	Number of Literary and Artistic Creations	个 unit	1 169	1 228	998
获奖个数	Number of Prizes	个 unit	198	181	163
获奖人次	Number of Person-times Who Get the Prizes	人次 person-time	2 500	2 350	2 155
获奖单位	Number of Units Who Get the Prizes	个 unit	198	181	163

表15-10　公共图书馆基本情况
Statistics of Public Libraries

指　标	Indicators	单　位　Unit	2005	2010	2011	2012
机构数	Number of Institutions	个 unit	1	3	3	3
职工人数	Staff and Workers	人 person	110	188	195	201
公用房屋建筑面积	Floor Space of Buildings for Public Use	平方米 sq·m	18 343	74 221	74 221	74 221
#书　库	Stack Rooms	平方米 sq·m	6 040	16 515	5 297	5 650
阅览室面积	Floor Space of Reading Rooms	平方米 sq·m	7 550	38 882	27 464	28 130
阅览室座席	Seats in Reading Rooms	个 unit	1 366	3 764	4 535	4 149
总藏书量	Total Book Volume	万册 10 000 volumes	126	290	351	453
#本年新购藏书	New Books Purchased in Current Year	万册 10 000 volumes	12	24	43	29
发放借书证	Library Cards Distributed	张 in number	10 524	56 598	51 962	67 086
图书流通人次	Books Circulation Persons-Time	万人次 10 000 person-times	150	242	324	300
图书外借册次	Borrowed Books-time	万册次 10 000 volume-times	99	177	315	277

表15－11 广播电视事业基本情况
Statistics of Broadcasting and Television

指 标	Indicators	单位 Unit	2005	2010	2011	2012
区广播电视台	PNA Radio and TV Station	座 unit	1	1	1	1
区有线网络中心	PNA Cabled Networking Center	座 unit	1	1	1	1
市属有线电视管理站	Municipal CATV Management Station	个 unit	10	10	10	10
区属有线电视管理站	PNA CATV Management Station	个 unit	3	7	6	6
镇广播电视站	Town Radio & TV Station	个 unit	13	24	24	23
广电工作从业人员	Persons Employed in Sectors of Broadcasting and Television	人 person	342	544	537	559
区台无线广播发射塔	Radio Broadcasting and TV Tower of PNA	座 unit	1	1	1	1
区台使用频率	Frequency Occupied by PNA	兆赫 MHz	106.5	106.5/100.1	106.5/100.1	106.5/100.1
区台无线广播覆盖率	Radio Broadcasting Coverage of PNA	%	100.0	100.0	100.0	100.0
有线广播电视专线	Cabled Broadcasting and Television Line	杆公里 pole. km	1 858	6 097	6 774	7 015
有线电视管道干线	CATV Trunk Line	公里 km	223	1 211	1 345	1 776
广播电视台播出节目时间	Broadcasting Duration of Radio and Television Stations	小时/日 hour/day		18	18	18
有线电视用户	CATV Subscribers	万户 10 000 households	73	131	135	140
村通播率	Rate of Villages Access to Broadcasting	%	100.0	100.0	100.0	100.0
区台平均日播音时间	Average Broadcasting Hours of PNA Radio Stations	小时 hour	1/14.5	1/21.0	2/36.0	2/36.0
镇广播电视站日播放时间	Airing/Broadcasting Hours of Town Radio & TV Stations	小时 hour	14.5	21.0	21.0	21.0

表 15－12 文化馆基本情况
Statistics of Cultural Centers
(2012)

指 标	Indicators	单 位 Unit	合 计 Total	浦东文化馆 Pudong Cultural Center	浦南文化馆 Punan Cultural Center	川沙文化馆 Chuansha Cultural Center	文化艺术指导中心 Art Consulting Center
机构数	Number of Centers	个 unit	4	1	1	1	1
职工人数	Staff and Workers	人 person	185	32	26	29	98
公用房屋建筑面积	Floor Space of Buildings for Public Use	平方米 sq・m	35 100	6 180	2 500	4 920	21 500
组织文艺活动次数	Performances Organized	次 time	470	35	257	28	150
举办业余文艺训练班班次	Training Courses for Amateurs	班次 class-time	713	11	650	6	46
结业人数	Persons Graduated	人次 person-time	28 264	150	20 550	400	7 164

表 15－13 参加市级以上体育竞赛成绩情况
PNA in State-level and International-level Competitions
(2012)

单位:次 (time)

指 标	Indicators	第 1 名 First Place Winners	第 2 名 Second Place Winners	第 3 名 Third Place Winners	第 4 名 Fourth Place Winners	第 5 名 Fifth Place Winners	第 6 名 Sixth Place Winners	第 7 名 Seventh Place Winners
合 计	**Total**	**401**	**383**	**336**	**100**	**91**	**63**	**48**
市 级	Municipal Level	365	350	305	99	87	63	47
全 国	State Level	36	33	31	1	4		1
团 体	**Team**	**24**	**26**	**24**	**7**	**14**	**5**	**6**
市 级	Municipal Level	22	24	21	6	12	5	5
全 国	State Level	2	2	3	1	2		1
个 人	**Individual**	**377**	**357**	**312**	**93**	**77**	**58**	**42**
市 级	Municipal Level	343	326	284	93	75	58	42
全 国	State Level	34	31	28		2		

表15－14 举(承)办各级体育比赛情况
Sports Games of All Levels Held or Undertaken
(2012)

比赛级别	Levels	次数(次) Times (in number)	参加人次数(人次) Athletes (person-time)
总 计	**Total**	**203**	**53 913**
区级比赛	PNA Games	133	28 084
市级比赛	Shanghai Games	57	22 167
全国比赛及以上	National or Above Games	13	3 662

表15－15 等级运动员和裁判员情况
Graded Athletes and Referees
(2012)

单位:人 (person)

项 目	Item	二级运动员 Grade-Ⅱ Athletes	裁判员 Referees	
			二级 Grade-Ⅱ	三级 Grade-Ⅲ
合 计	**Total**	**129**	**118**	**204**
田 径	Track and Field	16	30	40
排 球	Volleyball	6		
武 术	Martial Art	17	24	21
篮 球	Basketball	4	37	49
射 击	Shooting	7		
足 球	Soccer			
游 泳	Swimming	25		
棒 球	Baseball	6		
散 打	Free Boxing	3		
击 剑	Fence-play	5		
围 棋	Go	7	1	29
象 棋	Chinese Chess			
国际象棋	Chess	1		
乒乓球	Table Tennis	10	5	
举 重	Weight Lifting			
垒 球	Softball			
羽毛球	Badminton		12	46
台 球	Billiards			
门 球	Croquet			
健美操	Aerobics			
皮划艇	Canoeing/Kayaking	11		
赛 艇	Racing Boat	2		
摔 跤	Wrestling	4		
中国式摔跤	Chinese-style Wrestling	3		
花样游泳	Synchronized Swimming	1		
网 球	Tennis	1		
风 筝	Kite Flying		3	
航空模型	Model Plane		2	
车辆模型	Model Vehicle		2	
体育舞蹈	Ballroom Dancing		2	19

表 15-16　全民健身活动设施情况
Facilities for Fitness Activities

指　标 Indicators		单　位 Unit	2010	2011	2012
农民健身家园	**Fitness Garden for Farmers**				
篮球场	Basketball Court	片 in number	206	227	239
羽毛球场	Badminton Court	片 in number	5	5	5
网球场	Tennis Court	片 in number	2	2	2
门球场	Croquet Court	片 in number	68	77	80
社区公共运动场	**Community Public Sports Ground**				
篮球场	Basketball Court	片 in number	69	74	81
门球场	Croquet Court	片 in number	26	34	36
网球场	Tennis Court	片 in number	16	17	18
足球场	Soccer Field	片 in number	1	1	1
羽毛球场	Badminton Court	片 in number	3	3	3
健身苑(点)数量	**Number of Fitness Court (Center)**	**个 in number**	**1 689**	**1 689**	**1 689**
健身苑	Fitness Court	个 in number	67	67	67
街道、镇	Subdistrict or Town	个 in number	63	63	63
体育系统	Sports System	个 in number	2	2	2
学　校	School	个 in number	2	2	2
健身点	Fitness Center	个 in number	1 622	1 622	1 622
街道、镇	Subdistrict or Town	个 in number	1 622	1 622	1 622
健身苑(点)面积	**Floor Space for Fitness Court (Center)**	**万平方米 10 000 sq·m**	**91.95**	**91.95**	**91.95**
健身苑	Fitness Court	万平方米 10 000 sq·m	15.15	15.15	15.15
街道、镇	Subdistrict or Town	万平方米 10 000 sq·m	14.00	14.00	14.00
体育系统	Sports System	万平方米 10 000 sq·m	0.60	0.60	0.60
学　校	School	万平方米 10 000 sq·m	0.55	0.55	0.55
健身点	Fitness Center	万平方米 10 000 sq·m	76.80	76.80	76.80
街道、镇	Subdistrict or Town	万平方米 10 000 sq·m	76.80	76.80	76.80
健身器材配置数	**Number of Body Fitness Apparatus**	**件 set**	**20 803**	**20 803**	**20 803**
街　道	Subdistrict	件 set	6 125	6 125	6 125
镇	Town	件 set	14 582	14 582	14 582
专业体育场馆	Professional Stadium and Gymnasium	件 set	60	60	60
学　校	School	件 set	36	36	36

表 15-17 各类卫生机构、床位及人员数
Healthcare Institutions, Hospital Beds and Professionals by Institution Type (2012)

指 标	Indicators	机构数(个) Institution (unit)	床位数(张) Beds (bed)	人员数(人) Staff (person)	# 卫生技术人员 Healthcare Professional	管理人员 Administrator
总 计	**Total**	**1 091**	**18 151**	**30 026**	**24 466**	**1 415**
卫生部门合计	**Total by Healthcare Departments**	**176**	**14 139**	**23 978**	**19 691**	**1 089**
医院合计	Total of Hostpitals	25	10 806	16 596	13 856	779
综合性医院	Comprehensive Hospital	11	6 635	11 882	9 949	557
中医医院	Hospital of Traditional Chinese Medicine	4	1 415	2 175	1 797	135
专科医院	Special Hospital	8	2 442	2 013	1 672	80
妇幼保健院	Maternity and Pediatric Hospital	2	314	526	438	7
社区卫生服务中心(站)	Community Healthcare Service Center (Station)	144	3 333	6 296	5 178	266
妇幼保健所	Maternity and Pediatric Clinic	1		71	61	1
眼病牙病防治所	Visual and Dental Clinic	1		32	27	5
疾病预防控制中心	Disease Prevention and Control Center	1		284	245	2
卫监监督所	Health Supervision Institute	1		144	129	2
急救中心	First-Aid Center	1		392	101	10
采供血机构	Blood Sampling and Supply Institute	1		75	45	12
其 他	Others	1		88	49	12
工业及其他部门合计	**Total by Industry and other Departments**	**915**	**4 012**	**6 048**	**4 775**	**326**
医院合计	Total of Hospitals	35	4 012	3 898	2 893	326
工业医院	Industrial Hospital	5	2 212	1 267	904	199
综合性医院	Comprehensive Hospital	3	673	778	500	174
专科医院	Special Hospital	1	420	130	80	12
护理院	Nursing Home	1	1 119	359	324	13
民办医院	Private Hospital	30	1 800	2 631	1 989	127
# 护理院	Nursing Home	1	83	54	28	4
诊所(含内设医疗机构)	Clinic (medical establishments inside)	561		2 150	1 882	
村卫生室	Village Health Room	319				

注：以上含浦东区域内市属三级医院及分院数据
Note: The above-mentioned data include those of municipal Grade III hospitals and their affiliated hospitals located in Pudong.

表15-18 各类卫生技术人员数
Number of Healthcare Professionals
(2012)

单位:人 (person)

指标	Indicators	合计 Total	执业医师 Medical Practitioners	执业助理医师 Assistant Medical Practitioners	注册护士 Registered Nurses	药师(士) Pharmacist	检验技师(士) Inspect technician	摄像技师(士) Video technician	其他卫生技术人员 Other Healthcare Professionals
总计	**Total**	**24 466**	**8 864**	**366**	**10 391**	**1 423**	**1 063**	**349**	**2 010**
卫生部门合计	**Total by Healthcare Departments**	**19 691**	**6 825**	**277**	**8 522**	**1 212**	**889**	**312**	**1 654**
医院合计	Hostpitals	13 856	4 494	24	6 766	717	551	252	1 052
综合性医院	Comprehensive Hospital	9 949	3 346	7	4 800	435	381	173	807
中医医院	Hospital of Traditional Chinese Medicine	1 797	613	7	822	181	76	46	52
专科医院	Special Hospital	1 672	404	9	880	91	75	33	180
妇幼保健院	Maternity and Pediatric Hospital	438	131	1	264	10	19		13
社区卫生服务中心(站)	Community Healthcare Service Center (Station)	5 178	2 077	245	1 706	490	237	59	364
妇幼保健所	Maternity and Pediatric Clinic	61	41		11	3	4	1	1
眼病牙病防治所	Visual and Dental Clinic	27	16		9	1	1		
疾病预防控制中心	Disease Prevention and Control Center	245	148		6	1	36		54
卫监监督所	Health Supervision Institute	129							129
急救中心	First-Aid Center	101	45	7					49
采供血机构	Blood Sampling and Supply Institute	45	4	1	24		15		1
其他	Others	49					45		4
工业及其他部门合计	**Total by Industry and other Departments**	**4 775**	**2 039**	**89**	**1 869**	**211**	**174**	**37**	**356**
医院合计	Hospitals	2 893	979	24	1 313	158	121	21	277
工业医院	Industrial Hospital	904	212	7	439	48	49	9	140
综合性医院	Comprehensive Hospital	500	163	6	213	33	39	5	41
专科医院	Special Hospital	80	15	1	57	4	2	1	
护理院	Nursing Home	324	34		169	11	8	3	99
民办医院	Private Hospital	1 989	767	17	874	110	72	12	137
#护理院	Nursing Home	28	5		13		1		9
诊所(含内设医疗机构)	Clinic (medical establishments inside)	1 882	1 060	65	556	53	53	16	79

注：以上含浦东区域内市属三级医院及分院数据

Note: The above-mentioned data include those of municipal Grade III hospitals and their affiliated hospitals located in Pudong.

表 15－19　区级医院基本情况
Statistics of PNA-level Hospitals
(2012)

指　标	Indicators	人员数（人）Staff (person)	#卫生技术人员 Healthcare Professionals	建筑面积（平方米）Floor Space (sq·m)	#业务用房 Floor Space for Treatment	床位数（张）Beds (bed)	全年诊疗人次（万人次）Annual Patients Treated (10 000 person-times)
总　计	**Total**	**11 009**	**9 253**	**568 404**	**492 522**	**7 684**	**1160.24**
综合医院	**Comprehensive Hospitals**	**8 995**	**7 583**	**444 940**	**390 668**	**4 908**	**930.00**
东方医院	Oriental Hospital	2 128	1 789	65 788	54 363	802	184.86
第七人民医院	No. 7 People's Hospital	1 238	1 097	79 603	78 104	690	119.73
华山医院南汇分院	Nanhui Branch of Huashan Hospital	1 263	1 116	91 015	91 015	950	137.06
浦东新区人民医院	PNA People's Hospital	1 294	1 121	91 561	56 998	806	147.01
浦东新区公利医院	PNA Gongli Hospital	1 273	1 061	60 905	60 228	586	153.98
第九人民医院周浦分院	Zhoupu Branch of Shanghai No. 9 People's Hospital	838	643	23 608	17 500	463	99.35
浦南医院	Punan Hospital	961	756	32 460	32 460	611	88.01
专科医院	**Specialized Hospitals**	**2 014**	**1 670**	**123 464**	**101 854**	**2 776**	**230.24**
传染病院	Infectious Disease Control Hospital	88	68	7 380	4 500	100	3.86
浦东新区中医医院	Hospital of Traditional Chinese Medicine, PNA	511	414	24 331	22 531	275	86.02
妇幼保健院	Maternity and Pediatric Hospital	360	315	20 031	15 770	250	39.53
光明中医医院	Guangming Chinese Medicine Hospital	423	370	16 000	13 800	318	81.12
南汇精神卫生中心	Nanhui Mental Health Center	104	84	12 500	10 725	320	2.03
浦东新区精神卫生中心	Mental Health Centre, PNA	205	171	21 771	17 634	800	7.85
南华医院	Nanhua Hospital	116	98	7 398	6 101	153	6.53
老年医院	Laonian Hospital	122	82	7 800	6 600	400	1.86
肺科医院	Pulmonary Disease Hospital	85	68	6 253	4 193	160	1.44

表 15-20 综合医院工作质量情况
Workload in Comprehensive Hospitals

指 标	Indicators	手术人数(人次) Operations (person-time)		入院病人数(人次) Inpatients(person-time)		出院病人数(人次) Inpatients Leaving for Home(person-time)	
		2011	2012	2011	2012	2011	2012
总 计	**Total**	**77 411**	**91 557**	**156 899**	**177 335**	**156 846**	**177 316**
东方医院	Oriental Hospital	18 625	22 351	30 926	36 658	30 948	36 753
第七人民医院	No. 7 People's Hospital	7 455	9 079	16 671	18 510	16 671	18 462
华山医院南汇分院	Nanhui Branch of Huashan Hospital	13 638	16 291	32 306	34 905	32 350	34 831
浦东新区人民医院	PNA People's Hospital	11 941	14 104	24 899	29 142	24 807	29 142
浦东新区公利医院	PNA Gongli Hospital	11 940	13 392	20 601	22 689	20 564	22 646
第九人民医院周浦分院	Zhoupu Branch of Shanghai No. 9 People's Hospital	7 503	9 797	14 852	18 209	14 857	18 182
浦南医院	Punan Hospital	6 309	6 543	16 644	17 222	16 649	17 300

表 15-20 续表 Continued

指 标	Indicators	出院者平均住院日数(日) Average Days of Inpatients at Hospital(day)		平均病床工作日(日) Average Beds Exploitation(day)		病床使用率(%) Rate of Beds Exploitation(%)	
		2011	2012	2011	2012	2011	2012
总 计	**Total**	**10.36**	**9.77**	**355.37**	**352.00**	**97.36**	**96.44**
东方医院	Oriental Hospital	9.85	8.06	368.49	371.12	100.96	101.68
第七人民医院	No. 7 People's Hospital	13.12	12.53	337.21	338.86	92.39	92.84
华山医院南汇分院	Nanhui Branch of Huashan Hospital	9.72	9.60	386.82	356.30	105.98	97.62
浦东新区人民医院	PNA People's Hospital	9.59	9.66	338.08	346.61	92.63	94.96
浦东新区公利医院	PNA Gongli Hospital	9.26	8.99	328.41	347.77	89.97	95.28
第九人民医院周浦分院	Zhoupu Branch of Shanghai No. 9 People's Hospital	9.87	8.92	375.59	349.29	102.90	95.70
浦南医院	Punan Hospital	12.73	12.92	347.49	348.01	95.20	95.35

注：老年医院 2011 年起调整为专科医院

Note: Laonian Hopsital was readjusted as one of special hospitals since 2011.

表15-21 医院诊疗人次和入院人数
Outpatients and Inpatients Treated
(2012)

指 标	Indicators	诊疗人次（万人次）Total Patients Treated (10 000 person-times)	#门、急诊 Outpatients or Emergency Treatment	入院人数（万人次）Inpatients (10 000 person-times)	每百诊次的入院人数(人) Inpatients Per 100 Total Patient/time (person)	出院人数（万人次）Inpatients Leaving for Home (10 000 person-times)
总 计	**Total**	**3 811.54**	**3 745.88**	**312 756**	**0.82**	**425 998**
卫生部门合计	**Total by Healthcare Departments**	**3 258.48**	**3 210.56**	**271 778**	**0.83**	**385 015**
医院合计	Hostpitals	1 715.59	1 692.24	240 251	1.40	353 161
综合性医院	Comprehensive Hospital	1 165.04	1 141.69	178 536	1.53	247 749
中医医院	Hospital of Traditional Chinese Medicine	336.53	336.53	15 757	0.47	49 802
专科医院	Special Hospital	167.56	167.56	28 196	1.68	33 104
妇幼保健院	Maternity and Pediatric Hospital	46.46	46.46	17 762	3.82	22 506
社区卫生服务中心(站)	Community Healthcare Service Center(Station)	1 536.20	1 511.63	31 527	0.21	31 854
专业公共卫生机构	Special Public Health Institution	6.69	6.69			
工业及其他部门合计	**Total by Industry and other Departments**	**553.06**	**535.32**	**40 978**	**0.74**	**40 983**
医院合计	Hospitals	354.92	337.18	40 978	1.15	40 983
工业医院	Industrial Hospital	47.67	47.67	11 448	2.40	11 430
综合性医院	Comprehensive Hospital	45.71	45.71	7 247	1.59	7 259
专科医院	Special Hospital			23		20
护理院	Nursing Home	1.96	1.96	4 178	21.32	4 151
民办医院	Private Hospitals	307.25	289.51	29 530	0.96	29 553
#护理院	Nursing Home			438		438
诊 所（含门诊部）	Clinics (including health rooms)	198.14	198.14			

注：1、业务指标不包括诊所(含内设机构)、村卫生室
2、以上数据除入院人数指标外均包含浦东地域市属三级医院分院数据

Note: 1、Business indicators exclude those of clinics (medical establishments inside) and village health rooms.
2、Except the number of inpatients, the above-mentioned data include those of municipal Grade III hospitals and their affiliated hospitals located in Pudong.

表15－22　医疗业务效益指标
Indicators of Medical Results

指　标 Indicators		单　位 Unit	2005	2010	2011	2012
医院(卫生部门)	**Hospitals (Healthcare Departments)**					
手术人次数	Operation Person－times	人次 person-time	32 404	69 354	93 519	108 832
病床周转率	Turnover of Beds	次/床 time/bed	26.77	24.95	26.71	28.45
病床平均工作日	Average Bed in Service	日/床 day/bed	374.72	344.26	355.15	355.92
病床使用率	Rate of Bed Exploitation	%	102.66	94.32	97.30	97.51
出院者平均住院日	Average Days of Inpatient at Hospital	日 day	13.37	13.06	12.17	11.8
平均每张处方费用	**Average Fee for Each Prescription**	**元 yuan**	**93.66**			
#综合医院	Comprehensive Hospitals	元 yuan	106.56			
专科医院	Specialized Hospitals	元 yuan	101.84			
街道、镇医院	Subdistrict/Town Hospitals	元 yuan	85.77			
其他部门医院	Other Hospitals	元 yuan	110.23			
综合医院出院病人平均医疗费	**Average Medical Fee of Inpatients at Comprehensive Hospitals**	**元/人 yuan/person**	**7 499.06**	**10 362.34**	**10 983.72**	**11 515.19**

注：1、2009年始，平均每张处方费用不作统计。
　　2、本表不含浦东区域内市属三级医院分院数据

Note：1、The average expense of every medical prescription has not been put into statistics since 2009.
　　2. Data in this table exclude those of municipal Grade III hospitals and their affiliated hospitals located in Pudong.

表15－23　公民义务献血、用血情况
Voluntary Blood Donation and Blood Transfusion

指　标 Indicators		单　位 Unit	2010	2011	2012
献血人次	Number of Person-times Who Voluntarily Donate Their Blood	人份 in number	49 902	47 959	49 112
无偿献血占献血人次比重	Ratio of Person-times Who Voluntarily Donate Their Blood in Total Number of Blood Donations	%	93.0	96.0	97.0
用血量	Amount of Blood Transfusion				
#全　血	Whole Blood	人次 person-time	96	52	40
红细胞	Red Blood Cell	人次 person-time	41 729	41 666	47 101
血　浆	Blood Plasma	人次 person-time	37 740	45 739	46 093

表 15－24 主要年份前十五位疾病死亡原因及构成
Death Causes of 15 Major Diseases and Their Composition in Main Years

单位：%　　(%)

疾病死亡原因	Cause of Death	构成比 Composition Rate					
		1997	2000	2005	2010	2011	2012
循环系统病	Circulatory System Disease	35.85	32.40	34.55	34.24	34.25	36.06
肿　瘤	Tumor	26.87	30.40	31.04	32.52	32.65	31.31
呼吸系病	Respiratory Disease	16.11	13.80	11.00	9.66	10.05	10.07
损伤和中毒	Trauma & Toxicosis	5.86	6.30	5.48	5.73	5.42	4.52
消化系病	Digestive Disease	2.57	2.90	2.70	2.78	2.84	4.23
内分泌代谢免疫病	Internal Secretion, Metabolic and Immunity Diseases	2.64	2.70	4.10	4.03	4.16	2.90
传染病寄生虫病	Infectious Disease and Pardsitic Disease	1.94	2.10	1.52	1.19	1.20	1.14
精神病	Mental Disease	1.66	1.90	0.97	0.65	0.45	1.06
泌尿生殖系病	Genitourinary Disease	1.10	1.11	0.93	0.85	0.95	0.68
神经系病	Neuro Disease	0.66	0.62	0.78	1.05	1.07	0.39
先天异常	Congenital Anomaly	0.48	0.35	0.27			
血液造血器官疾病	Haematopoietic Tissue Disease	0.24	0.29	0.34			
新生儿病	Disease of the New-borns	0.22	0.11	0.10			
妊娠分娩产褥症	Pregnancy/Childbirth/ Puerperium Disease	0.01					
其他疾病	Others Diseases	3.79	5.02	6.22			

表 15-25　家庭病床情况
Patients Staying in Family Ward Beds

指　标	Indicators	单　位　Unit	2005	2010	2011	2012
中西医师(士)赴家庭病床诊疗总人次	Total Number of Doctors of Traditional Chinese Medicine and of Western Medicine Treating Patients in Family Ward Beds	人次 person-times	109 579	162 608	139 092	143 381
期初原有家庭病床数	Number of Family Ward Beds at Beginning of Term	张 bed	2 097	2 555	2 604	2 437
期内新建家庭病床数	Number of New Established Family Ward Beds During the Term	张 bed	4 340	5 005	4 732	4 918
期内撤床病人数	Number of Patients Leaving Family Ward Beds During the Term	人 person	4 260	4 928	4 859	5 000
治　愈	Patients Cured	人 person	1	2	8	4
好　转	Patients Getting Better	人 person	149	264	163	300
稳　定	Patients Turning Stablized	人 person	3 452	3 711	3 582	3 415
转　院	Patients Turning to Another Hospital	人 person	419	618	696	803
要求撤床	Patients Asking to Cancel the Ward Beds	人 person	204	279	339	357
死　亡	Dead Patients	人 person	35	54	71	121
期末实有家庭病床数	Acutual Number of Family Ward Beds at End of Term	张 bed	2 177	2 632	2 477	2 355
期内家庭病床病人住床总床日数	Total Bed-days of Patients Staying in Familiy Ward Beds During the Term	天 day	777 590	1 042 073	1 100 242	979 514
期内撤床病人住床总床日数	Total Bed-days of Patients Who Have Stayed in Ward Beds Asking to Cancel Ward Beds During the Term	天 day	610 522	589 302	557 883	563 942
期内撤床病人诊疗总人次数	Total person-times of Patients Who Have Taken Medical Care Asking to Cancel Ward Beds During the Term	人次 person-times	90 942	100 068	84 545	104 022

主要统计指标解释

学　校

指按国家规定的设置标准和审批程序批准设立的，招收适龄人口实施各级各类教育活动的教育机构。

普通高等学校

指按照国家规定的设置标准和审批程序批准举办的，通过全国普通高等学校统一招生考试，招收高中毕业生为主要培养对象，实施高等教育的全日制大学、独立设置的学院和高等专科学校、高等职业学校和其他机构。

大学、独立设置的学院主要实施本科层次以上教育，高等专科学校、高等职业学校实施专科层次教育，其他机构是承担国家普通招生计划任务不计校数的机构。包括普通高等学校分校和批准筹建的普通高等学校等。

成人高等学校

指按国家规定的设置标准和审批程序举办的，通过全国成人高等教育统一招生考试，招收高中毕业或同等学历的人员为主要培养对象，利用函授、业余、脱产的多种形式对其实施高等学历教育的学校。包括：职工高等学校、农民高等学校、管理干部学院、教育学院、独立函授学院、广播电视大学、其他机构等。

民办的其他高等教育机构

指经省、自治区、直辖市教育行政部门审批并颁发办学许可证，但不具有颁发学历文凭资格的实施高等教育的单位。学历文凭考试机构是指民办的经教育行政部门专门批准，进行全日制高等教育的其他高等教育机构。

中等专业学校

指经县或县以上教育行政部门批准设立，招收初中毕业生实施中等专业课程教育的教学机构。

职业中学（职业高中、职业初中）

指经县或县以上教育行政部门批准设立，招收小学或初中毕业生实施中等职业技术教育的教学机构。按学校性质类别可分为：独立设置的职业中学（包括：职业初中、职业高中、职业初高中合设学校）；附设有普通中学班的职业中学。

普通中学（普通高中、普通初中）

普通中学分为普通高级中学和普通初级中学两个阶段。普通初级中学是指独立设置的招收小学毕业的适龄人口进行初级中等基础教育的机构；普通高级中学是指独立设置的招收初中毕业的适龄人口进行高级中等基础教育的机构；完全中学是指普通初、高中合设的教育机构；一贯制学校是指在一所学校连续实施中小学教育的机构。其中包括实施九年义务教育的九年一贯制学校和实施高中教育的十二年一贯制学校。（说明：一贯制学校的办学条件如能划分为小学、初中、高中，则分开填报；如不能划分清楚，可按就高不就低的方法填入初中、高中报表中，不能重复填写。）

普通小学

指由区或区以上教育行政部门批准，招收学龄儿童实施初等教育的教学机构。

幼儿园

指招收三周岁以上（含三周岁）学龄前幼儿，对其进行保育和教育的单位。

特殊教育学校

指本市独立设置的招收盲聋哑和智残儿童，以及其他特殊需要的儿童、青少年进行普通或职业初、中等教育的教学机构。

文化机构

是指专门从事文化工作具有法人资格，独立核算的事业，企业单位，以及单独核算，附属于事业单位的经营性专业文化活动单位。包括从事艺术、图书馆、档案馆、群众文化、文物保护、艺术教育、艺术研究、文化娱乐、新闻出版等机构，以及其他文化机构。

等级运动员人数

指经考核正式批准授予等级运动员称号的人数。运动员等级分为国际级运动健将、运动健将、一级运动员、二级运动员、三级运动员、少年级运动员。该指标主要反映运动员队伍的技术质量水平。

等级裁判员人数

指经考核正式批准授予等级裁判员称号的人数。裁判员等级分为国际裁判、国家级裁判、一级裁判、二级裁判、三级裁判。该指标主要反映裁判员队伍的技术质量水平。

卫生机构

卫生机构是指从卫生行政部门取得《医疗机构执业许可证》，或从民政、工商行政、机构编制管理部门取得法人单位登记证书，为社会提供医疗保健、疾病控制、卫生监督服务或从事医学研究、医学教育等卫生单位和卫生社会团体。

医疗机构

医疗机构是指根据《医疗机构管理条例》的规定，经登记取得《医疗机构执业许可证》的机构。包括医院、社区卫生服务中心(站)、卫生院、门诊部、诊疗所、医务室、村卫生室、妇幼保健院(所、站)、专科疾病防治院(所、站)、急救中心、临床检验中心。

医　院

医院指设有固定床位，能收容病人住院并能为病人提供医疗、护理服务的医疗机构，包括县及县以上医院、农村乡卫生院和其他医院三部分。县及县以上医院按业务性质不同分为综合医院和专科医院。

卫生技术人员

卫生技术人员指从事卫生技术工作并在卫生事业机构领取劳动报酬的专业人员。包括中医师、西医师、中西医结合高级医师、护师、中药师、西药师、检验师、其他技师、中医士、西医士、护士、助产士、中药剂士、西药剂士、检验士、其他技士、其他中医、护理员、中药剂员、西药剂员、检验员、其他初级卫生技术人员。

医　生

医生指在医疗、预防保健机构工作且取得《执业医师证书》的执业医师和执业助理医师。

EXPLANATORY NOTES TO MAJOR STATISTICAL INDICATORS

School Institutions

School Institutions refer to education establishment set up according to the government evaluation and approval procedures, enrolling population of the right age, providing various phase education activity.

Regular Institutions of Higher Education

Regular Institutions of Higher Learning refer to educational establishments set up according to the government evaluation and approval procedures, enrolling graduates from senior secondary schools and providing higher education courses and training for senior professionals. They include full-time universities, colleges, high professional schools, high professional vocational schools and others.

Universities and colleges are mainly providing undergraduate courses; those high professional schools and high professional vocational schools are mainly providing professional trainings; and others refer to educational establishments, which are responsible for enrolling students but not covered in the total number of schools, including: branch schools of universities and colleges, and universities and colleges that have been proved and prepared to construct.

Institutions of Higher Education for Adults

Institution of Higher Learning for Adults refer to educational establishments, set up in line with relevant rules approved by the government, enrolling personnel with senior secondary schools or equivalent education, and providing higher education courses in many forms of correspondence, spare time, or full time for adults. Institutions of higher schools for adults include schools of higher educations for staff and workers, schools of higher education for peasants, colleges for management cadres, pedagogical colleges, independent correspondence colleges, Radio and TV universities and other educational establishment, etc.

Civil Other Institution of Higher Education

Civil Other Institution of Higher Education refer to educational establishment set up according to rules approved and permitted by educational administration department of municipal government and not be provided with qualification to awarding diploma.

Specialized Secondary schools

Specialized Secondary Schools refer to educational establishment set up according to approval and permission by educational administration department of district and above government, enrolling graduates from junior secondary schools and providing secondary professional education courses.

Vocational Secondary Schools (senior secondary schools and junior secondary schools)

Vocational Secondary Schools (senior secondary schools and junior secondary schools) refer to educational establishment set up according to approval and permission by educational administration department of district and above government, enrolling graduates from primary schools and junior secondary schools and providing secondary vocational education courses.

Regular Secondary Schools (senior secondary schools and junior secondary schools)

Regular Secondary Schools (senior secondary schools and junior secondary schools) are classified as senior secondary schools and junior secondary schools. Junior Secondary Schools refer to educational establishment enrolling graduates from primary schools and providing junior secondary educational courses. Senior Secondary Schools refer to educational establishment enrolling graduates from junior secondary schools and providing higher secondary educational courses.

Regular Primary Schools

Regular Primary Schools refer to educational establishment set up according to approval and permission by educational administration department of district and above government, enrolling graduates from children of school age and providing primary educational courses.

Kindergartens

Kindergartens refer to nursery and education establishment, enrolling children in 3 years old and above.

Special Education Schools

Special Education Schools refer to educational establishments set up independently, enrolling blind, deaf, dumb, amentia or other special children, and educational establishment, providing regular or vocational junior and senior secondary education for hobbledehoy.

Cultural Institutions

Cultural Institution refers to undertaking and business institutions which specialize in cultural work and have legal personality and independent accounting system, and those professional cultural institutions attached to undertaking institutions and have independent accounting system. It includes institutions specialize in art, library, archives, mass culture, historical relic protection, art education, art research, entertainment, news and publication and other cultural institutions.

Number of Athletes in Grades

Number of Athletes in Grades refers to the number of athletes who have been given titles through examination. The titles of athletes include international masters of sports, masters of sports, first-grade, second-grade and third-grade sportsmen and young athletes. This indicator reflects skill of the athletes.

Number of Referees in Grades

Number of Referees in Grades refers to the number of referees who have been given titles after examination. They are classified as international referees, national referees and referees of the first, second and third grades. This indicator reflects the skill of referees.

Health Care Institutions

Health Care Institution refers to medical institutions and corporations providing health care, disease control and medical supervision service or engaged in medical research and medical education, which obtain Medical Institution Practice License from Medical Administration or Corporative Registration Certificate from Civil Administration, Commercial Administration or Organizational Management Administration.

Medical Organizations

Medical Institution refers to institutions which register Medical Institution Practice License according to Medical Institution Management Regulation, including hospitals, community medical service centers, medical house, clinics, dispensaries, medicine rooms, village medicine rooms, hospitals for maternity and kids care, special disease cure hospitals, first-aid center, clinical inspection centers.

Hospitals

Hospitals refer to medical institutions with permanent hospital beds, which are able to take in patients and provide them with medical and nursing services. Hospitals are classified into three categories: hospitals at or above the county level, hospitals of rural townships, and other hospitals. Hospitals at or above county level are divided into comprehensive and specialized hospitals.

Medical Professionals

Medical Professionals refers to those professionals engaged in medical work and receive salaries from medical institutions, including doctors of Chinese and Western medicine, senior doctors of integrated Chinese-Western medicine, head nurses, pharmacists of Chinese and Western medicine, laboratory specialists , other specialists, junior doctors of Chinese and Western medicine, nurses, midwives, druggists of Chinese and Western medicine, laboratory technicians, other technicians, other practitioners of Chinese medicine, nursing attendants, pharmacological workers of Chinese and Western medicine, laboratory workers and other primary medical personnel.

Doctors

Doctors refer to certified physicians and certified assistant physicians with certifications working in medical and health care and prevention agencies.

第十六篇

CHAPTER 16

法律、社会治安及其他

LAWS, PUBLIC ORDER AND OTHERS

表16-1　主要年份律师、公证及调解工作基本情况
Lawyers, Notaries and Mediations in Main Years

指　标	Indicators	单位 Unit	2010	2011	2012
律师事务所	**Law and Lawyers' Offices**	**个 unit**	**214**	**217**	**215**
合伙所	Partner Offices	个 unit	172	171	170
个人所	Individual Offices	个 unit	42	46	45
律师工作人员	**Lawyer Staff**	**人 person**	**2 958**	**3 269**	**3 571**
#专职律师	Full-time Lawyers	人 person	2 842	3 144	3 423
兼职律师	Part-time Lawyers	人 person	116	125	148
律师办理各类法律事务	**All Kinds of Legal Affairs Handled by Lawyers**				
担任法律顾问	Legal Advisers	家 unit	9 170	9 252	9 090
刑事诉讼辩护及代理	Litigation Defense and Legal Representation in Criminal Cases	件 unit	2 392	3 077	4 090
民事案件诉讼代理	Legal Representation in Civil Cases	件 unit	6 152	6 193	7 482
行政案件诉讼代理	Legal Representation in Administrative Cases	件 unit	98	90	110
非诉讼法律事务	Non-Litigation Legal Affairs	件 unit	5 741	5 814	6 949
公证工作	**Notarization**				
公证处	Notary Offices	个 unit	1	1	1
公证人员	Notarization	人 person	40	52	49
#公证员	Notaries	人 person	26	36	37
办理各类公证文件	All Kinds of Notarial Documents Conducted	件 unit	27 535	25 233	35 193
国内公证	Notarization for Domestic Affairs	件 unit	13 205	10 228	16 910
涉外公证	Notarization Concerning Foreign Affairs	件 unit	13 447	14 270	17 502
涉港澳台公证	Notarization Concerning Affairs in Macao, Hong Kong and TaiWan	件 unit	883	735	781
人民调解工作	**Mediation Work**				
专职司法助理员	Full-time Judicial Assistants	人 person	124	124	146
人民调解委员会	People's Mediation Commission	个 person	1 142	1 142	1 260
调解员	Mediators	人 person	5 386	6 066	6 064
调解民间纠纷	Mediation for Disputes among the People	件 unit	41 622	46 971	47 397

表 16-2 道路交通事故
Road Traffic Accidents

指 标	Indicators	单 位 Unit	2010	2011	2012
次 数	Number of Traffic Accidents	起 in number	726	838	760
死亡人数	Death Toll	人 person	242	215	222
伤残人数	Number of Wounded and Disabled	人 person	633	755	746
损失折款	Amount Converted from the Losses	万元 10 000 yuan	240	251	297

表 16-3 火灾事故
Fire Accidents

指 标	Indicators	单 位 Unit	2010	2011	2012
次 数	Number	起 in number	1 274	1 305	1 029
#纵 火	Arson	起 in number	19	12	7
电 气	Electric	起 in number	500	544	485
违章操作	False Operations	起 in number	59	60	55
吸 烟	Cigarette Smoking	起 in number	38	51	36
生活用火不慎	Careless Use of Fire in Daily Life	起 in number	218	245	201
玩 火	Playing with Fire	起 in number	33	32	13
自 燃	Spontaneous Ignition	起 in number	8	24	11
死亡人数	Death Toll	人 person	8	8	9
伤残人数	Number of Wounded and Disabled	人 person	6	14	6
损失折款	Amount Converted from the Losses	万元 10 000 yuan	1 083	1 729	1 052

表 16-4 社会治安
Public Order

指 标	Indicators	单 位 Unit	2010	2011	2012
刑事案件立案数	Number of Registered Criminal Cases	件 piece	23 517	26 070	27 552
行政(治安)案件查处	Investigation and Prosecution of Administrative (Public Order) Cases	件 piece	622 580	958 881	1 244 253
治安案件查处数	Number of Investigation and Prosecution of Public Order Cases	件 piece	95 669	104 609	112 362

表16-5 档案管理
Archives Management

指 标	Indicators	单 位 Unit	2010	2011	2012
机构数	**Number of Institutions**	**个 Unit**	**1**	**1**	**1**
档案局(馆)	Archives Bureaus (Chanceries)	个 unit	1	1	1
从业人员	**Employees**	**人 person**	**93**	**88**	**89**
专 职	Full-time Employees	人 person	93	88	89
馆藏档案	**Collected Files**				
全 宗	Whole File	个 unit	359	360	362
案 卷	Rolls	万卷 10 000 rolls	235	239	260
录音、录像、影片档案	Archives of Records, Videos and Films	万盘 10 000 discs	0.16	0.16	0.16
照片档案	Photo Archives	万张 10 000 pieces	12.91	13.07	15.01
底 图	Base Maps	万张 10 000 pieces	0.21	0.21	0.21
电子档案	**Electric Archives**				
磁 盘	Discs	万盘 10 000 discs	0.03	0.03	0.03
光 盘	Compact Discs	万盘 10 000 discs	0.43	0.43	0.43
微缩胶片	**Microfiches**				
平 片	Plain Films	万张 10 000 Pieces	0.20	0.20	0.20
卷 片	Coiled Films	万米 10 000 meters	12.93	12.93	12.93
档案利用情况	**Utilization of Archives**				
利用卷次	Number of Roll-times Utilized	万卷次 10 000 roll-times	6.89	6.20	4.89
利用人次	Number of Person-times Utilized	万人次 10 000 Person-times	5.71	6.23	5.28
综合档案开放利用情况	**Open and Utilization of Comprehensive Archives**				
建国前案卷	Rolls Archived Before Liberation	卷 roll	425	425	1308
建国后案卷	Rolls Archived After Liberation	万卷 10 000 rolls	5.88	5.88	5.88
建筑面积	**Floor Space**	**平方米 sq·m**	**17 524**	**17 524**	**17 524**
#库 房	Storeroom	平方米 sq·m	8 200	8 200	8 200

表16-6 信访情况
Complaint Letters and Visits

指标	Indicators	单位 Unit	2010	2011	2012
信访办受理人民来信、来访	**People's Letters and Visits Handled by Offices of Complaint Letters and Visits**	**件(批) piece (batch)**	**27 741**	**26 786**	**22 553**
来信数	Number of People's Letters	件(批) piece (batch)	12 453	8 981	17 146
#电子邮件	E-mails	件(批) piece (batch)	9 452	12 318	8 206
来访数	Number of Visits	件(批) piece (batch)	1 893	2 377	3 057
#来电数	Number of Calls	件(批) piece (batch)	3 943	3 110	2 350
进京非正常上访人次数	Number of Person-times Visiting Beijing in Secret	人次 person-times		242	124
到市政府集体上访批次	Number of Patch-times Visiting Municipal Government	批次 batch-times	145	231	107
到市政府集体上访人次数	Number of Person-times with Three and More Persons Visiting Municipal Government	人次 person-times	2 947	4 875	2 700

表16－7　法院收、结案情况
Cases Accepted and Ended by Courts

指　标　Indicators		单位 Unit	2010	2011	2012
法院收案数	Number of Cases Accepted by Courts	件 piece	76 028	83 897	85 289
#刑　事	Criminal	件 piece	3 406	3 571	5 756
民　事	Civil	件 piece	52 356	57 106	55 655
#经　济	Economic	件 piece	11 091	9 645	12 350
婚姻家庭类	Marriage and Family	件 piece	6 746	6 419	5 684
行　政	Administrative	件 piece	381	350	336
法院结案数	Number of Cases Ended by Courts	件 piece	75 899	84 077	85 380
法院未结案数	Number of Cases Not Ended by Courts	件 piece	8 556	8 378	8 286
法院结案率	Rate of Cases Ended by Courts	%	89.8	90.9	91.1
法院上诉率	Rate of Appeals by Courts	%	23.4	21.1	21.6
法院实际执行率	Rate of Actual Executions by Courts	%	82.5	87.4	90.1
法院审限内结案率	Rate of Cases Ended by Courts Within Time Limit	%	98.3	98.5	99.3

表16-8 外事活动情况
Activities in Foreign Affairs

指标	Indicators	2011		2012	
		批数(批) Delegations (in number)	人数(人) Visitors (person)	批数(批) Delegations (in number)	人数(人) Visitors (person)
接待外国人来访总计	**Foreigners Received**	**219**	**2 247**	**256**	**1 219**
#副总理以上国宾团	Deputy Prime Ministers and Above	2	24	1	12
部长级(含副部长)团	Ministers (Including Deputy Ministers)	4	60	2	28
其他政界人士团	Persons of Other Political/Government Circles	50	1 249	65	499
经贸界团	Businessmen	128	611	100	350
新闻界团	Newsreporters	15	120	10	113
其他团	Others	20	183	78	217
邀请外国人来访总计	**Foreigners Invited**	**9 732**	**10 382**	**9 812**	**11 078**
按签证性质分	By Type of Visa				
多次签证	Multi-Entry	1 931	2 015	2 017	2 127
一次性签证	One-Entry	6 679	7 428	5 901	6 795
按国别(地区)分	By Country/Region				
#美　国	United States of America		1 193		1 238
德　国	Germany		745		921
日　本	Japan		2 179		1 935
审批因公出国访问总计	**Approved Overseas Visits on State Missions**	**1 190**	**3 884**	**1 234**	**3 815**
按出国性质分	By Purpose				
经　贸	Business	973	3 083	996	3 023
非经贸	Non-Business	42	247	52	279
按出访国家(地区)分	By Country/Region				
#美　国	United States of America	153		186	
日　本	Japan	41		36	
中国香港	Hong Kong, China	49		79	

表16-9 主要年份人大情况
Statistics of Deputies to the People's Congress in Main Years

指 标	Indicators	单 位 Unit	2005	2010	2011	2012
全国人大代表人数	Number of Deputies to the National People's Congress	人 person	1			
全国人大代表提出议案	Proposals Suggested by Deputies to NPC	件 piece	5			
市人大代表人数	Number of Deputies to the Municipal People's Congress	人 person	80	118	116	121
#女 性	Female	人 person	19	37	37	48
市人大常委人数	Number of Standing Committee Members in MPC	人 person	4	6	6	6
市人大代表提出议案	Proposals Suggested by Deputies to MPC	件 piece	4	8	6	8
新区人大代表人数	Number of Deputies to PNA People's Congress	人 person	436	443	444	445
#女 性	Female	人 person	158	136	143	143
新区人大常委人数	Number of Standing Committee Members in PPC	人 person	28	34	31	34
#女 性	Female	人 person	4	11	9	9
新区人大代表提出议案	Proposals Suggested by Deputies to PPC	件 piece	9	4	7	8

表16-10 主要年份政协情况
Statistics of Political Consultative Conference Affairs in Main Years

指 标	Indicators	单 位 Unit	2005	2010	2011	2012
全国政协委员人数	National Political Consultative Conference Commissioners	人 person	7	10	10	15
市政协委员人数	Municipal Political Consultative Conference Commissioners	人 person	58	66	63	71
#女 性	Female	人 person	6	8	7	13
新区政协委员人数	PNA Political Consultative Conference Commissioners	人 person	379	645	644	535
#女 性	Female	人 person	84	161	161	145
新区政协常委人数	Standing Commissioners of PNA Political Consultative Conference	人 person	55	93	93	85
#女 性	Female	人 person	8	13	13	17
新区政协委员提案	Proposals Submitted by PNA Political Consultative Conference Commissioners	件 piece	205	528	302	267
#被采纳提案	Proposals Accepted	件 piece	165	467	274	228

注:"全国政协委员人数"和"市政协委员人数"均指在浦东工作的政协委员人数。
Note: Both the item of National Political Consultative Conference Commissioners and that of Municipal Political Consultative Conference Commissioners refer to those who work in Pudong New Area.

表16-11 主要年份精神文明建设情况
Construction of Role Models in Main Years

单位:个 (unit)

指 标	Indicators	2005	2010	2011	2012
市级文明社区	Model Communities at Municipal Level	6	12	10	8
市级文明镇	Model Towns at Municipal Level	6	16	16	16
文明小区	Model Quarters	393	908	908	729
#市 级	Municipal-level	208	414	414	291
文明村	Model Villages	101	254	254	209
#市 级	Municipal-level	53	112	112	78
文明开发园区	Model Development Parks	6	11	11	10
文明大厦	Model Mansions	22	45	45	47
文明单位	PNA Model Institutions	484	1 081	1 081	1 039
#市 级	Municipal-level	113	245	245	277
军民共建先进集体(对)	Model Collectives of Army-civilian (pair)	76	97	97	103
#市 级	Municipal-level	24	22	22	
五好文明家庭(户)	Model Families (household)	203	241	480	610
"三八"红旗手(人)	Female Models (person)	306	192		39
#国 家	State Level		1		
市 级	Municipal-level	32	41		39
"三八"红旗集体	Female Model Groups	99	88		10
#国 家	State Level		3		
市 级	Municipal-level	11	10		10
文明班组	Model Crews	338	479	478	508
#市 级	Municipal-level	12		4	
区文明岗位	PNA-level Model Posts	202	227	232	254
市级文明岗	Municipal Model Posts			129	

注:1. 除"文明班组"和"红旗文明岗"外,表列各项均为每两年评选一次。
2. 为规范"三八"红旗手和红旗集体的评选标准,2011 年新区未举行该类活动评选。

Note: 1. Except "Model Grew" and "Model Post", all the items in the listed table are choosen through public appraisal every two years.
2. To normalize the stardards for choosing female models and model groups, we did not organize these activities in 2011.

主要统计指标解释

律　师

指依法取得律师执业证书,担任法律顾问,民事(刑事、行政)案件代理人、刑事案件辩护人、办理非诉讼业务,解答法律询问,代写法律事务文书等,为社会提供法律服务的人员。

公证人员

指在国家机关依法办理公证事务的司法人员。包括公证员、助理公证员和在公证处工作的其他人员。

公证文书

指公证处根据当事人申请,依照事实和法律,按照法定程序制作的,具有法律效力的司法证明文书。根据公证书用途和使用地,公证书分为国内公证书、国内经济公证书、涉外民事公证书、涉外经济公证书四类。

调解民间纠纷

指调解委员会按照法律规定,根据自愿原则,用说服教育的方法调解民间发生的有关民事权利和义务争执的件数,包括调解成功数和调解未成功数。该指标主要反映人民调解委员会的工作量。

立　案

指人民检察院对受理的报案、控告、举报或自首及自行发现的犯罪线索、犯罪嫌疑人进行初步调查后,认为存在职务犯罪事实和应追究刑事责任,并决定作为刑事案件进行侦查的诉讼活动,是追究犯罪的开始。该指标主要反映人民检察院依法将职务犯罪线索作为刑事案件进行侦查的诉讼活动。

EXPLANATORY NOTES TO MAJOR STATISTICAL INDICATORS

Lawyers

Lawyers are certified legal workers according to law, and who are employed by legal counseling firms to act as legal advisers, agents in criminal or civil lawsuits, or defenders in criminal lawsuits, or to handle non-litigious legal affairs, to advise on matters of law or to write legal papers for others, and provide service to the public.

Notary Personnel

Notary Personnel are judicial workers of the state notary organs handling notarization work according to law. They include notaries, assistant notaries, and other people working in notary firms.

Notary Documents

Notary Documents refer to the judicatory notary documents drawn up by the request of the party and are in accordance with facts and laws and following certain legal proceedings. According to usage and locality, the notary documents are divided into following 4 types: domestic notary documents, domestic economic notary documents, foreign-related civil notary documents and foreign-related economic notary documents.

Mediation of Civil Disputes

Mediation of Civil Disputes refers to number of cases made by mediation committees in mediating in civil disputes concerning civil rights and duties through persuasion and education in accordance with the provisions of law on a voluntary basis, so as to solve disputes by helping the parties involved come to an agreement and understanding, including those unsuccessful ones. This indicator reflects the workload of the mediation committees.

Acceptance of Case

Acceptance of Case refers to the decision made by the people's procuratorate office on reported cases, prosecution, impeachment, surrender, self-found criminal clues or suspects after initial investigation to confirm the act of crime and to start legal proceedings of the case as criminal case.

第十七篇

CHAPTER 17

城市建设和环境保护

URBAN CONSTRUCTION
AND ENVIRONMENTAL PROTECTION

表 17－1　历年各类房屋构成情况

Composition of all Kinds of Buildings in Main Years (2007 ~2012)

单位:万平方米　　(10 000 sq·m)

指　标	Indicators	2007	2008	2009	2010	2011	2012
总　计	**Total**	**11 504.03**	**12 567.85**	**17 399.80**	**18 760.72**	**19 600.71**	**19 619.48**
居住房屋	**Residential Buildings**	**7 147.99**	**7 835.57**	**11 039.96**	**11 971.31**	**12 544.30**	**13 453.09**
花园住宅	Garden Residence	333.67	357.77	459.02	518.00	534.83	573.52
公　寓	Apartments	19.62	19.62	20.81	23.81	11 371.36	12 381.79
新公房	Public Housing	6 747.57	7 411.05	10 150.56	10 982.28		
联列住宅	Terrace Housing					137.09	147.12
新式里弄	New-styled Lanes	2.25	2.25	162.32	165.90	165.90	7.19
旧式里弄	Old-styled Lanes	37.45	37.45	237.70	142.20	142.20	218.96
低标住宅	Low-standard Housing					53.80	79.77
简　屋	Simple Housing	7.37	7.37	7.98	8.30	8.30	16.14
其　他	Others	0.06	0.06	1.57	130.82	130.82	28.60
非居住房屋	**Non-residential Buildings**	**4 356.04**	**4 732.28**	**6 359.84**	**6 789.41**	**7 056.41**	**6 166.39**
工　厂	Factories	724.14	786.25	1 448.45	1 458.00	1 547.00	1 880.36
学　校	Schools	278.94	297.94	470.70	463.19	532.44	635.63
仓库堆栈	Warehouses	92.78	108.58	125.70	130.14	78.00	60.60
办公建筑	Office Buildings	1 517.69	1 599.39	1 825.14	1 781.05	1 858.19	1 908.23
商场店铺	Emporiums and Shops	1 212.75	1 379.53	1 707.29	1 760.50	1 760.50	1 049.94
医　院	Hospitals	73.27	86.68	126.93	117.09	128.90	121.64
旅　馆	Hotels	141.02	151.22	165.89	203.22	203.22	162.57
影剧院	Theatres and Cinemas	12.80	12.80	17.24	18.16	18.02	17.72
其　他	Others	302.65	309.89	472.50	858.06	930.14	329.70

表17-2 八层以上房屋分布(至2012年累计)
Distribution of 8-storey and Above Buildings (Total by the End of 2012)

单位:万平方米 (10 000 sq · m)

指 标	Indicators	总 计 Total	8~10层 8~10 Storeys	11~15层 11~15 Storeys	16~19层 16~19 Storeys	20~29层 20~29 Storeys	30层及以上 30 Storeys and Above
幢	In number	7 697	868	4 229	1 736	657	207
面 积	Area	6 946	604	2 776	1 499	1 255	812

表17-3 市政工程设施
Public Utilities

指 标	Indicators	单 位 Unit	2005	2010	2011	2012
城市道路长度	Length of Urban Roads	公里 km	960	1 224	1 255	1 282
城市道路面积	Area of Urban Roads	万平方米 10 000 sq · m	1 704	2 463	2 666	2 603
城市桥梁	Urban Bridges	座 unit	169	370	495	507
雨水、污水泵站	Pump Stations for Rain/Sewage	座 unit	148	176	176	234
雨水、污水管长度	Length of Rain/Sewage Pipe	公里 km	1 858	2 805	2 805	3 200
公路里程	Length of Rural Highways	公里 km	905	1 937	1 983	2 072
公路面积	Area of Rural Highways	万平方米 10 000 sq · m	1 360	3 173	3 285	3 002
公路桥梁	Highway Bridges	座 unit	635	1 533	1 616	1 723

注：1. 2007年起道路长度和道路面积统计口径改变。
2. 雨水、污水泵站数据不包含南片,因南片排水所已撤销;公路里程、面积、桥梁包括农村在内。

Note: 1. The statistical approach has changed for the length and coverage of roads since 2007.
2. The data of pump stations for rain water and sewage exclude those of the southern part because the discharge stations in the southern part have been cancelled. The data of the length and coverage of roads, and the bridges include those in the rural area.

表 17-4　环境保护
Environmental Protection

指　标	Indicators	单　位 Unit	2005	2010	2011	2012
工业固体废物产生量	Amount of Industrial Solid Waste	万吨/年 10 000 tons/year	250	268	268	224
工业固体废物综合利用量	Comprehensive Utilization of Industrial Solid Waste	万吨/年 10 000 tons/year	242	243	248	212
工业废水排放量	Discharge of Industrial Waste Water	万吨/年 10 000 tons/year	7 103	6 679	6 895	6 284
#符合排放标准	Up to the Standards	万吨/年 10 000 tons/year	6 900	6 560	5 896	5 562
工业废气排放总量	Total Emission of Industrial Waste Gases	亿标立方米/年 100 million cu · m/year	1 112	1 696	1 865	1 811
二氧化硫日平均值	Daily Average Amount of Sulphur Dioxide	毫克/立方米 milligram / cu · m	0.056	0.035	0.030	0.028
二氧化氮日平均值	Daily Average Amount of Nitrogen Dioxide	毫克/立方米 milligram / cu · m	0.046	0.041	0.039	0.036
可吸入颗粒物日平均值	Daily Average Amount of Inhalable Particles	毫克/立方米 milligram / cu · m	0.081	0.071	0.069	0.060
区域环境噪声平均值	Average Value of Regional Ambient Noise	分贝 decibel	57.4	54.8	55.6	55.9
空气质量优良率	Rate of Fine Air Quality	%	89.3	92.6	94.2	96.2
污水纳管率	Rate of Sewage Piping	%	70.4	81.9	82.5	83.9

表 17-5 城市环境卫生
Urban Environmental Sanitation

指 标 Indicators		单 位 Unit	2005	2010	2011	2012
清运垃圾	**Garbage Disposal**	**万吨 10 000 tons**	**104.22**	**169.86**	**168.92**	**172.10**
生活垃圾	Domestic Waste	万吨 10 000 tons	103.10	168.98	158.86	154.78
建筑垃圾	Construction Refuse	万吨 10 000 tons	1.12	0.88	10.06	17.32
清运粪便	**Night Soil Disposal**	**万吨 10 000 tons**	**31.45**	**35.31**	**31.82**	**31.57**
环境卫生设施	**Facilities of Environmental Sanitation**					
公共厕所	Public Restrooms	所 unit	219	900	934	1 011
垃圾箱	Garbage Bins/Cans	只 unit	9 216	4 013	3 962	3 913
废物箱	Litterbins	只 unit	8 317	19 384	22 183	23 936
倒粪站	Manure – Dumping Stations	个 unit	89	102	104	104
化粪池	Septic Tanks	个 unit	4 711	5 855	5 850	5 802
垃圾处理	**Trash Disposal**					
垃圾焚烧	Trash Burning	万吨 10 000 tons	44.49	44.40	44.14	44.07
焚烧垃圾发电量	Power Output by Trash Burning	万千瓦·时 10 000 kw·h	10 841	12 619	13 217	13 576
环卫机械总数	**Machineries Used in Environmental Sanitation**	**辆 set**	**598**	**1 191**	**1 211**	**1 085**

注：2009 年起，垃圾箱统计口径作调整。
Note: The statistical approach for garbage bins has been readjusted since 2009.

表 17-6 园林绿化
Parks,Gardens and Green Space

指 标	Indicators	单 位 Unit	2005	2010	2011	2012
园林绿地面积	Total Area of Parks, Gardens and Green Space	万平方米 10 000 sq · m	8 439.52	12 019.49	12 518.60	12 879.50
#公共绿地	Public Green Space	万平方米 10 000 sq · m	4 154.71	5 565.51	5 951.40	6 065.00
单位附属绿地	Green Space of Organizations	万平方米 10 000 sq · m	1 508.15	2 479.00	2 519.78	2 628.63
居住区绿地	Residential Green Space	万平方米 10 000 sq · m	1 139.81	2 834.12	2 893.34	3 031.50
建成区绿化覆盖面积	Green Coverage of Built Area	万平方米 10 000 sq · m	6 426.88	12 283.46	12 923.80	13 287.40
建成区绿化覆盖率	Coverage Rate of Urban Green Areas (%) in PNA	%	37.8	36.1	36.1	36.1
新辟、扩大各类绿地	New and Extended Green Space	万平方米 10 000 sq · m	199.50	516.76	344.78	411.00
#公共绿地	Public Green Space	万平方米 10 000 sq · m	78.97	294.71	244.76	164.00
公园个数	Parks	个 unit	17	20	24	25
#免费公园	Ticket-free Parks	个 unit	15	17	20	21
公园面积	Area of Parks	万平方米 10 000 sq · m	214.25	486.27	493.42	551.17
#免费公园	Ticket-free Parks	万平方米 10 000 sq · m	68.88	78.31	113.06	143.21
人均公共绿地	Public Green Space Per Capita	平方米/人 sq · m/person	24.42	22.71	23.94	24.04
行道树年末累计数	Accumulated Trees on Streets at Year-end	万株 10 000 pcs	36.79	23.20	31.67	33.02

表17-7 水、电、煤气供应
Supply of Tap Water, Electricity and Gas

指 标	Indicators	单 位 Unit	2005	2010	2011	2012
自来水	**Tap Water**					
水厂生产能力	Capacity of Tap Water Plants	万立方米/日 10 000 cu·m/day	171.20	241.00	234.00	228.00
供水管道总长度	Length of Water Supply Pipes	公里 km	3 100	8 471	9 597	10 610
全年售水总量	Total Annual Volume of Water Sold	万立方米 10 000 cu·m	41 926	60 088	59 418	58 694
#工业用水	Industrial Water	万立方米 10 000 cu·m	10 526	14 541	12 063	11 341
生活用水	Domestic Water	万立方米 10 000 cu·m	21 749	21 876	20 710	21 602
每日平均售水量	Average Daily Tap Water Consumption	万立方米 10 000 cu·m	115	165	163	161
电 力	**Electricity**					
用电最高日负荷	Maximum Daily Load of Electricity	万千瓦 10 000 kw	285.70	553.00	556.00	574.10
全年售电量	Annual Electricity Sold	亿千瓦·时 100 million kwh	128.19	229.71	239.00	247.75
各类用电户数	Various Electricity Users	万户 10 000 households	117.91	190.03	193.70	203.30
天然气	**Natural Gas**					
管线长度	Length of Gas Pipes	公里 km	3 574	6 463	6 766	7 096
全年销售量	Annual Volume of Gas Sold	万立方米 10 000 cu·m	44 300	64 200	66 800	69 500
#生活用气	Domestic Use	万立方米 10 000 cu·m	18 700	23 926	25 900	28 083
家庭用天然气户数	Natural Gas-using Households	万户 10 000 households	75.50	121.25	127.42	133.62
液化石油气	**Liquified Petroleum Gas (LPG)**					
全年销售量	Annual Volume of Gas Sold	吨 ton	52 000	66 700	57 400	55 700
#生活用气	Domestic Use	吨 ton	50 000	54 000	44 100	44 000
家庭用液化气户数	LPG-using Households	万户 10 000 households	45.90	69.11	73.39	75.64

表17-8　交通运输
Transportation

指　标	Indicators	单　位 Unit	2005	2010	2011	2012
公共交通	**Public Transport**					
年末实有公交线路条数	Routes of Public Transport at year-end	条 route	108	232	252	278
年末运营线路长度	Length of Public Transport Routes at year-end	公里 km	2 125	4 770	5 019	5 108
年末运营公共车辆	Buses in Operation at year-end	辆 vehicle	2 041	3 450	3 550	3 622
全年运客量	Annual Passengers Carried	万人次 10 000 person-times	34 894	60 317	57 591	62 617
专线客运	**Public Feeder Bus System**					
专线客运线路条数	Routes of Public Feeder Buses	条 route	68	43	43	31
年末营运线路长度	Length of Routes in Operation at year end	公里 km	2 069	1 623	1 647	1 303
运营专线车辆	Public Feeder Buses in Operation	辆 vehicle	1 575	1 023	1 377	764
全年运客量	Annual Passengers Carried	万人次 10 000 person-times	28 293	14 879	22 252	15 761
隧道大桥	**Tunnels and Bridges**					
越江隧道条数	Tunnels across the Huangpu River	条 route	6	12	12	12
越江大桥座数	Bridges across the Huangpu River	座 in number	4	4	4	4
越江桥隧道车道数	Number of Lanes on Tunnels and Bridges across the Huangpu River	条 lane	54	84	84	84
轨　道	**City Railways**					
运营条数	Number of Railways in Operation	条 route		7	7	7
运营线路里程	Length of Routes in Operation	公里 km		109	109	109
站点数	Number of City Railway Stations	个 Unit		73	73	73
港　口	**Ports**					
港口货物吞吐量	Volume of Cargo Handled at Ports	万吨 10 000 tons		22 470	26 332	27 232
外高桥港区货物吞吐量	Volume of Cargo Handled at Waigaoqiao Port	万吨 10 000 tons		13 570	14 596	14 263
洋山港货物吞吐量	Volume of Cargo Handled at Yangshan Port	万吨 10 000 tons		8 900	11 736	12 969
集装箱吞吐量	Volume of Containers Handled	万标箱 10 000 TEUs		2 510	2 881	2 951
外高桥港区集装箱吞吐量	Volume of Containers Handled at Waigaoqiao Port	万标箱 10 000 TEUs		1 499	1 571	1 536
洋山港集装箱吞吐量	Volume of Containers Handled at Yangshan Port	万标箱 10 000 TEUs		1 011	1 310	1 415
民用航空	**Civil Aviation**					
浦东机场旅客吞吐量	Passenger Capacity at Pudong International Airport	万人次 10 000 person-times	2 358	4 041	4 144	4 486
浦东机场货邮吞吐量	Volume of Cargo and Post Handled at Pudong International Airport	万吨 10 000 tons	185	322	311	295

表 17－9 邮电通信设施和邮电业务量
Post and Telecommunications Facilities and the Volume of Business

指 标 Indicators		单 位 Unit	2005	2010	2011	2012
邮政设施	**Postal Facilities**					
邮电局、所	Post Offices	个 unit	93	136	124	102
信筒、信箱	Mailboxes	处 unit	624	641	1 076	665
报刊发行站	Newpaper and Magazine Distributors	个 unit	728	392	1 049	1 103
邮路单程长度	Length of Single-Way Post	公里 km	3 282	822	902	644
农村投递路线总长度	Total Length of Postal Routes	公里 km	3 691	6 688	9 373	5 950
邮运汽车	Postal Vehicle	辆 vehicle	108	144	205	264
邮政业务总量	**Business Value of Postal Service**					
邮政业务收入	Postal Service Income	万元 10 000 yuan	35 300	43 990	52 288	46 908
函　件	Mails	万件 10 000 pieces	5 409	15 112	20 201	21 070
包　件	Parcels	万件 10 000 pieces	94	93	90	92
汇　票	Drafts	万张 10 000pieces	98	162	173	172
订销报刊累计数	Accumulated Circulation of Newspapers and Magazines	万份 10 000 pieces	11 750	7 326	18 050	18 263
特快专递	Special Express	万份 10 000 pieces	281	618	87	76
集邮业务	Stamp-collecting Business	万枚 10 000 pieces	354	663	863	535
邮政储蓄年末收储余额	Postal Savings Balance at Year-end	万元 10 000 yuan	235 230	1 008 020	1 171 274	1 351 179
电讯设施、用户及业务收入	**Telecommunication Facilities, Subscribers and Operating Income**					
本地电话局用交换机容量	Urban Switchboard Capacity	万门 10 000 units	146	218	222	225
本地电话用户数	Local Telephone Users	万户 10 000 households	118	161	158	152
电信宽带用户数	Subscribers of Telecommunication Broad-Band	门 unit	281 408	806 341	900 796	921 190
电信业务收入	Telecommunication Income	万元 10 000 yuan	119 250	353 092	363 919	382 198
网络互动电视(IPTV)	Internet Interactive TV Network	线 Line		263 280	299 216	379 174
“我的 e 家”用户	“My e-Home” Subscribers	户 Household		625 799	627 829	696 551
光纤入户(FTTH)	Fiber To The Home(FTTH)	户 Household		53 731	271 913	513 581

注：电信业务收入，不包括移动通信和中国联通以及与其结算的业务量。报刊发行站、邮路单程长度、订销报刊不包括邮政投递的业务量。

Note: The business value of China Mobile and China Unicom as well as the related business is not included in the Telecommunication Income. Fields of newspaper distribution stations, one-way length of postal routes, subscriptions and unsubscriptions of newspapers and magazines exclude the postal delivery volume.

表17-10 房屋拆迁情况
Housing Demolition and Resettlement

指 标 Indicators		单 位 Unit	2005	2010	2011	2012
房屋完成拆迁总户数	**Total Households Domolished and Resettled**	**户 household**	**23 294**	**3 725**	**2 011**	**429**
重大项目拆迁	Demolished Because of Key Investment Projects	户 household	18 288	1 175	1 474	95
企事业单位	Enterprises and Institutions	户 household	351	77	128	2
公 房	Public Housing	户 household	4 487			
私 房	Private Housing	户 household	13 361	1 085	1 346	93
个体工商	Individuals Engaged in Industry and Commerce	户 household	89	13		
旧城改造拆迁	Demolished Because of Renovation of Old Towns	户 household	211			
其 他	Others	户 household	4 795	2 550	537	334
完成拆迁总面积	**Tota Area of Demolition Finished**	**万平方米 10 000 sq·m**	**474.63**	**139.78**	**101.83**	**9.55**
重大项目拆迁	Demolished Because of Key Investment Projects	万平方米 10 000 sq·m	363.14	26.79	68.18	2.05
企事业单位	Enterprises and Institutions	万平方米 10 000 sq·m	59.67	5.06	41.06	0.16
公 房	Public Housing	万平方米 10 000 sq·m	22.34			
私 房	Private Housing	万平方米 10 000 sq·m	277.46	18.83	27.12	1.89
个体工商	Individuals Engaged in Industry and Commerce	万平方米 10 000 sq·m	3.67	2.90		
旧城改造拆迁	Demolition Because of Renovation of Old Towns	万平方米 10 000 sq·m	5.83			
#企事业单位	Enterprises and Institutions	万平方米 10 000 sq·m	3.81			
其 他	Others	万平方米 10 000 sq·m	105.66	112.99	33.65	7.50

主要统计指标解释

城市基础设施

城市基础设施包括电力建设、交通运输、邮电通信、市内公共交通、自来水、煤气、市政建设、园林绿化、环境卫生等。

道路长度

道路长度指除土路外,路面经过铺装宽度在3.5米以上的道路,包括高级、次高级道路和普通道路。

城市园林绿地面积

指报告期末用作园林和绿化的各种绿地面积。包括公共绿地、居住区绿地、单位附属绿地、防护绿地、生产绿地、道路绿地和风景林地面积。

不包括:

(1)屋顶绿化、垂直绿化、阳台绿化和室内绿化。

(2)以物质生产为主的林地、耕地、牧草地、果园和竹园等。

(3)城市总体规划中不列入绿地的水域。

公共绿地

公共绿地指向公众开放的市级、区级、居住区级各类公园、街旁游园,包括其范围内的水域。其中居住区级公园应不小于1万平方米,街旁游园的宽度不小于8米,面积不小于400平方米。

供水管道长度

指从送水泵至用户水表之间所有管道的长度。不包括新安装尚未使用的管道。

生活用水

生活用水包括公共服务用水和居民家庭用水。公共服务用水指为城市社会公共生活服务的用水。包括行政事业单位、部队营区和公共设施服务、社会服务业、批发零售贸易业、旅馆饮食业以及其他公共服务业等单位的用水。居民家庭用水指城市范围内所有居民家庭的日常生活用水。包括城市居民、农民家庭、公共供水站用水。

工业固体废弃物产生量

指报告期内企业在生产过程中产生的固体状、半固体状和高浓度液体状废弃物的总量,包括危险废物、冶炼废渣、粉煤灰、炉渣、煤矸石、尾矿、放射性废物和其他废物等;不包括矿山开采的剥离废石和掘进废石(煤矸石和呈酸性或碱性的废石除外)。酸性或碱性废石指采掘的废石其流经水、雨淋水的pH值小于4或pH值大于10.5者。

工业固体废物综合利用量

指通过回收、加工、循环、交换等方式,从固体废物中提取或者使其转化为可以利用的资源、能源和其他原材料的固体废物量(包括当年利用往年的工业固体废物累计贮存量),如用作农业肥料、生产建筑材料、筑路等。综合利用量由原产生固体废物的单位统计。

工业废水排放量

工业废水排放量指经过企业厂区所有排放口排到企业外部的工业废水量。包括生产废水、外排的直接冷却水、超标排放的矿井地下水和与工业废水混排的厂区生活污水,不包括外排的间接冷却水(清污不分流的间接冷却水应计算在内)。

工业废水排放达标量

指报告期内废水中各项污染物指标都达到国家或地方排放标准的外排工业废水量,包括未经处理外排达标的,经废水处理设施处理后达标排放的,以及经污水处理厂处理后达标排放的。

工业废气排放量

工业废气排放量指企业厂区内燃料燃烧和生产工艺过程中产生的各种排入空气的含有污染物的气体总量,按标准状态〔273K,101 325Pa〕计算。测算公式为:

工业废气排放量 = 燃料燃烧过程中废气排放量 + 生产工艺过程中废气排放量

生活垃圾清运量

指报告期内收集和运送到垃圾处理厂(场)的生活垃圾数量。生活垃圾指城市日常生活或为城市日常生活提供服务的活动中产生的固体废物以及法律行政规定的视为城市生活垃圾的固体废物。包括:居民生活垃圾、商业垃圾、集市贸易市场垃圾、街道清扫垃圾、公共场所垃圾和机关、学校、厂矿等单位的生活垃圾。

运营公交车辆数

指年末公交企业(单位)用于运营业务的全部车辆数。以企业(单位)固定资产台帐中已投入运营的车辆数为准。

邮政业务总量

指以货币表现的邮政部门用于邮政服务的总数量。它综合反映了一定时期邮政工作的总成果，是研究邮政业务量构成和发展趋势的重要指标。它用各种邮政分类业务量，如函件件数、电报份数、订销报刊累计份数等，分别乘以相应的平均单位（不变价），加总后再加上其他业务收入求得。

局用交换机容量

指安装在电信企业用于接续本地固定电话的电话交换机容量。

住宅电话用户

指安装在居民住宅或农民家里并按照住宅电话用户登记注册和收费的电话用户。包括私人付费、单位付费和按规定免费安装的住宅电话用户。

EXPLANATORY NOTES TO MAJOR STATISTICAL INDICATORS

Urban Infrastructure Facilities

Urban Infrastructure Facilities include facilities for power generating, transportation, post and telecommunication, urban public transportation, supply of tap water and gas, development of municipal engineering, city landscaping and sanitation.

Length of Roads

Length of Roads refers to the roads with a paved surface, and with a width of more than 3 – 5 meters, including high quality, medium quality and ordinary roads.

Area of Urban Gardens and Green Areas

Area of Urban Gardens and Green Areas refers to the total area occupied for green projects at the end of the reference period, including public green land, green land in residential quarters, green land attached to institutions, protection green land, production green land, roadside green land and forest in scenic spots. It does not include the following:

(1) Greenery and plants on roofs, balconies, indoors and vertical green areas;

(2) Forest, cultivated land grassland, orchards and bamboo grooves that are for production purpose and etc.;

(3) Water areas that are not included in urban master plan as green land.

Public Green Area

Public Green Area refers to green areas open to the public such as municipal, community and neighborhood parks and roadside parks, including waters within parks. Neighborhood parks should occupy an area larger than 10,000 square meters, and the width of roadside parks should occupy an area larger than 400 square meters, with a width of more that 8 meters.

Length of Water Supply Pipelines

Length of Water Supply Pipelines refers to the total length of all the pipelines between the water pumps and the user's water meters, excluding pipelines newly installed but not used yet.

Consumption of Water for Residential Use

Consumption of Water for Residential Use refers to the water consumption of households for daily life and the water consumption of public service facilities. The latter refers to water consumption for urban public services, including the consumption of government agencies and public institutions, military barracks, public facilities, wholesale and retail outlets, restaurants, hotels, and other units providing public services. Household water consumption refers to consumption of water for daily life of all households in the boundary of cities, including households of urban residents and farmers, and public water supply stations.

Industrial Solid Wastes Produced

Industrial Solid Wastes Produced refers to total volume of solid, semi-solid and high concentration liquid residues produced by industrial enterprises from production process in a given period of time, including hazardous wastes, slag, coal ash, gangue, tailings, radioactive residues and other wastes, but excluding stones stripped or dug out in mining (gangue and acid or alkaline stones not included). A stone is acid or alkaline depending on the pH value of the water below 4 or above 10.5 when the stone is in, or soaked by, the water.

Volume of Industrial Solid Wastes Utilized in a Comprehensive Way

Volume of Industrial Solid Wastes Utilized in a Comprehensive Way refers to the volume of solid wastes from which useful materials can be extracted or which can be changed into utilizable resources, energy or other materials, including the volume of industrial solid wastes stored up in previous years and utilized in the current year, such as the solid wastes utilized as fertilizers, building materials, for making roads or for other purposes. Statistical data on utilization of industrial solid wastes are collected by solid wastes producing units.

Volume of Industrial Waste Water Discharged

Volume of Industrial Waste Water Discharged refers to the volume of industrial waste water discharged, through all outlets, to the outside of industrial enterprises, including waste water produced, direct-cooling water, underground water from mines that does not meet the standard of discharge, and the domestic sewage mixed up with industrial waste water when discharged, but excluding discharged indirect-cooling water.

Industrial Waste Water Meeting Discharge Standards

Industrial Waste Water Meeting Discharge Standards refers to volume of industrial waste water discharge which, with or without treatment, reaches national or local standards with regard to all pollutants.

Volume of Waste Industrial Gas Emission

Industrial Waste Air Emission refers to discharge into atmosphere of waste air containing pollutants generated from fuel burning and production process in enterprises within a given period of time. It is calculated at standard status (273K, 101325Pa) as:

Industrial waste air emission = emission through fuel burning + emission through production process

Consumption Wastes Transported

Consumption Wastes Transported refers to volume of consumption wastes collected and transported to disposal factories or sites. Consumption Wastes are solid wastes produced from urban households or from seryice activities for urban households , and solid wastes regarded by laws and regulations as urban consumption wastes, including those from households, commercial activities, markets cleaning of streets, public sites, offices, schools, factories, mining units and other sources.

Number of Vehicles under Operation

Number of Vehicles under Operation refers to the total number of vehicles under operation by public transport enterprises (units) at the end of the year, based on the records of operational vehicles by the enterprises (units).

Volume of Post Business

Volume of Post Business refers to the total amount of post services provided by the post department, which reflects the total achievements by the post departments during a given period of time in a comprehensive way, and is an important indicator to study the composition and development of the post business. It is arrived by first multiplying the business volume of different types, such as number of letters, telegrams and accumulated number of newspaper and journals subscribed and sold, etc. by their respective average unit price (fixed price) and then adding these products together, plus the income from other business revenues.

Capacity of Office Telephone Exchanges

Capacity of Office Telephone Exchanges refers to the capacity of telephone exchanges installed in the office of telecommunication service providers for communication between fixed telephones.

Household Telephone Subscribers

Household Telephone Subscribers refer to telephone sets installed in the dwelling units of urban or rural residents, and registered as residence subscribers for payment, including 3 types of payment for the service: private payment, public payment and free service.

第十八篇

CHAPTER 18

重点开发区和镇

KEY DEVELOPMENT ZONES AND TOWN

表18-1 陆家嘴金融贸易区主要经济指标
Major Economic Indicators in Lujiazui Finance and Trade Zone

指 标 Indicators		单 位 Unit	2011	2012
税收总额(税务部门口径)	Total Amount of Tax Revenues (from the Tax Departments)	亿元 100 million yuan	380.87	477.70
地方财政收入	Local Fiscal Revenue	亿元 100 million yuan	122.84	134.98
固定资产投资额	Investment in Fixed Assets	亿元 100 million yuan	177.57	193.91
#房地产开发投资额	Investment in Real Estate	亿元 100 million yuan	120.71	125.22
#办公楼及商业营业用房	Office and Commercial Buildings	亿元 100 million yuan	70.73	75.38
房地产新开工面积	Floor Space of New Construction of Buildings	万平方米 10 000 sq·m	83.87	58.88
房地产竣工面积	Floor Space of Completed Buildings	万平方米 10 000 sq·m	93.14	106.43
外商直接投资项目	Projects of Foreign Direct Investment	个 unit	294	266
外商直接投资合同金额	Contracted Amount of Foreign Direct Investment	亿美元 USD 100 million	28.74	21.13
外商直接投资实际到位金额	Actual Paid Amount of Foreign Direct Investment	亿美元 USD 100 million	24.10	14.64
新增内资企业注册户数	Number of New Domestic Enterprises Registered	个 unit	1 442	1 287
新增内资企业注册资本	Capital of New Domestic Enterprises Registered	亿元 100 million yuan	247.51	251.10
金融业增加值	Added Value of Finance Industry	亿元 100 million yuan	845.12	895.64
期末金融机构数	Number of Financial Institutions at End of Term	个 unit	630	662
#外资银行法人行	Foreign Banks and Corporate Banks	个 unit	18	18
基金总公司	Head Office of Funds	个 unit	30	31
期末认定跨国公司地区总部个数	Number of Approved Regional Headquarters of Transnational Companies at End of Term	个 unit	71	81
举办展览(博览)次数	Number of Exhibitions (Fairs) Hosted	次 time	119	99
商品销售总额(限额以上)	Gross Sales of Commodities (Above Quota)	亿元 100 million yuan	8 166.82	9 056.35
社会消费品零售总额(限额以上)	Total Volume of Retail Sales for Social Consumer Goods (Above Quota)	亿元 100 million yuan	292.35	354.59
期末星级宾馆个数	Number of Star Hotels at End of Term	个 unit	32	34
主要景点接待人次	Person-times Received by Main Sight Spots	万人次 10 000 persom-times	1 554.99	1 713.30
商办楼宇数	Number of Office Buildings	幢 in number	201	220
商办楼宇建筑面积	Floor Space of Office Buildings	万平方米 10 000 sq·m	1 196.85	1 314.87
商办楼宇平均入驻率	Average Occupancy Rate of Office Buildings	%	94.4	91.3

注：地方财政收入即为原“地方税收”口径，后续相关指标口径相同。
Note: The local fiscal revenue is the former local tax approach. The relevant indicators hereinafter have the same statistical approach.

表18－2　金桥出口加工区主要经济指标
Major Economic Indicators in Jinqiao Export Processing Zone

指　标	Indicators	单　位 Unit	2011	2012
税收总额(税务部门口径)	Total Amount of Tax Revenues (from the Tax Departments)	亿元 100 million yuan	79.45	310.70
地方财政收入	Local Fiscal Revenue	亿元 100 million yuan	18.83	23.27
固定资产投资额	Investment in Fixed Assets	亿元 100 million yuan	62.85	80.19
#房地产开发投资额	Investment in Real Estate	亿元 100 million yuan	10.96	19.90
工业投资额	Investment in Industries	亿元 100 million yuan	47.04	45.45
房地产新开工面积	Floor Space of New Construction of Buildings	万平方米 10 000 sq·m	73.69	8.59
房地产竣工面积	Floor Space of Completed Buildings	万平方米 10 000 sq·m	12.93	
外商直接投资项目	Projects of Foreign Direct Investment	个 unit	26	30
外商直接投资合同金额	Contracted Amount of Foreign Direct Investment	亿美元 USD 100 million	3.05	4.43
外商直接投资实际到位金额	Actual Paid Amount of Foreign Direct Investment	亿美元 USD 100 million	2.20	4.00
新增内资企业注册户数	Number of New Domestic Enterprises Registered	个 unit	227	221
新增内资企业注册资本	Capital of New Domestic Enterprises Registered	亿元 100 million yuan	19.81	4.82
工业总产值	Gross Value of Industrial Output	亿元 100 million yuan	2 275.66	1 886.76
#高技术产业产值	Output Value of High-tech Industries	亿元 100 million yuan	734.15	604.57
工业重点发展行业产值	Output Value of Key Industrial Sectors for Development	亿元 100 million yuan	1 859.65	1 537.96
#电子信息产品制造业	Manufacturing of Electronic and Information Products	亿元 100 million yuan	683.32	529.79
汽车制造业	Automobile Industry	亿元 100 million yuan	909.67	742.17
成套设备制造业	Manufacturing of Complete Equipment	亿元 100 million yuan	143.52	135.16
生物医药制造业	Manufacturing of Biological Medicine	亿元 100 million yuan	26.71	35.25
工业出口交货值	Delivery Value of Industrial Exports	亿元 100 million yuan	422.61	322.80
生产性服务业经营收入	Operating Income of Productive Services	亿元 100 million yuan	415.51	2 092.46
期末从业人员数	Number of Employed Persons at End of Term	万人 10 000 persoms		15.76

注：工业总产值为规模以上口径。后续相关指标口径相同。
Note: The gross value of industrial output has the approach for enterprises with above-certain scales. The relevant indicators hereinafter have the same statistical approach.

表 18-3　南汇工业园区主要经济指标
Main Economic Indicators in Nanhui Industrial Park

指　标 Indicators		单　位 Unit	2011	2012
税收总额(税务部门口径)	Total Amount of Tax Revenues (from the Tax Departments)	亿元 100 million yuan	7.22	6.32
地方财政收入	Local Fiscal Revenue	亿元 100 million yuan	1.92	1.58
固定资产投资额	Investment in Fixed Assets	亿元 100 million yuan	18.04	15.14
#工业投资额	Investment in Industries	亿元 100 million yuan	16.11	12.78
外商直接投资项目	Projects of Foreign Direct Investment	个 unit	7	5
外商直接投资合同金额	Contracted Amount of Foreign Direct Investment	亿美元 USD 100 million	0.80	0.70
外商直接投资实际到位金额	Actual Paid Amount of Foreign Direct Investment	亿美元 USD 100 million	0.47	0.56
新增内资企业注册户数	Number of New Domestic Enterprises Registered	个 unit	161	66
新增内资企业注册资本	Capital of New Domestic Enterprises Registered	亿元 100 million yuan	5.09	14.29
工业总产值	Gross Value of Industrial Output	亿元 100 million yuan	132.18	134.49
#高技术产业产值	Output Value of High-tech Industries	亿元 100 million yuan	32.84	24.25
工业重点发展行业产值	Output Value of Key Industrial Sectors for Development	亿元 100 million yuan	84.94	81.02
#电子信息产品制造	Manufacturing of Electronic and Information Products	亿元 100 million yuan	46.72	39.36
汽车制造业	Automobile Industry	亿元 100 million yuan	12.12	14.14
成套设备制造业	Manufacturing of Complete Equipment	亿元 100 million yuan	21.20	23.61
生物医药制造业	Manufacturing of Biological Medicine	亿元 100 million yuan	3.68	2.60
工业出口交货值	Delivery Value of Industrial Exports	亿元 100 million yuan	30.79	38.75
工业利润总额	Total Amount of Industrial Profits	亿元 100 million yuan	6.51	4.19

表 18－4 张江高科技园区主要经济指标
Major Economic Indicators in Zhangjiang High-tech Park

指 标 Indicators		单 位 Unit	2011	2012
税收总额(税务部门口径)	Total Amount of Tax Revenues (from the Tax Departments)	亿元 100 million yuan	132.72	149.79
地方财政收入	Local Fiscal Revenue	亿元 100 million yuan	37.98	41.26
固定资产投资额	Investment in Fixed Assets	亿元 100 million yuan	146.83	131.88
#房地产开发投资额	Investment in Real Estate	亿元 100 million yuan	15.68	10.88
工业投资额	Investment in Industries	亿元 100 million yuan	100.45	103.19
外商直接投资项目	Projects of Foreign Direct Investment	个 unit	93	101
外商直接投资合同金额	Contracted Amount of Foreign Direct Investment	亿美元 USD 100 million	9.27	9.71
外商直接投资实际到位金额	Actual Paid Amount of Foreign Direct Investment	亿美元 USD 100 million	8.36	9.06
新增内资企业注册户数	Number of New Domestic Enterprises Registered	个 unit	683	573
新增内资企业注册资本	Capital of New Domestic Enterprises Registered	亿元 100 million yuan	174.97	59.33
工业总产值	Gross Value of Industrial Output	亿元 100 million yuan	555.70	583.94
#高技术产业产值	Output Value of High-tech Industries	亿元 100 million yuan	339.55	364.09
工业重点发展行业产值	Output Value of Key Industrial Sectors for Development	亿元 100 million yuan	505.68	528.28
#电子信息产品制造业	Manufacturing of Electronic and Information Products	亿元 100 million yuan	203.58	206.27
汽车制造业	Automobile Industry	亿元 100 million yuan	137.09	140.21
生物医药制造业	Manufacturing of Biological Medicine	亿元 100 million yuan	134.67	146.88
工业出口交货值	Delivery Value of Industrial Exports	亿元 100 million yuan	210.81	214.23
信息传输、计算机服务和软件业营业收入	Operating Income of Information Transmission, Computer Services and Software Industry	亿元 100 million yuan	475.58	529.88
文化产业营业收入	Operating Income of Cultural Industry	亿元 100 million yuan	595.43	640.13
知识产权授权数	Number of Authorizations for Intellectual Property	件 item	3 753	2 673
#专利授权数	Number of Patent Authorizations	件 item	2 823	2 251
技术交易数量	Number of Technology Transfers	件 item	1 298	1 094
技术合同金额	Contracted Value of Technologies	亿元 100 million yuan	50.80	67.83
经认定高新技术企业数	Number of Approved High-tech Enterprises	个 unit	366	443
在孵企业数	Number of Enterprises Being Incubated	个 unit	783	830
经认定研发机构数	Number of Approved Research and Development Institutions	个 unit	134	137
公共服务平台服务企业次数	Number of Enterprises Served by Public Service Platforms	次 time	317 081	317 777
期末从业人员数	Number of Employed Persons at End of Term	万人 10 000 persons	18.95	20.98

表18-5 康桥工业开发区主要经济指标
Main Economic Indicators in Kangqiao Industrial Development Zone

指 标 Indicators		单 位 Unit	2011	2012
税收总额(税务部门口径)	Total Amount of Tax Revenues (from the Tax Departments)	亿元 100 million yuan	24.71	36.67
地方财政收入	Local Fiscal Revenue	亿元 100 million yuan	6.79	9.10
固定资产投资额	Investment in Fixed Assets	亿元 100 million yuan	67.04	65.94
#工业投资额	Investment in Industries	亿元 100 million yuan	22.55	26.66
外商直接投资项目	Projects of Foreign Direct Investment	个 unit	8	12
外商直接投资合同金额	Contracted Amount of Foreign Direct Investment	亿美元 USD 100 million	0.86	1.01
外商直接投资实际到位金额	Actual Paid Amount of Foreign Direct Investment	亿美元 USD 100 million	0.75	0.87
新增内资企业注册户数	Number of New Domestic Enterprises Registered	个 unit	407	331
新增内资企业注册资本	Capital of New Domestic Enterprises Registered	亿元 100 million yuan	6.69	11.94
工业总产值	Gross Value of Industrial Output	亿元 100 million yuan	1 372.58	1 669.01
#高技术产业产值	utput Value of High-tech Industries	亿元 100 million yuan	882.10	1 193.04
工业重点发展行业产值	Output Value of Key Industrial Sectors for Development	亿元 100 million yuan	1 115.63	1 430.01
#电子信息产品制造	Manufacturing of Electronic and Information Products	亿元 100 million yuan	897.35	1 196.87
汽车制造业	Automobile Industry	亿元 100 million yuan	91.52	96.26
成套设备制造业	Manufacturing of Complete Equipment	亿元 100 million yuan	104.67	112.41
工业出口交货值	Delivery Value of Industrial Exports	亿元 100 million yuan	881.30	1 132.35
工业利润总额	Total Amount of Industrial Profits	亿元 100 million yuan	70.88	70.10

表18-6 国际医学园区主要经济指标
Main Economic Indicators in International Medical Park

指 标 Indicators		单 位 Unit	2011	2012
税收总额(税务部门口径)	Total Amount of Tax Revenues (from the Tax Departments)	亿元 100 million yuan	2.30	2.69
地方财政收入	Local Fiscal Revenue	亿元 100 million yuan	0.65	0.92
固定资产投资额	Investment in Fixed Assets	亿元 100 million yuan	20.59	28.06
# 工业投资额	Investment in Industries	亿元 100 million yuan	4.53	5.38
# 医疗仪器设备及器械投资额	Investment in Medical Equipment, Apparatus and Appliances	亿元 100 million yuan	4.53	5.38
外商直接投资项目	Projects of Foreign Direct Investment	个 unit	2	7
外商直接投资合同金额	Contracted Amount of Foreign Direct Investment	亿美元 USD 100 million	0.36	0.44
外商直接投资实际到位金额	Actual Paid Amount of Foreign Direct Investment	亿美元 USD 100 million	0.25	0.20
新增内资企业注册户数	Number of New Domestic Enterprises Registered	个 unit	37	59
新增内资企业注册资本	Capital of New Domestic Enterprises Registered	亿元 100 million yuan	4.80	5.00
工业总产值	Gross Value of Industrial Output	亿元 100 million yuan	26.97	31.97
# 高技术产业产值	Output Value of High-tech Industries	亿元 100 million yuan	24.85	29.64
工业重点发展行业产值	Output Value of Key Industrial Sectors for Development	亿元 100 million yuan	26.76	31.77
# 生物医药制造业	Manufacturing of Biological Medicine	亿元 100 million yuan	23.55	28.60
工业出口交货值	Delivery Value of Industrial Exports	亿元 100 million yuan	13.53	15.33
生物医药产业营业收入	Operating Income of Bio-medicine Industry	亿元 100 million yuan	54.33	64.00
期末生物医药企业签约个数	Number of Contracted Bio-medicine Enterprises at End of Term	个 unit	67	84
期末医院签约个数	Number of Contracted Hospitals at End of Term	个 unit	8	8
期末在建医院个数	Number of Hospitals under Construction at End of Term	个 unit	2	2

表18-7　外高桥保税区主要经济指标
Major Economic Indicators in Waigaoqiao Free Trade Zone

指　标	Indicators	单　位　Unit	2011	2012
税收总额(税务部门口径)	Total Amount of Tax Revenues (from the Tax Departments)	亿元 100 million yuan	351.81	404.97
地方财政收入	Local Fiscal Revenue	亿元 100 million yuan	77.28	86.21
海关部门税收	Tax Revenues by Customs Departments	亿元 100 million yuan	587.20	607.10
固定资产投资额	Investment in Fixed Assets	亿元 100 million yuan	25.35	23.42
外商直接投资项目	Projects of Foreign Direct Investment	个 unit	127	131
外商直接投资合同金额	Contracted Amount of Foreign Direct Investment	亿美元 USD 100 million	7.36	14.64
外商直接投资实际到位金额	Actual Paid Amount of Foreign Direct Investment	亿美元 USD 100 million	5.83	5.26
新增内资企业注册户数	Number of New Domestic Enterprises Registered	个 unit	222	288
新增内资企业注册资本	Capital of New Domestic Enterprises Registered	亿元 100 million yuan	9.35	9.22
港口货物吞吐量	Cargo Handling Capacity	万吨 10 000 tons	14 596	14 263
集装箱吞吐量	Container Handling Capacity	万标箱 10 000 TEUs	1 571	1 536
商品销售总额(限额以上)	Gross Sales of Commodities (Above Quota)	亿元 100 million yuan	923.53	1 922.10
商品销售总额(注册地口径)	Gross Sales of Commodities (Approach of Registered Place)	亿元 100 million yuan	9 690.00	10 800.00
保税市场交易额	Volume of Transactions in Free Trade Markets	亿美元 USD 100 million	1 152.20	1 191.30
交通运输业营业收入(注册地口径)	Operating Income of Transportation Industry (Approach of Registered Place)	亿元 100 million yuan	96.00	98.00
仓储业营业收入(注册地口径)	Operating Income of Storage Industry (Approach of Registered Place)	亿元 100 million yuan	63.00	72.00
工业总产值	Gross Value of Industrial Output	亿元 100 million yuan	731.47	727.78
#高技术产业产值	Output Value of High-tech Industries	亿元 100 million yuan	491.28	504.21
工业重点发展行业产值	Output Value of Key Industrial Sectors for Development	亿元 100 million yuan	642.03	642.86
#电子信息产品制造业	Manufacturing of Electronic and Information Products	亿元 100 million yuan	506.00	506.84
汽车制造业	Automobile Industry	亿元 100 million yuan	38.20	50.57
石化及精细化工制造业	Manufacturing of Petrochemical Industry and Refined Industry	亿元 100 million yuan	47.67	41.84
工业出口交货值	Delivery Value of Industrial Exports	亿元 100 million yuan	149.40	149.77
进出口总额	Total Volume of Foreign Trade	亿美元 USD 100 million	915.00	1 017.00
出口额	Amount of Exports	亿美元 USD 100 million	200.00	218.50
进口额	Amount of Imports	亿美元 USD 100 million	715.00	798.50
期末从业人员数(注册地口径)	Number of Employed Persons at End of Term (Approach of Registered Place)	万人 10 000 persoms	23.70	25.05
期末历年累计竣工房屋面积	Floor Space of Accumulated Completed Buildings in Main Years at End of Term	万平方米 10 000 sq·m	824.84	857.07

表18-8 洋山保税港区主要经济指标
Major Economic Indicators in Yangshan Bonded Area Port

指标 Indicators		单位 Unit	2011	2012
税收总额(税务部门口径)	Total Amount of Tax Revenues (from the Tax Departments)	亿元 100 million yuan		
地方财政收入	Local Fiscal Revenue	亿元 100 million yuan	0.12	
海关部门税收	Tax Revenues by Customs Departments	亿元 100 million yuan	332.70	387.10
固定资产投资额	Investment in Fixed Assets	亿元 100 million yuan	0.77	2.82
外商直接投资项目	Projects of Foreign Direct Investment	个 unit	19	26
外商直接投资合同金额	Contracted Amount of Foreign Direct Investment	亿美元 USD 100 million	1.01	1.11
外商直接投资实际到位金额	Actual Paid Amount of Foreign Direct Investment	亿美元 USD 100 million		0.23
新增内资企业注册户数	Number of Actual Registered Domestic Enterprises at End of Term	个 unit	103	281
新增内资企业注册资本	Registered Capital of Actual Domestic Enterprises at End of Term	亿元 100 million yuan	19.93	14.82
港口货物吞吐量	Cargo Handling Capacity at Port	万吨 10 000 tons	11 736	12 969
集装箱吞吐量	Container Handling Capacity	万标箱 10 000 TEUs	1 309.90	1 415.00
#洋山港国际中转量	International Transferring Amount at Yangshan Port	万标箱 10 000 TEUs	93.00	120.30
#洋山港水水中转	Ship-to-ship Transferring Amount at Yangshan Port	万标箱 10 000 TEUs	601.50	660.80
进出口总额	Total Volume of Foreign Trade	亿美元 USD 100 million	59.00	93.00
出口额	Amount of Exports	亿美元 USD 100 million	30.00	38.50
进口额	Amount of Imports	亿美元 USD 100 million	29.00	54.50

表 18-9　临港产业区主要经济指标
Main Economic Indicators in Lingang Industrial Park

指　标 Indicators		单　位 Unit	2011	2012
税收总额(税务部门口径)	Total Amount of Tax Revenues (from the Tax Departments)	亿元 100 million yuan	6.22	8.93
地方财政收入	Local Fiscal Revenue	亿元 100 million yuan	1.58	2.13
固定资产投资额	Investment in Fixed Assets	亿元 100 million yuan	44.88	93.88
#工业投资额	Investment in Industries	亿元 100 million yuan	35.60	54.81
外商直接投资项目	Projects of Foreign Direct Investment	个 unit	2	7
外商直接投资合同金额	Contracted Amount of Foreign Direct Investment	亿美元 USD 100 million	0.80	0.85
外商直接投资实际到位金额	Actual Paid Amount of Foreign Direct Investment	亿美元 USD 100 million	0.34	0.52
新增内资企业注册户数	Number of New Domestic Enterprises Registered	个 unit	55	77
新增内资企业注册资本	Capital of New Domestic Enterprises Registered	亿元 100 million yuan	5.69	2.77
工业总产值	Gross Value of Industrial Output	亿元 100 million yuan	204.89	221.56
#高技术产业产值	Output Value of High-tech Industries	亿元 100 million yuan	1.58	1.24
工业重点发展行业产值	Output Value of Key Industrial Sectors for Development	亿元 100 million yuan	95.20	93.43
#汽车制造业	Automobile Industry	亿元 100 million yuan	7.77	11.57
成套设备制造业	Manufacturing of Complete Equipment	亿元 100 million yuan	82.88	77.09
工业出口交货值	Delivery Value of Industrial Exports	亿元 100 million yuan	46.60	53.82
工业利润总额	Total Amount of Industrial Profits	亿元 100 million yuan	2.36	2.62

表18-10 各镇财政收入及工业总产值
Financial Revenue and Gross Output Value of Industry in Towns

单位:亿元 100 million yuan

镇 Town		财政收入 Financial Revenue			工业总产值 Gross Output Value of Industry		
		2010	2011	2012	2010	2011	2012
总 计	**Total**	**302.16**	**334.08**	**384.69**	**2 261.09**	**2 193.86**	**2 134.52**
川沙新镇	Chuansha New Town	26.35	29.14	19.41	203.82	186.41	142.14
高桥镇	Gaoqiao Town	18.71	17.78	18.21	122.12	126.89	122.83
北蔡镇	Beicai Town	19.08	27.70	25.62	67.89	64.52	61.23
合庆镇	Heqing Town	10.52	12.08	12.39	177.77	174.61	178.97
唐 镇	Tangzhen Town	14.41	17.60	23.08	63.52	63.42	50.42
曹路镇	Caolu Town	21.19	21.74	22.82	180.49	182.99	176.93
金桥镇	Jinqiao Town	25.01	25.32	24.80	24.87	20.42	18.01
高行镇	Gaohang Town	24.36	22.26	23.04	181.17	193.84	171.63
高东镇	Gaodong Town	16.54	17.07	28.13	346.95	363.27	343.79
张江镇	Zhangjiang Town	14.25	17.25	16.29	46.11	43.62	40.67
三林镇	Sanlin Town	18.18	18.08	27.70	57.28	43.27	39.36
惠南镇	Huinan Town	9.53	9.44	9.76	19.00	15.38	13.86
周浦镇	Zhoupu Town	13.18	13.87	15.53	89.33	85.91	85.34
新场镇	Xinchang Town	4.76	5.93	7.54	91.71	82.85	85.55
大团镇	Datuan Town	2.93	3.36	3.27	19.57	13.45	14.08
芦潮港镇	Luchaogang Town	6.31	7.25	6.32	13.11	14.53	13.57
康桥镇	Kangqiao Town	17.19	21.44	26.56	199.88	211.56	198.49
航头镇	Hangtou Town	10.24	11.31	13.56	92.71	79.37	85.25
祝桥镇	Zhuqiao Town	8.01	10.64	33.00	110.09	90.10	145.80
泥城镇	Nicheng Town	5.79	8.32	9.88	18.75	12.43	11.28
宣桥镇	Xuanqiao Town	6.10	5.21	4.23	53.85	49.54	54.97
书院镇	Shuyuan Town	4.23	5.18	5.77	26.21	22.10	21.04
万祥镇	Wanxiang Town	2.73	3.60	4.79	18.66	20.31	20.52
老港镇	Laogang Town	2.56	2.49	2.99	36.23	33.06	38.82

主要统计指标解释

货物流量包括货物运输总量和货物进出仓量

货物运输总量

指在报告期内，以重量单位吨位计算的各种运输工具实际完成运输过程的货物数量，公路和水路的货运量按报告期到达货物数量统计，即报告期内已送达目的地并投卸完的货物数量为该报告期的货物运输总量。

货物进仓量

指在报告期内进入本企业仓库和堆放场地的各种货物的重量。按来源分为来自国外、来自国内一般地区和来目国内特殊监管区域（即保税区、出口加工区、保税物流园区等海关特殊监管区域）。

货物出仓量

指在报告期内运出本企业仓库和堆放场地的各种货物的重量。按流向分为流向国外、流向国内一般地区和流向国内特殊监管区域（即保税区，出口加工区、保税物流园区等海关特殊监管区域）。

上海市高新技术企业认定条件

（一）在本市注册的企业，近三年内通过自主研发、受让、受赠、并购等方式，或通过在全球范围内5年以上的独占许可方式，对其主要产品（服务）的核心技术拥有在中国内地得到中国法律保护的自主知识产权；

（二）产品（服务）属于高新技术企业认定管理办法的附件《国家重点支持的高新技术领域》规定的范围；

（三）具有大学专科以上学历的科技人员占企业当年职工总数的30%以上，其中研发人员占企业当年职工总数的10%以上；

（四）企业为获得科学技术（不包括人文、社会科学）新知识，创造性运用科学技术新知识，或实质性改进技术、产品（服务）而持续进行了研究开发活动，且近三个会计年度的研究开发费用总额占销售收入总额的比例符合如下要求：

1、最近一年销售收入小于5000万元的企业，比例不低于8%；

2、最近一年销售收入在5000万元至20000万元的企业，比例不低于4%；

3、最近一年销售收人在20000万元以上的企业，比例不低于3%。

其中，企业在中国内地发生的研究开发费用总额占全部研究开发费用总额的比例不低于60%。企业注册成立时间满一年但不足三年的，按实际经营年限计算；

（五）高新技术产品（服务）收入占企业当年总收入的60%以上；

（六）企业研究开发组织管理水平、科技成果转化能力、自主知识产权数量、销售与总资产成长性等指标符合《高新技术企业认定管理工作指引》的要求。

EXPLANATORY NOTES TO MAJOR STATISTICAL INDICATORS

The Flow of Goods Includes the Total of Goods and the Amount of Goods Entered and Left the Warehouse

Total of Cargo Transport

Refers to the number of cargoes that have been completely finished by all kinds of transportation means that are calculated by weight with the unit of ton during the reference period. The transport volume by road and that by water are calculated by the number of cargoes that have actually arrived during the reference period, namely the volume of goods that has been transported to its destination and discharged during the reference period is the total of cargo transport during the reference period.

Amount of Goods Entered the Warehouse

Refers to the weight of all kinds of goods that have entered the warehouse and storage space of this enterprise during the reference period.. Grouped by its sources, they are from the overseas, ordinary domestic regions and specially-supervised domestic regions (namely special regions supervised by the Customs House such as bonded zones, export processing zones, bonded logistics parks).

Amount of Goods Left the Warehouse

Refers to the weight of all kinds of goods that have left the warehouse and storage space of this enterprise during the reference period. Grouped by its flows, they are to the overseas, ordinary domestic regions and specially-supervised domestic regions (namely special regions supervised by the Customs House such as bonded zones, export processing zones, bonded logistics parks).

Conditions for Identification of High-tech Enterprises in Shanghai

(I) Enterprises, which have registered in Shanghai, possess independent intellectual property rights protected by Chinese laws in China for the core technology of their main products or services, by means of independent research and development, transferring, donation and purchasing, or in possession of exclusive licenses for over five years all over the world.

(II) Their products or services belong to the scope specified in the Appendix: High-tech Fields Key Supported by the State of Identification and Management Methods of High-tech Enterprises.

(III) High-tech employees with education levels of college degrees or above occupy over 30% of the total number of employees in that year, in which R&D persons are over 10%.

(IV) In order to obtain the new knowledge of science and technology (excluding human studies), take advantage of the new knowledge of science and technology in a creative way, or improve their products or services in a substantial way, enterprises have continued to conduct R&D activities and the ratios of the sum of expenses for research and development in the total sales revenue during the current three fiscal years should accord with the following requirements:

1. This ratio is not less than 8% for enterprises with its sales revenue of the previous year less than RMB 50 million.

2. This ratio is not less than 4% for enterprises with its sales revenue of the previous year between RMB 50 million and RMB 200 million.

3. This ratio is not less than 3% for enterprises with its sales revenue of the previous year over RMB 200 million.

Which the sum expenses for research and development in domestic regions of China of the enterprise should account for more than 60% of the total R&D expenses. If the enterprise has registered for more than one year and less than three years, we will calculate its actual operation period.

(V) The revenue of high-tech products or services accounts for over 60% of the total income of the enterprise at the year.

(VI) Indicators such as the level of R&D organization and management, the transferring capability of scientific and technical achievements, the number of independent intellectual property rights, and sales and total assets growth accord with the requirements of the Working Guidance of Identification and Management for High-tech Enterprises.

第十九篇

CHAPTER 19

上海市统计资料

STATISTICS OF SHANGHAI MUNICIPALITY

表19-1　主要年份人口、从业人员、工资和婚姻情况
Population,Employment,Wages and Marriage in Main Years

指　标	Indicators	1990	2000	2010	2011	2012
年末总人口（万人）	**Year-end Population(10 000 persons)**	**1 283.35**	**1 321.63**	**1 412.32**	**1 419.36**	**1 426.93**
按性别分	Grouped by Sex					
男	Male	647.13	665.51	703.57	706.37	709.62
女	Female	636.22	656.12	708.75	712.99	717.31
按农业、非农业分	Grouped by Agriculture and Non-agriculture					
农业人口	Agriculture	418.89	335.47	157.37	151.60	146.11
非农业人口	Non-agriculture	864.46	986.16	1 254.95	1 267.76	1 280.82
常住人口(万人)	Year-end Resident Population(10 000 persons)	1 334.00	1 608.60	2 302.66	2 347.46	2 380.43
人口密度(人/平方公里)	Density of Population (persons/sq. km)	2 104	2 537	3 632	3 702	3 754
总户数(万户)	Total Households (10 000 household)	415.28	475.73	519.27	522.01	524.31
每户平均人口(人)	Average Persons Per Household (persons)	3.1	2.8	2.7	2.7	2.7
人口自然变动	**Natural Change**					
出生人口(万人)	Number of Birth (10 000 persons)	13.12	6.95	10.02	10.15	12.11
出生率(‰)	Birth Rate (‰)	10.20	5.30	7.13	7.17	8.51
死亡人口(万人)	Number of Death (10 000 persons)	8.63	9.45	10.87	11.11	11.74
死亡率(‰)	Death Rate (‰)	6.70	7.20	7.73	7.85	8.25
自然增长率(‰)	Natural Growth Rate (‰)	3.51	-2.50	-0.60	-0.68	0.26
人口迁徙变动	**Migration Change**					
迁入人口(万人)	Inflows (10 000 persons)	12.18	15.16	17.22	13.15	12.96
迁入率(‰)	Rate of Inflows (‰)	9.52	11.51	12.24	9.29	8.11
迁出人口(万人)	Outflows (10 000 persons)	10.72	5.32	4.97	5.33	5.89
迁出率(‰)	Rate of Outflows (‰)	8.38	4.04	3.53	3.76	4.14
从业人员(万人)	**Employment (10 000 persons)**	**787.72**	**828.35**	**1 090.76**	**1 104.33**	**1 115.5**
职工人数(万人)	Staff and Workers (10 000 persons)	508.10	390.14	648.49	868.42	944.47
职工工资总额(亿元)	Wages of Staff and Workers (100 million yuan)	146.78	614.53	3 018.55	4 505.57	5 347.99
职工年平均工资(元)	Average Annual Wages of Staff and Workers (yuan)	2 917	15 420	46 757	51 968	56 300
婚姻登记	**Registered Marriage**					
准予登记结婚(万对)	Marriage Registration Permitted (10 000 couples)	10.77	9.31	13.03	14.89	14.42
初婚(万人)	First Marriage (10 000 persons)	19.49	15.08	20.10	23.94	22.96
再婚(万人)	Remarriage (10 000 persons)	2.04	2.89	5.96	5.84	5.88
离婚登记(万人)	Divorce (10 000 persons)	3.27	6.36	9.34	9.57	10.57

表 19-2 主要年份上海市生产总值和指数
Value Added And Indices in Main Years

指　标	Indicators	1990	2000	2010	2011	2012
上海市生产总值(亿元)	**Gross Domestic Product (100 million yuan)**	**781.66**	**4 771.17**	**17 165.98**	**19 195.69**	**20 181.72**
第一产业	Primary Industry	34.24	76.68	114.15	124.94	127.80
第二产业	Secondary Industry	505.60	2 207.63	7 218.32	7 927.89	7 854.77
工　业	Industry	469.83	1 998.96	6 536.21	7 208.59	7 097.76
建筑业	Construction	35.77	208.67	682.11	719.30	757.01
第三产业	Tertiary Industry	241.82	2 486.86	9 833.51	11 142.86	12 199.15
构　成(%)	**Composition (%)**					
第一产业	Primary Industry	4.3	1.8	0.7	0.7	0.6
第二产业	Secondary Industry	63.8	47.6	42.0	41.3	39.0
工　业	Industry	59.1	43.0	38.0	37.6	35.2
建筑业	Construction	4.7	4.6	4.0	3.7	3.8
第三产业	Tertiary Industry	31.9	50.6	57.3	58.0	60.4
人均生产总值(元)	**Average GDP Per Capita (yuan)**	**5 911**	**30 047**	**76 074**	**82 560**	**85 373**
上海市生产总值指数(以1990年为100)	**Indices of GDP (1990=100)**	**100.0**	**319.1**	**953.0**	**1 031.1**	**1 108.4**
第一产业	Primary Industry	100.0	126.8	112.8	112.0	110.4
第二产业	Secondary Industry	100.0	305.0	915.8	975.3	999.9
第三产业	Tertiary Industry	100.0	375.9	1 143.6	1 252.2	1 391.2
上海市生产总值指数(以上年为100)	**Indices of GDP (preceding year=100)**	**103.5**	**111.0**	**110.3**	**108.2**	**107.5**
第一产业	Primary Industry	104.3	103.4	93.4	99.3	103.5
第二产业	Secondary Industry	102.8	109.8	116.8	106.3	103.1
第三产业	Tertiary Industry	105.3	113.5	105.7	109.6	110.6

表 19-3　主要年份全社会固定资产投资主要指标
Major Indicators Of Total Investment in Fixed Assets in Main Years

指　标	Indicators	1990	2000	2010	2011	2012
投资总额(亿元)	**Total Investment (100 million yuan)**	**227.08**	**1 869.67**	**5 317.67**	**5 067.09**	**5 254.38**
#房地产	Real Estate	8.16	566.17	1 980.68	2 170.31	2 381.36
在投资总额中按构成分	In Total Investment Grouped by Use of Funds					
#建筑安装工程	Construction and Installation	127.63	882.91	2 820.17	2 991.95	3 097.79
设备、工具、器具购置	Purchase of Equipment, Tools and Instrument	79.51	482.47	991.10	834.17	851.13
按建设性质分	Grouped by Type of Construction					
#新　建	New Construction	78.01	730.76	2 052.69	1 764.74	1 715.93
改建和技改	Reconstruction and Technical Renovation	70.48	216.40	513.80	413.81	427.08
扩　建	Expansion	47.50	216.71	368.07	348.73	368.51
按三次产业分	Grouped by Type of Industry					
第一产业	Primary Industry	3.20	7.87	16.40	18.62	11.20
第二产业	Secondary Industry	133.00	615.94	1 435.37	1 295.83	1 294.14
第三产业	Tertiary Industry	90.88	1 245.86	3 865.90	3 752.64	3 949.04
按经济类型分	Grouped by Economic Types					
#国有经济	State-owned	192.24	829.98	2 234.12	1 875.48	1 855.24
集体经济	Collective-owned	18.29	156.34	183.07	133.33	112.41
联营经济	Joint Owned		41.20	11.52	10.62	8.99
股份制经济	Share-holding		421.53	1 200.26	1 349.65	1 417.80
外商投资经济	Foreign Funded		222.86	439.28	473.28	528.06
港澳台投资经济	Hong Kong, Macao and Taiwan Funded		96.19	247.67	253.29	230.02
房屋建筑面积(万平方米)	**Floor Space of Buildings (10 000 sq. m)**					
施工面积	Floor Space Under Construction	3 801.46	8 636.31	15 020.76	16 572.36	16 874.72
#住　宅	Residential Housing	2 269.06	4 804.12	7 344.07	8 441.61	8 350.83
竣工面积	Floor Space Completed	2 138.44	3 266.52	2 776.21	2 926.28	2 838.97
#住　宅	Residential Housing	1 339.02	1 724.02	1 415.44	1 581.03	1 626.73
房屋建筑面积竣工率(%)	Rate of Floor Space of Buildings Completed (%)	56.3	37.8	18.5	17.7	16.8
资金来源合计(亿元)	**Total Capital Source (100 million yuan)**	**261.46**	**2 061.66**	**7 997.62**	**7 969.18**	**8 749.17**
上年末结余资金	A Balance at End of Previous Year	28.85	241.05	1 440.57	1 679.64	1 635.40
当年资金来源小计	Sub-total Capital Source of the Year	232.61	1 820.61	6 557.05	6 289.54	7 113.77
国家预算内资金	Capital Within the State Budget	14.39	48.30	116.71	75.89	406.08
国内贷款	Domestic Loans	62.52	379.21	1 568.79	1 330.99	1 554.53
债　券	State Treasury Bond		4.85	10.06	3.47	
利用外资	Foreign Capital Absorbed	35.46	161.83	239.18	158.31	165.89
自筹资金	Self-raised Capital	94.13	905.46	3 273.11	3 352.48	3 348.77
其他资金	Other Capital	26.11	320.96	1 349.21	1 368.40	1 638.50

表19-4 主要年份城市基础设施投资额和公用事业
Investment in Urban Infrastructure And Public Utilities in Main Years

指 标	Indicators	1990	2000	2010	2011	2012
城市基础设施投资额（亿元）	**Investment in Urban Infrastructure (100 million yuan)**	**47.22**	**449.90**	**1 497.46**	**1 157.34**	**1 038.61**
电力建设	Electric Construction	17.53	64.61	148.50	118.81	110.06
交通邮电	Traffic and Post	10.06	117.52	866.20	668.52	570.37
公用设施	Public Facilities	19.63	267.77	482.76	370.01	358.18
公用事业	Public Utilities	10.83	104.43	86.58	54.22	56.45
自来水	Tap Water	1.06	5.35	61.63	41.85	40.75
燃 气	Gas	1.81	6.88	24.95	12.37	15.70
市政建设	Municipal Construction	8.80	163.34	396.18	315.80	301.74
#园林建设	Parks, Gardens and Green Areas	0.11	38.76	35.87	44.71	20.99
环境卫生	Environment Sanitation	0.37	19.34	10.80	23.91	23.74
市政工程	Urban Municipal Engineering	8.31	102.36	349.27	247.15	256.73
自来水	**Tap Water**					
自来水管道长度（公里）	Length of Tap Water Pipelines (km)	3 483	15 943	31 182	32 217	34 904
自来水供应能力（万立方米/日）	Tap Water Supply (10 000 cu · m/day)	462	1 048	1 131	1 150	1 145
售水量（亿立方米）	Sales of Tap Water (100 milion cu · m)	12.25	19.75	24.44	24.41	24.35
#生产用水	Industrial Use	5.90	5.49	5.80	5.60	5.18
生活用水	Residential Use	6.11	11.88	18.64	18.81	19.17
燃气、液化气	**Gas and Liquefied Gas**					
管道燃气	Pipeline Gas					
管线长度（公里）	Length of Gas Pipelines (km)	2 700	6 606	5 517	4 710	3 596
燃气销售量（亿立方米）	Sales of Coal Gas (100 million cu · m)	12.15	20.56	55.51	62.29	68.19
#家庭用	Family Use	7.63	16.22	14.07	13.95	13.84
家庭用液化气户数（万户）	Household of Family Use Petroleum Gas (10 000 households)	113.19	255.89	316.37	310.62	328.22
道 路	**Road**					
铺装道路长度（公里）	Length of Road Paved (km)	1 631	6 641	16 687	16 792	17 316
铺装道路面积（万平方米）	Area of Road Paved (10 000 sq. m)	1 787	8 147	25 607	26 176	26 813
交 通	**Traffic**					
年末实有公交线路条数（条）	Lines of Public Traffic (year-end) (route)	390	978	1 165	1 202	1 257
年末实有公交线路长度（公里）	Lines of Public Traffic Routes (year-end) (km)	18 593	23 260	23 131	22 906	23 190
年末运营公交车辆（辆）	Public Transportation Vehicles (year-end) (vehicle)	6 264	17 939	17 455	16 589	16 695
客运总量（亿人次）	Passengers Carried (100 million person-times)	54.37	26.49	28.08	28.11	28.04
出租汽车运营车辆数（辆）	Taxi in Operation (vehicle)	11 298	42 943	50 007	50 438	50 683
隧 道	**Tunnels**					
越江隧道条数（条）	Routes of Tunnels Across the Huangpu River (route)	2	2	12	13	13
越江大桥座数（座）	Number of Bridges Across the Huangpu River (unit)	1	5	10	10	10
城市绿化	**Urban Greenbelt**					
城市绿地面积（公顷）	Area of Parks, Gardens and Green Areas (hectare)	3 570	12 601	120 148	122 283	124 204
人均公共绿地面积（平方米/人）	Public Green Area Per Capita (sq. m/person)	1.02	4.60	13.00	13.10	13.29
绿化覆盖率（%）	Green Area Coverage (%)	12.4	22.2	38.2	38.2	38.3
公园数（个）	Number of Parks (unit)	83	122	148	153	157

注：2009年起原园林绿地面积改为城市绿地面积，统计分类作了调整。
Note: As the field of green-land area was changed into that of urban green space since 2009, the classification has been readjusted thereafter.

表19-5 主要年份农业主要指标
Major Indicators of Agriculture in Main Years

指标	Indicators	1990	2000	2010	2011	2012
农业总产值(亿元)	**Gross Output Value of Agriculture (100 million yuan)**	**68.16**	**216.50**	**287.03**	**314.58**	**321.73**
#种植业	Planting	29.09	89.82	155.27	165.07	171.48
林业	Forestry	0.37	1.41	7.53	7.62	9.55
牧业	Animal Husbandry	30.25	87.35	62.90	77.44	72.59
渔业	Fishery	8.04	37.92	52.62	54.72	57.45
主要农副产品产量	**Output of Major Farm and Sideline Products**					
粮食(万吨)	Grain (10 000 tons)	244.36	174.00	118.40	121.95	122.39
油菜籽(万吨)	Rapeseed (10 000 tons)	18.17	15.71	2.04	1.64	1.51
蔬菜(万吨)	Vegetables (10 000 tons)	186.79	377.00	398.08	408.24	406.93
水果(万吨)	Fruit (10 000 tons)	9.42	22.54	44.16	40.22	48.15
年末圈存量(万头)	Hogs at year-end (10 000 in number)	237.53	241.60	171.87	180.65	172.71
猪肉产量(万吨)	Pork (10 000 tons)	23.32	25.96	17.87	19.12	17.57
牛奶产量(万吨)	Cow Milk (10 000 tons)	22.68	25.95	24.71	29.08	26.31
鲜蛋上市量(万吨)	Poulty Eggs (10 000 tons)	15.07	16.64	6.28	6.30	5.90
水产品(万吨)	Aquatic Products (10 000 tons)	27.36	28.87	28.97	28.37	27.21
淡水产品	Freshwater Aquatic Products	10.32	16.64	16.82	16.57	13.21
海水产品	Seawater Aquatic Products	17.04	12.23	12.15	11.80	14.00
农业机械总动力(万千瓦)	**Total Power of Agricultural Machinery (10 000 kw)**	**276.50**	**142.50**	**28.97**	**105.58**	**112.72**

表 19－6　规模以上工业企业主要指标
Major Indicators of the City's Above-Certain-Scale Industrial Enterprises (2012)

指　标 Indicators		单位数（个）Number of Enterprises (unit)	从业人员（万人）Employees (10 000 persons)	工业总产值（亿元）Gross Output Value of Industry (100 million yuan)	年末资产总计（亿元）Total Assets (year-end) (100 million yuan)	利润总额（亿元）Total After-tax Profits (100 million yuan)	税金总额（亿元）Total Tax and Duties (100 million yuan)
总　计	**Total**	**9 772**	**264.97**	**31 896.88**	**31 160.89**	**2 149.42**	**1 660.52**
按隶属关系分	**Grouped by Subordination**						
#中央工业	Central Government	162	16.95	6 806.16	8 103.02	341.44	849.50
市(局)属工业	Municipality	576	34.29	6 260.07	7 305.09	862.22	391.68
区属工业	District	310	6.99	706.94	630.56	37.01	16.39
镇属工业	Town	485	12.93	795.29	829.07	50.62	23.38
乡属工业	Township	46	1.29	116.85	92.37	5.51	3.25
村委会属工业	Village Committee	210	4.16	293.32	194.73	14.06	7.04
按登记注册类型分	**Grouped by Registration Categories**						
内　资	Domestic	5 407	107.21	12 480.23	15 895.81	887.19	1 004.70
国　有	State-owned	174	8.20	1 296.84	2 385.89	35.59	54.27
集　体	Collective-owned	155	2.65	174.80	119.10	6.10	5.42
股份合作	Share-holding Coorperation						
联　营	Joint Owned						
有限责任公司	Companies with Limited Liabilities	916	29.05	4 598.60	5 454.71	290.05	683.04
股份有限公司	Share-holding Companies with Limited Liabilities	151	10.09	2 658.34	4 489.77	374.75	155.84
私　营	Private	3712	51.96	3 327.11	3 090.51	161.03	92.52
其　他	Others						
港澳台商投资	Hong Kong, Macao and Taiwan Funded	1 208	42.03	4 944.57	3 624.72	195.14	127.89
外商投资	Foreign Funded	3 157	115.73	14 472.08	11 640.36	1 067.09	527.93
按轻、重工业分	**Grouped by Light and Heavy Industry**						
轻工业	Light Industry	3 429	85.86	6 924.54	6 757.10	635.36	821.22
重工业	Heavy Industry	6 343	179.11	24 972.33	24 403.79	1 514.06	839.30
按企业规模分	**Grouped by Size of Enterprises**						
大型企业	Large	325	96.08	17 325.89	16 873.11	1 312.87	1 249.45
中型企业	Medium	1 498	80.73	7 188.89	6 748.91	436.28	201.05
小型企业	Small	7 949	88.17	7 382.10	7 538.88	400.27	210.02

注：本表为国有企业及销售收入在2000万元以上的非国有企业。
Note: Data in this table is collected from state-owned enterprises and non-state-owned enterprises with revenue of sales more than 20 million yuan.

表19－7　主要年份国内外贸易主要指标
Major Indicators of Domestic and Foreign Trade in Main Years

指　标	Indicators	1990	2000	2010	2011	2012
社会消费品零售总额(亿元)	**Total Retail Sales Value of Consumer Goods (100 million yuan)**	**333.86**	**1 865.28**	**6 070.50**	**6 814.80**	**7 412.30**
按用途分	Grouped by Type of Goods					
吃的商品	Food	142.15	743.31	1 830.64	2 036.14	2 107.08
穿的商品	Clothing	52.33	248.94	686.15	760.31	862.56
用的商品	Articles	137.23	858.33	3 197.85	3 590.39	3 990.29
烧的商品	Fuels	2.15	14.70	355.86	427.96	452.36
按行业分	Grouped by Sector					
#批发零售贸易业	Wholesale and Retail Trade	265.67	1 493.13	5 391.59	6 100.99	6 653.10
餐饮业	Catering Trade	17.08	134.12	678.91	713.81	759.20
外贸出口商品总额(亿美元)	**Total Value of Exports (USD 100 million)**	**53.21**	**253.54**	**1 807.84**	**2 097.89**	**2 068.07**
外贸进口商品总额(亿美元)	Total Value of Imports (USD 100 million)	21.10	293.56	1 880.85	2 276.47	2 299.51
外商直接投资签约项目数(个)	Projects of Foreign Direct Investment (unit)	203	1 814	3 906	4 329	4 043
#中外合资	Joint Venture	161	441	445	511	592
中外合作	Cooperative Operation	12	226	14	13	8
外商独资	Foreign Enterprise	30	1 146	3 443	3 801	3 437
外商直接投资合同金额(亿美元)	Contracted Foreign Capital of Foreign Direct Investment (USD 100 million)	3.75	63.90	153.07	201.03	223.38
#中外合资	Joint Venture	1.98	13.86	21.54	23.85	39.76
中外合作	Cooperative Operation	0.40	5.86	1.11	14.85	7.29
外商独资	Foreign Enterprise	1.36	44.14	128.17	160.22	172.16

表19-8 主要年份口岸进出口商品总额
Total Export and Import at Port in Main Years

单位:亿美元 (USD 100 million)

指 标	Indicators	1990	2000	2010	2011	2012
口岸进出口总额	**Total Value of Import and Export**	**172.89**	**1 093.11**	**6 846.45**	**8 123.14**	**8 013.10**
出口总额	**Total Value of Export**	**86.62**	**615.72**	**4 233.40**	**4 999.64**	**4 911.56**
#一般贸易	Original Trade	51.39	341.02	2 183.98	2 691.93	2 722.62
来料加工装配贸易	Processing and Assembly Trade	3.20	64.21	178.52	151.78	137.52
进料加工贸易	Processing Trade of Imported Material	30.67	205.13	1 639.70	1 846.59	1 718.06
对外承包工程货物	Contracted Projects in Foreign Countries	0.41	1.25	60.55	77.70	72.14
进口总额	**Total Value of Import**	**86.27**	**477.39**	**2 613.05**	**3 123.50**	**3 101.54**
#一般贸易	Original Trade	51.79	212.65	1 209.42	1 558.35	1 516.96
来料加工装配贸易	Processing and Assembly Trade of Import	2.40	44.87	169.36	135.68	123.06
进料加工贸易	Processing Trade of Imported Material	19.70	125.13	552.83	610.32	553.38
租赁贸易	International Leasing		2.47	18.56	13.69	10.79
外商投资进口设备	Imported Equipment of Foreign Funded Enterprise	6.11	40.26	43.81	51.18	33.00

表19-9　主要年份财政和保险
Major Indicators of Finance,Cash Balance and Insurance in Main Years

单位:亿元　　(100 million yuan)

指　标	Indicators	1990	2000	2010	2011	2012
全市财政收入	**Financial Revenue**	**284.36**	**1 752.70**			
#中央财政收入	Central Financial Revenue	114.33	1 246.47			
地方财政收入	Local Government Revenue	170.03	497.96	2 873.58	3 429.83	3 743.71
#增值税	Value-added Tax		93.55	388.62	416.70	667.13
营业税	Sales Tax		153.81	933.91	1 041.49	897.92
企业所得税	Enterprise Income Tax		103.03	606.05	731.05	806.77
个人所得税	Individual Income Tax		60.24	261.20	314.95	318.10
#市级财政收入	Financial Revenue at Prefectural Level		215.81	1 393.23	1 675.79	1 831.64
区县级财政收入	Financial Revenue at District (Country) Level		282.15	1 480.35	1 754.05	1 912.07
地方财政支出	**Local Government Expenditure**	**75.56**	**622.84**	**3 302.89**	**3 914.88**	**4 184.02**
保险费收入	**Premium Income**	**8.99**	**127.23**	**883.86**	**753.11**	**820.64**
赔款及给付	Indemnity Expenditure and Payment	2.23	36.20	194.54	260.71	255.79
赔款率(%)	Indemnity and Premium Ratio(%)	24.7	28.5	22.0	34.6	31.2

表 19-10 主要年份交通运输
Transportaion in Main Years

指 标	Indicators	1990	2000	2010	2011	2012
铁路运输	**By Railway**					
运营里程(公里)	Operations in Length (km)	259	257	414	453	457
正线延展里程(公里)	Extension of Main Tracks in Length (km)	356	397	697	774	826
旅客发送量(万人次)	Volume of Passengers Carried (10 000 person-times)	2 476	2 980	6 095	6 198	6 758
旅客周转量(亿人・公里)	Volume of Passengers Circulated (100 million persons・km)	26.85	35.40	60.16	63.11	68.38
货物运输量(万吨)	Volume of Goods Transported (10 000 tons)	1 257	1 055	959	888	825
货物周转量(亿吨・公里)	Volume of Goods Circulated (100 million tons・km)	111	122	26	21	18
公路运输	**By Road**					
通车里程(公里)	Available for Traffic in Length (km)	3 050	6 078	11 974	12 084	12 541
#高速公路	Expressway	36	98	775	806	806
旅客发送量(万人次)	Volume of Passengers Carried (10 000 person-times)	605	2 482	3 634	3 477	3748
旅客周转量(亿人・公里)	Volume of Passengers Circulated (100 million persons・km)	8.42	16.44	115.44	106.74	112.72
货物运输量(万吨)	Volume of Goods Transported (10 000 tons)	605	2 482	40 890	42 685	42 911
货物周转量(亿吨・公里)	Volume of Goods Circulated (100 million tons・km)	11	56	266	284	288
水路运输	**By Water**					
旅客周转量(亿人・公里)	Volume of Passengers Circulated (100 million persons・km)	40.84	6.77	3.69	1.02	0.99
货物运输量(万吨)	Volume of Goods Transported (10 000 tons)	12 864	18 442	38 803	49 389	50 302
#远洋运输(万吨)	Ocean Transportation (10 000 tons)	2 246	7 022	15 172	16 044	17 491
货物周转量(亿吨・公里)	Volume of Goods Circulated (100 million tons・km)	3 236	6 430	15 818	20 005	20 067
#远洋运输(亿吨・公里)	Ocean Transportation (100 million tons・km)	1 957	5 285	14 535	15 654	16 086
港 口	**Ports**					
港口旅客发送量(万人次)	Volume of Passengers Carried at Ports (10 000 person-times)	555	539	85	78	66
民用航空	**Civil Aviation**					
旅客发送量(万人次)	Volume of Passengers Carried (10 000 person-times)	199	892	3 642	3 766	3 974
旅客周转量(亿人・公里)	Volume of Passengers Circulated (100 million persons・km)	37.84	176.11	1 034.96	1 136.69	1 040.97
货物运输量(万吨)	Volume of Goods Transported (10 000 tons)	13	88	371	356	338
货物周转量(亿吨・公里)	Volume of Goods Circulated (100 million tons・km)	1	12	63	57	54

注：港口旅客发送量从2006年起不包含海港到内河部分。
Note: The volume of Passenger Departures excludes those from seaports to freshwater since 2006.

表 19－11　主要年份教育、卫生事业情况
Statistics of Education and Healthcare in Main Years

	指　标　Indicators	1990	2000	2010	2011	2012
学校(所)	**School (unit)**					
高等学校	Institutions of Higher Education	50	37	66	66	67
中等专业学校	Special Secondary Schools	110	84	65	64	61
职业中学	Vocational Middle Schools	80	60	26	28	28
普通中学	Regular Secondary Schools	712	861	755	754	760
小　学	Primary Schools	2 630	1 021	766	764	761
特殊教育学校	Special Schools	29	34	29	29	29
在校学生数(万人)	**Student Enrollment (10 000 persons)**					
高等学校	Institutions of Higher Education	12.13	22.68	51.57	51.13	50.66
中等专业学校	Special Secondary Schools	6.17	11.89	10.91	10.22	9.88
职业中学	Vocational Middle Schools	3.66	8.48	3.77	3.52	3.55
普通中学	Regular Secondary Schools	48.31	79.54	59.44	59.17	59.04
小　学	Primary Schools	110.19	78.86	70.16	73.11	76.04
特殊教育学校	Special Schools	0.33	0.54	0.50	0.49	0.49
教职员工(万人)	**Staff and Workers (10 000 persons)**					
高等学校	Institutions of Higher Education	7.06	6.08	7.42	7.41	7.33
中等专业学校	Special Secondary Schools	1.49	1.27	0.91	0.89	0.85
职业中学	Vocational Middle Schools	0.53	0.66	0.43	0.42	0.40
普通中学	Regular Secondary Schools	6.62	7.66	6.73	7.53	7.58
小　学	Primary Schools	7.48	6.13	5.58	4.82	4.90
特殊教育学校	Special Schools	0.11	0.16	0.16	0.16	0.16
卫生机构数(个)	**Health Care Institutions(unit)**	**7 690**	**4 400**	**3 270**	**3 358**	**3 465**
#医　院	Hospital	462	459	306	308	317
医院床位数(张)	**Hospital Beds (bed)**	**69 636**	**75 334**	**105 083**	**107 130**	**109 612**
卫生技术人员(万人)	**Medical Technical Personnel (10 000 persons)**	**15.85**	**10.71**	**13.54**	**13.91**	**14.61**
#执业医生	Medical Parctitioners	5.82	4.99	5.13	5.21	5.42
护师、护士	Senior and Junior Nurses	3.27	3.68	5.59	5.89	6.32
医院治疗人次(万人次)	**Total Patients Treated (10 000 person-times)**	**8 395.00**	**8 631.67**	**21 002.46**	**20 205.30**	**21 402.13**
#门、急诊	Out-patients and Emergency Patients		8 432.29	20 676.24	19 964.97	21 114.29
医院入院人数(万人次)	**In Patients (10 000 person-times)**	**95.28**	**122.79**	**285.68**	**268.28**	**298.80**
医院每百诊次的入院人数(人)	**In Patients Per 100 Patient-times (person)**	**1.10**	**1.40**	**1.40**	**1.33**	**1.40**

表19-12 居民消费价格指数(以上年价格为100)
Consumer Price Indices of Residents(Preceding Year = 100)

指标	Indicators	2012
居民消费价格指数	**Overall Residents Consumer Price Index**	**102.8**
食　品	**Food**	**105.8**
粮　食	Grain	102.9
淀粉及制品	Starch and Related Products	109.5
干豆类及豆制品	Dry Beans and Bean Products	109.5
油　脂	Oil and Fat	103.8
肉禽及其制品	Meat Poultry and Their Products	105.1
蛋	Eggs	98.2
水产品	Aquatic Products	105.8
菜	Vegetables	111.1
#鲜　菜	Fresh Vegetables	113.3
调味品	Flavoring	103.5
糖	Sugar	103.5
茶及饮料	Tea and Beverages	103.1
干鲜瓜果	Dried and Fresh Fruits	102.8
#鲜瓜果	Fresh Fruits	100.8
糕点饼干面包	Cakes, Biscuits and Bread	102.8
液体乳及乳制品	Milk and Its Products	103.8
在外用膳食品	Out-of-home Food	107.8
其他食品	Other Food	108.1
烟酒及用品	**Tobacco, Alcohol and Related Products**	**101.4**
烟　草	Tobacco	100.0
酒	Liquor	105.0
衣　着	**Clothing**	**103.0**
服　装	Garments	103.9
男式服装	Men's Wear	103.9
女式服装	Women's Wear	103.8
儿童服装	Children's Wear	104.1
衣着材料	Clothing Materials	104.9
鞋袜帽	Shoes, Socks and Hats	99.3
#鞋	Shoes	99.0
衣着加工服务	Garment Processing Service	105.5
家庭设备用品及维修服务	**Home Appliances and Required Service**	**103.5**
耐用消费品	Durable Consumer Goods	103.0
室内装饰品	Interior Decorations	105.0
床上用品	Bed Articles	99.1
家庭日用杂志	Daily Use Household Articles	103.0
家庭服务及加工维修服务	Other Daily Use Articles	109.1
医疗保健和个人用品	**Medicine, Medical Services and Personal Articles**	**100.6**
医疗保健	Medicine and Medical Services	99.9
#中药材及中成药	Chinese Medicinal Crop and Patent Medicine	102.3
西　药	Western Medicine	95.6
保健器具及用品	Healthcare and Equipment	106.9
医疗保健服务	Medical and Healthcare Services	99.8
个人用品及服务	Personal Articles and Service	101.3
交通和通信	**Means of Transportation and Communication**	**100.8**
交　通	Transport	102.6
#交通工具	Transport Tools	99.3
通　信	Communications	96.5
通信工具	Communications Tools	73.5
通信服务	Communications Service	100.3
娱乐教育文化用品及服务	**Recreation, Education and Culture Articles**	**99.3**
文娱用耐用消费品及服务	Durable Consumer Goods for Recreational Use	87.8
教　育	Education	102.0
文化娱乐用品	Recreation and Culture Articles	101.8
旅　游	Tourism	102.1
居　住	**Residence**	**102.8**
建房及装修材料	Housing Construction And Finishing Materials	105.0
租　房	House Leasing	100.2
自有住房	Self-owned House	103.2
水电燃料	Tap Water, Electricity and Fuels	101.4
#水	Tap Water	100.0
电	Electricity	102.4
液化石油气	LPG	105.1
管道燃气	Pipelined Gas	100.0

表19-13 主要年份商品零售价格指数(以上年价格为100)
Classified Retail Price Index in Main Years (Preceding Year = 100)

指 标	Indicators	2001	2004	2005	2010	2011	2012
商品零售价格指数	**Overall Retail Price Index**	**98.6**	**100.9**	**99.4**	**101.7**	**104.1**	**101.2**
食品类	Food	98.4	108.6	104.7	107.6	111.0	105.9
粮　食	Grain	100.1	128.8	102.1	112.0	113.3	103.0
淀粉及制品	Starch and Related Products	100.4	107.2	105.2	95.5	106.6	109.5
干豆类及豆制品	Dry Beans and Bean Products	111.3	124.8	103.6	108.7	114.7	109.5
油　脂	Oil or Fat	81.4	114.4	91.2	105.6	117.3	103.8
肉禽及其制品	Meat Poultry and Their Products	100.4	117.6	105.5	104.2	119.9	105.1
蛋	Eggs	110.7	118.6	105.8	106.1	113.5	98.2
水产品	Aquatic Products	90.1	107.7	114.4	116.1	113.7	105.8
菜	Vegetables	107.1	95.5	103.4	111.0	99.8	111.1
调味品	Flavoring	99.5	103.0	102.1	106.5	107.5	103.5
糖	Sugar	104.4	103.1	103.8	103.8	104.8	103.5
干鲜瓜果	Dried and Fresh Fruits	107.3	118.3	99.4	112.1	114.5	102.8
糕点饼干面包	Cakes, Biscuits and Bread	99.8	100.9	98.4	100.5	108.8	102.8
奶及奶制品	Milk and Its Products	99.8	99.6	100.8	102.3	108.2	103.8
在外用膳食品	Out-of-home Food	100.7	103.1	104.4	105.6	107.9	107.8
其它食品	Other Food	99.5	96.9	101.1	105.0	107.4	108.1
饮料、烟酒	Beverages, Tobacco and Liquor	98.4	98.8	99.6	101.9	102.3	102.1
服装、鞋帽类	Garments, Shoes and Hats	107.7	93.9	92.6	98.4	103.9	102.9
纺织品类	Textiles	98.8	102.2	99.4	103.9	117.6	99.5
家用电器及音像器材	Household Appliances and Audio-video Appliances	95.0	93.4	93.1	92.4	96.0	96.2
文化办公用品	Cultural and Office Articies	98.7	91.9	91.6	97.7	94.7	94.1
日用品	Daily Use Articles	99.0	98.4	100.5	100.3	106.2	102.1
体育娱乐用品	Sports and Recreation Goods	99.1	96.8	94.7	95.9	103.8	100.0
交通、通信用品	Transportation and Communication Goods	97.4	90.2	88.5	94.0	98.3	95.4
家　具	Furniture	90.4	98.2	100.1	101.1	104.2	103.3
化妆品类	Cosmetics	100.7	99.0	96.1	101.0	104.8	101.1
金银珠宝类	Jewelry	87.2	107.9	107.3	111.7	107.9	99.2
中西药品及医疗保健用品类	Traditional Chinese and Western Medicines	98.7	95.6	97.7	99.8	99.4	100.0
书报杂志及电子出版物类	Books, Newspapers, Magazines and Electronic Publications	99.5	99.6	98.0	103.2	102.1	102.1
燃料类	Fuels	111.4	107.0	109.1	112.8	107.2	102.0
建筑材料及五金电料类	Building Materials and Hardwares	101.8	104.7	104.0	103.3	104.2	102.6

主要统计指标解释

居民消费价格指数

居民消费价格指数是度量一组代表性消费商品及服务项目价格水平随着时间而变动的相对数，反映居民家庭购买的消费品及服务价格水平的变动情况。它是宏观经济分析和决策、价格总水平监测和调控以及国民经济核算的重要指标。其按年度计算的变动率通常被用来作为反映通货膨胀或紧缩程度的指标。

现行的居民消费价格指数按用途分为八个大类，包括食品、烟酒及用品、衣着、家庭设备用品及维修服务、医疗保健和个人用品、交通和通信、娱乐教育文化用品及服务、居住。

商品零售价格指数

商品零售价格指数是反映一定时期内城乡商品零售价格变动趋势和程度的相对数。商品零售价格的变动直接影响城乡居民的生活支出和国家的财政收入，影响居民购买力和市场供需的平衡，影响消费与积累的比例关系。因此，该指数可以从一个侧面对上述经济活动进行观察和分析。

EXPLANATORY NOTES TO MAJOR STATISTICAL INDICATORS

Consumer Price Index

The Consumer Price Index is an index that reflects the time-based change of prices of a group of representative consumption commodities and services. It is an important reference factor for macro-economic analysis and strategy, monitoring and adjustment of overall price level and the national economic budgeting. The year-on-year change of the index is often a norm reflecting the inflation or deflation.

The current CPI covers eight categories of goods and services: food; tobacco, liquor and related articles; garments; household facilities, articles and repair services; medical and health care and personal items; traffic and telecommunications; education, culture and recreation articles and services and residence.

Retail Price Indices

Retail Price Indices reflect the trend and degree of change in retail prices of commodities during a given period. The change in retail prices of commodities directly affect the living expenditure of urban and rural residents, government revenue, purchasing power of residents and the equilibrium of market supply and demand, and the ratio of consumption to accumulation. Therefore, the retail price indices are useful to analyze the changes of the above economic activities.

图书在版编目（CIP）数据

上海浦东新区统计年鉴. 2013／上海浦东新区统计局，国家统计局浦东调查队编.
——北京 ：中国统计出版社，2013.8
ISBN 978-7-5037-6875-0

Ⅰ. ①上…
Ⅱ. ①上… ②国…
Ⅲ. ①统计资料－浦东新区－2013－年鉴
Ⅳ. ①C832.513-54

中国版本图书馆CIP数据核字(2013)第169053号

上海浦东新区统计年鉴—2013

作　　者／上海市浦东新区统计局　国家统计局浦东调查队
责任编辑／陈越月
执行编辑／施湘君　计勤敏
封面设计／蔡旭洲
出版发行／中国统计出版社
通信地址／北京市西城区月坛南街57号
邮　　编／100826
办公地址／北京市丰台区西三环南路甲6号
邮政编码／100073
电　　话／邮购（010）63376909　书店（010）68783171
网　　址／http://csp.stats.gov.cn
印　　刷／上海万卷印刷有限公司
经　　销／新华书店
开　　本／890×1240毫米1/16
字　　数／95.68万字
印　　张／23
印　　数／1～1500册
版　　别／2013年8月第1版
版　　次／2013年8月第1次印刷
书　　号／ISBN 978-7-5037-6875-0
定　　价／320.00元

如有印装错误，本社发行部负责调换。